Architecture T

Architecture Theory
A Reader in Philosophy and Culture

Andrew Ballantyne

CONTINUUM
The Tower Building   15 East 26th Street
11 York Road   New York
London SE1 7NX   NY 10010

© Andrew Ballantyne 2005

All rights reserved. No part of this publication may be reproduced or transmittted in any form or by any means, electronic or mechanical, including photocopying, recording, or any information storage or retrieval system, without prior permission in writing from the publishers.

British Library Cataloguing-in-Publication Data
A catalogue record for this book is available from the British Library.

ISBN: HB: 0–8264–6409–2
       PB: 0–8264–6408–4

Library of Congress Cataloging-in-Publication Data
A catalog record for this book is available from the Library of Congress.

Typeset by Servis Filmsetting Ltd, Manchester.
Printed and bound in Great Britain by Antony Rowe, Chippenham, Wiltshire.

Contents

Acknowledgements	vii
Preface	ix
Section 1: Powers of Ten	1
Georges Bataille	15
Percy Bysshe Shelley	26
Ralph Waldo Emerson	30
Section 2: Groundwork	33
Gaston Bachelard and Michel Tournier	42
William James	48
John Dewey	61
Charles Sanders Peirce	67
Gregory Bateson	71
Walter Benjamin, Louis Aragon and Karl Marx	88
Diane Favro	93
Section 3: Individual	107
Sigmund Freud, Julia Kristeva and Slavoj Žižek	118
Samuel Butler	126
Donna Haraway	144
Henry David Thoreau	150
Section 4: Pluralities	157
Paul Ricoeur and Nelson Goodman	169
Michel Serres	182
Edgar Allen Poe	203
Mabel O. Wilson and Le Corbusier	210
Section 5: Relations	231
Gilles Deleuze	245
Brian Massumi	253
Patsy Healey	259
Ian Buchanan and Fredric Jameson	272
Heinrich von Kleist	301
Index	307

Acknowledgements

'Architecture' by Georges Bataille, reprinted by permission of Sage Publications Ltd from Michael Richardson (ed.), *Georges Bataille: Essential Writings*, © Michael Richardson, 1998.

'The Obelisk', from *Visions of Excess: Selected Writings, 1927–1939*, Georges Bataille, translated by Allan Stoekl, with Carl R. Lovvitt and Donald M. Leslie, Jr., University of Minnesota Press (© 1985 by the University of Minnesota).

The Poetics of Space, Gaston Bachelard, translated by Maria Jolas (Boston: Beacon Press, 1969).

Le miroir des idées, Michel Tournier (Paris: Mercure de France, 1996).

Paris Peasant, Louis Aragon, translated by Simon Watson Taylor (London: Jonathan Cape, 1971).

'Paris, Capital of the Nineteenth Century', Walter Benjamin, translated by Howard Elland and Kevin McLaughlin, in *The Arcades Project*, (Cambridge, MA: Belknap, 1999).

Capital, Karl Marx, translated by Samuel Moore and Edward Aveling (New York: International Publishers, 1967).

'Of Cells and Selves', Slavoj Žižek, in *The Žižek Reader*, edited by Elizabeth Wright and Edmond Wright (London: Blackwell, 1999).

Experience and Nature, John Dewey. Reprinted by permission of Open Court Publishing Company, a division of Carus Publishing Company, Peru, IL, from *Experience and Nature* by John Dewey, © 1925 by John Dewey.

Art as Experience by John Dewey, © 1934 by John Dewey, renewed 1973 by The John Dewey Foundation. Used by permission of G.P. Putnam's Sons, a division of Penguin Group (USA) Inc.

'Bali: The Value System of a Steady State', in *Steps to an Ecology of Mind: Collected Essays in Anthropology, Psychiatry, Evolution and Epistemology*, Gregory Bateson (London: Granada Publishing, 1973).

'The Street Triumphant: The Urban Impact of Roman Triumphal Parades', Diane Favro, in *Streets: Critical Perspectives on Public Space*, ed. by Zeynep Çelik *et al.* (Berkeley, Los Angeles and London: University of California Press, 1994).

'Civilization and its Discontents', Sigmund Freud © The Institute of Psycho-Analysis and The Hogarth Press for permission to quote from *The Standard Edition of the Complete Psychological Works of Sigmund Freud*, translated and edited by James Strachey. Reprinted by permission of The Random House Group Ltd.

'In Times Like These, Who Needs Pschoanalysts?', in *New Maladies of the Soul*, by Julia Kristeva, translated by Ross Guberman © 1995 Columbia University Press. Reprinted with the permission of the publisher.

'A Cyborg Manifesto: Science, Technology, and Socialist-Feminism in the Late

Twentieth-Century', in *Simians, Cyborgs, and Women*, Donna Haraway (New York: Free Association Books, 1996).

'Review of *Ways of Worldmaking* by Nelson Goodman', Paul Ricoeur, in *Philosophy and Literature* 4:1 (1980), 107–20, The Johns Hopkins University Press. Reprinted with permission of The Johns Hopkins University Press.

'In the City: Agitated Multiplicity', from Michael Serres, *Rome: The Book of Foundations*, translated by Felicia McCarren. © 1991 by the Board of Trustees of the Leland Stanford Jr. University; 1983 by Editions Grasset & Fasquelle. All rights reserved. Used with permission of Stanford University Press.

'Dancing in the Dark', Mabel O. Wilson, in *Places Through the Body*, ed. by Heidi J. Nast and Steve Pile (London and New York: Routledge, 1998).

'Postscript on Control Societies', in *Negotiations, 1972–1990*, Gilles Deleuze, trans. by Martin Joughin (New York: Columbia University Press, 1995). Reprinted with the permission of the publisher.

'Strange Horizon', in *Parables for the Virtual: Movement, Affect, Sensation*, Brian Massumi (Durham and London: Duke University Press, 2002).

'Planning in Relational Space and Time: Responding to New Urban Realities', Patsy Healey, in *Companion to the City*, ed. by Gary Bridge and Sophie Watson (London: Blackwell, 2002).

'Schizophrenic Utopianism', in *Deleuzism: A Metacommentary*, Ian Buchanan (Edinburgh: Edinburgh University Press, 2000).

'The Puppet Theatre', in *Heinrich von Kleist: Selected Writings*, ed. and trans. by David Constantine (London: Weidenfeld & Nicolson, 1997).

Preface

This book is designed to help the reader think creatively about architecture. The idea of a theory is to simplify things, so that it is possible to act. Architecture is complicated, and stands in need of theories. The arguments presented here should stand up for themselves, without needing support from higher authorities. I have pointed to evidence where I think it is needed, and have tried to root everything in the particular – in an example of one kind or another – to help make the points clearly and directly.

I have drawn on two major resources in my commentary. One of them is the philosophical writings of Gilles Deleuze and Félix Guattari, whose work I have found endlessly stimulating – sometimes absorbing, sometimes baffling, but now certainly ingrained in my ways of thinking. The other is the work of the American pragmatist philosophers, including Richard Rorty, whose writing is a model of clarity. I am not the first to have noticed that there are links between these two bodies of thought, and the links are far from being exhausted in my use of them here. What I am aware of above all in presenting these papers is a sense of incompleteness, which is how it should be in presenting a framework. Why *this* and not *that*? For some of the papers there would certainly be alternatives that could have made the same point, and with them I have tried to use examples that are particularly clear or in some other way particularly delightful. I have preferred essays that left me feeling that they turned my head when I first encountered them.

A book like this cannot aim to be exhaustive, but offers a reorientation. There is an invitation to the reader to continue, to see what can be done with these ideas, and how they can prompt other ideas to follow in turn. I have made use of ideas drawn from Deleuze and Guattari in trying to understand and explain what is going on, but I have not tried to present their ideas systematically. My use of their concepts is opportunist and pragmatic. Most of the time I have avoided the metaphysical aspect of their work, and have preferred their pragmatic side, which will give an impression of them being less finely nuanced than in fact they are. Just as builders need mainly blunt instruments, so architects are well equipped to deal with bold ideas, linked either by the grip of logic, by more nebulous associations of ideas, or by habit – which takes a fierce hold on patterns of thought and makes us see the world through it, persuading us that we see the truth when we see only commonplaces. This book will shake your habits of mind, and help you to think fresh thoughts.

Between the lines, and not in sequence, it feels as though there is an autobiography in these pages, as some of the essays have been with me for many years. Trying to think things through has taken me back to them, as I found them compelling and persuasive when I encountered them, and have subsequently absorbed their lessons and forgotten them. Other essays have been written more recently. It might be important to my reception of them that none of the essays included came my way as a set text, and so collectively they add up to an attempt to piece together a world outside the curriculum. They are presented here as a group, making them into a textbook that has the hope of actualizing that world, as it opens it up for others to inhabit.

I would like to thank Tristan Palmer whose enthusiasm initiated the project, and thank two of my friends in particular, Mark Lockett and Peter Klein, who introduced me to texts included here that changed my ways of thinking, and my life. My more recent intellectual development has been helped along by conversations with Gerard Loughlin and Dana Arnold, both of them creative thinkers with far-reaching ideas and a sound knowledge of how to live.

Along the way various colleagues and friends have helped me to rehearse ideas that are presented here. They include Niran Abbas, Martin Beattie, Hanjo Berressem, Nathaniel Coleman, Christiane Collins, Alan Day, Graham Farmer, Simon Guy, Paul Andre Harris, Vaughan Hart, Gill Ince, Stephen Kite, Neil Leach, Di Leitch, Hentie Louw, Jules Lubbock, Sarah Menin, John Paul Ricco, Simon Richards, Chris Smith, Joseph Tabbi, Robert Tavernor and William Tavernor.

Section 1
Powers of Ten

Local, national, international

I am writing on a terrace, sitting out of doors, under a roof that gives me enough shade to be able to see the computer screen. I look out across a landscape that was not designed for the sake of its visual effect. There are trees in the foreground, planted by my neighbours, or their forebears. Some of these trees, the smaller ones, will bear fruit later in the year. It is spring at the moment, and the fruit trees are blossoming. The whiteness scattered across their foliage makes it seem that the effects of frost – which touched the valley in the night – are lingering on into the day, even after the early-morning mists have cleared. Now in the afternoon, there is honey in the air, and noises. There are hens, pigeons, sheep, lambs (with their all-too-human bleating) and from time to time a barking dog; but the most persistent sound is the cawing of rooks – a restless and grating sound – that is centred on a line of tall trees in the middle distance. The leaves have not yet grown, so the branches make a tracery of dark lines against both the bright sky and a hill beyond them. There is a parasitic growth on some of the lower branches of the trees – mistletoe – and these growths echo in shape the rooks' nests that are in the higher branches, a little smaller but denser than the growths below. The rooks (because of work I have done in the past) put me in mind of a passage in Richard Payne Knight's poem, *The Landscape*, where he describes a colony of rooks as illustrating the beginnings of civil society:

> e'en these little politicians know
> The ills that from a social compact flow.
> Here, while I view their feuds of petty strife,
> I learn, unfelt, the ills of public life;
> And see well acted, in their little state,
> All that ambition aims at in the great.[1]

It's not great poetry, but it is a memorable image, drawn from the everyday furniture of the countryside, seeing the local wildlife as emblematic of the impulses that drive a greater world, of impressive statesmen. It is a passage that deliberately calls to mind Thomas Gray's much better-known *Elegy* (written in a country churchyard) and Knight used his rural imagery to make the same point as Gray's poem – that obscure and unnoticed lives can draw on the same passions and drives as the lives of the great.[2] The people buried in the country churchyard are unknown, but they would – if circumstances had put them in positions of power and influence – have been just as capable of good and evil as were the people who achieved fame and notoriety in history. Whether through accident of birth, or through lack of ambition, these obscure people never connected with the world of power and influence and their qualities went with them to the grave, unnoticed by the wider world. I am elaborating this reading of the colony of rooks – the colony that is here before my eyes – because I want to use it to make the point that even a scene like this one can be (and in this case genuinely is) invested with a significance that is not immediately apparent, and which indeed is not inherent in it. In this case, the associations of ideas spring readily to my mind and would have vanished just as fleetingly had I not decided to dwell on the point and explain it. Normally this would be one of the ghosts that I carry round with me, haunting the things I think, but without making itself fully audible or visible.

However there is no need to turn to literary allusion in order to draw political inferences from the place. The landscape is full of them, if we care to notice, and the great world is drawn into the local scene in multifarious ways. Already in order to sustain the idea of my working in a bucolic idyll, I have edited out the thunderous low-flying fighter jets that tore the serenity apart a couple of hours ago. It was uncharacteristic, and therefore seemed better not mentioned. However if I were telling a different story about the place, then the aircraft might seem to be a highly pertinent detail, not so much for the sake of what the planes were doing here, but for the sake of what they were practising for, which would connect with international affairs of state, not excluding warfare or the threat of it. My telephone is on the table, and it rang earlier, putting me in touch with someone I had thought from her 'AOL' e-mail address was in America, but she turned out to be in the west of England. She phoned me thinking that I was in England, but the call was automatically diverted to me here in central France. The electricity in the house comes from somewhere far away, and invisible to me, and it may well have been generated at a nuclear power station, run on principles discovered by Einstein and unleashed to practical ends in the 1940s. The fuel that powers the villagers' vehicles comes from one political hot-spot or another, whether Texas or the Middle East. There is something going on in this part of the world – and not only here – that means the area is depopulating, as people move towards the towns where there are jobs; I have managed to move here and pursue my studies while remaining connected back to an urban world of academic activity, networked round the world, so that I like to think that it hardly matters where I am. Things are not what they seem. The countryside looks traditional, and there are things going on here that have continued for generations, but the traditional rural practices are now self-consciously nurtured, and are put on display as curiosities, rather than being the unquestioned fabric of life. Even the weather is changing – the farmers want there to be rain at the moment, while everything is starting to grow, but despite an unseasonably wet summer last year, and flooding through the winter, the spring has been rather dry. One school of thought in the village thinks that these things just happen. The other thinks that it is to some significant degree the fault of the president of the USA. The scene is shot through with real politics, not just symbolic inferences and associations of ideas in my idiosyncratically stocked mind. Of course one can ignore them, and see the scene (as Richard Payne Knight would have done) informed by paintings of Arcadian landscapes, relishing the play of light, especially as the scene is muted by mists or gilded by the low sun, making it look more than ever like the sort of thing painted by an old master; and people come to visit because of this traditionally cultivated sort of 'natural' beauty, but there is more to it than that.

In the village churchyard behind me, there are the obscure burials that one would expect to find in a remote place; but another church is visible through the trees where the rooks have built their nests. It is altogether different in its significance, because it is the Basilica of the Madeleine at Vézelay – the finest Romanesque church, and since Sunday 1 July 1984, a UNESCO-designated World Heritage Site, so there is no doubt of its more-than-local cultural importance.[3] It is marked out in the landscape as a special place, because despite being surrounded by hills, this particular hill is the steepest and perhaps the tallest. There has been a settlement nearby in the valley from Roman times, but the town on the hill did not come into its own until the middle ages, when the bones of Mary Magdalen were brought here. The authenticity of these relics is now doubted (not least by authoritative claimants in Provence at Sainte-Baume) but some bones are still on display in the crypt, and they are labelled as being hers. It may not have been the inherent properties of the bones, but the play of the imagination on them, that brought real wealth and real influence to the town. The construction of this importance might look improbable to those of us who are not steeped in the attitudes and belief-systems of the middle ages, but the consequences were real and tangible. There is a remarkably fine building here, produced with care, highly developed craft skills, and large amounts of money. It was one of the major starting points for the pilgrimage to Santiago di Compostella, and the second crusade set out from here. In the twelfth century it was on occasion at the centre of world events. Even later, there were things happening here that had influence beyond the region. In 1707 in a small village church on the other side of Vézelay, at a settlement called Bazoches, Louis XIV's general Sébastien Le Prestre, the Maréchal Vauban, was buried, after a long and illustrious career in the service of the state, designing and supervising the construction of defences around the kingdom. He travelled a good deal, but was based at his chateau at Bazoches.[4] Generations later, Napoleon found him such an inspiration that he had the body disinterred. The general's heart was cut out, put in a lead casket and reburied at Les Invalides, where Napoleon's own body was eventually brought, sharing the space marked by a refulgently self-confident baroque monument in the centre of Paris, domed in radiant gold and green lacquer, and even more prominent now that it is floodlit at night than it was in the time of Louis XIV.[5] At moments like this, the little world of the village is touched by the great world of affairs of state, and the individual is connected into a mechanism of wider significance. It was an accident that Vauban was attached to Bazoches, the location might have been anywhere, but what he did there made it a place that was of interest to people who wielded great power, and made of it a special place, while his snatched heart is part of an assemblage of military relics that irradiates the Parisian sky. There is no doubt about the authenticity of these relics, and they have never been supposed to be miraculous, but there is a survival of elements of the ancient ways of thinking. Here they are assembled into a machine that incorporates heroic bodies and solid geometry in order to focus and mobilize powerful forces of sentiment for the glory of the state. Somehow the body parts are necessary to power this engine of patriotism, raptured into the building.

Obelisk

This brings me to Georges Bataille, who is another local personage, as he is buried in the churchyard of the Madeleine's basilica, but his reputation is hardly local at all. He lived in Vézelay late in his life, in a very modest house in the middle of the town. His grave is exceptional in its austerity, the usual plot marked with a flat gravestone, like many other graves here, but in Bataille's case there is no inscription in the wide horizontal surface of the stone slab, no expression of sentiment in verse, no effusion of any kind, only the most meagre information (name and dates) carved into the vertical surface at the slab's edge, making a point of understatement. His house is marked with a plaque, but it goes for the most part unnoticed. The writer whose house is visited is Jules Roy, also buried in the churchyard, also with a notably austere headstone, though this one looks less neglected, partly perhaps because it is much newer. Roy has no reputation outside of France, but was a charming and skilful journalist who lived in a house that is open to the public, just next to the basilica. His books (unlike Bataille's) are on sale in the local bookshops, and his extensive gardens, arranged in sweeping terraces, have glorious panoramic views. His intellectual views were sufficiently commonplace to keep him in touch with the mainstream, and he was well rewarded for his efforts. Bataille, meanwhile, was a more independent thinker, driven by demons all his own, whose work often seems to be merely deranged; but from time to time it has moments of insight that seem to strip away all that conventional wisdom can offer, to see to the heart of a human condition, resisting the efforts of civilization to police what can be thought and felt. Nevertheless he felt that he was part of a social network, and that he was worthless outside of it. This is extraordinary, given that he seems to have been so independently minded. The society that he cared about and that validated his efforts was certainly not identical with the state. 'If I wish my life to have meaning for me, it is necessary that it have meaning for others: no one would dare give to life a meaning which he alone would perceive.'[6]

Some passages from Bataille's writings 'Architecture' and 'The Obelisk' are included here, the first for its general view of architecture and its place in society, the second as an example of the particular architectural monument being seen in relation to a wide cultural perspective – life, the universe and everything – as well as because the obelisk itself makes a good marker as a point of entry to the book. It is a solid monument with a particular well-defined concrete form, that occupies a place in the everyday world. The particular obelisk in question is in the Place de la Concorde, where the French president presides over an annual parade of military hardware, and where the guillotine was set up in the 1790s. The obelisk marks the spot where two axes cross – that of the Champs Elysées (which runs in a straight line from the Louvre to the Arc de Triomphe and beyond) and that of the parliament building, the Assemblée Nationale – both of them symbolic of nationhood and power.[7] The obelisk is an important symbolic presence in modern Paris, and is a familiar part of the scene, but from another perspective it is also an alien presence, bursting in from another culture and another time – a petrified sunbeam – with ramifications that spread out to the furthest reaches of the imagination. Its clear and simple geometry sits within a nebulous aura of cultural complexities, evoking a con-

Section 1: Powers of Ten

nection with the most distant past, by way of eighteenth-century revolution, nineteenth-century imperialism, and modern politics. Bataille's essay is disjointed and declamatory. That was his method. Formal polish is not the point here. Bataille could excoriate the very idea of form:

> A dictionary begins when it no longer gives the meaning of words, but their tasks. Thus *formless* [*informe*] is not only an adjective having a given meaning, but a term that serves to bring things down in the world, generally requiring that each thing have its form. What it designates has no rights in any sense and gets itself squashed everywhere, like a spider or an earthworm. In fact, for academic men to be happy, the universe would have to take shape. All of philosophy has no other goal: it is a matter of giving a frock coat to what is a mathematical frock coat. On the other hand, affirming that the universe resembles nothing and is only *formless* amounts to saying that the universe is something like a spider or spit.[8]

Bataille's thought had a pragmatist aspect, drawing attention to roles rather than forms – don't ask what it is, but ask what it does: we learn how to use a word or an idea, and when we use it with confidence then we feel that we 'understand' it. This was a key move in his thinking which enabled him to see things as equivalent when they played a comparable role in different social frameworks – things as superficially different as sunlight and excrement, or a nun intoxicated with God, and a fashion victim intoxicated with extravagant clothes, can be seen as performing much the same role in their different mechanisms.[9] To encounter Bataille seriously for the first time, is to feel one's world ripped apart. His images are often extremely violent or disgusting, sadistic and incoherent. It is the fact that they transgress the usual decorums that makes them unsuitable texts for the tourist bookshops: they rip through the petty gentility of such places; and perhaps more to the point, they would not sell – the only real transgression in a retail outlet. In photographs Bataille always looks neat and conventional, and some of his writings have that formality of presentation. Nevertheless I imagine Bataille snarling and flayed like a figure from a painting by Francis Bacon, chewing up our usual categories and ways of thinking. His is a vision of the abyss, and he howls into it with no returning echo.

Where does this leave architecture? 'Architecture,' says Bataille, 'is the expression of the very being of societies', therefore it is useful in giving us insight into the real values of a society.[10] It is virtually impossible for architecture to achieve anything other than what a society can condone, because it involves the marshalling of significant sums of money, or the equivalent in labour and ingenuity. The only substantial buildings will be those that accord with the society's values, and if there is a will to transgress then the would-be builder will probably turn out to be powerless to build, either for want of the means (being insufficiently rich) or because permission will not be granted (excluded from prominence in the social structure). Think of the dome of Les Invalides, and one knows immediately that it is a monument to the glory of the state; it could never have been built as a monument to a revolutionary group that was struggling to take over, or of a private individual with grandiose dreams. It would be out of the question for such a monument to upstage those of the 'legitimate' state that actually has power. In fact Bataille's 'take' on architecture is that it is designed to intimidate and oppress, in order to coerce into social conformity. There is some irony in the presentation of the idea, as he seems to suppose that this is architecture's right and proper role. It is indeed in general architecture's inescapable role, and it is impossible to promote a genuinely radical cause by way of putting up a large prominent monument to that cause – because at the moment when it becomes possible, the cause has become acceptable to the established powers, and its supposed radicalism evaporates like a lost illusion.

Harmony

This need not lead one to despair. Society exacts an obedience to its ways, and the architects who flourish are those who have no problems with conforming to these demands. There is no shortage of willing souls, who in a market economy are selected rather than coerced. There is no need to change the mind of someone who thinks like Bataille, because individuals like him are seen to marginalize themselves. The theme of the local and the universal is played out in a famous short film, called *Powers of Ten*, by Charles and Ray Eames, who were principally furniture designers, but they also designed themselves a house in California that is very well known among architects. It was assembled between 1945 and 1949 from factory-made component parts, rather than being crafted in any traditional way. As an idea, it sounds charmless but what we might expect of doctrinaire avant-garde architects working in those days. In the execution it turned out to be a very special place indeed, partly because of the building's transparency – which has the effect of placing the inhabitants in a eucalyptus grove, rather than in a traditional house – and partly because of the way in which it was inhabited. The house was furnished not only with the Eameses' own designs, but also with evocative objects brought back from their wide-ranging travels. It was also animated with their celebrated *joie de vivre*, so that even a simple everyday moment, like the arrival of a cup of tea, could turn into an informal but gracefully improvised event, with roses laid out across the tea tray. This was the realization of an experimentalist decorum, which was refreshing because it abandoned the formality of the usual received rules, and worked by beguiling rather than challenging. The Eameses also looked into the abyss, into the furthest reaches of our space, and the innermost heart of the atom, but somehow in doing so what they did was to enlist the whole universe into a new way of living the American dream. They are 'insiders' where Bataille is an 'outsider'. There is nothing threatening or untoward in their vision, and it is always fresh – informal rather than formless. It involved an intimate complicity with capitalism, but that was not a problem for them, the way it was for Bataille.[11] Everything in the Eameses' universe connects in a harmonious way, singing the same song.

Powers of Ten is composed of a sequence of images which move from the unimaginably large to the unimaginably small, with the human being as the reference point half way through. In fact, as ever, the middle is the real starting point. In the development of an understanding of the world, one starts with the things close at hand, perceptible to the sense-organs – skin, ears, eyes – and from there works

Section 1: Powers of Ten

outward in both directions. The rest of the universe quickly comes crowding in. I have tried to organize my thoughts in this chapter in that way – starting with the things close at hand, before my eyes, but the allusiveness that is possible in a sequence of writing could be confusing in a sequence of images, and the Eameses organized their material into a systematically linear narrative. The sequence begins and ends with empty space and points of light. When the image represents a space 10^{+23} metres across, our own galaxy, the Milky Way, is one spot of light among others. At 10^{-15} metres a single proton fills the frame. The images are presented dispassionately, but the vision is harmonious. The human being is clearest when the image is one metre across (10^{+0}) – a young man asleep at a picnic in Chicago, on a lawn between Lake Shore Drive and a marina. His companion, a young woman, is sitting up and is reading a book or journal that is open at a double-page spread of images of the sky with clouds. There are copies of scientific journals on the picnic rug (*Scientific American* and *Science*), a journal with an image of a clock face boldly on its cover, and a copy of *The Voices of Time*, a book edited by T.J. Fraser (1968). This is no casual picnic, but a carefully staged event, that is styled so as to show two human beings at home in the universe. 'I am a part of all that I have met,' said Alfred, Lord Tennyson, quoted by Fraser, and this sequence of images seems to show it.[12]

The two visions of the world and our place in it are in some ways opposed, as the Eameses' vision is harmonious where the Bataille vision is disjunctive; but what they share is the ability to see the small part as a symptom of a larger whole, and the larger whole as a warranted extrapolation from limited experience (the writer's own). This has been a theme in architecture for thousands of years, as monuments have been made to reflect various ideas of the heavens and our place beneath them. We always work with a limited range of concepts, and can apply them at various scales of operation. It was the Florentine Renaissance architect and polymath Leon Battista Alberti who asked, 'What is a house, but a small city? And what is a city, but a large house?'.[13] To go back to the Eameses' example from a comparison of scale, we move from 10^{+1} metres, which could be about the size of a house, to 10^{+5} metres, which includes the whole of the greater Chicago area (though the kind of city that Alberti had in mind would have been closer to 10^{+3} metres across). In the case of the house, we need to think about how to conceptualize its parts, and we can do that by thinking of some areas as 'public' spaces, while others are securely 'private' – even though this is all out of sight behind closed doors, away from the real public in the street, and the only people who would come in are the people we would invite. Alberti of course would have been thinking of a *palazzo*, with servants, visitors, and power-brokers all finding a place in the scheme of things. By contrast, thinking about the city, we need to simplify, and can do so by thinking of a central square as a public 'living room', or an out-of-centre area where people seem to do little more than sleep, as a 'dormitory'. The particular importance of the temple of Vesta in ancient Rome was that it was the place where Aeneas was supposed to have brought his gods from Troy, and which in turn gave Rome its special destiny. Just as if, in the house, the flame of the domestic altar went out, then death would visit the house, so, if the flame at the temple of Vesta went out, there would be death in the city – on a commensurate scale. Therefore the priestesses, the Vestal virgins, who had neglected the flame, would have to be put to death. The hearth of the home compared with the hearth of the city, and the same superstitions attached, but amplified as appropriate.

Metaphor

We explain things to ourselves by using images that compare the unknown with things that are already part of our experience. Thinking about the house, we can imagine it as a small city. Thinking about the city, we can think of it as a large house. Thinking about atoms, we can image that they behave rather like billiard balls – but only for some sorts of interactions. For others it is better to call to mind clouds, or other things altogether. The images are in our language, and they disappear from view once we are inured to them, and the meanings of words seem to be too obvious to need to hesitate and call an image to mind. However a little time scrutinizing the etymological information in a good dictionary can put one in touch with the image again, and awaken an awareness of the poetry that lurks unnoticed in even our most commonplace exchanges. I have just used images of 'awakening' and 'lurking', so as to bring to mind respectively the idea of seeing something that went unnoticed before, and the idea that the meanings might not co-operate in revealing themselves, but might be content to remain forever out of sight. These are metaphorical uses of words, to mean things that they do not literally mean. But even a word like 'obvious', which has a seemingly self-evident sense, carries within it an image of blocking the way (from *ob* – as in 'obstruct' – and *via*, a path). There must once have been a time when such a word was coined, and the person who used it would have been thinking like a poet – would have been a poet, according to Percy Shelley's conception. Shelley's great essay 'A Defence of Poetry', is insufficiently appreciated, but it made an argument that reality as we live it is a socially constructed phenomenon, built up from the images of poets, both living and the long dead. He composed these thoughts in 1821, a generation before Nietzsche. His project was as radical as Bataille's but seen from another perspective. He was a political radical with private means and an aristocratic outlook. Therefore although he lived wildly and unreliably, he identified with the law-makers rather than the victims of laws. The point for Shelley was not trangression, but making the world new, recognizing that 'Poets are the unacknowledged legislators of mankind'.[14] To live as an innovator, facing events afresh with a repertoire of newly minted metaphors, is to live as a poet. We may not notice poets' efforts, but we make use of concepts that they made, whether recently or long ago. If the concept was formed in the distant past and has been in use ever since, then it is likely that today it will not be noticed as poetic, but will be a straightforward statement of self-evident truth. Also one does not need to consider oneself a poet in order to fall into Shelley's category. Many a commonplace versifier would not qualify, if the verses were just repeating established ideas, turning them into well-mannered clichés. On the other hand a military strategist like Vauban can be seen as a poet when he coined a fresh idea. His ideal military towns were organized on a hexagonal plan. It is a commonplace of contemporary French journalism to refer to the country, France, as *l'hexagone*. This image stems from Vauban's strategy for the defence of the realm, seeing the whole country as a fortified town – taking the image from a town of 10^{+3} metres and applying it at 10^{+6} metres – a metaphor, understanding one thing in terms of another, a thousand times different in size. Moreover France is not really hexagonal, and one could as easily imagine it to be round or square – the hexagon is an approximation, which fits well enough, and the expression has gone beyond being a cliché, now being taken as a statement of fact, but France would not have been hexagonal if Vauban had not conceptualized it in that way. Similarly the image would not have persisted had it not been apt.

In wanting to say that Vauban was, in effect, a poet when he was making a fresh conception, I am developing a line of thought that is there in Shelley's essay, and one which has been taken up more recently. The American philosopher, Richard Rorty, explained how he took up the idea of the 'strong poet' from the literary critic, Harold Bloom.[15] Bloom claimed that

> 'every poet begins (however "unconsciously") by rebelling more strongly against the fear of death than all other men and women do'. I assume [said Rorty] that Bloom would be willing to extend the reference 'poet' beyond those who write verse, and to use it in the large generic sense in which I am using it – so that Proust and Nabokov, Newton and Darwin, Hegel and Heidegger, also fall under the term. Such people are also to be thought of as rebelling against 'death' – that is, against the failure to have created – more strongly than most of us.[16]

What I want to do here is to claim that acts of conceptual creativity are very similar sorts of acts, whether they occur in the work of writers, artists, military strategists or architects. The coining of a fresh metaphor is as vital an act in architecture as it is in verse. If we see our buildings as reflecting important aspects of the way we see the world, then to propose a fresh sort of architecture is to propose dwelling in a fresh universe. In fact I can find authority for the move by going back to Shelley, who included architecture among the works he gathered together as the works of 'poets'.[17] Or alternatively, there are fresh ways of living that re-orientate us more harmoniously or more effectively in the world. Charles Jencks in his book *The Architecture of the Jumping Universe*, has described how certain contemporary architects (not least himself) are trying to make architecture and its imagery connect with the current state of knowledge among scientists.[18] The enterprise is the most traditional that we can imagine. Even when we have little evidence to support our conjectures, we find it impossible to avoid the intuition that the great silent monuments of the past were erected with a view to relating mundane activity with the ancients' conceptions of the universe and the heavens. No one supposes that Stonehenge and the great pyramids were built for purely utilitarian purposes, but it is not clear exactly what they were seen to express, by the people who built them. However we find them so powerfully evocative, that we imagine that they were powerfully evocative for their builders also; and they consumed such vast resources that we can infer that they must have been important. If we try to think of ourselves giving expression to matters of comparable importance, it is difficult to conceive of the appropriate parallel. If we use traditional architectural languages, then we reiterate tired or dead metaphors, that have the virtues of familiarity and immediate comprehensibility, but the disadvantage that they point to 'truths' in which we no longer genuinely believe.

Shelley's position was distinctly modernist, seeing the value of the life – its very vitality – in its moments of creativity (rather than for example in its goodness, or in its role as a pillar of society, promoting the continuing viability of a society or culture). However it has its precursor within classicism, as it seems remarkably like Winckelmann's highly idealized conception of the ancient Greek – someone who was closely in touch with nature, and who used that contact to inform his civilized discourse, unaffectedly responding afresh to the world.[19] In recent philosophy the person who promoted such a conception most clearly was Gilles Deleuze, who defined the role of the philosopher as that of the inventor of concepts.[20] There is no doubt that in such works as *Anti-Oedipus* and *A Thousand Plateaus*, working with Félix Guattari, Deleuze reconfigured the world and experience of it, prompting thousands of creative engagements with the text, and of engagements of its concepts with the world. Something of Shelley's impassioned restlessness is there in the thought that Deleuze calls 'nomadic' – creating concepts, remaking oneself by way of them, moving on.[21]

The Personal and the Universal

The most general point to make in this introduction is that ideas are our tools for dealing with the world. If we have new concepts, then we can do new things. We can also do new things if we find new ways to deploy old concepts. We interrogate our experience and by doing so develop concepts that can be taken out of their initial context and put to use in new contexts. One of the techniques that this collection of texts takes as axiomatic is that ideas in its essays – which are not necessarily themselves about buildings – will be taken up by readers and creatively used in ways that were unanticipated by the authors and editor. The vision of an ordered and harmonious universe is normative in the architecture-world, because – as Bataille points out in his analysis – large and prominent monuments, however egalitarian their gestures, are naturally in the hands of the rich and powerful who have their hands on the apparatus of state. Vauban, who was at the heart of the state, commissioned dozens of buildings and lived in a splendid chateau, from where (some of the time) he ran the nation's corps of military engineers. A statue of him is set in a prominent position in the centre of Avallon, in a square named after him. The local cinema is named after him. Bataille had altogether more sophisticated ideas, but he was remote from the corridors of power, and from a popular power-base, so while he has a wider reputation in the international intellectual world, he was never in a position to build anything at all. He rented a very modest house (in Vézelay because it was cheaper than Paris). Professional architects in need of commissions need the patronage of people like Vauban, whereas striking up a friendship with someone like Bataille could only ever have been a personal indulgence – and, given his self-loathing and his preoccupation with death and violence, an uneasy sort of personal indulgence at that. My point is that I believe that what Bataille says is accurate, and valuable for someone who wants to say things about

Section 1: Powers of Ten

architecture, but that it is entirely unhelpful to architects, who are bound to have other preoccupations. By contrast the Eameses have been held in high regard by architects, because what they achieved was to show a way of behaving that made the values of corporate America look cool. In this, they were acting in a way that Shelley would have recognized as poetic. They were acting in a way that other architects could learn from, whereas from Bataille architects could only learn to feel self-conscious and uncomfortable about their activity, because, feeling himself to be one of society's victims, his rhetoric defies one to endorse the values of a state. Nevertheless states will find their architects, and ambitious architects have been prepared, if not willing, to make the necessary compromises – if compromises they feel them to be. Mies van der Rohe famously did not leave Nazi Germany until after he had realized that he would not be able to realize his designs under that regime. Le Corbusier would have worked with the Nazis when they occupied France, if they had asked him. When faced with real choices of this kind, it is a rare architect who turns down the opportunity of a lifetime for the sake of an abstract principle, and if one does turn it down then one is not the architect for that particular commission. Bataille's logic works inexorably. How fortunate the Eameses, then, to be able to position themselves in a society whose values they could unreservedly endorse, and see the whole universe as singing along. Albert Speer achieved the same in a more centralized state, and we feel that he should have known better.[22] Buildings are always symptomatic of larger and smaller forces, operating at different levels of influence, from the personal to the global. If an architect tries to give expression to these forces, in order to show in a harmonious or critical way, a conception of how this modest part fits into the whole, then the building will be influenced by what the architect's vision of the universe happens to be, and a vision of the ways in which the individual relates to that whole. If we can project the hunter Orion striding across the northern skies, when we look up and see nothing more than empty space and points of light, how much easier it is to see our own values and interpretations reflected in something so much closer to us, like a building. I can curl up into a space that is no more than 10^{+0} metres square, and could live very comfortably in a house that was 10^{+1} metres square, whereas 'Orion' is perhaps 10^{+18} metres across (about 100 light years, say). Our houses are almost as much part of us as are our clothes, and are approximately the same size. In fact they are probably more a part of us than our clothes are, as we change our houses much less often. The public buildings in a city centre are not personal, but project an idea of a corporate civic identity, which means that we feel that we are in a culturally significant place if we find good cultural institutions in prominent places there. If, by contrast, we find low-grade commercial activity and nothing more, then we know that the place is nowhere special. Architects on the whole would prefer to be the designers of the cultural landmarks, and those commissions do not go to designers who want to find a means of expressing the society's sickness – such things find expression readily enough, without the need for special commissions – but to those who can endorse and imagine ways of giving form to buildings that promote the society's worth and enhance the place that they produce.

Buildings are both designed and interpreted as symptoms. The essays gathered together in this volume are here because they make or illustrate various points about either the world we live in and how we could conceive it, or about buildings in relation to those conceptions. The universal is implicit in the detail. The personal is the political. What architects can do in proposing a design for a building, is to propose a fragment of a world. It might be that the design is persuasive because it seems to be an appropriate part of the world that we already inhabit; or it might be persuasive because it seems to make it possible to live in a world that we do not yet know, but which seems to be an improvement. The first of these approaches is conservative and decorous, and is what most of a society would want from buildings most of the time. The second approach is visionary, and is what is needed for special occasions, or to mark out the fact that we are embarking on a new epoch, ushering in a brave new world – not so much 'representing' it as making it possible. There is a stanza by Willam Blake:

> To see a World in a Grain of Sand
> And Heaven in a Wild Flower,
> Hold Infinity in the palm of your hand
> And Eternity in an hour.[23]

The architect can directly influence only a miniscule part of the world, but the kinds of decisions that are taken in that molecular fragment embody sets of priorities and assumptions that refract the rest of the universe in its perspective, and sets the person who dwells here in a particular set of relations to a plurality of worlds.

Notes

1. Richard Payne Knight, *The Landscape, a Didactic Poem* (London: 1794) book I, lines 363–4 and 373–6 of the second edition (1795). See Andrew Ballantyne, *Architecture, Landscape and Liberty: Richard Payne Knight and the Picturesque* (Cambridge University Press, 1997) p. 200.
2. Gray's *Elegy* is one of the most anthologized of all English poems. It can be found with authoritative editorship in *The Poems of Gray, Collins and Goldsmith*, edited by Roger Lonsdale (New York: Longman, 1969).
3. Guy Lobrichon, 'Vézelay', in *Les lieux de mémoire*, edited by Pierre Nora, 3 vols (Paris: Gallimard, 1997) vol. 3, pp. 4141–76.
4. Bernard Pujo, *Vauban* (Paris: Albin Michel, 1991).
5. There is an illustration of the plan of this building on the final page of Le Corbusier's *The City of Tomorrow*, captioned as follows: 'Louis XIV commanding the building of the Invalides. Homage to a great town planner. This despot conceived immense projects and realized them. Over all the country his noble works still fill us with admiration. He was capable of saying, "We wish it", or "Such is our pleasure".' Le Corbusier, *Urbanisme* (Paris: 1924) translated by John Rodker, *The City of Tomorrow and its Planning* (London: Architectural Press, 1929) p. 302.
6. Georges Bataille, translated by Leslie Anne Boldt, *Inner Experience* (Albany:

Section 1: Powers of Ten

State University of New York, 1988) p. 42, in Michael Richardson, *Georges Bataille: Essential Writings* (London: Sage, 1998) p. 37.
7. There is an account by Sarah Bonnemaison of an event staged at the foot of this obelisk, 'Places and Memory: Multiple Readings of a Plaza in Paris During the Commemoration of the French Revolution', in *Architecture as Experience*, edited by Dana Arnold and Andrew Ballantyne (London: Routledge, 2004) pp. 153–70.
8. Georges Bataille, 'Informe', *Oeuvres Complète*, vol. I, p. 217; translated Yve-Alain Bois and Rosalind E. Krauss, *Formless: A User's Guide* (Cambridge, Mass.: MIT Press, 1997). See also by Michael Richardson, *Georges Bataille: Essential Writings* (London, Thousand Oaks, California, and New Delhi: SAGE, 1998) pp. 25-6.
9. Georges Bataille, translated by Alan Stoekl, 'Solar Anus', in *Visions of Excess: Selected Writings 1927–1939* (Minneapolis: Minnesota University Press, 1985) pp. 5–9; Georges Bataille, translated by Robert Hurley, 'Sovereignty', in *The Accursed Share Vols II and III* (New York: Zone, 1991) p. 313.
10. Georges Bataille, 'Architecture' in *Oeuvres Complètes*, vol. 1, pp. 171–2; translated by Michael Richardson, 'Architecture' in *Georges Bataille: Essential Writings*, op. cit., pp. 37–8.
11. Hal Foster, *Design and Crime* (London: Verso, 2002) draws attention to various designers who combine radical posturing with complicity in global capitalism. 'Radicalism' is a marketable commodity. For a reader of Bataille the surprise is not that this sort of thing happens, but that the designers can really suppose themselves to be 'radical' by designing novelties for clients who are able to pay well.
12. J.T. Fraser, *Time, Conflict, and Human Values* (Chicago: University of Illinois Press, 1999) p. 26.
13. Leon Battista Alberti, *De re aedificatoria libri decem . . .* (1486) translated by Joseph Rykwert, Neil Leach and Robert Tavernor, *On the Art of Building in Ten Books* (Cambridge, Massachusetts: MIT, 1988) p. 23.
14. This is the last line of 'A Defence of Poetry'. See p. 28, below.
15. Harold Bloom, *The Anxiety of Influence* (Oxford: Oxford University Press, 1973) pp. 80 and 10.
16. Richard Rorty, *Contingency, Irony, and Solidarity* (Cambridge: Cambridge University Press, 1989) p. 24n.
17. Percy Bysshe Shelley, in 'A Defence of Poetry', included below, p. 27.
18. Charles Jencks, *The Architecture of the Jumping Universe* (London: Academy, 1997).
19. Johann-Joachim Winckelmann, *Geschichte der Kunst des Alterthums* (Dresden: 1774) translated by G.H. Lodge, *The History of Ancient Art*, 2 vols (London: 1881) vol. 1, pp. 286, 312–13.
20. Gilles Deleuze and Félix Guattari, *Qu'est-ce que la philosophie?* (Paris: Editions de Minuit, 1991) translated by Graham Burchell and Hugh Tomlinson, *What is Philosophy?* (London: Verso, 1994) p. 2.
21. Gilles Deleuze and Félix Guattari, *Mille plateaux* (Paris: Editions de Minuit, 1987) translated by Brian Massumi, *A Thousand Plateaus: Capitalism and*

Schizophrenia 2 (London: Athlone, 1988), pp. 351–423: 'Treatise on Nomadology – the War Machine'.
22. Gitta Sereny, *Albert Speer: His Battle With Truth* (New York: Knopf, 1995).
23. William Blake, from 'Auguries of Innocence', in *William Blake*, edited by Jacob Bronowski (Harmondsworth: Penguin, 1958) p. 67.

Georges Bataille

What matters about the writings of Georges Bataille (1897–1962) is their vitality, and the way in which the world is presented in them in a fresh perspective – or rather in a series of fresh perspectives, because although there is a certain coherence in his vision, his presentation is far from systematic, and some parts of it seem to be far removed from others. His greatest achievement was *La Part Maudite* (*The Accursed Share*), a sociological study that understood societies through their consumption and production of excess, so that the idea of the exuberant burning up of surplus was seen as a key element in the working of a society. The form that this sacrifice takes is different from one society to another, but it is always there. Architecture can be implicated in this process, as we very commonly ask our buildings to do more than meet our utilitarian needs. Alternatively, perhaps the way we spend our money, as a society, shows us that we value other things. Bataille had a traumatic childhood, and his personal psychology was nightmarish. The range of his writings covers much that is cruel, death-oriented, erotic and scandalously obscene. He reportedly destroyed one book, *W.C.*, a cry of horror, 'violently opposed to all dignity', the reading of which prompted one of his friends to arrange for Bataille to have psychoanalytic treatment.[1] Bataille was interested in surrealism, and came into contact with Parisian intellectuals such as Michel Leiris, André Breton, Roger Caillois and Maurice Blanchot. It was Bataille who first welcomed Walter Benjamin to Paris.[2] Bataille supported himself uncertainly, his steadiest employment being while he worked as a librarian at the Bibliothèque Nationale between 1922 and 1942, but he retired early, having contracted tuberculosis. He moved to Vézelay in 1943. Much of his writing remained unpublished during his lifetime, and given its character it comes as a surprise to see Bataille in photographs looking sympathetic and respectable, even polished – as seems to have been his habit. Martin Heidegger described Bataille as 'the most important contemporary thinker in France',[3] which is extraordinary given the differences in their attitudes and their approaches to philosophy – Heidegger highly systematic, Bataille all over the place. 'I am not a philosopher,' said Bataille, 'but a *saint*, perhaps a madman.'[4]

Notes

1. Georges Bataille, quoted by Allan Stoekl, in his Introduction to Georges Bataille, *Visions of Excess: Selected Writings 1927–1939* (Minneapolis: University of Minnesota Press, 1985) p. x.
2. According to Pierre Missac, quoted in Michel Surya, *Georges Bataille, la mort à l'oeuvre* (Paris: Gallimard, 1992), translated by Krzysztof Fijalkowski and

Michael Richardson, *Georges Bataille: An Intellectual Biography* (London: Verso, 2002) p. 266.
3. Michael Richardson, in his Introduction to Georges Bataille, *Essential Writings* (London: SAGE, 1998) p. 1.
4. Georges Bataille, 'Méthode de méditation' in *Oeuvres complètes*, vol. 5, pp. 217–18; quoted by Michael Richardson, Georges Bataille, *Essential Writings*, op. cit., p. 1.

Architecture

Architecture is the expression of the very being of societies, just as human physiognomy is the expression of the being of individuals. Yet, this comparison especially refers to the physiognomy of officials (prelates, magistrates, admirals). In fact, only society's ideal being (that which authoritatively orders and prohibits) is expressed in actual architectural constructions. Thus great monuments rise up like dams, opposing all disturbed elements to a logic of majesty and authority. This is in the form of cathedrals and palaces through which the Church or the State addresses and imposes silence on the multitude. In fact, monuments clearly inspire social sobriety and often even veritable fear. The fall of the Bastille is symbolic of this state of things. It is difficult to explain such a flow of the crowd except by popular hostility to monuments that are their veritable masters. Equally, whenever architectural composition is found otherwise than in monuments (whether in physiognomy, dress, music, or painting) we can infer a prevalent taste for human or divine authority. The large-scale compositions of certain painters express the will to constrain the spirit to an official ideal. With the disappearance of academic composition in painting, in contrast, the way opens to the expression (and so the exaltation) of psychological animated reaction that, for more than half a century, the progressive transformation of painting (hitherto characterized by a sort of hidden architectural skeleton) has provoked.

In any case, it is clear that mathematical order imposed upon stone is just the fulfilment of an evolution of terrestrial forms, whose direction is revealed in the biological order by the passage from simian to human form, the latter already exhibiting all the elements of architecture. Man apparently represents merely an intermediary stage in the morphological process between monkey and large edifices. Forms have increasingly become static and dominant. From the start human and architectural orders are associated with one another, architecture being only the development of the human order. To attack architecture, whose monumental productions are now the real monsters of the whole earth, grouping servile multitudes under their shadow, imposing admiration and amazement, order and constraint, is also, so to speak, an attack on man. Today all earthly activity, and probably the most intellectually brilliant, tends towards such a direction, denouncing the insufficiency of human dominance. Thus as strange as it may seem when it is a question of a creature as elegant as the human being, a path (traced by the painters) opens up towards bestial monstrosity, as though there were no other possibility of escaping the architectural straitjacket.

The Obelisk

The Mystery of the Death of God

A 'mystery' cannot be posited in the empty region of spirit, where only words foreign to life subsist. It cannot result from a confusion between obscurity and the abstract void. The obscurity of a 'mystery' comes from images that a kind of lucid dream borrows from the realm of the crowd, sometimes bringing to light what the guilty conscience has pushed back into the shadows, sometimes highlighting figures that are routinely *ignored*. From Louis XVI's guillotine to the obelisk, a spatial arrangement is formed on the PUBLIC SQUARE, in other words, on all the public squares of the 'civilized world' whose historical charm and monumental appearance prevail over everything else. For it is nowhere but THERE that a man, in some ways bewitched, in some ways overtaken by frenzy, expressly presents himself as 'Nietzsche's madman' and illuminates with his dream-lantern the mystery of the DEATH OF GOD.

The Prophecy of Nietzsche

'Have you not heard,' cried Nietzsche, 'of that madman who lit a lantern in the bright morning hours, ran to the marketplace, and cried incessantly: "I seek God! I seek God!"' – As many of those who did not believe in God were standing around just then, he provoked much laughter. Has he got lost? asked one. Did he lose his way like a child? asked another. Or is he hiding? Is he afraid of us? Has he gone on a voyage? emigrated? – Thus they yelled and laughed.

The madman jumped into their midst and pierced them with his eyes. 'Whither is God?' he cried; 'I will tell you. *We have killed him* – you and I. All of us are his murderers. But how did we do this? How could we drink up the sea? Who gave us the sponge to wipe away the entire horizon? What were we doing when we unchained this earth from its sun? Whither is it moving now? Whither are we moving? Away from all suns? Are we not plunging continually? Backward, sideward, forward, in all directions? Is there still any up or down? Are we not straying as through an infinite nothing? Do we not feel the breath of empty space? Has it not become colder? Is not night continually closing in on us? Do we not need to light lanterns in the morning? Do we hear nothing as yet of the noise of the gravediggers who are burying God? Do we smell nothing as yet of the divine decomposition? Gods, too, decompose. God is dead. God remains dead. And we have killed him.

'How shall we comfort ourselves, the murderers of all murderers? What was holiest and mightiest of all that the world has yet owned has bled to death under our knives: who will wipe this blood off us? What water is there for us to clean ourselves? What festivals of atonement, what sacred games shall we have to invent? Is not the greatness of this deed too great for us? Must we ourselves not become gods simply to appear worthy of it? THERE HAS NEVER BEEN A GREATER DEED; AND WHOEVER IS BORN AFTER US – FOR THE SAKE OF THIS DEED HE WILL BELONG TO A HIGHER HISTORY THAN ALL HISTORY HITHERTO.'[1]

Mystery and the Public Square

While the existence of human beings may have importance within their own lives and within the limits of their personal destinies, it has none in the eyes of others. Beyond these limits – where human meaning begins – existence matters to the extent that they attract and, apart from this attraction, they are less than shadows, less than specks of dust. And the attraction of an isolated human being is itself nothing but a shadow, a pitiful fleeting apparition. It is but the tentative incarnation of WHAT IS ONLY HUMAN LIFE, which has no name and which the agitation of countless multitudes obscurely demands and constructs, in spite of appearances to the contrary. Who knows what bitterness and sanctity are exhaled in this agitation, which is horror, violence, hatred, sobs, crime, disgust, laughter, and human love. Each individual is but one of the specks of dust that gravitate around this bitter existence. The dust so effectively obscures the condensation around which it orbits that many clear minds, whose reality, however, is only a kind of residue formed wherever activity is condensed (and not a stormy light produced in the shelterless solitude of the individual), imagine human existence as inaccurately as someone who would judge the reality of a capital by the appearance of a suburb, who would think that that life must be examined in its empty and peripheral forms, rather than in the monuments and the monumental vistas that are its center.

The Obelisk

Clausewitz writes in *On War*: 'Like the obelisks that are raised at the points where the major roads of a country begin, the energetic will of the leader constitutes the center from which everything in military art emanates.' The *Place de la Concorde* is the space where the death of God must be announced and shouted precisely because the obelisk is its calmest negation. As far as the eye can see, a moving and empty human dust gravitates around it. But nothing answers so accurately the apparently disordered aspirations of this crowd as the measured and tranquil spaces commanded by its geometric simplicity.

The obelisk is without a doubt the purest image of the head and of the heavens. The Egyptians saw it as a sign of military power and glory, and just as they saw the rays of the setting sun in their funeral pyramids, so too they recognized the brilliance of the morning sun in the angles of their splendid monoliths: the obelisk was to the armed sovereignty of the pharoah what the pyramid was to his dried-out corpse. It was the surest and most durable obstacle to the drifting away of all things. And even today, wherever its rigid image stands out against the sky, it seems that sovereign permanence is maintained across the unfortunate vicissitudes of civilizations.

The old obelisk of Rameses II is thus, at the central point from which the avenues radiate, both a simpler and a more important apparition than any other; is it not worthy of renewed astonishment that, from remote regions of the earth and from the dawn of the ages, this Egyptian image of the IMPERISHABLE, this petrified sunbeam, arrives at the center of urban life?

The Obelisks Respond to the Pyramids

If one considers the mass of the pyramids and the rudimentary means at the disposal of their builders, it seems evident that no enterprise cost a greater amount of labor than this one, which wanted to halt the flow of time.

The Egyptian pharoah was surely the first to give the human individual the structure and the measureless *will to be* that set him upright above the surface of the earth as a kind of luminous and living edifice. When individuals – long after the era of the great pyramids – have wanted to acquire immortality, they have had to appropriate the Osirian myths and the funeral rites that formerly had been the privilege of the sovereign. For it was only to the extent that a considerable mass of power had been concentrated in a single head that the human being raised to the heavens his greed for eternal power, something that had surely never taken place before the *pschent* designated the head of the pharoah to the holy terror of a vast populace. But once it did, each time death struck down the heavy column of strength the world itself was shaken and put in doubt, and nothing less than the giant edifice of the pyramid was necessary to reestablish the order of things: the pyramid let the god-king enter the eternity of the sky next to the solar Râ, and in this way existence regained its unshakable plenitude in the person of the one it had *recognized*. The existing pyramids still bear witness to this calm triumph of an unwavering and hallucinating resolve: they are not only the most ancient and the vastest monuments man has ever constructed, but they are still, even today, the most enduring. The great triangles that make up their sides 'seem to fall from the sky like the rays of the sun when the disk, veiled by the storm, suddenly pierces through the clouds and lets fall to earth a ladder of sunlight.' Thus they assure the presence of the unlimited sky on earth, a presence that never ceases to contemplate and dominate human agitation, just as the immobile prism reflects every one of the things that surrounds it. In their imperishable unity, the pyramids – endlessly – continue to crystallize the mobile succession of the various ages; alongside the Nile, they rise up like the totality of centuries, taking on the immobility of stone and watching all men die, one after the other: they transcend the intolerable void that time opens under men's feet, for all possible movement is halted in their geometric surfaces: IT SEEMS THAT THEY MAINTAIN WHAT ESCAPES FROM THE DYING MAN.

The 'Sensation of Time' Sought by Glory

A moving perspective, represented by the shadows and traces of the successive generations of numberless dead, extends from the banks of the Nile to those of the Seine, from the angles of the pyramids to those of the monolith erected before the Gabriel palace. The long span that stretches from the Ancient Empire of Egypt to the bourgeois monarchy of the Orleans – which raised the obelisk on the Place de la Concorde 'to the applause of the immense crowd' – was necessary for man to set the most stable limits on the deleterious movement of time. The mocking universe was slowly given over to the severe *eternity* of its almighty Father, guarantor of profound stability. The slow and obscure movements of history took place here at the heart and not at the periphery of being, and they represent the long and inexpiable struggle of God against time, the combat of 'established sovereignty' against the destructive and creative madness of things. Thus history endlessly repeats the immutable stone's response to the Heraclitean world of rivers and flames.

But from the development of this changing perspective over the centuries, a specific result that dominates even the monstrous accumulation of forms has come to light: the boundaries raised in opposition to the atrocious 'sensation of time' were tied to this sensation in exactly the same way that all work is tied to a sensation of 'need.' Whereas 'need' and poverty endlessly use up the results of useful labor, the interminable obstinacy of men eventually managed to distance from communal existence the 'sensation of time,' and the shameful malaise it introduced. Moderation and platitude slowly took over the world; more and more accurate clocks replaced the old hourglasses that retained a funereal meaning. The grim reaper went the way of all other phantoms. The earth has been so perfectly emptied of everything that made night terrifying that the worst misfortunes and war itself can no longer alter its comfortable perception. The result is that human striving is no longer directed at powerful and majestic limits; it now aspires, on the contrary, to anything that can deliver it from established tranquillity. *Everything indicates that it was impossible for man to live without the 'sensation of time' that opened his world like a movement of breathtaking speed – but what he lived in the past as fear he can only live now as pride and glory.*

To this vision, whose consequences must be projected before us, is added the fact that life ceaselessly gravitates around limits that up to now held back agitation and dread. It would seem that sovereign protection has sometimes been shaken, sometimes violently toppled, and sometimes ignored – but the horizon none the less remains bound by these great figures. And when someone is carried by glory to meet time and its cutting explosion, he comes upon them again, and it is precisely at that moment that death is revealed. From the very fact that they had become, for the mass of tranquilized lives, increasingly useless, empty, and fragile shadows, the figures stand under the threat of collapse and thus reveal, far more thoroughly than in the fearful obsessions of the past, the despairing fall of lives. They are no longer obstacles to the lost obsessive 'sensation of time,' but are instead the high places from which the breakneck speed of the fall is possible: and the high places themselves topple, to ensure a total revelation. The lands stray from their sun, the horizon is annihilated. And now, rising before the man who carries within himself the naive uproar of conquest of the 'death of God,' the very stone that earlier had sought to limit storms is nothing more than a milestone marking the immensity of an unlimitable catastrophe. A feeling of explosion and a vertiginous weightlessness surround an imperious and heavy obelisk.

The 'Tragic Time of Greece'

Starting with the immense masonry of the pyramids, this reversal of signs is not, however, the result of a uniform and regular course of things. Time has not been the object of a simple feeling of fear. In the attraction exercised by the majestic figures that impose its limit, a now solid time is no less fascinating than the explosive charge packed in a steel shell. And the affinities between happiness and explosion are so profound that fiery catastrophes have always been at the mercy of transports of joy. Combat has always been preferable to tranquillity, a sudden fall to stability. Thus Greece in its earliest days already revealed the possibilities of affinity between man and violence.

It even seems that ancient Greece was engendered by wounds and crime, just as the strength of Cronus was engendered by the bloody mutilation of his father Uranus, in other words, of precisely the divine sovereignty of the heavens. Cronus, the very 'human' god of the golden age, was celebrated in saturnalia; Dionysus, whose coming into the world depended on the murder of his mother by his father – the criminal Zeus striking down Semele in a blast of lightning – this tragic Dionysus, broken in joy, started the sudden flight of the bacchantes. And the least explained of all the 'mysteries,' TRAGEDY, like a festival given in honor of horror-spreading time, depicted for gathered men the signs of delirium and death whereby they might recognize their true nature.

This happy yet somber receptiveness of life was answered by the aggressive vision of Heraclitus. Nietzsche said that this vision was the equivalent of an earthquake, robbing the earth of its stability. He described it in images that he used ten years later to describe the death of God, images of a total yet brilliantly glorious fall. Thus in the death of God, whose whirlwind tears everything from the past, we find once again this 'nostalgia for a lost world' which so painfully riveted the eyes of Nietzsche on Greece in the tragic era.

And which, in the same movement, directed Nietzsche's rage against Socrates: what Socrates introduced to a tumultuous humanity was nothing less than the principle, still weak but bearing with it the quality of *immutability*, whose obligatory value would put an end to the *levity* of combat. What Socrates introduced was the GOOD: it was GOD, and already the gravity of Christianity, which dominated the tragedy of the *passion* of the heavens and reduced 'the death of God' to the debasement of men and to sin, and turned TIME into EVIL.

The Obelisk and the Cross

The obelisks of Rome are capped with crosses, which add their metallic fragility to the pyramidal peaks of these great stone figures.

The equivocal image of the 'death of God' more than any other shatters the order that had fixed the features of immutable sovereignty. The irritated amusement that derives from this botched copulation captures the essence of the malaise that results from the accumulation of successive forms necessary to the lives of men. Thus are revealed the happy shortcuts of Roman Christianity in which, without logic, life attempts to reconcile its impossible moods. But at the same time it becomes clear that the crafty, baroque edifice that resulted was elevated only to fall. For this occidental world, whose fevers were first exhausted and contained in the terrible expiation of saints, only seems to have torn apart its childhood before God in order to be rid of this father, once it had the strength. Whereas the development of ancient life little by little allowed the divine shadow to grow and rejected tragic time, the movement of occidental life strikes down, one after the other, the risky constructions that the will to endure never maintained in correct propositions. Thus, going in the opposite direction on the road traveled by the ancient world, this world, as its riches accumulate and everything in it decomposes, aspires in its depths to the tragic deliverances of primitive Greek naiveté. It is true that everything takes place in an almost empty expanse, in a world which, in its entirety, is leveled and depressed by rational destruction. But in each place where the massive destiny of men is formed, the rhythm of life and death accelerates and attains a speed so great that it results only in the vertigo of the fall.

Hegel against the Immutable Hegel

What makes this movement difficult to represent is the fact that it is accelerated by increases in the sensation of rest. This is what first became apparent when the vicissitudes of human life were traced back from an obelisk. In particular, the rest attained by means of this shadow was necessary for the intellect to approach time with a light heart.

This movement was not at first clear or assured. Even Hegel describing the movement of Spirit as if it excluded all possible rest made it end, however, at HIMSELF as if he were its necessary conclusion. Thus he gave the movement of time the *centripetal* structure that characterizes sovereignty, Being, or God. Time, on the other hand, dissolving each center that has formed, is fatally known as *centrifugal* – since it is known in a being whose center is already there. The dialectical idea, then, is only a hybrid of time and its opposite, of the death of God and the position of the immutable. But it nevertheless marks the movement of a thought eager to destroy what refuses to die, eager to break the bonds of time as much as to break the law through which God obligates. It is manifestly clear that the liberty of time traverses the heavy Hegelian process, precisely to the feeble extent that Socratic irony introduced into this world an eternal Being imposing man.

The Pyramid of Surlei

Nietzsche is to Hegel what a bird breaking its shell is to a bird contentedly absorbing the substance within. The crucial instant of fracture can only be described in Nietzsche's own words:

Section 1: Powers of Ten

'The intensity of my feelings makes me both tremble and laugh ... I had cried too much ... these were not tears of tenderness, but tears of jubilation ... That day I was walking through the woods, along the lake of Silva-plana; at a powerful pyramidal rock not far from Surlei I stopped ...'[2]

Nietzsche's thought, which resulted in the sudden ecstatic vision of the eternal return, cannot be compared to the feelings habitually linked to what passes for profound reflection. For the object of the intellect here exceeds the categories in which it can be represented, to the point where as soon as it is represented it becomes an object of ecstasy – object of tears, object of laughter ... The *toxic* character of the 'return' is even of such great importance that, if for an instant it were set aside, the formal content of the 'return' might appear empty.

In order to represent the decisive break that took place – freeing life from the humilities of fear – it is necessary to tie the sundering vision of the 'return' to what Nietzsche experienced when he reflected upon the explosive vision of Heraclitus, and to what he experienced later in his own vision of the 'death of God': this is necessary in order to perceive the full extent of the bolt of lightning that never stopped shattering his life while at the same time projecting it into a burst of violent light. TIME is the object of the vision of Heraclitus. TIME is unleashed in the 'death' of the One whose eternity gave Being an immutable foundation. And the audacious act that represents the 'return' at the summit of this rending agony only wrests from the dead God his *total* strength, in order to give it to the deleterious absurdity of time.

A 'state of glory' is thus deftly linked to the feeling of an endless fall. It is true that a fall was already a part of human ecstasy, on which it conferred the intoxication of that which approximates the nature of time – but that fall was the *original* fall of man, whereas the fall of the 'return' is FINAL.

The Guillotine

'The very stone that earlier had sought to limit storms is now nothing more than a milestone marking the immensity of an unlimitable catastrophe ...' Near Surlei, a rock in the form of a pyramid still bears witness to the fall of the 'return' ...

Only protracted futility – attached to servile or useful objects – can today shelter existence from the feeling of violent absurdity. The great dead shadows have lost the magical charm that made their protection so effective. And when an extreme chance wills that they still make up the center of destiny, they protect only to the extent that there is daily indifference.

The obelisk of Luxor has, after a hundred years, become the measured navel of the land of moderation: its precise angles now belong to the essential figure that radiates from its base. But the timelessness given to it is due to the absence of any intelligible affirmation: it endures by virtue of its discreet value. Where monuments that had clearly affirmed principles were razed, the obelisk remains only so long as the sovereign authority and command it symbolizes do not become conscious. There was some difficulty in finding an appropriate symbol for the Place de la Concorde, where the images of royalty and the Revolution had proven powerless. But it was contrary to the majesty of the site to leave an empty space, and agreement was reached on a monolith brought back from Egypt. Seldom has a gesture of this type been more successful; the apparently meaningless image imposed its calm grandeur and its pacifying power on a location that always threatened to recall the worst. Shadows that could still trouble or weigh upon the conscience were dissipated, and neither God nor time remained: total sovereignty and the guillotine-blade that put an end to it no longer occupied any place in the minds of men.

This is the deceitful and vague response of exalted places to the fathomless multitude of insignificant lives that, for as far as the eye can see, orbit around them – and the spectacle only changes when the lantern of a madman projects its absurd light on stone.

At that moment, the obelisk ceases to belong to the present and empty world, and it is projected to the ends of time. It rises, immutable – there – dominating time's desperate flight. But even while it is blinded by this domination, madness, which flits about its angles in the manner of an insect fascinated by a lamp, recognizes only endless time escaping in the noise of successive explosions. And there is no longer an image before it, but it *hears* this noise of successive explosions. To the extent that the obelisk is now, with all this dead grandeur, *recognized*, it no longer facilitates the flight of consciousness; it focuses the attention on the guillotine.

The Place de la Concorde is dominated, from the height of the palace balustrades, by eight armored and acephalic figures, and under their stone helmets they are as empty as they were on the day the executioner decapitated the king before them. After the execution, Marly's two horses were brought from the nearby forest and set up at the entrance to the exalted places, before which they rear without end. The central point of the triangle formed by the two horses and the obelisk marks the location of the guillotine – an empty space, open to the rapid flow of traffic.

Nietzsche/Theseus

The pure image of the heavens, the purified image of the king, of the chief, of the *head* and of his firmness, this pure image of the sky crossed by rays, commands the concord and the assurance of those who do not *look at it*, and who are not struck by it; but a mortal torment is the lot of the one before whom its reality becomes naked.

The purified head, whose unshakable commands lead men, takes on in these conditions the value of a derisive and enigmatic figure placed at the entrance to a labyrinth, where those who naively *look* are led astray without guidance, overcome with uneasy torment and glory. It is the 'breath of empty space' that one inhales THERE – there where interpretations based on immediate political events no longer have any meaning; where the isolated event is no more than the symbol of a much greater event. For it is the *foundation* of things that has fallen into a bottomless void. And what is fearlessly conquered – no longer in a duel where the death of the hero is risked against that of the monster, in exchange for an indifferent duration – is not an isolated creature; it is the very void and the vertiginous fall, it is TIME. The movement of all life now places the human being before the alternatives of either this conquest or a disastrous retreat. The human being arrives at the threshold: there he must throw himself headlong into that which has no foundation and no head.

Section 1: Powers of Ten

Notes

1. *The Gay Science*, section 125, trans. W. Kaufmann (New York: Random House, 1974), p. 181. Tr.
2. *Ecce Homo*, section on *Thus Spake Zarathustra*, trans. W. Kaufmann (New York: Random House, 1967), p. 295.

Percy Bysshe Shelley

Shelley (1792–1822) was a monster and a genius, who lived his brief life with intensity and devotion to the cause of art, leaving broken hearts and suicides in his wake, along with a body of poetry that can still inspire, but which is read now less than it was. Indeed his popular reputation is now outshone by that of his second wife, Mary, of whose novel *Frankenstein* there will be something to say in the next chapter. Shelley is the very type of the culture hero, a role in which he cast himself, and which he theorized in a general way in his essay *A Defence of Poetry*, extracts from which appear below. He wrote at a time of social upheaval and radical change, and had sympathy with the progressive politics of the era, growing up as he did in the wake of the French Revolution, with the industrial revolution re-shaping the world around him. It was plain to him that the world needed making anew, and that it fell to poets to re-imagine it for the future – but his conception of the 'poet' included all creative thinkers (he mentions 'authors of language and of music, of the dance and architecture and statuary and painting'). It was also plain that the world would continue to change and would continue to need to be reconfigured in future – this is a vision of the role of art as the premonition of social change, as the poet infers from the evidence in current circumstances the shape of things to come, and by making that inference actually gives shape to the emergent life. There is an idea of the poet as being in touch with eternity – an idea that the values of art are unchanging – but it is overlaid with an assumption of a continuing and perpetual need for metaphors to be refreshed and for society and thought to evolve and progress. It is worth being patient with Shelley's now archaic language, as its exalted ambition and lyrical charge can be thrilling, and persuasive. The style of argument – imagining the formation of the primitive origins of language and society – has its precedents in ancient literature (such as Vitruvius) and in Rousseau's speculations about the origins of language, which he imagined to have developed out of music, and which was the very reverse of progressive in its intentions, seeking to recapture the lost merits of primitive practices.[1] Shelley's intuitions would be taken further and extended in scope by Friedrich Nietzsche and others,[2] so he can be seen as part of a tradition that has sought to make a link between the activity of the imagination and the forms of life – the ways of living – that become possible on account of seeing things afresh.

Notes

1. Vitruvius (Marcus Vitruvius Pollio), *De architecture libri x*, translated by Morris Hickey Morgan, *The Ten Books on Architecture* (1914, reprinted New York: Dover, 1960) pp. 38–9; Jean-Jacques Rousseau, translated by John H.

Moran, *Essay on the Origin of Languages, which treats of Melody and Musical Imitation* (Chicago: University of Chicago Press, 1966).
2. See Alexander Nehamas, *Nietzsche: Life as Literature* (Cambridge, Mass.: Harvard University Press, 1985).

From *A Defence of Poetry*

In the youth of the world, men dance and sing and imitate natural objects, observing in these actions (as in all others) a certain rhythm or order. And although all men observe a similar, they observe not the same order in the motions of the dance, in the melody of the song, in the combinations of language, in the series of their imitations of natural objects. For there is a certain order or rhythm belonging to each of these classes of mimetic representation, from which the hearer and the spectator receive an intenser and purer pleasure than from any other. The sense of an approximation to this order has been called taste by modern writers. Every man in the infancy of art observes an order which approximates more or less closely to that from which this highest delight results. But the diversity is not sufficiently marked as that its gradations should be sensible, except in those instances where the predominance of this faculty of approximation to the beautiful (for so we may be permitted to name the relation between the highest pleasure and its cause) is very great. Those in whom it exists in excess are poets, in the most universal sense of the word – and the pleasure resulting from the manner in which they express the influence of society or nature upon their own minds, communicates itself to others, and gathers a sort of reduplication from that community. Their language is vitally metaphorical; that is, it marks the before unapprehended relations of things, and perpetuates their apprehension, until the words which represent them become through time signs for portions or classes of thoughts, instead of pictures of integral thoughts; and then if no new poets should arise to create afresh the associations which have thus been disorganized, language will be dead to all the nobler purposes of human intercourse. These similitudes or relations are finely said by Lord Bacon to be 'the same footsteps of nature impressed upon the various subjects of the world'[1] – and he considers the faculty which perceives them as the storehouse of axioms common to all knowledge. In the infancy of society every author is necessarily a poet, because language itself is poetry; and to be a poet is to apprehend the true and the beautiful, in a word the good which exists in the relation subsisting first between existence and perception, and secondly between perception and expression. Every original language near to its source is in itself the chaos of a cyclic poem: the copiousness of lexicography and the distinction of grammar are the works of a later age, and are merely the catalogue and form of the creations of poetry.

But poets, or those who imagine and express this indestructible order, are not only the authors of language and of music, of the dance and architecture and statuary and painting; they are the institutors of laws, and the founders of civil society, and the inventors of the arts of life, and the teachers who draw into a certain propinquity with the beautiful and the true that partial apprehension of the agencies of the invisible world which is called religion. Hence all original religions are allegorical, or susceptible of allegory, and like Janus have a double face of false and true. Poets, according to the circumstances of the age and nation in which they appeared, were called in the earlier epochs of the world legislators and prophets. A poet essentially comprises and unites both these characters. For he not only beholds intensely the present as it is, and discovers those laws according to which present things ought to be ordered, but he beholds the future in the present, and his thoughts are the germs of the flower and the fruit of latest time. Not that I assert poets to be prophets in the gross sense of the word, or that they can foretell the form as surely as they foreknow the spirit of events – such is the pretence of superstition which would make poetry an attribute of prophecy, rather than prophecy an attribute of poetry.

A poet participates in the eternal, the infinite, and the one; as far as relates to his conceptions, time and place and number are not. The grammatical forms which express the moods of time, and the difference of persons and distinction of place are convertible with respect to the highest poetry without injuring it as poetry, and the choruses of Aeschylus, and the Book of Job, and Dante's *Paradiso* would afford, more than any other writings, examples of this fact, if the limits of this paper did not forbid citation. The creations of sculpture, painting, and music, are illustrations still more decisive.

[. . .]

The first part of these remarks has related to poetry in its elements and principles; and it has been shown, as well as the narrow limits assigned them would permit, that what is called poetry in a restricted sense has a common source with all other forms of order and of beauty according to which the materials of human life are susceptible of being arranged, and which is poetry in an universal sense.

The second part will have for its object an application of these principles to the present state of the cultivation of poetry, and a defence of the attempt to idealize the modern forms of manners and opinion, and compel them into a subordination to the imaginative and creative faculty. For the literature of England, an energetic development of which has ever preceded or accompanied a great and free development of the national will, has arisen, as it were, from a new birth. In spite of the low-thoughted envy which would undervalue contemporary merit, our own will be a memorable age in its intellectual achievements, and we live among such philosophers and poets as surpass beyond comparison any who have appeared since the last national struggle for civil and religious liberty. The most unfailing herald, companion, or follower of the awakening of a great people to work a beneficial change in opinion or institution, is poetry. At such periods there is an accumulation of the power of communicating and receiving intense and impassioned conceptions respecting man and nature. The persons in whom this power resides may often (as far as regards many portions of their nature) have little apparent correspondence with that spirit of the good of which they are the ministers. But even whilst they deny and abjure, they are yet compelled to serve the power which is seated upon the throne of their own soul. It is impossible to read the compositions of the most celebrated writers of the present day without being startled with the electric life which burns within their words. They measure the circumference and sound the depths of human nature with a comprehensive and all-penetrating spirit, and they are themselves perhaps the most sincerely astonished at its manifestation, for it is less their own spirit than the spirit of the age. Poets are the hierophants of an unapprehended inspiration, the mirrors of the gigantic shadows which futurity casts upon the present, the words which express what they understand not; the trumpets which sing to battle, and feel not what they inspire; the influence which is moved not, but moves. Poets are the unacknowledged legislators of the world.

Note

1. Francis Bacon, *Of the Advancement of Learning* (1605), Book III.

Ralph Waldo Emerson

Emerson (1803–82) published his first series of essays in 1841, and it is from there that the extract from 'Circles' is taken. Appropriately, given its theme, it seems impossible to discuss it except in relation to things that it anticipates – being as thoroughgoing in its way as Bataille or Nietzsche – and like them taking apart the established conventions of the day, seeing civilizations perish and decay. In Emerson's hands, though, this sounds far from nihilistic, as the vision is presented in the most optimistic terms, as a chance to make the world anew. Emerson welcomes the symptoms of the new, invites us to embrace them and to live as prophets of the age to come. Like Shelley in his defence of poetry, Emerson looks for the causes behind superficial appearances, and finds them in the hands that put up buildings, and in the will that guides the hands. In order to understand a culture it is not enough to describe its buildings, but one wants to know about the impulses that drove people to build them. These volitions, acting in different directions, balanced against one another, or working together in the same direction, are held in a relation that could be called the society's *ethos*. The circles that radiate out from these values are secondary and tertiary productions of the ethics that lies at the culture's heart, producing the ways of living and the material culture of the society as a set of consequences and by-products of the life of the community.

Trying to understand buildings in this way, as the consequence of systems of values, lies at the heart of the project represented in this book, which brings together texts that often have a bearing on the ethos that one would want an architect to have, rather than issuing instructions to build particular shapes. Architects cannot be convincing nihilists – as the positive activity of building involves investing in an imagined future, projecting one's insights and values into the world that is yet to come, and of which the new building will form a part, probably outliving the individuals who designed and built it, surviving in ways that are forever unfathomable. Emerson's optimism is far from superficial, and is valuable in lending support to the architects' enterprise of trying to see into the future and building it early. He inculcates part of a value-system for a new world, and his rhetoric is compelling. There is a need to apologize for some of his remarks (about women for example) which locate the writing back in its own time and did not anticipate the social change that we have seen more recently; but there is no doubt that he would have welcomed the changes had they been in sight.

From 'Circles'

The eye is the first circle; the horizon which it forms is the second; and throughout nature this primary figure is repeated without end. It is the highest emblem in the cipher of the world. St Augustine described the nature of God as a circle whose centre was everywhere, and its circumference nowhere. We are all our lifetime reading the copious sense of this first of forms. One moral we have already deduced, in considering the circular or compensatory character of every human action. Another analogy we shall now trace; that every action admits of being outdone. Our life is an apprenticeship to the truth, that around every circle another can be drawn; that there is no end in nature, but every end is a beginning; that there is always another dawn risen on mid-noon, and under every deep a lower deep opens.

This fact, as far as it symbolizes the moral fact of the Unattainable, the flying Perfect, around which the hands of man can never meet, at once the inspirer and the condemner of every success, may conveniently serve us to connect many illustrations of human power in every department.

There are no fixtures in nature. The universe is fluid and volatile. Permanence is but a word of degrees. Our globe seen by God is a transparent law, not a mass of facts. The law dissolves the fact and holds it fluid. Our culture is the predominance of an idea which draws after it this train of cities and institutions. Let us rise into another idea: they will disappear. The Greek sculpture is all melted away, as if it had been statues of ice; here and there a solitary figure or fragment remaining, as we see flecks and scraps of snow left in cold dells and mountain clefts in June and July. For the genius that created it creates now somewhat else. The Greek letters last a little longer, but are already passing under the same sentence, and tumbling into the inevitable pit which the creation of new thought opens for all that is old. The new continents are built out of the ruins of an old planet; the new races fed out of the decomposition of the foregoing. New arts destroy the old. See the investment of capital in aqueducts made useless by hydraulics; fortifications, by gunpowder; roads and canals, by railways; sails, by steam; steam by electricity.

You admire this tower of granite, weathering the hurts of so many ages. Yet a little waving hand built this huge wall, and that which builds is better than that which is built. The hand that built it can topple it down much faster. Better than the hand, and nimbler, was the invisible thought which wrought through it; and thus ever, behind the coarse effect, is the fine cause, which being narrowly seen, is itself the effect of a finer cause. Every thing looks permanent until its secret is known. A rich estate appears to women a firm and lasting fact; to a merchant, one easily created out of any materials and easily lost. An orchard, good tillage, good grounds, seem a fixture, like a gold mine, or a river, to a citizen; but to a large farmer, not much more fixed than the state of the crop. Nature looks provokingly stable and secular, but it has a cause like all the rest; and when once I comprehend that, will these fields stretch so immovably wide, these leaves hang so individually considerable? Permanence is a word of degrees. Every thing is medial. Moons are no more bounds to spiritual power than bat-balls.

The key to every man is his thought. Sturdy and defying though he look, he has a helm which he obeys, which is the idea after which all his facts are classified. He can only be reformed by showing him a new idea which commands his own. The life of man is a self-evolving circle, which, from a ring imperceptibly small, rushes on all sides outwards to new and larger circles, and that without end. The extent to which the generation of circles, wheel without wheel, will go, depends on the force or truth of the individual soul. For it is the inert effort of each thought, having formed itself into a circular wave of circumstance, – as for instance, an empire, rules of an art, a local usage, a religious rite, – to heap itself on that ridge, and to solidify and hem in the life. But if the soul is quick and strong, it bursts over that boundary on all sides, and expands another orbit on the great deep, which also runs up into a high wave, with attempt again to stop and to bind. But the heart refuses to be imprisoned; in its first and narrowest pulses, it already tends outward with a vast force, and to immense and innumerable expansions.

Every ultimate fact is only the first of a new series. Every general law only a particular fact of some more general law presently to disclose itself. There is no outside, no inclosing wall, no circumference to us. The man finishes his story, – how good! how final! how it puts a new face on all things! He fills the sky. Lo! on the other side rises also a man, and draws a circle around the circle we had just pronounced the outline of the sphere. Then already is out first speaker not man, but only a first speaker. His only redress is forthwith to draw a circle outside that of his antagonist. And so men do by themselves. The result of to-day, which haunts the mind and cannot be escaped, will presently be abridged into a word, and the principle that seemed to explain nature will itself be included as one example of a bolder generalization. On the thought of to-morrow there is a power to to upheave all thy creed, all the creeds, all the literatures, of the nations, and marshal thee to a heaven which no epic dream has yet depicted. Every man is not so much a workman of the world, as he is a suggestion of that he should be. Men walk as prophecies of the next age.

Step by step we scale this mysterious ladder: the steps are actions; the new prospect is power. Every several result is threatened and judged by that which follows. Every one seems to be contradicted by the new; it is only limited by the new. The new statement is always hated by the old, and, to those dwelling in the old, comes like an abyss of scepticism. But the eye soon gets wonted to it, for the eye and it are effects of one cause; then its innocency and benefits appear, and presently, all its energy spent, it pales and dwindles before the revelation of the new hour.

Fear not the new generalization. Does the fact look crass and material, threatening to degrade thy theory of spirit? Resist it not; it goes to refine and raise thy theory of matter just as much.

There are no fixtures to men, if we appeal to consciousness. Every man supposes himself not to be fully understood; and if there is any truth in him, if he rests at last on the divine soul, I see not how it can be otherwise. The last chamber, the last closet, he must feel, was never opened; there is always a residuum unknown, unanalysable. That is, every man believes that he has a greater possibility.

Our moods do not believe in each other. To-day I am full of thoughts, and can write what I please. I see no reason why I should not have the same thought, the same power of expression to-morrow. What I write, whilst I write it, seems the most natural thing in the world; but yesterday I saw a dreary vacuity in this direction in which I now see so much; and a month hence, I doubt not, I shall wonder who he was that wrote so many continuous pages. Alas for this infirm faith, this will not strenuous, this vast ebb of a vast flow! I am God in nature; I am a weed by the wall.

Section 2
Groundwork

Pragmatics

One meaning of the word 'pragmatic' suggests that a task is being done without any theory coming into play. However after reading Shelley, one would rather say that there is always a theory at work, but sometimes it is an old theory that has become so deeply ingrained that it is invisible to us. Such are the theories of common sense. 'Pragmatism' however is also the name of a philosophical movement (if 'movement' is quite the word) that is explicitly theoretical while being grounded in experience, and uninclined to be drawn into metaphysical abstractions. William James (1842–1912) was its clearest exponent, but the term had been coined by Charles Sanders Peirce (1834–1914) and would be taken up and applied to aesthetics by John Dewey (1859–1952) and more recently by Richard Shusterman.[1] Richard Rorty has been piecing together an idea of pragmatism as a philosophical tradition, in which his own work certainly belongs, and the idea has been appearing with increasing frequency in the analysis of architecture.[2] The great appeal of pragmatist aesthetics for anyone interested in architecture, is that it takes everyday experience as the basis from which to extrapolate. If architecture is concerned with the lives that it touches, and the kinds of life that become possible because it is there, then the centrality of this everyday experience feels right and proper in a discussion of architecture. There are, to be sure, special architectural experiences that deserve to be grouped with the kinds of experience that one has when confronting a work of art in a museum, but most often what we need from a building is for it to give an appropriate frame and support for our everyday habits. These habits make the structure of our lives and our identities, and so they assume a personal importance that we miss if we confine our discussion to geometry and the abstract forms of buildings. There is a cultural dimension to architecture, which is drawn out in the passages from Bachelard and Benjamin below, and it does not work all in one direction. When Peirce drafted a preface to a philosophical work (which never saw the light of day) he drew on his everyday experience of buildings, to give him a metaphor to convey the reliability of his enterprise.[3] In this characterization the familiar is commonsensical, while the unfamiliar is metaphysical, and worrying. What all the pragmatist philosophers share is a receptivity to thinking things afresh, not pretending to have arrived at a final truth, but being involved in a continuing development. The world, and especially our understanding of the world, is seen to be in an evolutionary state, and the point is to participate in a developing discourse in order to bring fresh understanding. There is no dogma, except a dogma of method – an appeal to experience and experiment. And different views are allowed to subsist side by side, where there is no experiment to conduct that would settle things one way or the other. The validity of an idea in a given set of circumstances is decided by seeing whether or not it helps us to achieve what we are trying to achieve. This implies a move away from trying to determine the 'real' innermost significance of an object by trying to contemplate it in isolation, but seeing it always in relation to other things (involved in processes) which can in turn generate a plurality of interpretations and experiences, which is the theme of Section 4 (Pluralities). There is also a very general point to be made here, about the importance of the relations of people and things. Relations between people conventionally fall under the heading of 'politics'. Relations between people and things could also fall under that heading – particularly if the 'things' in question significantly mediate the relations between people (if the things in question are for example weapons or money). Relations between parts of an environment can be conceived in a comparable way, so that there need be no particular need to switch to a different word to describe those relations.

Ethos

The idea of this book is not to promote a set of shapes for architects to use, but a set of ideas that can be brought into play. The overriding ideas that make the atmosphere in which decisions are taken make up a system of values – an *ethos* – and in this sense the book is a work of ethics. When John Ruskin set about a comparable task in the nineteenth century, he suggested a set of seven guiding principles, which he called the 'lamps' of architecture.[4] The kind of world in which we now live, looks in some ways very different from the world that Ruskin knew, and some fresh imperatives now face us. In some ways, though, much is the same. If we take Ruskin's 'lamps' and substitute a slightly different metaphor, the idea that there is a set of forces acting on a building's design, and the architect must try to give due attention to each of them, then Ruskin immediately begins to sound like Nietzsche. The lamps sound fanciful and old fashioned, whereas the forces sound bracing and modern, but they are different images for thinking about the same kind of thing. Nietzsche, Freud and Marx have between them had a colossal impact on the thought of the modern age, and their challenge to think through the implications for culture of power, sex and money has set the agenda for much social commentary in the last five decades and more, even if they now have to be read with a sense of their place in history, rather than as the last word on their subjects.

Despite the fact that questions of power, sex and money are certainly implicated in architecture, their analysis has been avoided until more recently, so that in architecture discussions of gender, identity, sexuality, power structures and the circulation of capital sound like still-contemporary developments. This is because practical architects need to endorse the cultural values of the building-commissioning classes, and the demands of gentility exclude challenging underlying questions from discussion, so polite discourse has gravitated around matters of style.[5] Histories of architecture have tended to be stories about one style succeeding another, and while these stories certainly have their validity, there are other stories also that can be told. One practical aspect of the stories about the successions of styles, is that if one has mastery of these stories then one can participate in the polite discourse of the day, which might be necessary for the pursuit of various goals. Another aspect is that the different approaches to design (that gave rise to the different architectural styles) give insight into the ways of thinking in cultures other than our own, and that gives us a more sophisticated understanding of the world and our place in it. At the heart of any architectural project there is a close connection between a solid object – the building – and the life that it was designed to support, or to make possible. Diane Favro's essay about ancient Roman triumphal parades is included here because it shows something of the vitality and validity of the connection between the Roman system of values and the buildings that their activity left behind – now in ruins. One reason for selecting this example is that the remains of antiquity have on occasion been treated with such reverence as pure objects, that architects have sometimes persuaded themselves that they were achieving something significant merely by emulating the ancient forms. Favro's essay shows something of the forces at work that gave rise to those forms, and how they connected. If we have agendas that are other than those of the ancient Romans it follows that we will be building with different ends in mind – even if (as does happen) there is an attempt to follow a Roman architectural style. The centre of Rome was the embodiment of a culture of centralization, with an extravagant display building up over the centuries as wealth poured into the imperial city from its colonies, and as the emperors and victors outdid one another with the magnificence of their monuments. The link between the concentration of power and wealth and the erection of monuments is very plain to see here, and the Romans were not reticent in letting it show – they were excited about their military achievements, and wanted to let each other know about their pride.

We do not see things in quite this way now, where our own societies' monuments are concerned. There is a concern not to demonstrate that we can coerce the world to our will, but that we have a duty to safeguard what is left of nature, and to live in harmony with other species on the planet. (The 'we' in this paragraph means 'I', but with the expectation that you, the reader, can be carried along in acquiescence – which may or may not be the case, as the view is not one that is universally held.) This idea has its precursors in nineteenth-century thinking, but has become mainstream in the last few decades. Gregory Bateson spoke with particular insight, as an anthropologist with a vocabulary to analyse the behaviour of societies, and with a wide range of intellectual concerns. 'Let us now consider,' he said,

> what happens when you make the epistemological error of choosing the wrong unit: you end up with the species versus the other species around it or versus the environment in which it operates. Man against nature. You end up, in fact, with Kaneohe Bay polluted. Lake Erie a slimy green mess, and 'Let's build atom bombs to kill off the next door neighbours.' *There is an ecology of bad ideas, just as there is an ecology of weeds*, and it is characteristic of the system that basic error propagates itself. It branches out like a rooted parasite through the tissues of life, and everything gets into a rather peculiar mess. [. . .] You forget that the eco-mental system called Lake Erie is part of your wider eco-mental system – and that if Lake Erie is driven insane, its insanity is incorporated in the larger system of your thought and experience.[6]

'Ecology' here is presented as a widely-drawn category that encompasses objects and ideas, organic species and their habitats, inseparably linked together. Where architecture is concerned, for 'habitats' we tend to mean buildings, rather than the natural landscape, but the principles at work are the same ones. As Félix Guattari said, commenting on Bateson:

> Now more than ever, nature cannot be separated from culture; in order to comprehend the interactions between eco-systems, the mecanosphere and social and individual Universes of reference, we must learn to think 'transversally'. Just as monstrous and mutant algae invade the lagoon of Venice, so our television screens are populated, saturated, by 'degenerate' images and statements. In the field of social ecology, men like Donald Trump are permitted to proliferate freely, like another species of algae, taking over entire districts of New York and Atlantic City; he 'redevelops' by raising rents, thereby driving out tens of thousands of poor families, most of whom are condemned to homelessness, becoming the equivalent of the dead fish of environmental ecology.[7]

The image of property tycoons as scum is startling. What Guattari was arguing for here, was to see the unit of survival, not as an individual organic species, but the species plus its habitat; and the habitat is likely to include other species. However there is a style of speaking at work in his texts, that fuses the inorganic parts of a habitat as part of the living 'unit of survival' (species plus habitat). So buildings are certainly included in the equation, and Guattari also mentioned 'incorporeal species such as music, the arts, cinema,'[8] in the company of which the gestural art of architecture certainly belongs. For practising architects who want to build large prominent buildings, and to earn a living while doing it, it is necessary to work with – or rather work for – people like Donald Trump, which makes the ideas above seem challenging. If an individual commercially-driven architectural practice were to take Guattari's image to heart, then the practice would certainly collapse. The property developer usually looks to maximize the profitability of a large development, and the architect has to play along. It is not necessarily that the developer as an individual feels the will to exploit assets to their maximum capacity; it is part of the system. If the company is not showing a good return on its investments, then its shareholders will move their money elsewhere – the process is quite abstract and impersonal, and the participants have their well-defined roles in this machine. It is beyond the capacity of an architectural practice to change the way that this machine works, but it might be possible to decide on the terms in which it is prepared to engage with it – or remain isolated from it – but that is likely to result in a loss of income. The idea that it is better to have more money is one of these ideas that takes root with great tenacity and spreads everywhere, and it is only with difficulty that people in its grip are to be persuaded otherwise.

Steady state

In Bataille's schema, society in general is not fundamentally inclined to endless hoarding, but to an everyday economy that builds up a surplus that is then extravagantly squandered in celebration – feasting, gifts, sacrifices. Buildings can certainly play a role in this sort of process, when an individual or a society decides that it desires a monument to commemorate a great event, or a cultural landmark to show what splendid things the society has achieved. These types of buildings fall outside the commercial mechanisms, and are ways of spending money that has been earned by other means – sometimes very large sums of it. In Bataille's description, these sacrificial mechanisms work as a way of restoring balance. The Roman triumphs would be a good example. The Royal Opera House at Covent Garden would be another, as would a national football stadium. In each case the society is made rich by other means – whether by conquest, or commerce, or a mixture of the two – and by this lavish non-commercial consumption, it displays to itself the fine qualities that it has. There is a profound cultural difference between the buildings that we erect in order to make money, and the buildings on which we spend the money that we have made. The first set is of buildings that are a means to an end. The second set is of buildings that, on the face of it, are an end in themselves, being some of the good things that the more general commercial activity has made possible (along with less noticeable public services). These highly visible projects are the flowerings of the culture, and different cultures make manifest their value-systems by way of them.

Gregory Bateson's essay on the culture of Bali, included here, is an attempt to describe a value-system that does not generate indefinite growth and ultimate catastrophe. It is a highly traditional and well-balanced culture, in which excess of any kind is discouraged, and even pleasure must not become too intense.

Michel Foucault tried to summarize the ethos of Deleuze and Guattari's first book together – *Anti-Oedipus* – in a series of bullet-points, designed to help turn the book into a manual for everyday life:

- Free political action from all unitary and totalizing paranoia.
- Develop action, thought, and desires by proliferation, juxtaposition, and disjunction, and not by subdivision and pyramidal hierarchization.
- Withdraw allegiance from the old categories of the negative (law, limit, castration, lack, lacuna), which Western thought has so long held sacred as a form of power and an access to reality. Prefer what is positive and multiple, difference over uniformity, flows over unities, mobile arrangements over systems. Believe that what is productive is not sedentary but nomadic.
- Do not think that one has to be sad in order to be militant, even though the thing one is fighting is abominable. It is the connection of desire to reality (and not its retreat into the forms of representation) that possesses revolutionary force.
- Do not use thought to ground a political practice in Truth; nor political action to discredit, as mere speculation, a line of thought. Use political practice as an intensifier of thought, and analysis as a multiplier of the forms and domains for the intervention of political action.
- Do not demand of politics that it restore the 'rights' of the individual, as philosophy has defined them the individual is the product of power. What is neded is to 'de-individualize' by means of multiplication and displacement, diverse combinations. The group must not be the organic bond uniting hierarchized individuals, but a constant generator of de-individualization.
- Do not become enamoured of power.[9]

The ethos that is shaped by such values is a long way from the world of perfect forms that was proposed by Plato, and which had so decisive an effect on Renaissance thought. This is a world of processes and politics, in which there are dynamic systems that interact with one another. The western architectural image that most clearly focuses intensity is that of the palace at Versailles, where the landscape for miles around is focused on the king's bedchamber, and gives expression to the concentration of power at the heart of a centralized state apparatus. The Baroque vista, along a symmetrical axis, to a culminating dome, has become unmistakeably an expression of power, whether of the church – as at St Peter's in Rome – or of the state – as at the end of the great mall in Washington DC. The most striking monuments of the past, from the pyramids to the Capitol, were shaped by architects who were close to concentrations of great power and who were trusted with the great commissions. The high-status architectural composition that comes closest to realizing the programme set down by Foucault is that of the Parc de la Villette, by Bernard Tschumi, a successful attempt to reclaim some blighted land just inside the Paris orbital motorway. Here an area of indefinite extent is defined by its being dotted with red cubes placed at regular intervals on a grid, so that when one is there they act as orientation devices and signal one's presence on that *plateau*. It is quite a different means of giving definition to the place than the baroque practice of marking out bounded geometric figures on the ground, and moving between them in organized ways. Here there is the systematic but arbitrary grid, and one wanders freely in it, one's movements impeded or encouraged by seemingly random acts of juxtaposition and dislocation, as the cubes are inhabited for various reasons – a café, a crèche, a hamburger bar, a cinema – with no controlling order disciplining the activities, where surreal adjacencies occur – the running track inside the piano bar, inside the winter garden.[10] Tschumi's 'event-cities' are also significant here, in that they signal the priority of events over monuments in the generation of urban space – a pragmatic turn (if it acts like a city, then we might as well call it a city, whether or not it has the usual urban fabric).[11] (Tschumi needs to be rescued from the 'deconstructivist' pigeon-hole into which he was put in the 1990s, just as Deleuze needs to be rescued from 'post-structuralism'.) The pragmatic move from objects to their uses is at the heart of Section 5 (Relations).

Rem Koolhaas in his book *S,M,L,XL* argues that when we are confronted with buildings that are executed on a very large scale, that we can no longer conceive of ourselves in relation to the whole building, but engage with it in a fragmentary way, paying attention to the relation between oneself and the parts of the building with which we are immediately surrounded.

> Beyond a certain critical mass, a building becomes a Big Building. Such a mass can no longer be controlled by a single architectural gesture, or even by a combination of architectural gestures. [. . .] The 'art' of architecture is useless in Bigness. [. . .] interior and exterior architectures become separate projects, one dealing with the instability of programmatic and iconographic needs, the other – agent of disinformation – offering the city the apparent stability of an object.[12]

This too is an experience of a *plateau* – a space without definite edges, or at least a space in which the edges are not a significant part of the experience. For example in

Section 2: Groundwork

a large department store, one finds oneself in a place where one has a clear relation to the goods that are on sale, and the place will be well lit and well served, but the sense of the quality of the space is not determined by its overall shape. By contrast the lessons we could learn from Bramante or Michelangelo would include lessons about how one feels in spaces of certain proportions, carefully balanced. The sense of the body and its relations with the world is explored in Section 3 (Individual). This section has been concerned with relations between people and places. The readings that follow draw attention firstly to the pragmatic issue that there are multiple, perhaps a great many, 'correct' responses to a given state of affairs. It is worth pointing out also – as these things are sometimes misrepresented – that there are many more possible 'incorrect' descriptions, which are demonstrably inaccurate in one way or another. The readings around Bachelard and Benjamin show responses at different scales – from the domestic, and domestic objects, to the city – and they are personal responses that have grown from particular cultural conditions. They are interesting at two levels; one because they give an account of a complex response to everyday conditions that could easily pass without comment and be taken to be much simpler; and two because to some degree we share in these responses. Bachelard and Benjamin might seem to be giving an account of personal idiosyncracies, but they are idiosyncracies that we all share – or else we have others of our own. The closer we are, culturally speaking, to Bachelard and Benjamin, the more their carefully nuanced responses will seem like descriptions that we might have written ourselves, but in each there is a struggle, because the realization that it was necessary to pay attention to these irrational aspects of things, was that they complicated the picture of objectivity that each was trying to build up (Bachelard with reference to scientific method, Benjamin with reference to Marxism). The utility value of a house is different from but not entirely to be separated from the sentimental value that builds up around a house where we have lived for a long time. Somehow it comes to matter, and at different scales of operation the same can apply to small inanimate objects – small tokens of one's childhood, that turn into personal *lieux de mémoire* as one outgrows them – or the city, the country, or the landscapes with which one has a rapport. When these things are purely personal, their value is purely idiosyncratic, but when they are introduced into a wider social realm, the issues become complicated. Certain sorts of landscapes, for example, can be valued by elite groups, who are taught to appreciate them, and then if one has knowledge of those landscapes and can demonstrate appreciation of them, then one has claim to a certain level of social distinction. Others who belong to the same social group will be able to lay claim to comparable experiences, and being able to demonstrate that one has them could be a factor in whether or not one feels that one belongs in a particular group, or wants to exclude oneself from it. The kinds of decisions I make about what sort of buildings to live and work in, may or may not change the sort of person I am, but they certainly influence how others see me, and architects need to be able to understand the cultural value of the gestures that their buildings will be seen to make. Good intentions are not enough. There plainly are interpersonal politics at work in architectural decisions, both in the development of the design and in the use of the building after it has been made. What kind of politics they are will be dependent on the kind of ethos that prevails – for whatever reason – and one might make a point of cultivating a certain set of values, or else would perpetuate unthinkingly the values that one has acquired through the accidents of upbringing and life. There are also politics to be analysed in the social forces at work that determine what degree of freedom I have to make choices about the kinds of places where I live and work. Some people have very little choice, while others have a great deal. To some extent this is connected with the power to control flows of money, but there are also sets of attitudes that can be brought to bear along with the ownership of property. If I have made a vast fortune in popular entertainment then I will probably feel myself free to buy what I like, and my personal taste could leave me very free to invent a way of living. If my possessions came to me by way of an ancient family lineage, I might feel a sense of duty to take care of the house and its furniture for another generation, and my purchases might be few and inconspicuous. In the domestic sphere, if my income is about average, then various sorts of consideration will have to come into play, as I try to weigh up whether it is better to rent a place to live or to buy it, and whether the money is well spent on a bigger house, or whether the increased expenditure so cramps my freedom to do other things than stay at home, that it is better to sacrifice some space and be able to travel (for example) or drive a more impressive car. Such factors inevitably have a bearing, and it is precisely because they do that our buildings tell us so clearly what we really care about as a society, as Bataille explained. If a public monument is to be built, then the money to build it will have to come from funds that would otherwise have helped to do other things. If I decide to have another room, rather than a better car, or a new kitchen rather than a large donation to a charity that helps homeless people, then that tells me something about the kind of person I am – and it is not always comfortable to realize it.

Notes

1. John Dewey, *Art as Experience* (1934, reprinted New York: Puttnam, 1980); Richard Shusterman, *Pragmatist Aesthetics: Living Beauty, Rethinking Art* (Oxford: Blackwell, 1992).
2. See for example *The Pragmatist Imagination*, edited by Joan Ockman (New York: Princeton Architectural Press, 2000).
3. See below, p. 69.
4. John Ruskin, *The Seven Lamps of Architecture* (London: 1849).
5. Diane Ghirardo, 'The Architecture of Deceit', in *What is Architecture?*, edited by Andrew Ballantyne (London: Routledge, 2002) pp. 63–71.
6. Gregory Bateson, 'Pathologies of Epistemology' in *Steps to an Ecology of Mind* (New York: Chandler, 1972), pp. 454–63; pp. 459–60; cited in Félix Guattari, *Les trois ecologies* (Paris: Galilée, 1989) translated by Ian Pindar and Paul Sutton, *The Three Ecologies* (London: Athlone, 2000) pp. 70–71.
7. Félix Guattari, *Three Ecologies*, op. cit., p. 43.
8. Félix Guatarri, *Chaosmose* (Paris: Galilée, 1992) translated by Paul Bains and Julian Pefanis, *Chaosmosis: an Ethico-Aesthetic Paradigm* (Sydney: Power, 1995) p. 120.
9. Michel Foucault, in the preface to Gilles Deleuze and Félix Guattari, *L'Anti-*

Section 2: Groundwork

Oedipe: capitalisme et schizophrénie (Paris: Editions de Minuit, 1972) translated by Robert Hurley, Mark Seem and Helen R. Lane, *Anti-Oedipus: Capitalism and Schizophrenia 1* (New York: Viking, 1977) pp. xiii–xiv.

10. Bernard Tschumi, *Architeture and Dislocation* (Cambridge, Mass.: MIT, 1994).
11. Bernard Tschumi, *Event-Cities (Praxis)* (Cambridge, Mass.: MIT, 1994). An expanded version of *Praxis Villes-Événements* (Paris: Le Fresnoy, 1993). See also Bernard Tschumi, *Event-Cities 2* (Cambridge, Mass.: MIT, 2000).
12. Rem Koolhaas, Office for Metropolitan Architecture and Bruce Mau, *S,M,L,XL*, edited by Jennifer Sigler (New York: Monacelli, 1995) pp. 499–501.

Gaston Bachelard and Michel Tournier

Gaston Bachelard (1884–1962) was born at Bar-sur-Aube, a small country town in the Champagne-Ardennes region, east of Troyes. His father was a cobbler, as had been his grandfather, and his intellectual life was that of an independent thinker, who very gradually achieved recognition and then great eminence, working as a scientist and as a theorist of science. Patrick Heelan begins his Foreword to the English translation of Bachelard's book *The New Scientific Spirit* by saying that 'Gaston Bachelard's writings are comparable in spirit and scope to those of Charles Sanders Peirce, the American founder of pragmatism.'[1] Northrop Frye suggests that Bachelard's style compares with Samuel Butler's.[2] What they share is a broad range of interests and a conviction that the established ways of understanding the world were missing some fundamental point.

From the *The New Scientific Spirit*

The Essential Complexity of the Philosophy of Science: An Outline

Since William James it has often been repeated that every cultivated man necessarily subscribes to some system of metaphysics. To my mind it is more accurate to say that every man who attempts to learn science makes use not of one but of two metaphysical systems. Both are natural and cogent, implicit rather than explicit, and tenacious in their persistence. And one contradicts the other. For convenience let us attach provisional names to the two fundamental philosophical attitudes that coexist so peacefully in the modern scientific mind: rationalism and realism, to use the classical terminology. Is proof required that such tranquil eclecticism does indeed exist? Consider, then the following proposition: 'Science is a product of the human mind, a product that conforms to both the laws of thought and the outside world. Hence it has two aspects, one subjective, the other objective; and both are equally necessary, for it is as impossible to alter the laws of the mind as it is to change the laws of the Universe'.[3] This rather odd metaphysical assertion can be pursued in two possible directions: the first leading to a rationalism at one remove, according to which the laws of the universe would merely reflect the laws of the mind; the second leading to a universal realism, one of whose principles would be that the laws of the mind, being instances of universal laws, must be absolutely invariable.[4]

[. . .]

Section 2: Groundwork

> The very fact that the philosophy of science is a philosophy that *applies* to another discipline means that it cannot preserve the unity and purity of speculative philosophy. Any work of science, no matter what its point of departure, cannot become fully convincing until it crosses the boundary between the theoretical and the experimental: *Experimentation must give way to argument, and argument must have recourse to experimentation*. Every application is a form of transcendence. I intend to show that this duality exists in even the simplest scientific investigations, that is, the phenomenology of science divides, according to one set of epistemological polarities, into two realms, that of the picturesque and that of the comprehensible (which is just another way of saying that science may be viewed in either realistic or rationalistic terms).[5]

The constant move between theory and practice is at the heart of Bachelard's enterprise, each having value on account of the other. A practice that does not engage with theory is meaningless, and a theory that does not engage with practice is metaphysical. The attitude is strikingly reflected in Deleuze's remarking that 'Practice is a set of relays from one theoretical point to another, and theory is a relay from one practice to another. No theory can develop without eventually encountering a wall, and practice is necessary for piercing this wall.[6]

Bachelard, having published many books and papers on scientific method, developing the idea of science as a human and cultural construct, made a remarkable departure in 1938 with *The Psychoanalysis of Fire*. It was this work, published when he was 54, and soon after he was invited to take the chair of History and Philosophy of Science at the Sorbonne in Paris. His later works gravitated around 'picturesque' themes, examining elements of the irrational in our responses to things – ways in which we fail to achieve the objectivity that would seem to be at the heart of scientific endeavour, but which, inescapably, is not. Bachelard's epigraph for *The Psychoanalysis of Fire* was from Paul Eluard: 'I must not look on reality as being like myself'.[7] He failed of course, as we all must, and Bachelard's later works are studies of the ways in which we project ourselves and our interests into the world, even when we think that we are being objective.

From *The Psychoanalysis of Fire*

> We have only to speak of an object to think that we are being objective. But, because we chose it in the first place, the object reveals more about us than we do about it. What we consider to be our fundamental ideas concerning the world are often indications of the immaturity of our minds. Sometimes we stand in wonder before a chosen object; we build up hypotheses and reveries; in this way we form convictions which have all the appearance of true knowledge. But the initial source is impure: the first impression is not a fundamental truth. In point of fact, scientific objectivity is possible only if one has broken first with the immediate object, if one has refused to yield to the seduction of the initial choice, if one has checked and contradicted the thoughts which arise from one's first observation. Any objective examination, when duly verified, refutes the

results of the first contact with the object. To start with, everything must be called into question: sensation, common sense, usage however constant, even etymology, for words, which are made for singing and enchanting, rarely make contact with thought. Far from marvelling at the object, objective thought must treat it ironically. Without this malign vigilance we would never adopt a truly objective attitude. When we are dealing with men, our equals and our brothers, our method should be based on sympathy. But when confronted with this inert world whose life is not ours, which suffers none of our sorrows nor is exalted by any of our joys, we must restrain our enthusiasms, we must repress our personal feelings. The axes of poetry and of science are opposed to one another from the outset. All that philosophy can hope to accomplish is to make poetry and science complementary, to unite them as two well-defined opposites.

[. . .]

We are going to study a problem that no one has managed to approach objectively, one in which the initial charm of the object is so strong that it still has the power to warp the minds of the clearest thinkers . . . this problem is the psychological problem posed by our convictions about fire. It seems to me so definitely psychological in nature that I do not hesitate to speak of a psychoanalysis of fire.[8]

Bachelard turned his attention to buildings in *The Poetics of Space*, first published in 1958 (by when he was 74). The range of his approach is well conveyed by a list of the chapter headings, which point to the evocative kinds of nooks, shelters and refuges where our imaginations rest and play:

- The House
- From Cellar to Garret
- The Significance of the Hut
- House and Universe
- Drawers, Chests and Wardrobes
- Nests
- Shells
- Corners
- Miniature
- Intimate Immensity
- The Dialectics of Outside and Inside
- The Phenomenology of Roundness

It is a list that reads like a poem in itself, and needs to be read slowly, so that some of the individual words have enough space around them for the imagination to bring into proximity the resonances of each idea.

From *The Poetics of Space*

> Our house is our corner of the world. As has often been said, it is our first universe, a real cosmos in every sense of the word. . . . But our adult life is so dis-

possessed of the essential benefits, its anthropocosmic ties have become so slack, that we do not feel their first attachment in the universe of the house.[9]

[...]

The real houses of memory, the houses to which we return in dreams, the houses that are rich in unalterable oneirism, do not readily lend themselves to description. . . . The first, the oneirically definitive house must retain its shadows.

[...]

A house constitutes a body of images that give mankind proofs or illusions of stability. We are constantly re-imagining its reality: to distinguish all these images would be to describe the soul of the house; it would mean developing a veritable psychology of the house.

To bring order into these images, I believe that we should consider two principal connecting themes: 1) A house is imagined as a vertical being. It rises upward. It differentiates itself in terms of its verticality. It is one of the appeals to our consciousness of verticality. 2) A house is imagined as a concentrated being. It appeals to our consciousness of centrality.[9]

For the sake of concision, I have allowed the very brief and abstract statement of Bachelard's programme to stand here, but what makes his writing persuasive are his examples, particularly the evocative descriptions of his own childhood home. The rural houses in his part of France would have had a few habitable rooms, and a series of ancilliary spaces. Often a barn would be part of the same building as the house, connecting with the attic space that would run along above the presentable well-decorated rooms below. Probably in the Bachelard household this would have been turned into a workshop for the shoes. The roof, supported by heavy timbers, and made of clay tiles or riven stones, would shelter the house below from rain and the sometimes-fierce sun. There would be some insulation – usually packed earth – above the ceiling of the rooms below, so the attic floor could feel very solid, and might well be covered in small square clay tiles. Below the principal rooms there would be stone vaulted cellars, used for storage of things more sensitive to heat. The heavy stone construction of the cellars, and their connection with the cool dark world under ground, makes them correlate in Bachelard's description with the unconscious, the primitive and the instinctual. By contrast the attic with its arrangement of tiles and joists is rational and intellectual, representing the home of the mind. As children there is no doubt: we find these places exciting, and they are somehow highly charged. But Bachelard unexpectedly resists personal reminiscence:

What would be the use, for instance, in giving the plan of the room that was really *my* room, in describing the little room at the end of the garret, in saying that from the window, across the indentations of the roofs, one could see the hill. I alone, in my memories of another century, can open the deep cupboard that still retains for me alone that unique odour, the odour of raisins drying on a wicker tray. The odour of raisins! It is an odour that is beyond description, one that takes a lot of imagination to smell. But I've already said too much. If I said more, the reader, back in his own room, would not open that unique wardrobe, with its unique smell, which is the signature of intimacy. Paradoxically, in order to suggest the values of intimacy, we have to induce in the reader a state of suspended reading. For it is not until his eyes have left the page that recollections of my room can become a threshold of oneirism for him.[10]

It is precisely this quality in Bachelard's text that makes it impossible to read him briskly. The text constantly deflects the attentive reader into day-dreams, as one space after another is evoked in the reader's own imagination. In the passages above there has been a clear link back to the previous section, mentioning images of the universe in the particularity of the house. There is a link to be made forward to the next section if we notice that there is a kind of anthopomorphism at work in Bachelard's analysis of the house's vertical orientation, with the activities of the mind being located at the top, with the instinctive and primitive things going on below. It is an image of a person sitting on the ground – an image of the sedentary – not standing up and walking around, and it is an image that is not based on form, but on the activity (the *praxes*) of the brain and the guts.

Bachelard's conception of the house is restated with great concision, and is imaginatively extended, in the following passage by Michel Tournier (born 1924) who studied philosophy alongside Gilles Deleuze, but whose career took him into broadcasting and novel writing (for which he won the Prix Goncourt for *Le Roi des aulnes*). His book *Le miroir des idées* (*The Mirror of Ideas*) is a series of short essays or reflections, which try to give clarity to some of life's fundamental ideas. In his Introduction he expresses his admiration for the great thinkers who have managed to attain a level of abstraction in their thought that means that they can manage with very few ideas. Aristotle distinguished ten. Leibniz managed six. Kant allowed twelve, four of them fundamental categories, each with three subordinates. Tournier's thought is much less abstract, so he needs more ideas: 114, presented in pairs of oppositions. The book is dedicated to the memory of Bachelard.

From Michel Tournier, *Le miroir des idées*

The Cellar and the Attic

Every true house has a cellar and an attic. These extreme places are equally obscure, but they have quite different obscurities. The glimmer of light, which in the cellar falls from a small window (a *soupirail*), comes from the earth and the soil – garden or street – and is hardly ever animated by a sunbeam. It is an impure gleam, subdued, deadened. By contrast the attic's dormer opens directly in the roof, giving on to the heavens, its blueness, its clouds, its moon and its stars. It is still the case even if the cellar is a place of life, and the attic a place of death. The attic always resembles those balconies in heaven, of which Baudelaire speaks, where the dead years lean over in superannuated robes. The air of the attic smells of dust and faded flowers. Here one finds the baby's pram, mutilated dolls, dented straw hats, the picture book with yellowed pages, newspapers celebrating the current events of a time infinitely long ago. The temperature swings here are enormous: one could be cooked in here in summer, but would freeze in winter. One must stop oneself exploring too much the contents of the chests and trunks that sleep here, as one runs the risk of awaking shameful or doleful family secrets.

If the stair that climbs to the attic has the dry and creaking lightness of wood, that which descends to the cellar is of cold damp stone, with a bloom of moisture and muddy earth. As the attic is turned towards the past, its function is to remember and conserve, while in the cellar the next season is ripening. The plait of shallots hangs under the vault; wine improves, embedded in iron racks . . .[11]

Notes

1. Patrick A. Heelan, in the Foreword to Gaston Bachelard, *Le nouvel ésprit scientifique* (Paris: Presses Universitaires de France, 1934) translated by Arthur Goldhammer, *The New Scientific Spirit* (Boston: Beacon Press, 1984) p. vii.
2. Northrop Frye, in the Introduction to *La psychanalyse du feu* (Paris: Gallimard, 1938) translated by Alan C. M. Ross, *The Psychoanalysis of Fire* (London: Quartet, 1987) p. vii. For Samuel Butler see the next Section of the present volume.
3. Edmond Bonty, *La vérité scientifique* (1908) p. 7.
4. Gaston Bachelard, *Scientific Spirit*, op. cit., pp. 1–2.
5. Ibid., pp. 3–4.
6. Gillese Deleuze in conversation with Michel Foucault in 1972, 'Intellectuels et pouvoir', in *L'Arc* 49, 1973, p. 3; translated by Donald F. Bouchard and Sherry Simon, 'Intellectuals and Power', in Michel Foucault, *Language, Counter-Memory, Practice* (Ithaca, New York: Cornell University Press, 1977) p. 206.
7. Gaston Bachelard, *Psychoanalysis of Fire*, op. cit., p. 1.
8. Ibid., pp. 1–2.
9. Gaston Bachelard, *La poétique de l'espace* (Paris: Presses Univérsitaires de France, 1958) translated by Maria Jolas, *The Poetics of Space* (Boston: Beacon Press, 1964) p. 4.
10. Ibid., p. 14.
11. Michel Tournier, *Le miroir des idées* (Paris: Mercure de France, 1996) p. 79.

William James

William James (1842–1910) was a philosopher, and the older brother of the novelist Henry James (there were five siblings in all). Their parents were Swedenborgians – believers and promoters of the ideas of Emmanuel Swedenborg (1688–1772) which must have been an embarrassment, and might account for some of the assumptions William made in his best-known book: *The Varieties of Religious Experience* (1902). Swedenborg's best-known books were extensive descriptions of the spirit world – *Heaven and its Wonders*, and *Hell* – written more or less as travel books, and taken surprisingly seriously. They sold well, and Swedenborg societies were established. What James's philosophy did was to make it possible for him to set aside the experience of the spirit world (to which people like his parents attested) because it made no practical difference to the things that he wanted to accomplish. He did not have to prove his parents wrong, just to set their beliefs to one side, as not being under discussion. He wrote with great clarity, which makes him worth quoting at some length as he is well able to explain himself. In the passage that follows he situates himself in relation to other thinkers of his own time. It is now possible to see that his ideas have been hugely influential, and are so well accepted that they hardly seem to need saying. He remarked that people who wanted to reject pragmatism did so by saying, in effect 'It's not true, and furthermore, we already know this stuff'.[1] His method of presenting ideas by embodying abstract principles in concrete examples is exemplary.

Note

1. William James, quoted by Louis Menand, in 'Pragmatists and Poets: A Response to Richard Poirier', in The Revival of Pragmatism (Duke University Press) p. 365.

What Pragmatism Means (1907)

Some years ago, being with a camping party in the mountains, I returned from a solitary ramble to find everyone engaged in a ferocious metaphysical dispute. The *corpus* of the dispute was a squirrel – a live squirrel supposed to be clinging to one side of a tree-trunk; while over against the tree's opposite side a human being was imagined to stand. This human witness tries to get sight of the squirrel by moving rapidly round the tree, but no matter how fast he goes, the squirrel moves as fast in the opposite direction, and always keeps the tree between himself and the man, so that never a glimpse of him is caught. The resultant metaphysical problem now is this: *Does the man go round the squirrel or not?* He goes round the tree, sure enough, and the squirrel is on the tree; but does he go round the squirrel? In the unlimited leisure of the wilderness, discussion had been worn threadbare. Everyone had taken sides, and was obstinate; and the numbers on both sides were even. Each side, when I appeared, therefore appealed to me to make it a majority. Mindful of the scholastic adage that whenever you meet a contradiction you must make a distinction, I immediately sought and found one, as follows: 'Which party is right,' I said, 'depends on what you *practically mean* by "going round" the squirrel. If you mean passing from the north of him to the east, then to the south, then to the west, and then to the north of him again, obviously the man does go round him, for he occupies these successive positions. But if on the contrary you mean being first in front of him, then on the right of him, then behind him, then on his left, and finally in front again, it is quite as obvious that the man fails to go round him, for by the compensating movements the squirrel makes, he keeps his belly turned towards the man all the time, and his back turned away. Make the distinction, and there is no occasion for any farther dispute. You are both right and both wrong according as you conceive the verb "to go round" in one practical fashion or the other.'

Although one or two of the hotter disputants called my speech a shuffling evasion, saying they wanted no quibbling or scholastic hair-splitting, but meant just plain honest English 'round,' the majority seemed to think that the distinction had assuaged the dispute.

I tell this trivial anecdote because it is a peculiarly simple example of what I wish now to speak of as the *pragmatic method*. The pragmatic method is primarily a method of settling metaphysical disputes that otherwise might be interminable. Is the world one or many? – fated or free? – material or spiritual? – here are notions either of which may or may not hold good of the world; and disputes over such notions are unending. The pragmatic method in such cases is to try to interpret each notion by tracing its respective practical consequences. What difference would it practically make to anyone if this notion rather than that notion were true? If no practical difference whatever can be traced, then the alternatives mean practically the same thing, and all dispute is idle. Whenever a dispute is serious, we ought to be able to show some practical difference that must follow from one side or the other's being right.

A glance at the history of the idea will show you still better what pragmatism means. The term is derived from the same Greek word πράγμα, meaning action, from which our words 'practice' and 'practical' come. It was first introduced into philosophy by Mr. Charles Peirce in 1878. In an article entitled 'How to Make Our Ideas Clear,' in the 'Popular Science Monthly' for January of that year.[1] Mr. Peirce, after pointing out that our beliefs are really rules for action, said that, to develop a thought's meaning, we need only determine what conduct it is fitted to produce: that conduct is for us its sole significance. And the tangible fact at the root of all our thought-distinctions, however subtle, is that there is no one of them so fine as to consist in anything but a possible difference of practice. To attain perfect clearness in our thoughts of an object, then, we need only consider what conceivable effects of a practical kind the object may involve – what sensations we are to expect from it, and what reactions we must prepare. Our conception of these effects, whether immediate or remote, is then for us the whole of our conception of the object, so far as that conception has positive significance at all.

This is the principle of Peirce, the principle of pragmatism. It lay entirely unnoticed by anyone for twenty years, until I, in an address before Professor Howison's philosophical union at the university of California, brought it forward again and made a special application of it to religion. By that date (1898) the times seemed ripe for its reception. The word 'pragmatism' spread, and at present it fairly spots the pages of the philosophic journals. On all hands we find the 'pragmatic movement' spoken of, sometimes with respect, sometimes with contumely, seldom with clear understanding. It is evident that the term applies itself conveniently to a number of tendencies that hitherto have lacked a collective name, and that it has 'come to stay.'

To take in the importance of Peirce's principle, one must get accustomed to applying it to concrete cases. I found a few years ago that Ostwald, the illustrious Leipzig chemist, had been making perfectly distinct use of the principle of pragmatism in his lectures on the philosophy of science, though he had not called it by that name.

'All realities influence our practice,' he wrote me, 'and that influence is their meaning for us. I am accustomed to put questions to my classes in this way: In what respects would the world be different if this alternative or that were true? If I can find nothing that would become different, then the alternative has no sense.'

That is, the rival views mean practically the same thing, and meaning, other than practical, there is for us none. Ostwald in a published lecture gives this example of what he means. Chemists have long wrangled over the inner constitution of certain bodies called 'tautomerous.' Their properties seemed equally consistent with the notion that an instable hydrogen atom oscillates inside of them, or that they are instable mixtures of two bodies. Controversy raged; but never was decided. 'It would never have begun,' says Ostwald, 'if the combatants had asked themselves what particular experimental fact could have been made different by one or the other view being correct. For it would then have appeared that no difference of fact could possibly ensue; and the quarrel was as unreal as if, theorizing in primitive times about the raising of dough by yeast, one party should have invoked a "brownie," while another insisted on an "elf" as the true cause of the phenomenon.'[2]

Section 2: Groundwork

It is astonishing to see how many philosophical disputes collapse into insignificance the moment you subject them to this simple test of tracing a concrete consequence. There can *be* no difference anywhere that doesn't *make* a difference elsewhere – no difference in abstract truth that doesn't express itself in a difference in concrete fact and in conduct consequent upon that fact, imposed on somebody, somehow, somewhere and somewhen. The whole function of philosophy ought to be to find out what definite difference it will make to you and me, at definite instants of our life, if this world-formula or that world-formula be the true one.

There is absolutely nothing new in the pragmatic method. Socrates was an adept at it. Aristotle used it methodically. Locke, Berkeley and Hume made momentous contributions to truth by its means. Shadworth Hodgson keeps insisting that realities are only what they are 'known-as.' But these forerunners of pragmatism used it in fragments: they were preluders only. Not until in our time has it generalized itself, become conscious of a universal mission, pretended to a conquering destiny. I believe in that destiny, and I hope I may end by inspiring you with my belief.

Pragmatism represents a perfectly familiar attitude in philosophy, the empiricist attitude, but it represents it, as it seems to me, both in a more radical and in a less objectionable form than it has ever yet assumed. A pragmatist turns his back resolutely and once for all upon a lot of inveterate habits dear to professional philosophers. He turns away from abstraction and insufficiency, from verbal solutions, from bad *a priori* reasons, from fixed principles, closed systems, and pretended absolutes and origins. He turns towards concreteness and adequacy, towards facts, towards action, and towards power. That means the empiricist temper regnant, and the rationalist temper sincerely given up. It means the open air and possibilities of nature, as against dogma, artificiality and the pretence of finality in truth.

At the same time it does not stand for any special results. It is a method only. But the general triumph of that method would mean an enormous change in what I called in my last lecture the 'temperament' of philosophy. Teachers of the ultra-rationalistic type would be frozen out, much as the courtier type is frozen out in republics, as the ultramontane type of priest is frozen out in protestant lands. Science and metaphysics would come much nearer together, would in fact work absolutely hand in hand.

Metaphysics has usually followed a very primitive kind of quest. You know how men have always hankered after unlawful magic, and you know what a great part, in magic, *words* have always played. If you have his name, or the formula of incantation that binds him, you can control the spirit, genie, afrite, or whatever the power may be. Solomon knew the names of all the spirits, and having their names, he held them subject to his will. So the universe has always appeared to the natural mind as a kind of enigma, of which the key must be sought in the shape of some illuminating or power-bringing word or name. That word names the universe's *principle*, and to possess it is, after a fashion, to possess the universe itself. 'God,' 'Matter,' 'Reason,' 'the Absolute,' 'Energy,' are so many solving names. You can rest when you have them. You are at the end of your metaphysical quest.

But if you follow the pragmatic method, you cannot look on any such word as closing your quest. You must bring out of each word its practical cash-value, set it at work within the stream of your experience. It appears less as a solution, then, than as a program for more work, and more particularly as an indication of the ways in which existing realities may be *changed*.

Theories thus become instruments, not answers to enigmas, in which we can rest. We don't lie back upon them, we move forward, and, on occasion, make nature over again by their aid. Pragmatism unstiffens all our theories, limbers them up and sets each one at work. Being nothing essentially new, it harmonizes with many ancient philosophic tendencies. It agrees with nominalism for instance, in always appealing to particulars; with utilitarianism in emphasizing practical aspects; with positivism in its disdain for verbal solutions, useless questions, and metaphysical abstractions.

All these, you see, are *anti-intellectualist* tendencies. Against rationalism as a pretension and a method, pragmatism is fully armed and militant. But, at the outset, at least, it stands for no particular results. It has no dogmas, and no doctrines save its method. As the young Italian pragmatist Papini has well said, it lies in the midst of our theories, like a corridor in a hotel. Innumerable chambers open out of it. In one you may find a man writing an atheistic volume; in the next someone on his knees praying for faith and strength; in a third a chemist investigating a body's properties. In a fourth a system of idealistic metaphysics is being excogitated; in a fifth the impossibility of metaphysics is being shown. But they all own the corridor, and all must pass through it if they want a practicable way of getting into or out of their respective rooms.

No particular results then, so far, but only an attitude of orientation, is what the pragmatic method means. *The attitude of looking away from first things, principles, 'categories,' supposed necessities; and of looking towards last things, fruits, consequences, facts.*

So much for the pragmatic method! You may say that I have been praising it rather than explaining it to you, but I shall presently explain it abundantly enough by showing how it works on some familiar problems. Meanwhile the word pragmatism has come to be used in a still wider sense, as meaning also a certain *theory of truth*. I mean to give a whole lecture to the statement of that theory, after first paving the way, so I can be very brief now. But brevity is hard to follow, so I ask for your redoubled attention for a quarter of an hour. If much remains obscure, I hope to make it clearer in the later lectures.

One of the most successfully cultivated branches of philosophy in our time is what is called inductive logic, the study of the conditions under which our sciences have evolved. Writers on this subject have begun to show a singular unanimity as to what the laws of nature and elements of fact mean, when formulated by mathematicians, physicists and chemists. When the first mathematical, logical and natural uniformities, the first *laws*, were discovered, men were so carried away by the clearness, beauty and simplification that resulted, that they believed themselves to have deciphered authentically the eternal thoughts of the Almighty. His mind also thundered and reverberated in syllogisms. He also thought in conic sections, squares and roots and ratios, and geometrized like Euclid. He made Kepler's laws for the planets to follow; he made velocity increase proportionally to the time in falling bodies; he made the law of the sines for light to obey when refracted; he established the classes, orders, families and genera of plants and animals, and fixed the distances between them. He thought the archetypes of all things, and devised their variations; and when we rediscover any one of these wondrous institutions, we seize his mind in its very literal intention.

Section 2: Groundwork

But as the sciences have developed farther, the notion has gained ground that most, perhaps all, of our laws are only approximations. The laws themselves, moreover, have grown so numerous that there is no counting them; and so many rival formulations are proposed in all the branches of science that investigators have become accustomed to the notion that no theory is absolutely a transcript of reality, but that any one of them may from some point of view be useful. Their great use is to summarize old facts and to lead to new ones. They are only a man-made language, a conceptual shorthand, as someone calls them, in which we write our reports of nature; and languages, as is well known, tolerate much choice of expression and many dialects.

Thus human arbitrariness has driven divine necessity from scientific logic. If I mention the names of Sigwart, Mach, Ostwald, Pearson, Milhaud, Poincaré, Duhem, Ruyssen, those of you who are students will easily identify the tendency I speak of, and will think of additional names.

Riding now on the front of this wave of scientific logic Messrs. Schiller and Dewey appear with their pragmatistic account of what truth everywhere signifies. Everywhere, these teachers say, 'truth' in our ideas and beliefs means the same thing that it means in science. It means, they say, nothing but this, *that ideas (which themselves are but parts of our experience) become true just in so far as they help us to get into satisfactory relation with other parts of our experience*, to summarize them and get about among them by conceptual short-cuts instead of following the interminable succession of particular phenomena. Any idea upon which we can ride, so to speak; any idea that will carry us prosperously from any one part of our experience to any other part, linking things satisfactorily, working securely, simplifying, saving labor; is true for just so much, true in so far forth, true *instrumentally*. This is the 'instrumental' view of truth taught so successfully at Chicago, the view that truth in our ideas means their power to 'work,' promulgated so brilliantly at Oxford.

Messrs. Dewey, Schiller and their allies, in reaching this general conception of all truth, have only followed the example of geologists, biologists and philologists. In the establishment of these other sciences, the successful stroke was always to take some simple process actually observable in operation – as denudation by weather, say, or variation from parental type, or change of dialect by incorporation of new words and pronunciations – and then to generalize it, making it apply to all times, and produce great results by summating its effects through the ages.

The observable process which Schiller and Dewey particularly singled out for generalization is the familiar one by which any individual settles into *new opinions*. The process here is always the same. The individual has a stock of old opinions already, but he meets a new experience that puts them to a strain. Somebody contradicts them; or in a reflective moment he discovers that they contradict each other; or he hears of facts with which they are incompatible; or desires arise in him which they cease to satisfy. The result is an inward trouble to which his mind till then had been a stranger, and from which he seeks to escape by modifying his previous mass of opinions. He saves as much of it as he can, for in this matter of belief we are all extreme conservatives. So he tries to change first this opinion, and then that (for they resist change very variously), until at last some new idea comes up which he can graft upon the ancient stock with a minimum of disturbance of the latter, some idea that mediates between the stock and the new experience and runs them into one another most felicitously and expediently.

This new idea is then adopted as the true one. It preserves the older stock of truths with a minimum of modification, stretching them just enough to make them admit the novelty, but conceiving that in ways as familiar as the case leaves possible. An *outrée* explanation, violating all our preconceptions, would never pass for a true account of a novelty. We should scratch round industriously till we found something less excentric. The most violent revolutions in an individual's beliefs leave most of his old order standing. Time and space, cause and effect, nature and history, and one's own biography remain untouched. New truth is always a go-between, a smoother-over of transitions. It marries old opinion to new fact so as ever to show a minimum of jolt, a maximum of continuity. We hold a theory true just in proportion to its success in solving this 'problem of maxima and minima.' But success in solving this problem is eminently a matter of approximation. We say this theory solves it on the whole more satisfactorily than that theory; but that means more satisfactorily to ourselves, and individuals will emphasize their points of satisfaction differently. To a certain degree, therefore, everything here is plastic.

The point I now urge you to observe particularly is the part played by the older truths. Failure to take account of it is the source of much of the unjust criticism leveled against pragmatism. Their influence is absolutely controlling. Loyalty to them is the first principle – in most cases it is the only principle; for by far the most usual way of handling phenomena so novel that they would make for a serious rearrangement of our preconceptions is to ignore them altogether, or to abuse those who bear witness for them.

You doubtless wish examples of this process of truth's growth, and the only trouble is their superabundance. The simplest case of new truth is of course the mere numerical addition of new kinds of facts, or of new single facts of old kinds, to our experience – an addition that involves no alteration in the old beliefs. Day follows day, and its contents are simply added. The new contents themselves are not true, they simply *come* and *are*. Truth is *what we say about* them, and when we say that they have come, truth is satisfied by the plain additive formula.

But often the day's contents oblige a rearrangement. If I should now utter piercing shrieks and act like a maniac on this platform, it would make many of you revise your ideas as to the probable worth of my philosophy. 'Radium' came the other day as part of the day's content, and seemed for a moment to contradict our ideas of the whole order of nature, that order having come to be identified with what is called the conservation of energy. The mere sight of radium paying heat away indefinitely out of its own pocket seemed to violate that conservation. What to think? If the radiations from it were nothing but an escape of unsuspected 'potential' energy, pre-existent inside of the atoms, the principle of conservation would be saved. The discovery of 'helium' as the radiation's outcome, opened a way to this belief. So Ramsay's view is generally held to be true, because, although it extends our old ideas of energy, it causes a minimum of alteration in their nature.

I need not multiply instances. A new opinion counts as 'true' just in proportion as it gratifies the individual's desire to assimilate the novel in his experience to his beliefs in stock. It must both lean on old truth and grasp new fact; and its success (as I said a moment ago) in doing this, is a matter for the individual's appreciation. When old truth grows, then, by new truth's addition, it is for subjective reasons. We are in the process and obey the reasons. That new idea is truest which performs most felicitously its function of satisfying our double urgency. It makes itself true, gets itself classed as true, by the way it works; grafting itself then upon the ancient body of truth, which thus grows much as a tree grows by the activity of a new layer of cambium.

Now Dewey and Schiller proceed to generalize this observation and to apply it to the most ancient parts of truth. They also once were plastic. They also were called true for human reasons. They also mediated between still earlier truths and what in those days were novel observations. Purely objective truth, truth in whose establishment the function of giving human satisfaction in marrying previous parts of experience with newer parts played no rôle whatever, is nowhere to be found. The reasons why we call things true is the reason why they *are* true, for 'to be true' *means* only to perform this marriage-function.

The trail of the human serpent is thus over everything. Truth independent; truth that we *find* merely; truth no longer malleable to human need; truth incorrigible, in a word; such truth exists indeed superabundantly – or is supposed to exist by rationalistically minded thinkers; but then it means only the dead heart of the living tree, and its being there means only that truth also has its paleontology and its 'prescription,' and may grow stiff with years of veteran service and petrified in men's regard by sheer antiquity. But how plastic even the oldest truths nevertheless really are has been vividly shown in our day by the transformation of logical and mathematical ideas, a transformation which seems even to be invading physics. The ancient formulas are reinterpreted as special expressions of much wider principles, principles that our ancestors never got a glimpse of in their present shape and formulation.

Mr. Schiller still gives to all this view of truth the name of 'Humanism,' but, for this doctrine too, the name of pragmatism seems fairly to be in the ascendant, so I will treat it under the name of pragmatism in these lectures.

Such then would be the scope of pragmatism – first, a method; and second, a genetic theory of what is meant by truth. And these two things must be our future topics.

What I have said of the theory of truth will, I am sure, have appeared obscure and unsatisfactory to most of you by reason of its brevity. I shall make amends for that hereafter. In a lecture on 'common sense' I shall try to show what I mean by truths grown petrified by antiquity. In another lecture I shall expatiate on the idea that our thoughts become true in proportion as they successfully exert their go-between function. In a third I shall show how hard it is to discriminate subjective from objective factors in Truth's development. You may not follow me wholly in these lectures; and if you do, you may not wholly agree with me. But you will, I know, regard me at least as serious, and treat my effort with respectful consideration.

You will probably be surprised to learn, then, that Messrs. Schiller's and Dewey's theories have suffered a hailstorm of contempt and ridicule. All rationalism has risen against them. In influential quarters Mr. Schiller, in particular, has been treated like an impudent schoolboy who deserves a spanking. I should not mention this, but for the fact that it throws so much sidelight upon that rationalistic temper to which I have opposed the temper of pragmatism. Pragmatism is uncomfortable away from facts. Rationalism is comfortable only in the presence of abstractions. This pragmatist talk about truths in the plural, about their utility and satisfactoriness, about the success with which they 'work,' etc., suggests to the typical intellectualist mind a sort of coarse lame second-rate makeshift article of truth. Such truths are not real truth. Such tests are merely subjective. As against this, objective truth must be something non-utilitarian, haughty, refined, remote, august, exalted. It must be an absolute correspondence of our thoughts with an equally absolute reality. It must be what we *ought* to think, unconditionally. The conditioned ways in which we *do* think are so much irrelevance and matter for psychology. Down with psychology, up with logic, in all this question!

See the exquisite contrast of the types of mind! The pragmatist clings to facts and concreteness, observes truth at its work in particular cases, and generalizes. Truth, for him, becomes a class-name for all sorts of definite working-values in experience. For the rationalist it remains a pure abstraction, to the bare name of which we must defer. When the pragmatist undertakes to show in detail just *why* we must defer, the rationalist is unable to recognize the concretes from which his own abstraction is taken. He accuses us of *denying* truth; whereas we have only sought to trace exactly why people follow it and always ought to follow it. Your typical ultra-abstractionist fairly shudders at concreteness: other things equal, he positively prefers the pale and spectral. If the two universes were offered, he would always choose the skinny outline rather than the rich thicket of reality. It is so much purer, clearer, nobler.

I hope that as these lectures go on, the concreteness and closeness to facts of the pragmatism which they advocate may be what approves itself to you as its most satisfactory peculiarity. It only follows here the example of the sister-sciences, interpreting the unobserved by the observed. It brings old and new harmoniously together. It converts the absolutely empty notion of a static relation of 'correspondence' (what that may mean we must ask later) between our minds and reality, into that of a rich and active commerce (that anyone may follow in detail and understand) between particular thoughts of ours, and the great universe of other experiences in which they play their parts and have their uses.

But enough of this at present? The justification of what I say must be postponed. I wish now to add a word in further explanation of the claim I made at our last meeting, that pragmatism may be a happy harmonizer of empiricist ways of thinking, with the more religious demands of human beings.

Men who are strongly of the fact-loving temperament, you may remember me to have said, are liable to be kept at a distance by the small sympathy with facts which that philosophy from the present-day fashion of idealism offers them. It is far too intellectualistic. Old fashioned theism was bad enough, with its notion of God as an exalted monarch, made up of a lot of unintelligible or preposterous 'attributes'; but, so long as it held strongly by the argument from design, it kept some touch with concrete realities. Since, however, darwinism has once for all displaced design from the minds of the 'scientific,' theism has lost that foothold; and some kind of an immanent or pantheistic deity working *in* things rather than above them is, if any, the kind recommended to our contemporary imagination. Aspirants to a philosophic religion turn, as a rule, more hopefully nowadays towards idealistic pantheism than towards the older dualistic theism, in spite of the fact that the latter still counts able defenders.

But, as I said in my first lecture, the brand of pantheism offered is hard for them to assimilate if they are lovers of facts, or empirically minded. It is the absolutistic brand, spurning the dust and reared upon pure logic. It keeps no connexion whatever with concreteness. Affirming the Absolute Mind, which is its substitute for God, to be the rational presupposition of all particulars of fact, whatever they may be, it remains supremely indifferent to what the particular facts in our world actually are. Be they what they may, the Absolute will father them. Like the sick lion in Esop's fable, all footprints lead into his den, but *nulla vestigia retrorsum*. You cannot redescend into the world of particulars by the Absolute's aid, or deduce any necessary consequences of detail important for your life from your idea of his nature. He gives you indeed the assurance that all is well with *Him*, and for his eternal way of thinking; but thereupon he leaves you to be finitely saved by your own temporal devices.

Far be it from me to deny the majesty of this conception, or its capacity to yield religious comfort to a most respectable class of minds. But from the human point of view, no one can pretend that it doesn't suffer from the faults of remoteness and abstractness. It is eminently a product of what I have ventured to call the rationalistic temper. It disdains empiricism's needs. It substitutes a pallid outline for the real world's richness. It is dapper; it is noble in the bad sense, in the sense in which to be noble is to be inapt for humble service. In this real world of sweat and dirt, it seems to me that when a view of things is 'noble,' that ought to count as a presumption against its truth, and as a philosophic disqualification. The prince of darkness may be a gentleman, as we are told he is, but whatever the God of earth and heaven is, he can surely be no gentleman. His menial services are needed in the dust of our human trials, even more than his dignity is needed in the empyrean.

Now pragmatism, devoted though she be to facts, has no such materialistic bias as ordinary empiricism labors under. Moreover, she has no objection whatever to the realizing of abstractions, so long as you get about among particulars with their aid and they actually carry you somewhere. Interested in no conclusions but those which our minds and our experiences work out together, she has no *a priori* prejudices against theology. *If theological ideas prove to have a value for concrete life, they will be true, for pragmatism, in the sense of being good for so much. For how much more they are true, will depend entirely on their relations to the other truths that also have to be acknowledged.*

What I said just now about the Absolute of transcendental idealism is a case in point. First, I called it majestic and said it yielded religious comfort to a class of minds, and then I accused it of remoteness and sterility. But so far as it affords such comfort, it surely is not sterile; it has that amount of value; it performs a concrete function. As a good pragmatist, I myself ought to call the Absolute true 'in so far forth,' then; and I unhesitatingly now do so.

But what does *true in so far forth* mean in this case? To answer, we need only apply the pragmatic method. What do believers in the Absolute mean by saying that their belief affords them comfort? They mean that since in the Absolute finite evil is 'overruled' already, we may, therefore, whenever we wish, treat the temporal as if it were potentially the eternal, be sure that we can trust its outcome, and, without sin, dismiss our fear and drop the worry of our finite responsibility. In short, they mean that we have a right ever and anon to take a moral holiday, to let the world wag in its own way, feeling that its issues are in better hands than ours and are none of our business.

The universe is a system of which the individual members may relax their anxieties occasionally, in which the don't-care mood is also right for men, and moral holidays in order – that, if I mistake not, is part, at least, of what the Absolute is 'known-as,' that is the great difference in our particular experiences which his being true makes for us, that is part of his cash-value when he is pragmatically interpreted. Farther than that the ordinary lay-reader in philosophy who thinks favorably of absolute idealism does not venture to sharpen his conceptions. He can use the Absolute for so much, and so much is very precious. He is pained at hearing you speak incredulously of the Absolute, therefore, and disregards your criticisms because they deal with aspects of the conception that he fails to follow.

If the Absolute means this, and means no more than this, who can possibly deny the truth of it? To deny it would be to insist that men should never relax, and that holidays are never in order.

I am well aware how odd it must seem to some of you to hear me say that an idea is 'true' so long as to believe it is profitable to our lives. That it is *good*, for as much as it profits, you will gladly admit. If what we do by its aid is good, you will allow the idea itself to be good in so far forth, for we are the better for possessing it. But is it not a strange misuse of the word 'truth,' you will say, to call ideas also 'true' for this reason?

To answer this difficulty fully is impossible at this stage of my account. You touch here upon the very central point of Messrs. Schiller's, Dewey's and my own doctrine of truth, which I cannot discuss with detail until my sixth lecture. Let me now say only this, that truth is *one species of good*, and not, as is usually supposed, a category distinct from good, and co-ordinate with it. The *true is the name of whatever proves itself to be good in the way of belief, and good, too, for definite, assignable reasons.* Surely you must admit this, that if there were *no* good for life in true ideas, or if the knowledge of them were positively disadvantageous and false ideas the only useful ones, then the current notion that truth is divine and precious, and its pursuit a duty, could never have grown up or become a dogma. In a world like that, our duty would be to *shun* truth, rather. But in this world, just as certain foods are not only agreeable to our taste, but good for our teeth, our stomach and our tissues; so certain ideas are not only agreeable to think about, or agreeable as supporting other ideas that we are fond of, but they are also helpful in life's practical struggles. If there be any life that it is really better we should lead, and if there be any idea which, if believed in, would help us to lead that life, then it would be really *better for us* to believe in that idea, *unless, indeed, belief in it incidentally clashed with other greater vital benefits.*

'What would be better for us to believe'! This sounds very like a definition of truth. It comes very near to saying 'what we *ought* to believe': and in *that* definition none of you would find any oddity. Ought we ever not to believe what it is *better for us* to believe? And can we then keep the notion of what is better for us, and what is true for us, permanently apart?

Pragmatism says no, and I fully agree with her. Probably you also agree, so far as

Section 2: Groundwork

the abstract statement goes, but with a suspicion that if we practically did believe everything that made for good in our own personal lives, we should be found indulging all kinds of fancies about this world's affairs, and all kinds of sentimental superstitions about a world hereafter. Your suspicion here is undoubtedly well founded, and it is evident that something happens when you pass from the abstract to the concrete, that complicates the situation.

I said just now that what is better for us to believe is true *unless the belief incidentally clashes with some other vital benefit*. Now in real life what vital benefits is any particular belief of ours most liable to clash with? What indeed except the vital benefits yielded by *other beliefs* when these prove incompatible with the first ones? In other words, the greatest enemy of any one of our truths may be the rest of our truths. Truths have once for all this desperate instinct of self-preservation and of desire to extinguish whatever contradicts them. My belief in the Absolute, based on the good it does me, must run the gauntlet of all my other beliefs. Grant that it may be true in giving me a moral holiday. Nevertheless, as I conceive it, – and let me speak now confidentially, as it were, and merely in my own private person, – it clashes with other truths of mine whose benefits I hate to give up on its account. It happens to be associated with a kind of logic of which I am the enemy, I find that it entangles me in metaphysical paradoxes that are inacceptable, etc., etc. But as I have enough trouble in life already without adding the trouble of carrying these intellectual inconsistencies, I personally just give up the Absolute. I just *take* my moral holidays; or else as a professional philosopher, I try to justify them by some other principle.

If I could restrict my notion of the Absolute to its bare holiday-giving value, it wouldn't clash with my other truths. But we cannot easily thus restrict our hypotheses. They carry supernumerary features, and these it is that clash so. My disbelief in the Absolute means then disbelief in those other supernumerary features, for I fully believe in the legitimacy of taking moral holidays.

You see by this what I meant when I called pragmatism a mediator and reconciler and said, borrowing the word from Papini, that she 'unstiffens' our theories. She has in fact no prejudices whatever, no obstructive dogmas, no rigid canons of what shall count as proof. She is completely genial. She will entertain any hypothesis, she will consider any evidence. It follows that in the religious field she is at a great advantage both over positivistic empiricism, with its anti-theological bias, and over religious rationalism, with its exclusive interest in the remote, the noble, the simple, and the abstract in the way of conception.

In short, she widens the field of search for God. Rationalism sticks to logic and the empyrean. Empiricism sticks to the external senses. Pragmatism is willing to take anything, to follow either logic or the senses, and to count the humblest and most personal experiences. She will count mystical experiences if they have practical consequences. She will take a God who lives in the very dirt of private fact – if that should seem a likely place to find him.

Her only test of probable truth is what works best in the way of leading us, what fits every part of life best and combines with the collectivity of experience's demands, nothing being omitted. If theological ideas should do this, if the notion of God, in particular, should prove to do it, how could pragmatism possibly deny God's existence? She could see no meaning in treating as 'not true' a notion that was pragmatically so successful. What other kind of truth could there be, for her, than all this agreement with concrete reality?

In my last lecture I shall return again to the relations of pragmatism with religion. But you see already how democratic she is. Her manners are as various and flexible, her resources as rich and endless, and her conclusions as friendly as those of mother nature.

Notes

1. Translated in the *Revue Philosophique* for January, 1879 (vol. vii).
2. 'Theorie und Praxis,' *Zeitsch. des Oesterreichischen Ingenieur u. Architecten-Vereines*, 1905, Nr. 4 u. 6. I find a still more radical pragmatism than Ostwald's in an address by Professor W. S. Franklin: 'I think that the sickliest notion of physics, even if a student gets it, is that it is "the science of masses, molecules and the ether." And I think that the healthiest notion, even if a student does not wholly get it, is that physics is the science of the ways of taking hold of bodies and pushing them!' (*Science*, January 2, 1903.)

John Dewey

John Dewey was born in Burlington, Vermont, and lived for 93 years (1859–1952). He is perhaps best known for his ideas about education – from 1894 he was Professor of Pedagogy at the University of Chicago – but his writings closely link democracy, science and philosophy; and he published prolifically. His reputation has been revived in recent years by Richard Rorty's interest in and development of his work, making similar links between philosophical and political imperatives.[1] For Dewey life and thought were bound up closely together, and the key move that he made in his great work on aesthetics, *Art as Experience*, was to point out that aesthetic experience is part of the commonplace world of everyday life, not something that is to be found only in art museums.[2] Dewey cited movies and 'jazzed music' as parts of the art-world brimming with vitality, and part of the fabric of everyday life in a way that the paintings in art museums no longer could be. This aspect of Dewey's aesthetics has been revisited and brought up to date by Richard Shusterman in his *Pragmatist Aesthetics*.[3] Buildings, of course, have a role as part of the fabric of everyday life, as well as being separated out from it as revered 'art-objects' from time to time – for example in the case of the Parthenon, in one of the passages below.

In Dewey's writings there is much that sounds like 'common sense', but it is underpinned with some firm logical distinctions that are thought through into the recognizable circumstances of everyday life. For example in one passage given below, Dewey makes the distinction between the artistic and the aesthetic, which is to say between the production of an art-object and appreciation of it. Translated into the architecture world this becomes the distinction between on one hand the design and production of buildings, and on the other their reception and cultural value. In architecture the process of production is complex and divided between individuals in such a way that it would be the 'building team' as an entity that should be identified with the productive artist in the passage below. The point with consequences that reach further, however, is Dewey's point that 'art' is not the same as the 'art-object' but is something that is produced in experiencing the art-object. In order for there to be art there must be experience of the object, and in order for there to be experience there has to be a person having it. It follows further that the experience that we have of ancient monuments – when we see them as carefully preserved museum pieces – is very different from the experience that the citizens of the ancient world had when they used them as part of their everyday lives. This point is explored further in *Architecture as Experience*, edited by Dana Arnold and Andrew Ballantyne.[4] The point of a building keeps changing as its circumstances keep changing. The point of a building for the builder is different from the point of it for the people financing it, or making use of it once it is complete, or finding a new use for it decades later. Dewey is acutely aware of the way in which buildings are caught up in the processes of life.

From *Experience and Nature* (1929)

Experience, with the Greeks, signified a store of practical wisdom, a fund of insights useful in conducting the affairs of life. Sensation and perception were its occasion and supplied it with pertinent materials, but did not of themselves constitute it. They generated experience when retention was added and when a common factor in the multitude of felt and perceived cases detached itself so as to become available in judgement and exertion. Thus understood, experience is exemplified in the discrimination and skill of the good carpenter, pilot, physician, captain-at-arms; experience is equivalent to art. Modern theory has quite properly extended the application of the term to cover many things the Greeks would hardly have called 'experience', the bare having of aches and pains, or a play of colours before the eyes. But even those who hold this larger signification would admit, I suppose, that such 'experiences' count only when they result in insight, or in an enjoyed perception, and that only thus do they define experience in its honorific sense.

Greek thinkers nevertheless disparaged experience in comparison with something called reason and science. The ground for depreciation was not that usually assigned in modern philosophy; it was not that experience is 'subjective'. On the contrary, experience was considered to be a genuine expression of cosmic forces, not quite an exclusive attribute or possession of animal or of human nature. It was taken to be a realization of inferior portions of nature, those infected with chance and change, the less *Being* part of the cosmos. Thus while experience meant art, art reflected the contingencies and partialities of nature, while science – theory – exhibited its necessities and universalities. Art was born of need, lack, deprivation, incompleteness, while science – theory – manifested fullness and totality of Being. Thus the depreciatory view of experience was identical with a conception that placed practical activity below theoretical activity, finding the former dependent, impelled from outside, marked by deficiency of real being, while the latter was independent and free because complete and self-sufficing: that is perfect.

In contrast with this self-consistent position we find a curious mixture in modern thinking. The latter feels under no obligation to present a theory of natural existence that links art with nature; on the contrary, it usually holds that science or knowledge is the only *authentic* expression of nature, in which case art must be an arbitrary addition to nature. But modern thought also combines exaltation of science with eulogistic appreciation of art, especially of fine or creative art. At the same time it retains the substance of the classical disparagement of the practical in contrast with the theoretical, although formulating it in somewhat different language: to the effect that knowledge deals with objective reality as it is in itself, while in what is 'practical', objective reality is altered and cognitively distorted by subjective factors of want, emotions and striving. And yet in its encomium of art, it fails to note the commonplace of Greek observation – that the fine arts as well as the industrial technologies are affairs of practice.

This confused plight is partly cause and partly effect of an almost universal confusion of the artistic and the aesthetic. On one hand, there is action that deals with materials and energies outside the body, assembling, refining, combining, manipulating them until their new state yields a satisfaction not afforded by their crude condition – a formula that applies to fine and useful arts alike. On the other hand, there is the delight that attends vision and hearing, an enhancement of the receptive appreciation and assimilation of objects irrespective of participation in the operations of production. Provided the difference of the two things is recognized, it is no matter whether the words 'aesthetic' and 'artistic' or other terms be used to designate the distinction, for the difference must be acknowledged.

The community in which Greek art was produced was small; numerous and complicated intermediaries between production and consumption were lacking; producers had a virtually servile status. Because of the close connection between production and enjoyable fruition, the Greeks in their perceptive uses and enjoyments were never wholly unconscious of the artisan and his work, not even when they personally were exclusively concerned with delightful contemplation. But since the artist was an artisan (the term artist having none of the eulogistic connotations of the present usage), and since the artisan occupied an inferior position, the enjoyment of works of any art did not stand upon the same level as enjoyment of those objects for the realization of which manual activity was not needed. Objects of rational thought, of contemplative insight were the only things that met the specification of freedom from need, labour, and matter. They alone were self-sufficient, self-existent, and self-explanatory, and hence enjoyment of *them* was on a higher plane than enjoyment of works of art.

These conceptions were consistent with one another and with the conditions of social life at the time. Nowadays we have a messy conjunction of notions that are consistent neither with one another nor with the tenor of our actual life. Knowledge is still regarded by most thinkers as direct grasp of ultimate reality, although the practice of knowing has been assimilated to the procedure of the useful arts; – involving, that is to say, doing that manipulates and arranges natural energies. Again while science is said to lay hold of a reality, yet 'art' instead of being assigned a lower rank is equally esteemed and honoured. And when within art a distinction is drawn between production and appreciation, the chief honour usually goes to the former on the ground that it is 'creative', while taste is relatively possessive and passive, dependent for its material upon the activities of the creative artist.

If Greek philosophy was correct in thinking of knowledge as contemplation rather than as a productive art, and if modern philosophy accepts this conclusion, then the only logical course is relative disparagement of all forms of production, since they are modes of practice which is by conception inferior to contemplation. The artistic is then secondary to the esthetic: 'creation', to 'taste', and the scientific *worker* – as we significantly say – is subordinate in rank and worth to the dilettante who enjoys the fruits of his labours. But if modern tendencies are justified in putting art and creation first, then the implications of this position should be avowed and carried through. It would then be seen that science is an art, that art is practice, and that the only distinction worth drawing is not between practice and theory, but between those modes of practice that are not intelligent, not inherently and immediately enjoyable, and those which are full of enjoyed meanings. When this perception dawns, it will be a commonplace that art – the mode of activity that is charged with meanings capable of immediately enjoyed possession – is the complete culmination of nature, and that 'science' is properly a handmaiden that conducts natural events to this happy issue.

Thus would disappear the separations that trouble present thinking: division of everything into nature *and* experience, of experience into practice *and* theory, art *and* science, of art into useful *and* fine, menial *and* free.

[...]

The modern mind has formally abjured belief in natural teleology because it found Greek and medieval teleology juvenile and superstitious. Yet facts have a way of compelling recognition of themselves. There is little scientific writing which does not introduce at some point or other the idea of tendency. The idea of tendency unites in itself exclusion of prior design and inclusion of movement in a particular direction, a direction that may be either furthered or counteracted and frustrated, but which is intrinsic. Direction involves a limiting position, a point or goal of culminating stoppage, as well as an initial starting point. To assert a tendency and to be fore-conscious of a possible terminus of movement are two names of the same fact. Such a consciousness may be fatalistic; a sense of inevitable march toward impending doom. But it may also contain a perception of meanings such as flexibly directs a forward movement. The end is then an end-in-view and it is in constant and cumulative re-enactment at each stage of forward movement. It is no longer a terminal point, external to the conditions that have led up to it; it is the continually developing meaning of present tendencies – the very things which as directed we call 'means'. The process is art and its product, no matter at what stage it be taken, it is a work of art.

To a person building a house, the end-in-view is not just a remote and final goal to be hit upon after a sufficiently great number of coerced motions have been duly performed. The end-in-view is a plan which is *contemporaneously* operative in selecting and arranging materials. The latter, brick, stone, wood and mortar, are means only as the end-in-view is actually incarnate in them, in forming them. Literally they *are* the end in its present stage of realization. The end-in-view is present at each stage of the process; it is present as the *meaning* of the materials used and acts done; without its informing presence, the latter are in no sense 'means'; they are merely extrinsic causal conditions. The statement is generic; it applies equally at every stage. The house itself, when building is complete, is 'end' in no exclusive sense. It marks the conclusion of the organization of certain materials and events into effective means; but these materials and events still exist in causal interaction with other things. New consequences are foreseen; new purposes, ends-in-view, are entertained; they are embodied in the coordination of the thing built, now reduced to material, although significant material, along with other materials, and thus transmuted into means. The case is still clearer, when instead of considering a process subject to as many rigid external conditions as is the building of a house, we take for illustration a flexibly and freely moving process, such as painting a picture or thinking out a scientific process, when these operations are carried on artistically. Every process of free art proves that the difference between means and end is analytic, formal, not material and chronologic.

Section 2: Groundwork

From *Art as Experience* (1934)

By common consent, the Parthenon is a great work of art. Yet it has aesthetic standing only as the work becomes an experience for a human being. And, if one is to go beyond personal enjoyment into the formulation of a theory about that large republic of art of which the building is one member, one has to be willing at some point in his reflections to turn from it to the bustling, arguing, acutely sensitive Athenian citizens, with civic sense identified with a civic religion, of whose experience the temple was an expression, and who built it not as a work of art but as a civic commemoration. The turning to them is as human beings who had needs that were a demand for the building and that were carried to fulfilment in it; it is not an examination such as might be carried on by a sociologist in search for material relevant to his purpose. The one who sets out to theorize about the aesthetic experience embodied in the Parthenon must realize in thought what the people into whose lives it entered had in common, as creators and as those who were satisfied with it, with people in our own homes and streets.

In order to understand the aesthetic in its ultimate and approved forms, one must begin with it in the raw; in the events that hold the attentive eye and ear of man, arousing his interest and affording him enjoyment as he looks and listens: the sights that hold the crowd – the fire-engine rushing by; the machines excavating enormous holes in the earth; the human-fly climbing the steeple-side; the men perched high in air on girders, throwing and catching red-hot bolts. The sources of art in human experience will be learned by him who sees how the tense grace of the ball-player infects the onlooking crowd; who notes the delight of the housewife in tending her plants and the intense interest of her Goodman in tending the patch of green in front of the house; the zest of the spectator in poking the wood burning on the hearth and in watching the darting flames and crumbling coals. These people, if questioned as to the reason for their actions, would doubtless return reasonable answers. The man who poked the sticks of burning wood would say he did it to make the fire burn better; but he is none the less fascinated by the colourful drama of change enacted before his eyes and imaginatively partakes in it. He does not remain a cold spectator. What Coleridge said of the reader of poetry is true in its way of all who are happily absorbed in their activities of mind and body: 'The reader should be carried forward, not merely or chiefly by the mechanical impulse of curiosity, not by a restless desire to arrive at the final solution, but by the pleasurable activity of the journey itself'.

[. . .]

The arts which today have the most vitality for the average person are things he does not take to be arts: for instance, the movie, jazzed music, the comic strip, and too frequently, newspaper accounts of love-nests, murders, and exploits of bandits. For, when what he knows as art is relegated to the museum and gallery, the unconquerable impulse towards experiences enjoyable in themselves finds such outlet as the daily environment provides. Many a person who protests against the museum conception of art, still shares the fallacy from which that conception springs. For the popular notion comes from a separation of art from the objects and scenes of everyday experience that many theorists and critics pride themselves upon holding and even elaborating. The times when select and distinguished objects are closely connected with the products of usual vocations are the times when appreciation of the former is most rife and most keen. When, because of their remoteness, the objects acknowledged by the cultivated to be works of fine art seem anaemic to the mass of people, aesthetic hunger is likely to seek the cheap and the vulgar.

Notes

1. Richard Rorty, *Contingency, Irony, and Solidarity* (Cambridge: Cambridge University Press, 1989); Richard Rorty, *Achieving Our Country: Leftist Thought in Twentieth-Century America* (Cambridge, Mass.: Harvard University Press, 1998).
2. John Dewey, *Art as Experience*, (New York: Putnam, 1934).
3. Richard Shusterman, *Pragmatist Aesthetics* (Oxford: Blackwell, 1992).
4. Dana Arnold and Andrew Ballantyne, *Architecture as Experience* (London: Routledge, 2004).

Charles Sanders Peirce

Peirce (1839–1914) had an unenviable life. He showed early signs of brilliance in chemistry, astronomy and surveying, and during his lifetime he published only one book: *Photometric Researches* (1878). He was a friend of William James, and a teacher of John Dewey and Thorstein Veblen, but the enduring image of him is as a wild man of the woods. He spent much of his later life in isolation, with his wife, writing and living in poverty. William James brought him to give some lectures at Harvard and did what he could to promote Peirce's work. The work on semiotics probably has the widest circulation currently, but it is his theorizing of practice that is represented here.

Following on from Shelley's insistence on the importance of the images we coin in our understanding of the world, the following passages from Peirce's unpublished writings make strong use of buildings as images of stability and sound construction. The first piece, on the architectonic construction of pragmatism, also makes the point that mathematics is a matter of seeking out images. In the mathematician's case the metaphors are formulae, which are seen to apply in particular practical or imaginative circumstances. What makes the mathematics work for an engineer is the aptness of the formula, and the imaginative leap to be made in selecting it is as much of an act of poetry as is the selection of an electrifying image by a wordsmith.

The second extract shows Peirce's wide reading, along with his brisk impatience. He mentions Aristotle – dismissively – alluding by the way to his school of philosophy (the peripatetics) and his birthplace (Stagira). These would have been commonplace allusions for the readership he would have anticipated – people with a classical education, which had not at that time melted away as Emerson had predicted it would (see above, p. 31). The classical allusions here, though, lend no support to Peirce's reasoning; they are just part of the furniture with which he expected a well-read mind to be stocked. Notoriously among the thinkers of the eighteenth-century Enlightenment, Aristotle was studied as a guide to the truth during the middle ages, and was displaced by experimental science where observations of practical matters took the place of texts that held unchallenged authority. Peirce was using Aristotle as a conventional emblem of the pre-scientific scholasticism of the medieval schools of thought – elements of which survive when we are swayed by the authoritative provenance of a text, rather than by the power of its arguments.

From *The Architectonic Construction of Pragmatism* (c. 1905)

Pragmatism was not a theory which special circumstances had led its authors to entertain. It had been designed and constructed, to use the expression of Kant,[1] architectonically. Just as a civil engineer, before erecting a bridge, a ship, or a house, will think of the different properties of all materials, and will use no iron, stone, or cement, that has not been subjected to tests; and will put them together in ways minutely considered, so, in constructing the doctrine of pragmatism the properties of all indecomposable concepts were examined and the ways in which they could be compounded. Then the purpose of the proposed doctrine having been analysed, it was constructed out of the appopriate concepts so as to fulfil that purpose. In this way, the truth of it was proved. There are subsidiary confirmations of its truth; but it is believed that there is no other independent way of strictly proving it . . .

But first, what is its purpose? What is it to be expected to accomplish? It is expected to bring to an end those prolonged disputes of philosophers which no observations of facts could settle, and yet in which each side claims to prove that the other side is in the wrong. Pragmatism maintains that in those cases the disputants must be at cross purposes. They either attach different meanings to words, or else one side or the other (or both) uses a word without any definite meaning. What is wanted, therefore, is a method for ascertaining the real meaning of any concept, doctrine, proposition, word, or other sign. The object of a sign is one thing; its meaning is another. Its object is the thing or occasion, however indefinite, to which it is to be applied. Its meaning is the idea which it attaches to that object, whether by way of mere supposition, or as a command, or as an assertion.

Now every simple idea is composed of one of three classes; and a compound idea is in most cases predominantly of one of those classes. Namely, it may, in the first place, be a quality of feeling, which is positively such as it is, and is indescribable; which attaches to one object regardless of every other; and which is *sui generis* and incapable, in its own being, of comparison with any other feeling, because in comparisons it is representations of feelings and not the very feelings themselves that are compared. Or, in the second place, the idea may be that of a single happening or fact, which is attached at once to two objects, as an experience, for example, is attached to the experiencer and to the object experienced. Or, in the third place, it is the idea of a sign or communication conveyed by one person to another (or to himself at a later time) in regard to a certain object well known to both . . . Now the bottom meaning of a sign cannot be the idea of a sign, since that latter sign must itself have a meaning which would thereby become the meaning of the original sign. We may therefore conclude that the ultimate meaning of any sign consists either in an idea predominantly of feeling or in one predominantly of acting and being acted on. For there ought to be no hesitation in assenting to the view that all those ideas which attach essentially to two objects take their rise from the experience of volition and from the experience of the perception of phenomena which resist direct efforts of the will to annul or modify them.

But pragmatism does not undertake to say in what the meanings of all signs consist, but merely to lay down a method of determining the meaning of intellectual concepts, that I, of those upon which reasonings may turn. Now all reasoning that is not utterly vague, all that ought to figure in a philosophical discussion involves, and turns upon, precise necessary reasoning. Such reasoning is included in the sphere of mathematics, as modern mathematicians conceive their science. 'Mathematics,' said Benjamin Peirce, as early as 1870, 'is the science which draws necessary conclusions';[2] and subsequent writers have substantially accepted this definition, limiting it, perhaps, to precise conclusions. The reasoning of mathematics is now well understood. It consists in forming an image of the conditions of the problem, associated with which are certain general permissions to modify the image, as well as certain general assumptions that certain things are impossible. Under the permissions, certain experiments are performed upon the image, and the assumed impossibilities involve their always resulting in the same general way. The superior certainty of the mathematician's results, as compared, for example, with those of the chemist, are due to two circumstances. First, the mathematician's experiments being conducted in the imagination upon objects of his own creation, cost next to nothing; while those of the chemist cost dear. Secondly, the assurance of the mathematician is due to his reasoning only concerning hypothetical conditions, so that his results have the generality of his conditions; while the chemist's experiments relating to what will happen as a matter of fact are always open to the doubt whether unknown conditions may not alter. Thus, the mathematician knows that a column of figures will add up the same, whether it be set down in black ink or in red; because he goes on the assumption that the sum of any two numbers of which one is M and the other one more than N will be one more than the sum of M and N; and this assumption says nothing about the colour of the ink. The chemist assumes that when he mixes two liquids in a test tube, there will or will not be a precipitate whether the Dowager Empress of China happens to sneeze at the time, because his experience has always been that laboratory experiments are not affected by such distant conditions. Still, the solar system is moving through space at a great rate, and there is a bare possibility that it may just then have entered a region in which sneezing has very surprising force.

Such reasonings and all reasonings turn upon the idea that if one exerts certain kinds of volition, one will undergo in return certain compulsory perceptions. Now this sort of consideration, namely, that certain lines of conduct will entail certain kinds of inevitable experiences is what is called a 'practical consideration'. Hence is justified the maxim, belief in which constitutes pragmatism; namely,

In order to ascertain the meaning of an intellectual conception one should consider what practical consequences might conceivably result by necessity from the truth of that conception; and the sum of these consequences will constitute the entire meaning of the conception.

Many plausible arguments in favour of this doctrine could easily be adduced; but the only way hitherto discovered of really proving its truth, without in any measure begging the question, is by following the thorny path that we have thus very roughly sketched.

From **a preface to an unpublished book**

To erect a philosophical edifice that shall outcast the vicissitudes of time, my care must be, not so much to set each brick with nicest accuracy, as to lay the foundations deep and massive. Aristotle built upon a few deliberately chosen concepts – such as matter and form, act and power – very broad, and in their outlines vague and rough, but solid, unshakeable, and not easily undermined; and thence it has come to pass that Aristotelianism is babbled in every nursery, that 'English Common Sense', for example, is thoroughly peripatetic, and that ordinary men live so completely within the house of the Stagyrite that whatever they see out of the windows appears to them incomprehensible and metaphysical. Long it has been only too manifest that, fondly habituated though we be to it, the old structure will not do for modern needs; and accordingly, under Descartes, Hobbes, Kant, and others, repairs, alterations, and partial demolitions have been carried on for the last three centuries. One system, also, stands upon its own ground; I mean the new Schelling-Hegel mansion, lately run up in the German taste, but with such oversights in its construction that, although brand new, it is already pronounced uninhabitable. The undertaking this volume inaugurates is to make a philosophy like that of Aristotle, that is to say, to outline a theory so comprehensive that, for a long time to come, the entire work of human reason, in philosophy of every school and kind, in mathematics, in psychology, in physical science, in history, in sociology, and in whatever other department there may be, shall appear as the filling up of its details. The first step toward this is to find simple concepts applicable to every subject.[3]

Notes

1. See *Kritik der reinen Vernunft*, A832, B860.
2. Benjamin Peirce, 'Linear Associative Algebra', #1, *American Journal of Mathematics*, vol. IV (1881), pp. 87–229. [Benjamin Peirce was C.S. Peirce's father.]
3. Charles Sanders Peirce, preface to an unwritten book (1898); in Alastair Gray, *A Book of Prefaces* (London: Bloomsbury, 2002) p. 606. See also 'The Architecture of Theories', in *The Philosophy of Peirce*, edited by Justus Buchler (London: Routledge and Kegan Paul, 1940) pp. 315–16.

Gregory Bateson

Bateson (1904–80) was an anthropologist and theorist, who is well known for his work with Margaret Mead, and for *Naven*, a study of ritualized transgression of the normal social codes of the Iatmul, a head-hunting tribe in New Guinea. There he remarked that 'We now have the beginnings of a general theory of process and change, adaptation and pathology; and, in terms of the general theory, we have to re-examine all that we thought we knew about organisms, societies, families, personal relationships, ecological systems, servo-mechanisms, and the like.'[1] Later in his life he published a work on the idea of evolution, and the mind's role in it.[2] In the essay on Balinese culture included here, he set out an ethical system that involved the cultivation of balance. The essay shows how it might be possible to have a culture in which the idea of balance was regulated by developing the taste for it from infancy. The child is steered away from pleasures that become too intense, and anything might have gone on for too long if it had become altogether fascinating. It seems as fantastical as Jonathan Swift's inventions in *Gulliver's Travels*, or Jorge Luis Borges' in *Doctor Brodie's Report*, but it is a carefully researched anthropological study.[3] Its importance is that it does more than satisfy prurient curiosity (which Freud suggested was the drive that lies behind and is sublimated into intellectual inquiry). It documents as fact a society that is regulated by an agenda other than acquisitiveness, which we are sometimes led to think is somehow intrinsic in human nature. Here is a society in which having more is not the be-all and end-all. The point is to have enough, and not more than enough, certainly not indefinitely more than enough. The system of global capital has generated a culture in which indefinite growth and the accumulation of as much as possible are endemic, and are productive of various sorts of catastrophe – sudden collapses, when an economic bubble bursts, or ecological disasters, as various cycles are thrown out of balance. The Balinese culture is highly traditional and well-balanced. The idea promoted in the essay is that the pattern of a gradual build-up of intensity that finds a sudden release in a moment of orgasm is a pattern that underpins much of the culture of the world, whether in games, war, or art. In Balinese culture it is different, and one finds instead a plateau of intensity, that builds up and falls away, shifts and transforms. This 'plateau' reappears in the title of Deleuze and Guattari's *Mille plateaux*, and Bateson's idea is cited as having a bearing on the structure of their book, which was self-consciously 'rhizomatic' – being composed in a network of associations, without a centralized core, or a linear narrative structure, but in a way that allowed any part to connect with any other.

> A plateau is always in the middle, not at the beginning or the end. A rhizome is made of plateaus. Gregory Bateson uses the word 'plateau' to designate

something very special: a continuous, self-vibrating region of intensities whose development avoids any orientation toward a culmination point or external end. Bateson cites Balinese culture as an example: mother–child sexual games, and even quarrels among men, undergo this bizarre intensive stabilization. 'Some sort of continuing plateau of intensity is substituted for [sexual] climax', war, or a culmination point. It is a regrettable characteristic of the Western mind to relate expressions and actions to exterior and transcendent ends, instead of evaluating them on a plane of consistency on the basis of their intrinsic value.[4]

And elsewhere they note:

Gregory Bateson uses the term *plateau* for continuous regions of intensity constituted in such a way that they do not allow themselves to be interrupted by any external termination, any more than they allow themselves to build toward a climax.[5]

As a structuring pattern this is best explained through music, as it is there that Bali's influence has been most clearly felt in the west, first in the shimmerings of Debussy, and more recently in the mesmerizing throbbing of the music of Lou Harrison, Philip Glass or Steve Reich, which work by very different means from those of the traditional western canon from Haydn to Mahler. 'Ravel and Debussy retain just enough form to shatter it', say Deleuze and Guattari,[6] but Ravel's *Bolero* (1928) is exemplary of an orgasmic structuration, whereas a piece like Debussy's *Pagodes* (1903) simply sits there, sparkling, with no sense of forward drive, only an atmosphere of rapt attention inspired by listening to Indonesian gamelan music.[7] 'Debussy...', exclaim Deleuze and Guattari, 'Music molecularizes sound matter...'.[8] For its form it is not answerable to anything beyond itself, but is music that organizes itself from within, finding its own form of life.

Notes

1. Gregory Bateson, *Naven: A Survey of the Problems Suggested by a Composite Picture of the Culture of a New Guinea Tribe Drawn from Three Points of View* (1958, Leland Stanford Junior University; 2nd edn; London: Wildwood House, 1980) p. vii.
2. Gregory Bateson, *Mind and Nature* (London: Wildwood House, 1979).
3. Jonathan Swift, *Gulliver's Travels* (1726) [originally published pseudonymously, as a first-person narrator's account of his travels: Lemuel Gulliver, *Travels into Several Remote Nations of the World*]; Jorge Luis Borges, translated by Norman Thomas di Giovanni, 'Doctor Brodie's Report' in *Doctor Brodie's Report* (Harmondsworth: Penguin, 1976) pp. 91–100.
4. Gilles Deleuze and Félix Guattari, *Mille plateaux: capitalisme et schizophrénie 2* (Paris: Editions de Minuit, 1980) translated by Brian Massumi, *A Thousand Plateaus: Capitalism and Schizophrenia 2* (London: Athlone, 1987) pp. 21–2.

Section 2: Groundwork

5. Ibid., p. 158.
6. Ibid., p. 270
7. Edward Lockspeiser, *Debussy* (London: Dent, 1963) pp. 146–7. There is an arrangement by Percy Grainger of this piece, which transfers it from the piano to Indonesian tuned gongs. At least two recordings of it are commercially available on CD.
8. Deleuze and Guattari, *Thousand Plateaus*, op. cit., p. 343.

Bali: The Value System of a Steady State[1]

'Ethos' and 'Schismogenesis'

It would be an oversimplification – it would even be false – to say that science necessarily advances by the construction and empirical testing of successive working hypotheses. Among the physicists and chemists there may be some who really proceed in this orthodox manner, but among the social scientists there is perhaps not one. Our concepts are loosely defined – a haze of chiaroscuro prefiguring sharper lines still undrawn – and our hypotheses are still so vague that rarely can we imagine any crucial instance whose investigation will test them.

The present paper is an attempt to make more precise an idea which I published in 1936[2] and which has lain fallow since that time. The notion of *ethos* had proved a useful conceptual tool for me, and with it I had been able to get a sharper understanding of Iatmul culture. But this experience by no means proved that this tool would necessarily be useful in other hands or for the analysis of other cultures. The most general conclusion I could draw was of this order: that my own mental processes had certain characteristics; that the sayings, actions and organization of the Iatmul had certain characteristics; and that the abstraction, 'ethos', performed some role – catalytic, perhaps – in easing the relation between these two specificities, my mind and the data which I myself had collected.

Immediately after completing the manuscript of *Naven*, I went to Bali with the intention of trying upon Balinese data this tool which had been evolved for the analysis of Iatmul. For one reason or another, however, I did not do this, partly because in Bali Margaret Mead and I were engaged in devising other tools – photographic methods of record and description – and partly because I was learning the techniques of applying genetic psychology to cultural data, but more especially because at some inarticulate level I felt that the tool was unsuitable for this new task.

It was not that ethos was in any sense disproved – indeed, a tool or a method can scarcely be proved false. It can only be shown to be not useful, and in this case there was not even a clear demonstration of uselessness. The method remained almost untried, and the most I could say was that, after that surrender to the data which is the first step in all anthropological study, ethological analysis did not seem to be the next thing to do.

It is now possible to show with Balinese data what peculiarities of that culture may have influenced me away from ethological analysis, and this demonstration will lead to a greater generalization of the abstraction, ethos. We shall in the process make certain heuristic advances which may guide us to more rigorous descriptive procedures in dealing with other cultures.

(1) The analysis of Iatmul data led to the definition of ethos as 'The expression of

Section 2: Groundwork

a culturally standardized system of organization of the instincts and emotions of the individuals.[3]

(2) Analysis of Iatmul ethos – consisting in the ordering of data so as to make evident certain recurrent 'emphases' or 'themes' – led to recognition of schismogenesis. It appeared that the working of Iatmul society involved *inter alia* two classes of regenerative[4] or 'vicious' circles. Both of these were sequences of social interaction such that A's acts were stimuli for B's acts, which in turn became stimuli for more intense action on the part of A, and so on, A and B being persons acting either as individuals or as group members.

(3) These schismogenic sequences could be classified into two classes: *(a) symmetrical schismogenesis*, where the mutually promoting actions of A and B were essentially similar, e.g., in cases of competition, rivalry and the like; and *(b) complementary schismogenesis*, where the mutually promoting actions are essentially dissimilar but mutually appropriate, e.g., in cases of dominance–submission, succouring–dependence, exhibitionism–spectatorship and the like.

(4) In 1939 a considerable advance was made in defining the formal relations between the concepts of symmetrical and complementary schismogenesis. This came from an attempt to state schismogenic theory in terms of Richardson's equations for international armaments races.[5] The equations for rivalry evidently gave a first approximation to what I had called 'symmetrical schismogenesis'. These equations assume that the intensity of A's actions (the rate of his arming, in Richardson's case) is simply proportional to the amount by which B is ahead of A. The stimulus term in fact is (B–A), and when this term is positive it is expected that A will engage in efforts to arm. Richardson's second equation makes the same assumption *mutatis mutandis* about B's actions. These equations suggested that other simply rivalrous or competitive phenomena – e.g., boasting – though not subject to such simple measurement as expenditure on armament, might yet when ultimately measured be reducible to a simply analogous set of relations.

The matter was, however, not so clear in the case of complementary schismogenesis. Richardson's equations for 'submission' evidently define a phenomenon somewhat different from a progressive complementary relationship, and the form of his equations describes the action of a factor 'submissiveness' which slows down and ultimately reverses the sign of war-like effort. What was, however, required to describe complementary schismogenesis was an equational form giving a sharp and discontinuous reversal of sign. Such an equational form is achieved by supposing A's actions in a complementary relationship to be proportional to a stimulus term of the type (A–B). Such a form has also the advantage of automatically defining the actions of one of the participants as negative, and thus gives some mathematical analogue for the apparent psychological relatedness of domination to submission, exhibitionism to spectatorship, succouring to dependence, etc.

Notably this formulation is itself a negative of the formulation for rivalry, the stimulus term being the opposite. It had been observed that symmetrical sequences of actions tend sharply to reduce the strain of excessively complementary relationships between persons or groups.[6] It is tempting to ascribe this effect to some hypothesis which would make the two types of schismogenesis in some degree psychologically incompatible, as is done by the above formulation.

(5) It is of interest to note that all the modes associated with the erogenous zones,[7] though not clearly quantifiable, define themes for *complementary* relationship.

(6) The link with erogenous zones suggested in 5, above, indicates that we ought, perhaps, not to think of simple rising exponential curves of intensity limited only by factors analogous to fatigue, such as Richardson's equations would imply; but rather that we should expect our curves to be bounded by phenomena comparable to orgasm – that the achievement of a certain degree of bodily or neural involvement or intensity may be followed by a release of schismogenic tension. Indeed, all that we know about human beings in various sorts of simple contests would seem to indicate that this is the case, and that the conscious or unconscious wish for release of this kind is an important factor which draws the participants on and prevents them from simply withdrawing from contests which would otherwise not commend themselves to 'common sense'. If there is any basic human characteristic which makes man prone to struggle, it would seem to be this hope of release from tension through total involvement. In the case of war this factor is undoubtedly often potent. (The real truth – that in modern warfare only a very few of the participants achieve this climactic release – seems hardly to stand against the insidious myth of 'total' war.)

(7) In 1936 it was suggested that the phenomenon of 'falling in love' might be comparable to a schismogenesis with the signs reversed, and even that 'if the course of true love ever ran smooth it would follow an exponential curve'.[8] Richardson[9] has since, independently, made the same point in more formal terms. Paragraph 6, above, clearly indicates that the 'exponential curves' must give place to some type of curve which will not rise indefinitely but will reach a climax and then fall. For the rest, however, the obvious relationship of these interactive phenomena to climax and orgasm very much strengthens the case for regarding schismogenesis and those cumulative sequences of interaction which lead to love as often psychologically equivalent. (Witness the curious confusions between fighting and lovemaking, the symbolic identifications of orgasm with death, the recurrent use by mammals of organs of offence as ornaments of sexual attraction, etc.)

(8) *Schismogenic sequences were not found in Bali.* This negative statement is of such importance and conflicts with so many theories of social opposition and Marxian determinism that, in order to achieve credibility, I must here describe schematically the process of character formation, the resulting Balinese character structure, the exceptional instances in which some sort of cumulative interaction can be recognized, and the methods by which quarrels and status differentiation are handled. (Detailed analysis of the various points and the supporting data cannot here be reproduced, but references will be given to published sources where the data can be examined.[10])

Balinese Character

(*a*) The most important exception to the above generalization occurs in the relationship between adults (especially parents) and children. Typically, the mother will start a small flirtation with the child, pulling its penis or otherwise stimulating it to interpersonal activity. This will excite the child, and for a few moments cumulative interaction will occur. Then just as the child, approaching some small climax, flings its arms around the mother's neck, her attention wanders. At this point the child will typically start an alternative cumulative interaction, building up towards temper tantrum. The mother will either play a spectator's role, enjoying the child's tantrum, or, if the child actually attacks her, will brush off his attack with no show of anger on her part. These sequences can be seen either as an expression of the mother's distaste for this type of personal involvement or as context in which the child acquires a deep distrust of such involvement. The perhaps basically human tendency towards cumulative personal interaction is thus muted.[11] It is possible that some sort of continuing plateau of intensity is substituted for climax as the child becomes more fully adjusted to Balinese life. This cannot at present be clearly documented for sexual relations, but there are indications that a plateau type of sequence is characteristic for trance and for quarrels (see *d*, below).

(*b*) Similar sequences have the effect of diminishing the child's tendencies towards competitive and rivalrous behaviour. The mother will, for example, tease the child by suckling the baby of some other woman and will enjoy her own child's efforts to push the intruder from the breast.[12]

(*c*) In general the lack of climax is characteristic for Balinese music, drama and other art forms. The music typically has a progression, derived from the logic of its formal structure, and modifications of intensity determined by the duration and progress of the working out of these formal relations. It does not have the sort of rising intensity and climax structure characteristic of modern Occidental music, but rather a formal progression.[13]

(*d*) Balinese culture includes definite techniques for dealing with quarrels. Two men who have quarrelled will go formally to the office of the local representative of the Rajah and will there register their quarrel, agreeing that whichever speaks to the other shall pay a fine or make an offering to the gods. Later, if the quarrel terminates, this contract may be formally nullified. Smaller – but similar – avoidances (*pwik*) are practised, even by small children in their quarrels. It is significant, perhaps, that this procedure is not an attempt to influence the protagonists away from hostility and towards friendship. Rather, it is a formal recognition of the state of their mutual relationship, and possibly, in some sort, a pegging of the relationship at that state. If this interpretation is correct, this method of dealing with quarrels would correspond to the substitution of a plateau for a climax.

(*e*) In regard to warfare, contemporary comment on the old wars between the Rajahs indicates that in the period when the comments were collected (1936–9) war was thought of as containing large elements of mutual avoidance. The village of Bajoeng Gede was surrounded by an old vallum and foss, and the people explained the functions of these fortifications in the following terms: 'If you and I had a quarrel, then you would go and dig a ditch around your house. Later I would come to fight with you, but I would find the ditch and then there would be no fight' – a sort of mutual Maginot Line psychology. Similarly the boundaries between neighbouring kingdoms were, in general, a deserted no-man's-land inhabited only by vagrants and exiles. (A very different psychology of warfare was no doubt developed when the kingdom of Karangasem embarked on the conquest of the neighbouring island of Lombok at the beginning of the eighteenth century. The psychology of this militarism has not been investigated, but there is reason to believe that the time perspective of the Balinese colonists in Lombok is today significantly different from that of Balinese in Bali.[14])

(*f*) The formal techniques of social influence – oratory and the like – are almost totally lacking in Balinese culture. To demand the continued attention of an individual or to exert emotional influence upon a group are alike distasteful and virtually impossible; because in such circumstances the attention of the victim rapidly wanders. Even such continued speech as would, in most cultures, be used for the telling of stories does not occur in Bali. The narrator will, typically, pause after a sentence or two, and wait for some member of the audience to ask him a concrete question about some detail of the plot. He will then answer the question and so resume his narration. This procedure apparently breaks the cumulative tension by irrelevant interaction.

(*g*) The principal hierarchical structures in the society – the caste system and the hierarchy of full citizens who are the village council – are rigid. There are no contexts in which one individual could conceivably compete with another for position in either of these systems. An individual may lose his membership in the hierarchy for various acts, but his place in it cannot be altered. Should he later return to orthodoxy and be accepted back, he will return to his original position in relation to the other members.[15]

The foregoing descriptive generalizations are all partial answers to a negative question – 'Why is Balinese society non-schismogenic?' – and from the combination of these generalizations we arrive at a picture of a society differing very markedly from our own, from that of the Iatmul, from those systems of social opposition which Radcliffe-Brown has analysed, and from any social structure postulated by Marxian analysis.

We started with the hypothesis that human beings have a tendency to involve themselves in sequences of cumulative interaction, and this hypothesis is still left virtually intact. Among the Balinese the babies, at least, evidently have such tendencies. But for sociological validity this hypothesis must now be guarded with a parenthetical clause stipulating that these tendencies are operative in the dynamics of society only if the childhood training is not such as to prevent their expression in adult life.

We have made an advance in our knowledge of the scope of human character formation in demonstrating that these tendencies towards cumulative interaction are subject to some sort of modification, deconditioning, or inhibition.[16] And this is an important advance. We know how it is that the Balinese are non-schismogenic and we know how their distaste for schismogenic patterns is expressed in various details of the social organization – the rigid hierarchies, the institutions for the handling of quarrels, etc. – but we still know nothing of the positive dynamics of the society. We have answered only the negative question.

Balinese Ethos

The next step, therefore, is to ask about Balinese ethos. What actually are the motives and the values which accompany the complex and rich cultural activities of the Balinese? What, if not competitive and other types of cumulative interrelationship, causes the Balinese to carry out the elaborate patterns of their lives?

Section 2: Groundwork

(1) It is immediately clear to any visitor to Bali that the driving force for cultural activity is *not* either acquisitiveness or crude physiological need. The Balinese, especially in the plains, are not hungry or poverty-stricken. They are wasteful of food, and a very considerable part of their activity goes into entirely non-productive activities of an artistic or ritual nature in which food and wealth are lavishly expended. Essentially, we are dealing with an economy of plenty rather than an economy of scarcity. Some, indeed, are rated 'poor' by their fellows, but none of these poor are threatened by starvation, and the suggestion that human beings may actually starve in great Occidental cities was, to the Balinese, unutterably shocking.

(2) In their economic transactions the Balinese show a great deal of carefulness in their small dealings. They are 'penny wise'. On the other hand, this carefulness is counteracted by occasional 'pound foolishness' when they will expend large sums of money upon ceremonials and other forms of lavish consumption. There are very few Balinese who have the idea of steadily maximizing their wealth or property; these few are partly disliked and partly regarded as oddities. For the vast majority the 'saving of pennies' is done with a limited time perspective and a limited level of aspiration. They are saving until they have enough to spend largely on some ceremonial. We should not describe Balinese economics in terms of the individual's attempt to maximize value, but rather compare it with the relaxation oscillations of physiology and engineering, realizing that not only is this analogy descriptive of their sequences of transactions, but that they themselves see these sequences as naturally having some such form.

(3) The Balinese are markedly dependent upon spatial orientation. In order to be able to behave they must know their cardinal points, and if a Balinese is taken by motor car over twisting roads so that he loses his sense of direction, he may become severely disorientated and unable to act (e.g., a dancer may become unable to dance) until he has got back his orientation by seeing some important landmark, such as the central mountain of the island around which the cardinal points are structured. There is a comparable dependence upon social orientation, but with this difference: that where the spatial orientation is in a horizontal plane, social orientation is felt to be, in the main, vertical. When two strangers are brought together, it is necessary, before they can converse with any freedom, that their relative caste positions be stated. One will ask the other, 'Where do you sit?' and this is a metaphor for caste. It is asking, essentially, 'Do you sit high or low?' When each knows the caste of the other, each will then know what etiquette and what linguistic forms he should adopt, and conversation can then proceed. Lacking such orientation, a Balinese is tongue-tied.

(4) It is common to find that activity (other than the 'penny wisdom' mentioned above) rather than being purposive, i.e., aimed at some deferred goal, is valued for itself. The artist, the dancer, the musician and the priest may receive a pecuniary reward for their professional activity, but only in rare cases is this reward adequate to recompense the artist even for his time and materials. The reward is a token of appreciation, it is a definition of the context in which the theatrical company performs, but it is not the economic mainstay of the troupe. The earnings of the troupe may be saved up to enable them to buy new costumes, but when finally the costumes are bought it is usually necessary for every member to make a considerable contribution to the

common fund in order to pay for them. Similarly, in regard to the offerings which are taken to every temple feast, there is no purpose in this enormous expenditure of artistic work and real wealth. The god will not bring any benefit because you made a beautiful structure of flowers and fruit for the calendric feast in his temple, nor will he avenge your abstention. Instead of deferred purpose there is an immediate and immanent satisfaction in performing beautifully, with everybody else, that which it is correct to perform in each particular context.

(5) In general there is evident enjoyment to be had from doing things busily with large crowds of other people.[17] Conversely there is such misfortune inherent in the loss of group membership that the threat of this loss is one of the most serious sanctions in the culture.

(6) It is of great interest to note that many Balinese actions are articulately accounted for in sociological terms rather than in terms of individual goals or values.[18]

This is most conspicuous in regard to all actions related to the village council, the hierarchy which includes all full citizens. This body, in its secular aspects, is referred to as *I Desa* (literally, 'Mr Village'), and numerous rules and procedures are rationalized by reference to this abstract personage. Similarly, in its sacred aspects, the village is deified as *Betara Desa* (God Village), to whom shrines are erected and offerings brought. (We may guess that a Durkheimian analysis would seem to the Balinese to be an obvious and appropriate approach to the understanding of much of their public culture.)

In particular all money transactions which involve the village treasury are governed by the generalization, 'The village does not lose' (*Desanne sing dadi potjol*). This generalization applies, for example, in all cases in which a beast is sold from the village herd. Under no circumstances can the village accept a price less than that which it actually or nominally paid. (It is important to note that the rule takes the form of fixing a lower limit and is not an injunction to maximize the village treasury.)

A peculiar awareness of the nature of social processes is evident in such incidents as the following: A poor man was about to undergo one of the important and expensive *rites de passage* which are necessary for persons as they approach the top of the council hierarchy. We asked what would happen if he refused to undertake this expenditure. The first answer was that, if he were too poor, *I Desa* would *lend* him the money. In response to further pressing as to what would happen if he really refused, we were told that nobody ever had refused, but that if somebody did, nobody would go through the ceremony again. Implicit in this answer and in the fact that nobody ever does refuse is the assumption that the ongoing cultural process is itself to be valued.

(7) Actions which are culturally correct (*patoet*) are acceptable and aesthetically valued. Actions which are permissible (*dadi*) are of more or less neutral value; while actions which are not permissible (*sing dadi*) are to be deprecated and avoided. These generalizations, in their translated form, are no doubt true in many cultures, but it is important to get a clear understanding of what the Balinese mean by *dadi*. The notion is not to be equated with our 'etiquette' or 'law', since each of these invokes the value judgement of some other person or sociological entity. In Bali there is no feeling that actions have been or are categorized as *dadi* or *sing dadi* by some human

or supernatural authority. Rather, the statement that such-and-such an action is *dadi* is an absolute generalization to the effect that under the given circumstances this action is regular.[19] It is wrong for a casteless person to address a prince in other than the 'polished language', and it is wrong for a menstruating woman to enter a temple. The prince or the deity may express annoyance, but there is no feeling that either the prince, the deity or the casteless person made the rules. The offence is felt to be against the order and natural structure of the universe rather than against the actual person offended. The offender, even in such serious matters as incest (for which he may be extruded from the society),[20] is not blamed for anything worse than stupidity and clumsiness. Rather, he is 'an unfortunate person' (*anak latjoer*), and misfortune may come to any of us 'when it is our turn'. Further, it must be stressed that these patterns which define correct and permissible behaviour are exceedingly complex (especially the rules of language) and that the individual Balinese (even to some degree inside his own family) has continual anxiety lest he make an error. Moreover, the rules are not of such a kind that they can be summarized either in a simple recipe or an emotional attitude. Etiquette cannot be deduced from some comprehensive statement about the other person's feelings or from respect for superiors. The details are too complex and too various for this, and so the individual Balinese is forever picking his way, like a tightrope walker, afraid at any moment lest he make some mis-step.

(8) The metaphor from postural balance used in the last paragraph is demonstrably applicable in many contexts of Balinese culture:

(*a*) The fear of loss of support is an important theme in Balinese childhood.[21]

(*b*) Elevation (with its attendant problems of physical and metaphorical balance) is the passive complement of respect.[22]

(*c*) The Balinese child is elevated like a superior person or a god.[23]

(*d*) In cases of actual physical elevation[24] the duty of balancing the system falls on the supporting lower person, but control of the direction in which the system will move is in the hands of the elevated. The little girl in the figure standing in trance on a man's shoulders can cause her bearer to go wherever she desires by merely leaning in that direction. He must then move in that direction in order to maintain the balance of the system.

(*e*) A large proportion of our collection of 1,200 Balinese carvings shows preoccupation on the part of the artist with problems of balance.[25]

(*f*) The Witch, the personification of fear, frequently uses a gesture called *kapar*, which is described as that of a man falling from a coconut palm on suddenly seeing a snake. In this gesture the arms are raised sideways to a position somewhat above the head.

(*g*) The ordinary Balinese term for the period before the coming of the white man is 'when the world was steady' (*doegas goemine enteg*).

Applications of the Von Neumannian Game

Even this very brief listing of some of the elements in Balinese ethos suffices to indicate theoretical problems of prime importance. Let us consider the matter in abstract terms. One of the hypotheses underlying most sociology is that the dynamics of the social mechanism can be described by assuming that the individuals constituting that mechanism are motivated to maximize certain variables. In conventional economic theory it is assumed that the individuals will maximize value, while in schismogenic theory it was tacitly assumed that the individuals would maximize intangible but still simple variables such as prestige, self-esteem or even submissiveness. The Balinese, however, do not maximize any such simple variables.

In order to define the sort of contrast which exists between the Balinese system and any competitive system, let us start by considering the premises of a strictly competitive Von Neumannian game and proceed by considering what changes we must make in these premises in order to approximate more closely to the Balinese system.

(1) The players in a Von Neumannian game are, by hypothesis, motivated only in terms of a single linear (sc. monetary) scale of value. Their strategies are determined: (*a*) by the rules of the hypothetical game; and (*b*) by their intelligence, which is, by hypothesis, sufficient to solve all problems presented by the game. Von Neumann shows that, under certain definable circumstances depending upon the number of players and upon the rules, coalitions of various sorts will be formed by the players, and in fact Von Neumann's analysis concentrates mainly upon the structure of these coalitions and the distribution of value among the members. In comparing these games with human societies we shall regard social organizations as analogous to coalition systems.[26]

(2) Von Neumannian systems differ from human societies in the following respects:

(*a*) His 'players' are from the start completely intelligent, whereas human beings learn. For human beings we must expect that the rules of the game and the conventions associated with any particular set of coalitions will become incorporated into the character structures of the individual players.

(*b*) The mammalian value scale is not simple and monotone, but may be exceedingly complex. We know, even at a physiological level, that calcium will not replace vitamins, nor will an amino acid replace oxygen. Further, we know that the animal does not strive to maximize its supply of any of these discrepant commodities, but rather is required to maintain the supply of each within tolerable limits. Too much may be as harmful as too little. It is also doubtful whether mammalian preference is always transitive.

(*c*) In the Von Neumannian system the number of moves in a given 'play' of a game is assumed to be finite. The strategic problems of the individuals are soluble because the individual can operate within a limited time perspective. He need only look forward a finite distance to the end of the play when the gains and losses will be paid up and everything will start again from a *tabula rasa*. In human society life is not punctuated in this way, and each individual faces a vista of unknowable factors whose number increases (probably exponentially) into the future.

(*d*) The Von Neumannian players are, by hypothesis, not susceptible either to economic death or to boredom. The losers can go on losing forever, and no player can withdraw from the game, even though the outcome of every play is definitely predictable in probability terms.

(3) Of these differences between Von Neumannian and human systems, only the

Section 2: Groundwork

differences in value scales and the possibility of 'death' concern us here. For the sake of simplicity we shall assume that the other differences, though very profound, can for the moment be ignored.

(4) Curiously, we may note that, although men are mammals and therefore have a primary value system which is multi-dimensional and non-maximizing, it is yet possible for these creatures to be put into contexts in which they will strive to maximize one or a few simple variables (money, prestige, power, etc.).

(5) Since the multi-dimensional value system is apparently primary, the problem presented by, for example, Iatmul social organization is not so much to account for the behaviour of Iatmul individuals by invoking (or abstracting) their value system; we should also ask how that value system is imposed on the mammalian individuals by the social organization in which they find themselves. Conventionally in anthropology this question is attacked through genetic psychology. We endeavour to collect data to show how the value system implicit in the social organization is built into the character structure of the individuals in their childhood. There is, however, an alternative approach which would momentarily ignore, as Von Neumann does, the phenomena of learning and consider merely the strategic implications of those contexts which must occur in accordance with the given 'rules' and the coalition system. In this connection it is important to note that competitive contexts – provided the individuals can be made to recognize the contexts as competitive – inevitably reduce the complex gamut of values to very simple and even linear and monotone terms.[27] Considerations of this sort, *plus* descriptions of the regularities in the process of character formation, probably suffice to describe how simple value scales are imposed upon mammalian individuals in competitive societies such as that of the Iatmul or twentieth-century America.

(6) In Balinese society, on the other hand, we find an entirely different state of affairs. Neither the individual nor the village is concerned to maximize any simple variable. Rather, they would seem to be concerned to maximize something which we may call stability, using this term perhaps in a highly metaphorical way. (There is, in fact, one simple quantitative variable which does appear to be maximized. This variable is the amount of any fine imposed by the village. When first imposed the fines are mostly very small, but if payment is delayed the amount of the fine is increased very steeply, and if there is any sign that the offender is *refusing* to pay – 'opposing the village' – the fine is at once raised to an enormous sum and the offender is deprived of membership in the community until he is willing to give up his opposition. Then a part of the fine may be excused.)

(7) Let us now consider a hypothetical system consisting of a number of identical players, plus an umpire who is concerned with the maintenance of stability among the players. Let us further suppose that the players are liable to economic death, that our umpire is concerned to see that this shall not occur and that the umpire has power to make certain alterations in the rules of the game or in the probabilities associated with chance moves. Clearly this umpire will be in more or less continual conflict with the players. He is striving to maintain a dynamic equilibrium or steady state, and this we may rephrase as the attempt to maximize the chances *against* the maximization of any single simple variable.

(8) Ashby has pointed out in rigorous terms that the steady state and continued

existence of complex interactive systems depend upon preventing the maximization of any variable, and that any continued increase in any variable will inevitably result in, and be limited by, irreversible changes in the system. He has also pointed out that in such systems it is very important to permit certain variables to alter.[28] The steady state of an engine with a governor is unlikely to be maintained if the position of the balls of the governor is clamped. Similarly a tightrope walker with a balancing pole will not be able to maintain his balance except by *varying* the forces which he exerts upon the pole.

(9) Returning now to the conceptual model suggested in paragraph 7, let us take one further step towards making this model comparable with Balinese society. Let us substitute for the umpire a village council composed of all the players. We now have a system which presents a number of analogies to our balancing acrobat. When they speak as members of the village council, the players by hypothesis are interested in maintaining the steady state of the system – that is, in preventing the maximization of any simple variable the excessive increase of which would produce irreversible change. In their daily life, however, they are still engaged in simple competitive strategies.

(10) The next step towards making our model resemble Balinese society more closely is clearly to postulate in the character structure of the individuals and/or in the contexts of their daily life those factors which will motivate them towards maintenance of the steady state not only when they speak in council, but also in their other interpersonal relations. These factors are in fact recognizable in Bali and have been enumerated above. In our analysis of why Balinese society is non-schismogenic, we noted that the Balinese child learns to avoid cumulative interaction, i.e., the maximization of certain simple variables, and that the social organization and contexts of daily life are so constructed as to preclude competitive interaction. Further, in our analysis of the Balinese ethos, we noted recurrent valuation: (*a*) of the clear and static definition of status and spatial orientation, and (*b*) of balance and such movement as will conduce to balance.

In sum it seems that the Balinese extend to human relationships attitudes based upon bodily balance, and that they generalize the idea that motion is essential to balance. This last point gives us, I believe, a partial answer to the question of why the society not only continues to function but functions rapidly and busily, continually undertaking ceremonial and artistic tasks which are not economically or competitively determined. This steady state is maintained by continual non-progressive change.

Schismogenic System versus the Steady State

I have discussed two types of social system in such schematic outline that it is possible to state clearly a contrast between them. Both types of system, so far as they are capable of maintaining themselves without progressive or irreversible change, achieve the steady state. There are, however, profound differences between them in the manner in which the steady state is regulated.

The Iatmul system, which is here used as a prototype of schismogenic systems,

Section 2: Groundwork

includes a number of regenerative causal circuits or vicious circles. Each such circuit consists of two or more individuals (or groups of individuals) who participate in potentially cumulative interaction. Each human individual is an energy source or 'relay', such that the energy used in his responses is not derived from the stimuli but from his own metabolic processes. It therefore follows that such a schismogenic system is – unless controlled – liable to excessive increase of those acts which characterize the schismogeneses. The anthropologist who attempts even a qualitative description of such a system must therefore identify: (1) the individuals and groups involved in schismogenesis and the routes of communication between them; (2) the categories of acts and contexts characteristic of the schismogeneses; (3) the processes whereby the individuals become psychologically apt to perform these acts and/or the nature of the contexts which force these acts upon them; and lastly, (4) he must identify the mechanisms or factors which control the schismogeneses. These controlling factors may be of at least three distinct types: (*a*) degenerative causal loops may be superimposed upon the schismogeneses so that when the latter reach a certain intensity some form of restraint is applied – as occurs in Occidental systems when a government intervenes to limit economic competition; (*b*) there may be, in addition to the schismogeneses already considered, other cumulative interactions acting in an opposite sense and so promoting social integration rather than fission; (*c*) the increase in schismogenesis may be limited by factors which are internally or externally environmental to the parts of the schismogenic circuit. Such factors which have only small restraining effect at low intensities of schismogenesis may increase with increase of intensity. Friction, fatigue and limitation of energy supply would be examples of such factors.

In contrast with these schismogenic systems, Balinese society is an entirely different type of mechanism, and in describing it the anthropologist must follow entirely different procedures, for which rules cannot as yet be laid down. Since the class of 'non-schismogenic' social systems is defined only in negative terms, we cannot assume that members of the class will have common characteristics. In the analysis of the Balinese system, however, the following steps occurred, and it is possible that some at least of these may be applicable in the analysis of other cultures of this class: (1) it was observed that schismogenic sequences are rare in Bali; (2) the exceptional cases in which such sequences occur were investigated; (3) from this investigation it appeared, (*a*) that in general the contexts which recur in Balinese social life preclude cumulative interaction and (*b*) that childhood experience trains the child away from seeking climax in personal interaction; (4) it was shown that certain positive values – related to balance – recur in the culture and are incorporated into the character structure during childhood, and, further, that these values may be specifically related to the steady state; (5) a more detailed study is now required to arrive at a systematic statement about the self-correcting characteristics of the system. It is evident that the ethos alone is insufficient to maintain the steady state. From time to time the village or some other entity does step in to correct infractions. The nature of these instances of the working of the corrective mechanism must be studied; but it is clear that this intermittent mechanism is very different from the continually acting restraints which must be present in all schismogenic systems.

Notes

1. This essay appeared in *Social Structure : Studies Presented to A. R. Radcliffe-Brown*, edited by Meyer Fortes, 1949. Preparation of the essay was aided by a Guggenheim Fellowship.
2. G. Bateson, *Naven*, Cambridge, Cambridge University Press, 1936.
3. op. cit., p. 118.
4. The terms 'regenerative' and 'degenerative' are borrowed from communications engineering. A regenerative or 'vicious' circle is a chain of variables of the general type: increase in A causes increase in B; increase in B causes increase in C; ... increase in N causes increase in A. Such a system, if provided with the necessary energy sources and if external factors permit, will clearly operate at a greater and greater rate or intensity. A 'degenerative' or 'self-corrective' circle differs from a regenerative circle in containing at least one link of the type: 'increase in N causes *decrease* in M'. The house thermostat or the steam engine with a governor are examples of such self-correcting systems. It will be noted that in many instances the same material circuit may be either regenerative or degenerative according to the amount of loading, frequency of impulses transmitted around the path, and time characteristics of the total path.
5. L. F. Richardson, 'Generalized Foreign Politics', *British Journal of Psychology*, Monograph Supplement xxiii, 1939.
6. *Naven*, p. 173.
7. E. H. Homburger, 'Configurations in Play: Psychological Notes', *Psychoanalytical Quarterly*, 1937, vi: 138–214. This paper, one of the most important in the literature seeking to state psychoanalytic hypotheses in more rigorous terms, deals with the 'modes' appropriate to the various erogenous zones – intrusion, incorporation, retention and the like – and shows how these modes may be transferred from one zone to another. This leads the writer to a chart of the possible permutations and combinations of such transferred modalities. This chart provides precise means of describing the course of the development of a large variety of different types of character structure (e.g., as met with in different cultures).
8. *Naven*, p. 197.
9. op. cit., 1939.
10. See especially G. Bateson and M. Mead, *Balinese Character: A Photographic Analysis*. Since this photographic record is available, no photographs are included in the present paper.
11. *Balinese Character: A Photographic Analysis*, pl. 47, and pp. 32–6.
12. Ibid., pls 49, 52, 53, and 69–72.
13. See Colin McPhee, 'The Absolute Music of Bali', *Modern Music*, 1935; and *A House in Bali*, London, Gollancz, 1947.
14. See G. Bateson, 'An Old Temple and a New Myth', *Djawa*, xvii, Batavia, 1937.
15. See M. Mead, 'Public Opinion Mechanisms among Primitive Peoples', *Public Opinion Quarterly*, 1937, i: 5–16.

16. As is usual in anthropology, the data are not sufficiently precise to give us any clue as to the nature of the learning processes involved. Anthropology, at best, is only able to *raise* problems of this order. The next step must be left for laboratory experimentation.
17. Bateson and Mead, op. cit., pl. 5.
18. Cf. *Naven*, pp. 250 ff., where it was suggested that we must expect to find that some peoples of the world would relate their actions to the sociological frame.
19. The word *dadi* is also used as a copula referring to changes in social status. *I Anoe dadi Koebajan* means 'So-and-so has become a village official'.
20. Mead, 'Public Opinion Mechanisms among Primitive Peoples', loc. cit, 1937.
21. Bateson and Mead, op. cit., pls 17, 67, and 79.
22. Ibid., pls. 10–14.
23. Ibid., pl. 45.
24. Ibid., pl. 10, fig. 3.
25. At present it is not possible to make such a statement in sharply defined quantitative terms, the available judgements being subjective and Occidental.
26. Alternatively, we might handle the analogy in another way. A social system is, as Von Neumann and Morgenstern point out, comparable to a non-zero sum game in which one or more coalitions of people play against each other and against nature. The non-zero sum characteristic is based on the fact that value is continually extracted from the natural environment. Inasmuch as Balinese society exploits nature, the total entity, including both environment and people, is clearly comparable to a game requiring coalition between people. It is possible, however, that that subdivision of the total game comprising the *people only* might be such that the formation of coalitions within it would not be essential – that is, Balinese society may differ from most other societies in that the 'rules' of the relationship between people define a 'game' of the type Von Neumann would call 'non-essential'. This possibility is not here examined. (See Von Neumann and Morgenstern, op. cit.)
27. L. K. Frank, 'The Cost of Competition', *Plan Age*, 1940, vi: 314–24.
28. W. R. Ashby, 'Effect of Controls on Stability', *Nature*, clv, no. 3930, 24 February 1945, 242–3.

Walter Benjamin, Louis Aragon and Karl Marx

With the rise of cultural studies on the curriculum, Walter Benjamin's influence is being felt as one of the cornerstones of modern sensibility. He was born in 1892 into a prosperous Jewish family in Berlin. He tried to support himself by writing, but his fine writing style and critical engagement with Marxist themes meant that it was only the small-circulation literary journals that would take his work, and to his mortification he remained dependent on an allowance from his father – an allowance that the father deliberately kept small in the hope that his son would settle down to a proper job. It never happened, and he lived a life of increasing desperation, brought to an end by his suicide in 1940 at the French–Spanish border, where he was detained while trying to escape the Nazis. Like Bachelard his thought moves between a fascination with the concrete objects of everyday life, and their place in an overarching world view. Benjamin could be fascinated by passing remarks in newspapers, by an object such as a lamp – which in Benjamin's description acquired a patination that is evocative of the lamp's passage through life – or by larger more complex objects such as buildings and machines. Above all Benjamin is a theorist of urban life and sensibility, and we catch him at his most characteristic when noticing the behaviour of a crowd, or documenting the *flâneur* – the young man with time on his hands, seeing the city as spectacle and entertainment. In his later years he assembled material for a book that was never written, about the Parisian arcades, which was his major engagement with architecture. This material is now available in English translation, but it is difficult to extract passages from it in a way that leaves them meaningful, because much of it is composed of scraps of press cuttings, transcriptions of passages from books, and jottings of Benjamin's own observations and comments in a very fragmentary form. It is heartily recommended for its power of suggestion but it is resistant to summary. The project was apparently initiated by Benjamin's reading of the description of the Passage de l'Opéra, in Louis Aragon's book *Paris Peasant*. Benjamin remarked that Aragon and André Breton (the founders of Surrealism) met their friends at a café in this arcade because they felt antipathy to the established artistic quarters around Montparnasse and Montmartre.[1] Aragon's writing is sumptuously evocative, and worth quoting. It too is interpolated with cuttings from advertisements, and notices that give an impression of the half-life going on in the *passages* at that time. 'Having been robbed,' said one, 'for the benefit of a finance company by an expropriation which has ruined the tradesmen of this passage, and being consequently unable to re-establish myself elsewhere, I am seeking a buyer for my bar equipment.'[2]

Section 2: Groundwork

Louis Aragon, from *Paris Peasant* (1926)

How oddly this light suffuses the covered arcades which abound in Paris in the vicinity of the main boulevards and which are rather disturbingly named *passages*, as though no one had the right to linger for more than an instant in those sunless corridors. A glaucous gleam, seemingly filtered through deep water, with the special quality of pale brilliance of a leg suddenly revealed under a lifted skirt. The great American passion for city planning, imported into Paris by a prefect of police during the Second Empire and now being applied to the task of redrawing the map of our capital in straight lines, will soon spell the doom of these human aquariums. Although the life that originally quickened them has drained away, they deserve, nevertheless, to be regarded as the secret repositories of several modern myths: it is only today when the pickaxe menaces them, that they have at last become the true sanctuaries of a cult of the ephemeral, the ghostly landscape of damnable pleasures and professions. Places that yesterday were incomprehensible, and that tomorrow will never know.[3]

Benjamin remarked that Aragon's writing remained 'impressionistic' and philosophically vague,[4] and his own writing was clearly anchored in a concern to see buildings as being implicated in social processes, and in the material culture of their production, without losing touch with the evocative qualities that are still to be valued. So, for example, in his analysis of the arcades in the opening of his essay, 'Paris, Capital of the Nineteenth Century' there is a much more concretely materialist sensibility at work.

Walter Benjamin, from **Paris, Capital of the Nineteenth Century** (1939)

Most of the Paris arcades are built in the fifteen years following 1822. The first condition of their development is the boom in the textile trade. *Magasins de nouveautés*, the first establishments to keep large stocks of merchandize on the premises, make their appearance. They are the forerunners of department stores. This is the period of which Balzac writes: 'The great poem of display chants its stanzas of colour from the Church of the Madeleine to the Porte Saint-Denis.' The arcades are centres of commerce in luxury items. In fitting them out, art enters the service of the merchant. Contemporaries never tire of admiring them. For a long time they remain an attraction for tourists. An *Illustrated Guide to Paris* says: 'These arcades, a recent invention of industrial luxury, are glass-roofed, marble-panelled corridors extending through whole blocks of buildings, whose owners have joined together for such enterprises. Lining both sides of the arcade, which gets its light from above, are the most elegant shops, so that the passage is a city, a world in miniature.' The arcades are the scene of the first attempts at gas lighting.

The second condition for the emergence of the arcades is the beginning of iron construction. Under the Empire, this technology was seen as a contribution to the revival of architecture in the classical Greek sense. The architectural theorist Boetticher expresses the general view of the matter when he says that, 'with regard to the art forms of the new system, the Hellenic mode' must come to prevail. The Empire style is the style of revolutionary terrorism, for which the state is an end in itself. Just as Napoleon failed to understand the functional nature of the state as an instrument of domination by the bourgeoisie, so the architects of his time failed to understand the functional nature of iron, with which the constructive principle begins its domination of architecture. These architects design supports resembling Pompeian columns, and factories that imitate residential houses, just as later the first railroad stations will assume the look of chalets. Construction plays the role of the subconscious. [. . .] – For the first time since the Romans, a new artifical building material appears: iron. It will undergo an evolution whose pace will accelerate in the course of the century.[5]

There is an attempt here to analyse cause and effect, to determine the necessary conditions for the development of the arcades (but this is not an exhaustive analysis of all the necessary conditions, just an attempt to show which new conditions have made the development possible). Also there is an understanding of the architecture as the product of processes – there is mention of the means of production, and an idea of evolutionary progress in the designs. There is also a wider range of reading here than is at first apparent. The statement that 'Construction plays the role of the subconscious', for example appears in an earlier draft in inverted commas, with a footnote referring us to Sigfried Giedion as the author of the words.[6] He noted elsewhere that his work 'has to develop to the highest degree the art of citing without quotation marks. Its theory is intimately related to that of montage.'[7] Curiously this is exactly the method of composition of the traditionally-trained architects of whose methods Benjamin seems to despair. For them, as for him, the idea would be to steep oneself in historical materials and then make a coherent composition that addresses the task in hand, that has an internal logic, an inner coherence, and which shows that it belongs in the realm of cultural accomplishment by making allusions to the approved stock of knowledge. Benjamin's compositional method is exactly comparable with that of a revered author like Montaigne, except that whereas Montaigne's citations would be almost entirely of ancient Latin and Greek authors, Benjamin's were from works of contemporary scholarship along with newspaper cuttings, and the ephemeral productions of the era that he was studying – textual productions from everyday life, that were untouched by any ambition to be seen as literature. The reference to Boetticher mentions one half of his distinction between 'core-form' and 'art-form' in buildings, the 'core-form' being what constructional necessity demands – lying unrealized in a virtual state – whereas the 'art-form' is the actual form of the building, determined by the architect who has an understanding of the 'core-form' but who must find one way or another of realizing it – it can be embodied in a number of ways.[8] Benjamin sought to refine Giedion's image of construction as being the unconscious of buildings, with reference to Boetticher's distinction, asking 'Wouldn't it be better to say "the role of bodily processes" – around which "artistic" architectures gather, like dreams around the framework of physiological processes?'[9] The body reappears when Benjamin compares the iron ribs of the arcades' roof structure to the whalebone ribs in a corset. The women who visited the arcades when they were new would have worn corsets, and the corset is the torso's arcade.[10] Dreams, bodies and the world are woven together in the fabric of Benjamin's view of architecture, which is nevertheless underpinned with an understanding of the practicalities of the means of production, and the political imperatives that he saw as consequent on his adoption of Communism. For example Benjamin collated the following passage from Karl Marx, which connects with a theme that will be introduced in the next section, but as it carries Benjamin's endorsement it can be included here. 'Simultaneity, the basis of the new style of living,' says Benjamin, 'comes from mechanical production',[11] and then he cites the following passage.

Karl Marx, from *Capital* (1867)

Each detail machine supplies the raw material to the machine next in order; and since they are all working at the same time, the product is always going through the various stages of its fabrication, and is also constantly in a state of transition from one phase to another. . . . The collective machine, now an organized system of various kinds of single machines, and of groups of single machines, becomes more and more perfect, the more the process as a whole becomes a continuous one – that is, the less the raw material is interrupted in its passage from its first phase to its last; in other words, the more its passage from one phase to another is effected not by the hand of man but by the machinery itself. In manufacture the isolation of each detail process is a condition imposed by the nature of division of labour, but in the fully developed factory the continuity of those processes is, on the contrary, imperative.[12]

Notes

1. Walter Benjamin, *Das Passagen-Werk*, edited by Rolf Tiedemann (Berlin: Suhrkamp, 1982) translated by Howard Eiland and Kevin McLaughlin, *The Arcades Project* (Cambridge, Mass.: Harvard University Press, 1999) p. 82.
2. Louis Aragon, *Le Paysan de Paris* (Paris: Gallimard, 1926) translated by Simon Watson Taylor, *Paris Peasant*, (London: Jonathan Cape, 1971) p. 25.
3. Louis Aragon, pp. 13–14; the last part of this quotation was cited by Walter Benjamin, *Arcades Project*, op. cit., p. 87.
4. Ibid., p. 458
5. Ibid., pp. 15–16.
6. The quotation is from Sigfried Giedion, *Bauen in Frankreich* (Leipzig, 1928) p. 3. Benjamin's earlier draft (of 1935) is given in Walter Benjamin, *Arcades Project*, op. cit., p. 4.
7. Walter Benjamin, *Arcades Project*, op. cit., p. 458.
8. Karl Heinrich von Boetticher, see Kenneth Frampton, Bötticher, Semper and

the Tectonic: Core Form and Art Form', what in *What is Architecture*, edited by Andrew Ballantyne (London: Routledge, 2002), pp. 138–52.
9. Walter Benjamin, *Arcades Project*, op. cit., p. 391.
10. Ibid., p. 492.
11. Ibid., p. 394
12. Karl Marx, *Das Kapital*, vol. 1 (Hamburg: 1922) p. 344; translated by Samuel Moore and Edward Aveling, *Capital* (1887; reprinted New York: International Publishers, 1967) pp. 359–60.

Diane Favro

This essay is included because it triumphantly displays some of the principles outlined above being put into action. It shows how compelling a reading can be made by linking objects – here buildings – with the culture that brought them into being. Favro draws on a wide range of scholarship, including traditional antiquarian knowledge, but puts it together in such a way as to bring out the pragmatist themes of the building in use, and in its dynamic relationship with the culture around it. As the buildings in question are in the public realm, there is also a Benjaminian theme of the crowd at work here – a collective entity, bringing the works into being and finding its needs met in the buildings that enable the group identity to be consolidated. The city of Rome is one of the most traditional objects of study for architectural historians, but Favro – who not only writes architectural history (including an important book on Augustan Rome)[1] but also teaches student architects – treats her subject with a characteristically twenty-first-century analysis, that could not have been made at a time when determining the forms of the ancient objects seemed to be the overriding concern of antiquarian discipline. The teleology of architectural history has moved, and will continue to move, in a manner that echoes the changing teleology of the buildings.[2] If we were to be faced with the need to make a description of a modern building, then the approach taken here would make the description meaningful and compelling, but with a building belonging to our own walk of life we would be unlikely to make such a description, because it would seem redundant. We know what we do with the familiar buildings around us, which ones we use as landmarks, which of them give shelter to our various activities, and which give us a sense of civic pride or national belonging. It is enough to show a picture of a national assembly or a rural homestead, and we have feelings about them that are predictably invoked. When we are dealing with a more remote past these overtones need to be reconstructed in a painstaking way, if we are to begin to empathize with the feelings that the places would have aroused in the people who commissioned, built and used them. As we become more sensitized to the variety of our own fragmenting and proliferating multiculture, it will become increasingly important to take note of such connotations in our own everyday surroundings, as our own common ground may be seen from radically distinct perspectives by other sectors in society that also have a claim on these places and interpret them unselfconsciously for their own ends.

Notes

1. Diane Favro, *The Urban Image of Augustan Rome* (Cambridge: Cambridge University Press, 1996).
2. See John Dewey above, pp. 65–6.

Rome: The Street Triumphant – The Urban Impact of Roman Triumphal Parades

> The people [of Rome] erected scaffolding in the theaters ... and round the Forum, occupied the other parts of the city which afforded a view of the procession, and witnessed the spectacle arrayed in white garments. Every temple was open and filled with garlands and incense, while numerous servitors and lictors restrained the thronging and scurrying crowds and kept the streets open and clear. Three days were assigned for the triumphal procession.
>
> <div align="right">Triumph of Aemilius Paullus, 167 B.C.E.
Plutarch, <i>Aemilius</i> 32</div>

A parade prescribes a distinct pathway through a city. In the case of ancient Rome, triumphal military parades had lasting implications for the city's plan. Delimited by human action, rather than flanking buildings, unifying paving, or set limits, a processional path creates a distinct urban route. A well-attended, lengthy parade transforms a series of interconnected thoroughfares into a new, independent processional street, with its own superseding identity. The triumphal route through ancient Rome is a premier example. Triumphal processions repeatedly energized the city during the period of the Republic, from 508 to 44 B.C.E. Lasting several days, each occasion elicited a powerful triumphal itinerary, defined by temporary seating, jostling crowds, and fluttering decorations.

Roman processions honoring successful generals have a long history, which Plutarch traces all the way back to Romulus.[1] The triumph was the highest attainable honor for a male citizen of the Republic. The Senate awarded a triumph based on complex criteria. The victor had to be a magistrate holding *imperium* who had been proclaimed triumphator in the field by his troops. The war whose victory was celebrated had to be a just, concluded confrontation involving the death of at least five thousand foes.[2] Since tradition forbade the discussion of war-related topics within the city proper, senators deliberated petitions for triumphs outside the *pomerium*, or sacred urban boundary. If all requirements were met, the Senate proclaimed the general a triumphator, acclaimed his troops as well, formally declared a holiday, and granted public resources to fund a parade and other festivities. At first, triumphs were infrequent and simple. Gradually, under the influence of extravagant Hellenistic celebrations and with an expanding power base, Rome developed impressive and numerous triumphs. Between 220 and 70 B.C.E., ceremonies occurred approximately once every year and a half.[3]

The triumph was trenchantly bound to the city as a cosmological and political necessity. No matter how far Roman authority extended, the city on the Tiber remained the focal point of power. Rome was the wellspring of *romanitas* and the home of Jupiter Optimus Maximus, to whom all triumphs were dedicated.[4] As a result, all communal ceremonies had to occur amid the seven hills. When Marcus Antonius celebrated a triumph in Alexandria, Romans reacted violently, considering this act a sacrilegious insult to the gods, the city, and the people.[5]

Descriptions of triumphs appear repeatedly in ancient literature; visual depictions are found in ancient art. Throughout, however, the emphasis is on the parade's participants and elaborate displays. Similarly, scholarly research on the Roman triumph focuses on the pageant as ritual. To date, the procession's considerable impact on the city's physical form has not been thoroughly considered.[6] Clearly, the relationship between the triumphal parade and the urban form was reciprocal. The temporary triumphal route drew strength from the power of place – that is, from the city locales through which it passed and from the historical moment in which it existed. At the same time, the processional practice affected building typologies, patronage, and siting.

The Roman triumph served three primary purposes, each associated with a select activity and a select sector of the city.[7] First, and probably oldest, was the ceremonial culmination of a successful military campaign, serving ritually to purify both the troops and the citizenry contaminated by war. Celebratory preparations began in the Campus Martius, northwest of the city center. Named after the war god Mars, this extrapomerial flood plain had a long military history. In the years before the creation of a standing army, the Romans had conducted military maneuvers and worshiped the war gods Bellona and Mars here. The Campus also accommodated foreign ambassadors, who resided in the Villa Publica while awaiting permission to enter the city.[8] A general petitioning for a triumph found ample room in the plain for his troops and appropriate shelter for himself in the porticoed public villa. There he waited anxiously for the decision of the Senate, convened in the Temple of Bellona. An affirmative vote resulted in raucous celebrations by the troops, along with solemn purification rituals, award ceremonies, and speeches by the new triumphator.[9] Immediately, preparations began for the triumphal procession into Rome.

During the Republic, the exact starting point of the triumphal parade varied greatly. Staging occurred throughout the southeastern Campus Martius. In particular, the unencumbered area known as the Circus Flaminius was conveniently located and large enough to be used for speeches, displays of captured goods, and the orchestration of the triumphal parade.[10] The procession gained definition as it left the Campus Martius and passed through the Porta Triumphalis. After years of study, this structure remains enigmatic, its precise date, form, and location hotly debated. The earliest literary references come from the late Republic. The term *porta* indicates a door or gatelike form. Located in the area of the Forum Holitorium, the Porta Triumphalis has been identified as either a gate in the Republican wall or a freestanding structure. Closed during most days of the year, the Porta was specifically opened for triumphal processions. Passage through the Porta Triumphalis both signified a symbolic purification and was a celebration of entry into the city.[11]

Conceptually, this choreography mimed Rome's topographical and functional realities. At its southern edge, the vast, flat Campus Martius gave way to the cramped hills and valleys of the city; in parallel, the free movement of masses possible in the plain gave way to the restricted activities allowed within the city's sacral and official boundaries. The teeming crowds of soldiers, prisoners, displays, and carts that swarmed over the Campus likewise were restrained within the city; there, an amorphous crowd became a visible and controlled urban line: the triumphal street.

The second aim of the triumph was to justify military campaigns to the Senate and populace who had remained at Rome. Wending through the dense city center, the procession had a large audience. At its head were Roman magistrates and senators, visible manifestations of State sanction. Behind them lumbered cartloads of booty, sacrificial animals, and captives, collectively vindicating the cost of war. Next came the triumphator in all his glory. Wrapped in a richly embroidered purple toga, he stood high in a gleaming chariot drawn by four white horses. Above his head a slave held a victory wreath, while whispering, 'Look behind you [i.e., look to the future] and remember that you are a man,' a cautionary reminder that the general acted on behalf of Rome. After the triumphator came his military officers, Roman citizens rescued from slavery, and the cheering (and jeering) troops.[12]

The parade formed the body of the triumph. Hour after hour over several days, spectators watched the flowing course of the pageant. The endlessly diverse triumphal extravaganzas drew enormous crowds from both Rome and throughout Italy.[13] Triumphal parades were as much didactic as celebratory. Through the exhibition of spoils, Rome's citizens learned not only about the prowess of their armies and generals, but also about the people, art, architecture, and fauna of their conquered foes. Along with the general and his rowdy troops came a panoply of exhibitions. The parade of Lucius Scipio in 189 B.C.E., for example, included 224 captured military standards, 134 *simulacra*, 231 ivory tusks, 234 gold crowns, 137,420 pounds of silver, and equally impressive quantities of gold, metal vases, coins, and prisoners. Particularly interesting are the *simulacra*, believed to be models of captured buildings, cities, or regions. In addition, large painted or woven panoramas several stories high tottered past the spectators; by depicting battles and related events, these allowed observers vicariously to experience being in the field. Often, the panels were later placed on permanent public display in Rome. Exhibits of captured exotica, ranging from jewel-encrusted furniture to elephants and other wild beasts, instructed the crowd about life and art in foreign lands.[14]

Moving with measured slowness, the pageant passed through the Forum Holitorium, the Velabrum, and the Forum Boarium, then circled around the base of the Palatine Hill, through the valley of the Circus Maximus, and into the Forum Romanum. Originally, spectators selected good viewing spots on the grassy hillsides. Later, as the slopes became densely built, they watched from porticoes, balconies, roofs, and windows. The poet Propertius describes lying in the arms of a paramour while gazing out an upper-story window at the banners of a passing triumphal parade.[15] At the base of the Capitoline Hill, the triumphal procession halted, and the chief captives were led off and killed, while the triumphator prepared for his ascent to the temple on the crown of the hill.

The route of the triumphal parade clearly followed Rome's earliest trails along the floors of connected valleys. In fact, each step drew upon the city's topographic history. For example, the loop through the Velabrum preserved the memory of the swamp that once had occupied the area northeast of the Forum Boarium. The encirclement of the Palatine brought to mind the limits of early Rome under Romulus.[16] At the same time, the path of the procession exhorted all observers to 'look behind' to the future. Each procession was part of an urban continuum, a street connected in time as well as in space with the past and future of the Roman state, the triumph ritual, and the topography of Rome.

The third purpose of the triumphal ceremony was to appease and honor the gods – in particular, Jupiter, guarantor of the Roman state. The expiatory nature of the event was evident in each phase. Religious sacrifices began with the offerings of the troops in the Campus Martius. In the city proper, the procession made an irregular loop; the counter-clockwise direction emulated the choreography of other rituals and may have been apotropaic. A similar protective power may have been associated with the Sacra Via, the Sacred Highway in the Forum Romanum, traversed by the triumphal parade. Activities on the Capitoline hill focused on the triumph's religious purpose. The triumphator proceeded on foot up the steep Clivus Capitolinus to the Temple of Jupiter Optimus Maximus.[17] Once at the huge temple, he solemnly sacrificed a white ox and laid a laurel branch and wreaths in the lap of Jupiter's statue; nearby, he offered selected spoils of war at the smaller shrine to Jupiter Feretrius. The ceremonies closed with the triumphator and Senate feasting in Jupiter's great temple.[18]

The *locus* on the Capitoline marked the end both of the improvised street and of an arduous military journey. Before leaving Rome on his campaign, the general had sacrificed to Jupiter on this same site; returning victorious, he came full circle. The procession drew upon the city's topography to recall his journey and prepare the triumphator for this potent terminus. Literally and figuratively, the parade left behind the field of Mars and passed through the civilizing urban zone. All along the way, participants caught glimpses of the Temple of Jupiter Optimus Maximus, hovering above the worldly realm of the city. Only a few, led by the triumphator, were allowed to ascend and face the god atop the Capitoline.

The triumphal street was powerful and enduring, yet it did not have a fixed itinerary. Three broad topographical components remained constant in all processions: the sorting out in the Campus Martius, the loop around the Palatine, and the terminus at the Capitoline. Within these areas, however, the route could vary. Each triumphator designed his parade to provide the greatest propagandistic benefit for his personal agenda. For example, he might direct the parade to pass by a monument erected by his family or himself. Due to this variability, the improvised street formed by the triumphal parade remained always new and vital, redefined periodically with each ceremonial event.

Celebration of a triumph transformed the urban realities of Rome. For a few hours or days, the parade route became the city's major thoroughfare, yet it was a street closed to use by urban residents. Lictors and other official attendants kept citizens off the processional path.[19] Made up of a series of connected thoroughfares, the triumphal street was recognizable as conceptual whole through the ephemeral trappings added to define its edges and length. Scaffolding for temporary seating and a solid wall of spectators formed the contours of the street at ground level. The gleaming white garb of the spectators contrasted greatly with the colorful dress of the figures in the parade, visually distinguishing the two groups.[20] Above the heads of the crowd, temporary decorations graced the buildings along the route, setting them apart from other structures in Rome. In addition to the usual floral garlands added to major structures on holidays, urban buildings received militaristic ornaments, the so-called *spolia*, commemorating battles. For example, in 308 B.C.E., the triumphator Papirius Cursor proudly displayed gilt shields on the shops of the silversmiths in the Forum Romanum.[21] Such ornaments visually and programmatically linked urban buildings associated with military victory.

The rituals of a triumph redefined the use of key buildings in Rome. For most of the year, the Porta Triumphalis stood as a mute billboard, its passageway blocked; on the days of a triumph, the barrier was torn away and the parade poured through. Thus, during the few hours of the ceremony, the monument actually functioned as an urban doorway. The celebration also transformed Rome's entertainment structures. To keep large audiences comfortable throughout the lengthy event, triumphators diverted processions directly into and through spectator buildings such as theaters and circuses.[22] The public perception of these structures thus changed temporarily from having a centralized focus to having a linear one. Theater orchestras and circus tracts became segments of the triumphal street, with the stone seating acting as a solid version of the temporary grandstands defining the processional route elsewhere in the city.

Significantly, Rome first acquired large permanent theaters in the first century B.C.E., a period when triumphs proliferated at an astonishing rate. The three that were built in the Campus Martius were all associated with triumphs.[23] In fact, the orientation of one of these, the Theater of Marcellus, may have directly responded to processional dictates. When clearing room for a stone theater near the Circus Flaminius in 44 B.C.E., Julius Caesar cavalierly destroyed temples erected by earlier triumphators. Dedicated by his heir as the Theater of Marcellus, this structure was not aligned on a east–west axis like other permanent theaters in the Republican city. Its skewed southwest–north–east orientation may have been chosen to facilitate the movement of triumphal processions from the Circus Flaminius, through the theater, and into the Forum Holitorium.[24]

Spectator events were an integral part of Roman life. Thus it is not surprising that they had a significant impact on building design. In the late first century B.C.E., Vitruvius explained the layout of the Roman fora as responding to the requirements of gladiatorial contests by including spacious colonnades, with balconies above for spectators.[25] All along the parade routes of Rome, buildings responded to spectators' needs. Thus, the open external arcades of theaters and circuses let light into interior galleries and simultaneously acted as platforms from which to view processions in the public streets below. Shady porticoes, high temple podia, balconies, and large upper-story windows likewise served parade watchers. The elevation of important Roman buildings upon podia may in part have been an attempt to keep facades visible above standing crowds.

The triumphal ceremony also promoted certain building types. The form most directly associated with the event is the commemorative arch. During the Republic, memorials took many forms in addition to buildings: single ornamented columns, statues atop viaducts, free standing sculptures, and *fornices*. Formed by freestanding piers connected by an arched lintel supporting sculpture, the *fornix* held special appeal for triumphators.[26] Like city gates or doorways, *fornices* compelled movement *through*, an act associated with purification. Victorious generals carefully sited their arches so that later triumphal parades would be compelled to pass through them and thus under their sculpted images, an effective means of demonstrating their linkage, if not superiority, to subsequent triumphators. Commemorating his Spanish victories in the early second century B.C.E., L. Stertinius shrewdly erected a *fornix* as the eastern gateway of the Circus Maximus, even though he had not formally been awarded a triumph.[27] All later triumphal processions had to exit the Circus through the Fornix Stertinii. Commemorative arches are valuable urban-design components; they divide one area from another, frame views, and mark shifts in street directions.[28] Yet without the persistence of the triumphal parade, this architectural form of street articulation might not have proliferated in Rome.

The requirements of triumphal ceremonies may also have strengthened the public resolve to maintain open areas within the city. Long after troops ceased to practice maneuvers in the Campus Martius, they mustered there for victory parades, along with captives, animals, and carts. This important activity called for ample open space, and thus promoted the preservation of unbuilt areas in the field of Mars. Elsewhere along the triumphal route, open urban land was continuously preserved for temporary seating, as well as post-parade events. Whenever possible, commemorative games and enormous feasts occupied facilities along the route. After his multiple triumph in 47 B.C.E., Caesar gave a great public banquet on twenty thousand dining couches. These must have occupied every open space in the Campus Martius, Forum Romanum, Circus Maximus, and Capitoline; maybe some couches also stood in Julius's new forum, then under construction, tangent to the triumphal path.[29] The needs of the triumph of course did not prevent the inexorable densification of Rome, yet they may have helped preserve open urban space as a planning priority.

Triumphal parades stimulated urban construction in other ways as well. During the Republic, the Romans felt culturally inferior to the Hellenistic world in all areas, including architecture and urban appearance. This feeling increased as triumphators displayed booty from conquests in the East, during the second and first centuries B.C.E. In a few instances, victorious generals carried back parts of Greek buildings for reuse in Rome.[30] The *simulacra* displayed in victory parades provided even more provocative exemplars of Hellenistic architecture and urban design. In his triumphal parade of 47 B.C.E., Julius Caesar included a model depicting one of the seven wonders of the ancient world, the enormous Pharos (lighthouse) of Alexandria, complete with the flames of its beacon. This display not only inspired architects, it also helped to justify Caesar's plans to erect similar extravagances in Rome.[31]

Every triumphator was expected to spend a portion of his booty on a public building in Rome. Thus, many of the city's magnificent structures, especially the temples, were windfalls of the triumphal ceremony. Furthermore, ambitious nontriumphators likewise sought permission to erect public buildings advertising their own successes. For maximum exposure and association, patrons of both kinds located their projects as closely as possible to the procession way. Since the exact parade route varied, such monuments clustered near the nodal points of the route, rather than along a specific urban line. During the Republic, a number of victory monuments appeared in the southwestern Campus Martius and the vicinity of the Circus Maximus.[32] For example, in the Forum Holitorium stood numerous statues, the *fornices* of Stertinius, and the temples of Janus, Juno Sospita, and Spes; near the Circus Maximus triumphators erected the column of Duilius and the temples of Juventas and Hercules.

Individuals were not the only patrons of triumph-related constructions. The Senate and People of Rome funded hundreds of triumphal commemoratives. After all, triumphs were a reaffirmation of the collective power of Rome. Memorials sponsored by individual victors provided exemplars for all Romans, but especially for participants in the parades. Passing monument after monument, the troops were reminded of their place within a victorious continuum. Simultaneously, the hundreds of captives were made aware of the overwhelming might of their conquerors – a memory that freed prisoners carried back to their homelands.[33] As a result, the State naturally took an active role in embellishing the ritual street. Most of the state-sponsored triumphal monuments stood in the areas of greatest public meaning and involvement, namely, the Forum Romanum and Capitoline, where they would reach the largest audience. In fact, the State exercised close control over these areas and periodically had to remove old commemoratives to make space for new ones.[34]

The concentration of memorial buildings, in turn, gradually shaped the choreography of the triumphal procession and of the city. For example, victorious generals erected several temples across from the Circus Flaminius, defining an impressive, straight street. The addition of surrounding porticoes by later triumphators further clarified the street edge and provided ground and rooftop space for spectators.[35] The street thus shaped by these buildings cut a straight line through the southwestern Campus. Here, a large segment of the parade could be orchestrated and viewed at one time. From the arcaded cavea of Pompey's theater, located to the north, observers, or even the triumphator himself, could look down and evaluate the relationships among various parts of the choreographed pageant before it moved through the Porta Triumphalis.[36]

At the end of an ephemeral event such as a Roman triumphal parade, much more remained than the detritus of marching troops, lumbering animals, and an immense crowd. The parade left an enduring imprint upon both urban structure and urban existence. After the last trumpet had sounded, residents found their understanding of the city's topography and history once more strengthened. They carried home a sense of security tangibly evidenced by the active presence of their impressive army and by the manifest power of the place where they lived. Those with the means and status to erect major structures in Rome noted the important rhetorical role buildings played in the triumph, and determined which sites, building types, and *simulacra* would have the greatest impact upon both spectators and participants. Throughout the rest of the year, concrete reminders kept the ritual alive. The impact of the procession remained clearly evident in the clustering of grand buildings, architectural forms accommodating spectators, militaristic ornamentation, and a thousand other symbolic reverberations. Collectively, the triumphal intervention clarified Roman urban imperatives: planning did not follow absolutist formal ideas, but was implemented in sympathy with the potent experience of a changing ritual.

Section 2: Groundwork

Notes

1. Plutarch, *Romulus* 16. The origins and history of the pre-Imperial triumph are covered in greater depth by L. Bonfante Warren, 'Roman Triumphs and Etruscan Kings,' *Journal of Roman Studies* 60 (1970): 49–66; R. Payne, *The Roman Triumph* (London, 1962), and H. S. Versnel, *Triumphus: An Inquiry into the Origin, Development, and Meaning of the Roman Triumph* (Leiden, 1970). Those of the Imperial triumph are handled by C. Barini, *Triumphalia: Imprese ed onori militari durante l'impero romano* (Turin, 1952); S. G. MacCormack, *Art and Ceremony in Late Antiquity* (Berkeley, 1981); and, most recently, E. Kunzl, *Der römische Triumph: Siegesfeiern im antiken Rom* (Munich, 1988). The best sources for the heady experience of a Roman triumph remain literary and cinematic recreations; for example, see L. Davis, *Silver Pigs* (New York, 1989), 200–206; and the 1951 MGM film 'Quo Vadis.'
2. These are but the most significant of many requirements to be met before the Senate would allow an armed force into the city. Exceptions were not infrequent and the criteria changed over time. In a few cases, the people overrode the Senate's decision and awarded triumphs themselves. Other options also existed. A few generals paid for victory celebrations at Monte Albano, thirteen miles southeast of Rome. A larger number accepted the *ovatio*, often called a lesser triumph. Awarded by the Senate and held in Rome, this event lacked the accoutrements and significance of the triumph; Versnel, *Triumphus*, 165–68; H. H. Scullard, *Festivals and Ceremonies of the Roman Republic* (London, 1981), 213–18.
3. Regarding Republican triumphs and their frequency, see J. S. Richardson, 'The Triumph, the Praetors and the Senate in the Early Second Century B.C.,' *Journal of Roman Studies* 65 (1975): 50–63; and L. Pietila-Castren, *Magnificentia Publica: The Victory Monuments of the Roman Generals in the Era of the Punic Wars* (Helsinki, 1987). Even in years when no triumph was awarded, the triumphal parade resonated in Republican Rome. Parades were a major component of many Roman rituals in addition to triumphs. Other *pompa* often followed a route very close to that of the triumph and likewise drew large crowds; Versnel, *Triumphus*, 94–131. The funeral processions of important citizens included figures in triumphal regalia, representing the ancestors of the deceased who had triumphed; these parades followed a route similar to that of a triumph, but in reverse, moving from the city center to tombs in the Campus Martius; Versnel, *Triumphus*, 115–29.
4. Regarding the complex relationship between the triumphator and Jupiter, see Versnel, *Triumphus*, 66–93; and Bonfante Warren, 'Roman Triumphs,' 53–63.
5. Plutarch, *Antonius* 50.2. A few foreign rulers staged their own triumphs, including Antiochus IV in Antioch; Polybius, *Histories* 30.25. Though grand, such imitative events remained inferior to those in Rome, for they could not draw upon the same power of place or cultural history.
6. A. Plattus deals with the triumphal parade's relationship to the city's image, rather than its physical form: 'Passages into the City: The Interpretive Function of the Roman Triumph,' *Princeton Journal* 1 (1983): 93–115.

7. This tripartite conceptualization of the city in relation to the ritual is especially clear in the writings of Josephus from the Imperial period; Josephus, *Jewish War* 7, 118–62.
8. Troops and foreign ambassadors approaching Rome from the south had to circle the city's *pomerium* to reach the approved waiting place in the Campus Martius. The form and functions of the Villa Publica are discussed by E. Makin, 'The Triumphal Route, with Particular Reference to the Flavian Triumph,' *Journal of Roman Studies* 11 (1921), 26–30.
9. One of the purificatory rituals may have involved walking one mile. Two Imperial inscriptions refer to a Porticus Triumphi, giving its length and the number of circumambulations necessary to complete a mile. In the late Republic, Caesar likewise built a marble portico one mile in length as part of the new Saepta, or voting enclosure, in the central Campus Martius; Cicero, *Ad Atticus* 4.16.14; Makin, 'Triumphal Route,' 28–9.
10. T. P. Wiseman has convincingly argued that the Circus Flaminius was not a built circus with permanent seats, but an open area defined by a low enclosure wall. Over the years, new buildings (many erected by triumphators) encroached upon this space. By the first century, the large Circus Flaminius area was reduced to a plaza; T. P. Wiseman, 'The Circus Flaminius,' *Papers of the British School at Rome* 42 (1974): 3–26; F. Coarelli, 'Il Campo Marzio occidentale: Storia e topografia,' *Mélanges de l'Ecole Française de Rome* 89 (1977): 807–46.
11. Originally, the Porta Triumphalis may have stood on Rome's pomerial line. Its role in purification is underscored by the fact that the *porta* was apparently opened only for triumphal parades; Cicero, *In Pisonem* 23.55; Festus, *Latin Glossary, Epitome* 104 L (117 M); Versnel, *Triumphus*, 135, 152, 394–6. For a contrasting interpretation of the Porta Triumphalis as a gate in daily use, see L. Richardson, Jr., *A New Topographical Dictionary of Ancient Rome* (Baltimore, 1992), 301. On the debates over the Porta Triumphalis, see the extensive research by F. Coarelli, 'La Porta Trionfale e la Via dei Trionfi,' *Dialoghi di Archeologia* 2 (1968): 55–103, and *Il Foro Boario dalle origini alla fine della repubblica* (Rome, 1988), 363–414; as well as Versnel, *Triumphus*, 132–63, and the analytical review by F. S. Kleiner, 'The Study of Roman Triumphal and Honorary Arches Fifty Years after Kähler,' *Journal of Roman Archaeology* 2 (1989): 201–4.
12. Zonaras, *Epitome* 7.21; cf. Tertullian, *Apologeticum* 33.4. In contrast to the modern linear, progressive view of time, some Romans perceived the future as coming from behind, rather than lying ahead; Seneca, *Ad Lucilium* 1.1–3; M. Bettini, *Kinship, Time, Images of the Soul* (Baltimore, 1991), 124–33. On Roman conceptions of cyclical time, see P. Holliday, 'Time, History, and Ritual on the Ara Pacis Augustae,' *Art Bulletin* 72 (1990): 542–57.

By shouting insults, the troops demonstrated their faith in the triumphator and his reliance upon them; Suetonius, *Caesar* 49. The sequence of components in triumphal parades varied slightly over time; that cited here is the one most commonly followed in the Republic. Naturally, the order had powerful implications. To demonstrate his superior standing, the first emperor, Augustus, placed himself, rather than the magistrates, at the head of his parade in 29 B.C.E.; Dio Cassius, *Roman History* 51.21.

13. Hundreds thronged to Rome in 47 B.C.E. to see Caesar's extravagant triumphal parade and entertainments. Since the city did not have enough available lodgings, visitors pitched tents on the streets, highways, and rooftops; two senators and several other individuals died in the press of the crowd; Suetonius, *Caesar* 39.
14. For Scipio's parade, see Livy, *From the Founding of the City* 37.59. For his triumph of 61 B.C.E., Pompey had gathered so much material that he could not show it all in the two days allotted; at an earlier triumph he had wanted elephants to draw his chariot, but the huge beasts would not fit through the city gate; Plutarch, *Pompey* 14.45.

    The exact meaning of *simulacra* is still under debate; generally it is assumed to mean three-dimensional representations. Regarding the depiction of architectural images in triumphal parades, see Appian, *Punic Wars* 66; Livy, *From the Founding of the City* 37.59. Triumphal parades also included statues of personifications representing cities and regions. In 264 B.C.E., M. Valerius Maximus Messala displayed a painting of his victory over the Carthaginians on a side wall of the Curia Hostilia in the Forum; Scipio, in 190 B.C.E., placed a picture of his Asiatic victory on the Capitoline; Pliny, *Natural History* 35.22–25. Pictures of actual triumphal celebrations appeared in the temples of Vertumnus and Consus as early as the fourth century B.C.E.; Festus, *Latin Glossary, Epitome* 228. The most detailed descriptions of the towering panoramas carried in triumphal parades come from the Imperial period; Josephus, *Jewish War* 5.123–60. In describing the triumphal parade of 275 B.C.E., Florus gives a sympathetic portrait of the elephants and carefully lists the diverse peoples included among the captives; *Vergilius orator* 1.13. In the Imperial period, Domitian allegedly hired actors in blond wigs to represent Germans in his triumph of 84 C.E.; Tacitus, *Agricola* 39; Dio Cassius, *Roman History* 67.8; Payne, *Roman Triumph*, 172.
15. Propertius, *Elegies* 3.4.15–18.
16. The route around the Palatine Hill essentially followed the presumed pomerial line of Rome's earliest settlement; Dionysius of Halicarnassus, *Roman Antiquities* 1.56. The counterclockwise movement of the procession may have been a kind of lustration; similar choreography occurred in a number of other Roman *pompa*, or processions; Scullard, *Festivals and Ceremonies*, 77; Coarelli, 'Porta Trionfale,' 59–66; Bonfante Warren, 'Roman Triumphs,' 54–5.
17. The triumphator did not go directly to Jupiter's temple, but instead apparently first went to the Arx, the northeastern mound of the Capitoline Hill; Bonfante Warren, 'Roman Triumphs,' 55. Julius Caesar added greater drama to his passage by climbing up the hill on his knees, accompanied by forty elephants bearing lamps; Suetonius, *Caesar* 37. For the Sacra Via, see Horace, *Epodes* 7.8; Ovid, *Tristia* 3.126–7.
18. The two consuls did not attend the feast atop the Capitoline, so that they would not draw attention away from the triumphator.

19. The triumphal pathway was technically a street, yet its inaccessibility led ancient observers to find alternative descriptors. For example, Josephus referred to the procession as a river running through Rome; Josephus, *Jewish War* 7.140. Triumphators also received permission to impose upon other urban streets throughout the year; Pliny notes that they were allowed to have the doors of their houses open outward onto the public thoroughfares; *Natural History* 36.112.
20. The Romans considered white the appropriate color for celebrations and formal occasions. This color coding possibly had social implications as well, since not every resident in Rome could afford a bleached toga; see Plutarch, *Aemilius* 32; Suetonius, *Augustus* 40; Juvenal, *Satires* 10.44–47.
21. Livy, *From the Founding of the City* 9.40.16. Not far from the Tabernae Veteres, the speakers' platform had earlier been decorated with captured ships' beaks or *rostra*; thereafter it became known by that name. *Rostra* also decorated a nearby column commemorating a naval victory over the Carthaginians in 260 B.C.E.; Pliny, *Natural History* 34.20; Livy, *From the Founding of the City* 8.14. When denied a triumph in 66 B.C.E. for political reasons, Lucullus displayed heaps of his booty in the Circus Flaminius; Plutarch, *Lucullus* 37.2.
22. Both the Circus Flaminius and the huge Circus Maximus (capacity 150 thousand) accommodated triumphal rituals at an early date; Livy, *From the Founding of the City* 39.5; Dionysius of Halicarnassus, *Roman Antiquities* 3.68. Before the construction of permanent theaters, temporary structures provided additional seating; Plutarch, *Aemilius* 32.
23. Pompey erected Rome's first permanent theater in 55 B.C.E. Although he was not triumphator that year, the huge stone complex had significant triumphal associations: it included a temple to Venus Victrix (Venus the Conqueror), statues representing the fourteen nations subdued by Pompey, and a hall where the Senate could meet to make extrapomerial decisions, such as the awarding of triumphs. The triumphator Caesar laid the foundations for a theater, dedicated by Augustus as the Theater of Marcellus in 13/11 B.C.E. Around the same time, L. Cornelius Balbus dedicated his own theater, commemorating his victories in Africa. Josephus describes an Imperial triumph of 70 C.E. as moving through several theaters, presumably those listed above; *Jewish War* 7.113. In addition to these permanent structures, Marcus Aemilius Scaurus erected a temporary theater when aedile in 58 B.C.E., in part to commemorate his eastern campaign; it remained standing for several years; Pliny, *Natural History* 34.36; 36.113–15.
24. The skewed angle may also be explained by the desire to present a dramatic façade to the river. Caesar's destruction of temples caused great consternation among Rome's highly religious citizenry; Dio Cassius, *Roman History* 43.49.
25. Vitruvius indicates that good seats in the balconies (*maeniana*) of fora could be sold to generate public revenue; *On Architecture* 5.1.1–2. The Forum Romanum in Rome was frequently the site of the gladiatorial games and other spectator events presented after triumphal parades.
26. Despite the popular misconception, not all Roman arches were associated with triumphs, nor did all straddle thoroughfares. For an overview of recent

literature on the subject, see Kleiner, 'Roman Triumphal and Honorary Arches,' 195–98. Regarding the change in terminology from *fornix* to *arcus* in the first century B.C.E., see G. A. Mansuelli, 'Fornix e arcus: Note di terminologia,' *Studi sull'arco onorario romano* (Rome, 1979), 15–18.

27. Since he was not an office holder at the time of his victory, Stertinius was not eligible for a triumph. His *fornix* in the Circus Maximus was later replaced by one commemorating the victories of the emperor Titus. Stertinius also erected two other *fornices* in the Forum Boarium; Livy, *From the Founding of the City* 33.27. Coarelli located these near the temples to Fortuna and Mater Matuta; Coarelli, 'La Porta Trionfale,' 91; Pietila-Castren, *Magnificentia publica*, 72–74.

28. D. Scagliarini Corlàita, 'La Situazione urbanistica degli archi onorari nella prima età imperiale,' *Studi sull'arco onorario romano*, 29–72.

29. Adjacent to the Forum Romanum, the crisply defined open space of the Forum Iulium readily accommodated triumph-related events. Caesar ended his triumphal celebrations and there and then proceeded home, accompanied by the entire populace of Rome, with elephants carrying torches; Dio Cassius, *Roman History* 43.22.

30. To celebrate his campaigns in Spain, in 173 B.C.E. Quintus Fulvius Flaccus, as censor, stripped the marble roof tiles off a temple in Croton in southern Italy; he was severely reprimanded by the Senate; Livy, *From the Founding of the City* 43.3. Marcus Antonius, triumphator in 100 B.C.E., used *spolia* on his victory monument, the so-called Ara Domitii Ahenobarbi; A. Kuttner, 'Some New Grounds for Narrative: The "Ara Domitii Ahenobarbi" and Other Republican Commemorative Bases,' in P. Holliday, ed., *Narrative and Event in Ancient Art* (New York, 1993). Similarly, the triumphator Sulla took Corinthian columns from the Olympeion in Athens for reuse on the great Temple of Jupiter Optimus Maximus on the Capitoline in Rome; Pliny, *Natural History* 36.45.

31. Florus 2.13.88. In the first century C.E., the emperor Claudius modeled his lighthouse at Ostia after the Pharos of Alexandria; Suetonius, *Claudius* 20.3. Hellenistic items displayed in triumphs influenced Roman aesthetics in many fields, including painting and furniture design; J. J. Pollitt, *The Art of Rome c. 753 B.C.–337 A.D.* (Englewood Cliffs, 1966), 29–53. Conversely, in the high Empire, the architectural and artistic images displayed in triumphs frequently demonstrated Roman cultural superiority, since the victories were over tribal societies in the West; for example, see the images on Trajan's Column.

32. The few projects not directly related to the triumphal route were built outside the Servian Wall, along major roadways into the city; Pietila-Castren, *Magnificentia publica*, 154–8; Coarelli, 'Il Campo Marzio occidentale,' 807–46.

33. In the triumph of Pompey alone there marched nearly three hundred important prisoners, including kings and other royalty, many of whom were later sent back to their homes; Appian, *Mithridates* 117. In the early Empire, Augustus put on permanent display in the Forum Romanum the impressive list of all triumphators in Rome's history.

34. In particular, the Rostra or speakers' platform in the Forum became a magnet for State triumphal memorials, including individual statues, columns, weapons, and of course *rostra*. The censors of 158 B.C.E. eliminated all statues in the Forum not authorized by decree of the People or Senate of Rome; Pliny, *Natural History* 34.30–31. Earlier, the censor Aemilius Lepidus removed statues from the Capitoline Hill; Livy, *From the Founding of the City* 40.51. The Senate apparently carefully controlled building in the Forum Romanum, since Roman generals did not erect structures there as triumphators, but as censors; Pietila-Castren, *Magnificentia publica*, 155–6.
35. Long, straight streets were rare in ancient Rome, and practically nonexistent inside the Servian Wall. The straight, lengthy edge of the Circus Flaminius was paralleled by the temples of Hercules Musarum (189 B.C.E.), Juno Regina (187 B.C.E.), and Jupiter Stator (148 B.C.E.); Pietila-Castren, *Magnificentia publica*, 154–6.

    Both Republican porticoes commemorate victories over Macedonia. That of Gnaeus Octavius celebrated his triumph of 168 B.C.E.; that of Q. Caecilius Metellus honored a triumph of 146 B.C.E., and surrounded the temples of Juno Regina and Jupiter Stator; B. Olinder, *Porticus Octavia in Circa Flaminio* (Stockholm, 1984), 83–124. The Porticus Triumphi may also have been in this area; Makin, 'Triumphal Route,' 28–9. Two more porticoes were added in the Augustan Age: the Porticus Philippi and the Porticus Octaviae. Due to their location, these structures were adopted for use during subsequent triumphs; Josephus, *Jewish War* 7.
36. A similar view could be had northward, once the Theater of Marcellus was completed in 13/11 B.C.E. In effect, the curving cavea of the two stone theaters framed this straight road.

Section 3
Individual

Carelessness and inattention

We all know perfectly well who we are, until we start thinking about it. One of the most serenely self-confident assertions of the Enlightenment understanding, Thomas Jefferson's draft of the Declaration of Independence, is both very close to, and a world away from, the understanding of David Hume. They were close together in time, and shared many of the same values, but Jefferson was moving in the world of political action – firstly in establishing his plantations in the Virginian hills, and then in building the USA, while Hume was acting as a librarian and an introspective philosopher in the cooler climate of Edinburgh. Each in his way made the world anew. 'As the sceptical doubt arises naturally from a profound and intense reflection,' said Hume, 'it always encreases, the farther we carry on our refections, whether in opposition or conformity to it. Carelessness and inattention alone can afford us any remedy. For this reason I rely entirely upon them'.[1] When he was plagued by doubt from his philosophical studies, then Hume, who was by all accounts a pleasant and sociable person, could join his friends for a game of backgammon, and his sense of well-being would very quickly return. Hume's scepticism led him to doubt the relations between cause and effect, and the idea of a unitary continuous self, but he could – like a good pragmatist – set these undecidable questions on one side, and could participate in the normal processes of society. At the time of Jefferson's declaration of self-evident truths, and Thomas Paine's *Rights of Man*,[2] Hume was entertaining philosophical doubts about the self-evidence of the self – a necessary pre-condition for the analysis of personality made by Nietzsche, and the construction of the Subject (which is more or less a 'given' in contemporary cultural studies). The most resonant version of this declaration of the contingency of the formation of the self was when Michel Foucault announced the death of man, in *The Order of Things*, and imagined the Enlightemnent idea of 'man' vanishing gradually, like an outline being washed away by an incoming tide on the beach.[3] In fact it has not been quite so straightforward, as there are different discourses in play, and dissolving the idea of 'man' also dissolves the idea of human rights, and there is still a need to be able to invoke this kind of rhetoric in practical politics, which means that 'man' has a continuing vitality, albeit outside the circles of advanced criticism.[4] The idea of the self as an identity that is constructed and performed is now well ingrained in the discourses that surround questions of identity-politics.

The idea of identity splits apart, when we find ourselves to be in two minds about a course of action. We can see why we should act in one way, and with another part of our minds can see why we should act in another. If our ingrained habits make our intuition lead us one way, and our reason leads us elsewhere, then we might find it difficult to act at all, as each course of action seems to be wrong. 'The test of a first-rate intelligence,' said F. Scott Fitzgerald, 'is the ability to hold two opposed ideas in the mind at the same time, and still retain the ability to function.'[5] This is the most observable kind of example, when the mental conflict is more or less conscious; but most of what goes on in the mind is unconscious, and many such conflicts are resolved without coming to the surface. Nearly always we follow habit, rather than calling every repetition of a comparable situation for a fresh judgement. In fact Deleuze and Guattari do not characterize the mind as being composed of two parts, but of crowds, swarms or tribes.

> The two of us wrote Anti-Oedipus together. Since each of us was several, there was already quite a crowd. Here we have made use of everything that came within range, what was closest as well as farthest away. We have assigned clever pseudonyms to prevent recognition. Why have we kept our own names? Out of habit, purely out of habit. To make ourselves unrecognizable in turn. To render imperceptible, not ourselves, but what makes us act, feel, and think. Also because it's nice to talk like everybody else, to say the sun rises, when everybody knows it's only a manner of speaking. To reach, not the point where one says I, but the point where it is no longer of any importance whether one says I. We are no longer ourselves. Each will know his own. We have been aided, inspired, multiplied.[6]

Robert Louis Stevenson's great short story about Dr Jekyll is a tale developed around the idea of the mind having different parts, that come into play with one another in various ways to produce different personalities. In the story a particular malign side to the good doctor's character comes to take over the proceedings, and to dominate the story, but the theory being advanced is that there are multiple possible personalities locked away in the mind, which find fleeting expression in the events of a life.[7] It is a theory of personality that makes sense in a novelist, accustomed to exploring the emotions and motivations of a range of characters, each of whom must be inhabited and must – if they are to have any psychological depth (and Stevenson's characters convincingly do have that) – to some degree be some part of the author.

The 'individual' starts to feel very far from being indivisible, if we start to take account of the various circumstances and roles in a life – from the infant in arms, to the school-child, from the prudent housekeeper, to the spendthrift shopper, from the staid professional to the passionate lover, one can find oneself engaging with different sets of emotions and impulses, that one learns to recognize and then perhaps to control. If in particular circumstances I know that I will, for example, gamble away sums of money that I cannot afford, then I will – if I have these things under control – ensure that I do not put myself into a situation where I will start feeling compelled to act in that way. There is a process that comes into play, and I can take decisions about it for as long as it does not have me in its grip, but after it has switched in, then I am in its grip and will take decisions that I cannot later defend. Crimes of passion work in this way, and the narrative of every novel or film of any dramatic weight will have a character taken out of their usual routines by the being seized by some unanticipated emotion or other. It is as if we have to witness these things acted out for us, so that we can continue with our well-regulated lives, exorcizing vicariously the difficult emotions that we can allow ourselves to feel in small doses, inoculating ourselves from these things when we encounter them ourselves, and can recognize the early symptoms. In Bateson's 'steady state', it would be hoped that we would act so as to preserve rather than destabilize an equilibrium. In conditions where life had become intolerable in one way or another, we might deliberately destabilize our circumstances in order to bring about a political upheaval or bring a more personal crisis to a head.

Machines and politics

The idea is that we would see the mind as dispersed, with connections between the various parts that work in a way that could be imagined as being like the workings of a machine, or of political groupings. Marvin Minsky tried to explain his work on artifical intelligence to a non-specialist audience in his book *The Society of Mind*, which manages to synthesize the two images, as we normally think of 'artificial intellegence' as involving machines – computers – and here, as the title makes plain, he imagines the mind as a 'society' of interconnected parts, each part of which has a very limited role that we would hesitate to call 'thinking', but when the whole set of multifarious parts is connected with an enormous number of links (such as are to be found in the brain) then it is capable of doing something very like thinking – so much like it that we might think it was not different from thinking.[8] Group identity has been an important part of the Deleuze-and-Guattari-world from the beginning of their collaborations. Their view of the personality (the subject) was that it is always multiple. And likewise there are group phenomena where parts of the personalities in the group form significant interactions, which makes for the development of a group 'personality' or subject. Guattari developed the idea particularly from reading Bateson. Guattari wrote:

> Gregory Bateson has clearly shown that what he calls the 'ecology of ideas' cannot be contained within the domain of the psychology of the individual, but organizes itself into systems or 'minds', the boundaries of which no longer coincide with the participant individuals.[9]

The key move in his thought is the linking of this perception with the description of the machine as found in Samuel Butler's 'Book of the Machines', collected here. The conception of the machine put forward by Butler should not be taken less seriously for being advanced in a work of fiction. It is a real conception of the machine, even though it appears as an imaginary work – supposedly in a library in Erewhon, and described at some length in Butler's novel of that name, published in 1872, when the industrial revolution was going at full throttle, and when Butler himself fled to New Zealand to farm sheep. In *Anti-Oedipus* – a book that works with glancing allusions to *recherché* texts – 'The Book of the Machines' is introduced as 'a profound text' and summarized at length.[10] Its inclusion is not incidental but necessary. The machine, by the time that Deleuze and Guattari have linked Bateson, Butler and Marx, becomes an indefinitely extensive assemblage of organic and inorganic parts, dispersed between organisms and their environments. Thus the machines in Erewhon have engineers as part of their reproductive cycle, but this is not in any way significantly different from the way in which the reproductive cycle of the red clover is dependent on the bumble bee, or the orchid on the male wasp that it attracts and intercepts by carrying on its flower the image and the odour of the female wasp.[11] As Butler says: 'Man's very soul is due to the machines; it is a machine-made thing; he thinks as he thinks, and feels as he feels, through the work that the machines have wrought upon him.'[12] And in Deleuze and Guattari: 'it becomes immaterial whether one says that machines are organs, or organs, machines'.[13] 'In a word,' they say, 'the real difference is not between the living and the machine, vitalism and mechanism, but between two states of the machine that are two states of the living as well. The machine taken in its structural unity, the living taken in its specific and even personal unity, are mass phenomena or molar aggregates.'[14] A mole, here, is the number of molecules dissolved in a litre of water to give a solution of a standard concentration, used by chemists in the laboratory. The number, Avogadro's number is unimaginably vast: 6.022×10^{23}. Which is to say that under this description, the 'individual' is a multiplicity of machines – a huge number – all working in their own little ways, building up into aggregates that are large enough to be visible to us, and which we then start to name as if they were unitary entities. This is true of entities such as individual human beings, and no less true of groups of people constituted for one purpose or another. It makes little difference to the operation of the 'machine' whether a project is carried out by an individual person, or by an interdisciplinary team. This is a world where the psyche is aggregated from thousands upon thousands of desiring machines, and where even a potato has a certain low cunning about him.[15]

Common sense

This is a world away from common sense. It involves making an imaginative leap, and then thinking through the consequences of it with a rigorous logic, that rarely forms part of our day-to-day activity. Peirce analysed three active elements in the world: chance, law, and habit;[16] and of all of them it is perhaps habit that is hardest to shift. Going back to Shelley's conception of knowledge, we can see that by the time that the poetic apprehension of the world has been so often repeated that it has come to seem that it is self-evident truth, then this truth – which is no more than a useful habit of mind – becomes almost impossible to dislodge and replace with a new idea, even if the new idea's explanatory power could, with development be helpful. Paul Feyerabend in discussing the ways in which a new scientific theory replaces an old one, compares the new theory with a defenceless baby, contrasting it with the well-defended old theory – a prize fighter, who can anticipate all the likely moves. The baby needs protecting and building up, if it is ever to stand a chance against the prize fighter. The old vocabulary, confirming the old description, will be grounded in common sense and will always sound sensible, even when reason has worked out an alternative.[17] We habitually put organic and inorganic machines in different categories, habitually say that an organism is an entity that is distinct from its surroundings, habitually separate out the natural and the manufactured. In the Deleuze and Guattari world all these distinctions blur together, and their vocabulary would make it possible to discuss topics that at the moment tend to send us into a panic. Common sense deals only very badly with such an issue as genetic engineering, where it seems that one category of being has been invaded by another. However if we allow identity to develop around such machinic assemblages as organism-plus-environment, allow that there is an ecology of ideas, and see the thing we call an 'individual' as an emergent property produced as an effect of relations between groups of machines (the habit of saying 'I') then some of the results are a challenge to common sense.

> No one has shown better than Samuel Butler that there is no continuity apart from that of habit, and that we have no other continuities apart from those of our thousands of superstitious and contemplative selves, so many claimants and satisfactions: 'for even the corn in the fields grows upon a superstitious basis as to its own existence, and only turns the earth and moisture into wheat through the conceit of its own ability to do so, without which faith it were powerless. . .'. Only an empiricist can happily risk such formulae.[18]

Once one has adopted this way of seeing things, then it becomes possible once again to use a more traditional vocabulary. If we can allow that it is practically useful for humans to have 'rights' then why can they not also have 'souls'? The soul was imagined as an emergent property of the body, somewhat akin to the centre of gravity, by Heinrich von Kleist, in his essay on the marionette theatre,[19] and is reappearing in contemporary criticism, such as Julia Kristeva's *New Maladies of the Soul*.[20] Similarly there is no reason why a place should not be seen to have a *genius loci*, and it is possible to imagine extending the vocabularies of human and animal rights even to mineral entities.[21] We come close to it with World Heritage Sites, and the preservation of historic buildings.

Buildings as organisms

Thinking at different scales of operation, using the same concepts, the entities that constitute machines and machinic assemblages can be molecular or sub-molecular in size, or could be universes. Our world nevertheless remains anthropocentric – our starting point has to be the data that our senses receive, and the sense that we make of those data. The architectural scale of operation is about the scale of the picnic on Lakeshore Drive, no smaller than that, but up to perhaps a hundred times larger. The image of the machine is already well ingrained in the culture of architecture, but it is a nineteenth-century idea of the machine, that has not taken on board its radicalization by Butler, with his premonition of intelligent and evolving machines – for him, seeing intelligence in steam engines, it was a much greater imaginative leap than it is for us. Just as for the hen, the nest and the eggshell are machines – one made internally in the body, the other made externally – so our houses are machines that help us to live, and we are parts of the mechanism that allow our houses to live. We are always already cyborgs. It is a matter of indifference under this description whether the parts of the machine are permanently connected (naturally developed within the body, or surgically implanted) or whether we just connect with them when we need them (as tools, casings, clothings, buildings).

Science fiction stories rehearse our hopes and fears, projecting contemporary developments into a distant future when they are more developed. *Erewhon* is one such story, projecting an idea about the development of machines which led the inhabitant of this imaginary place to reject the development of the machine and renounce all advances made after a certain date. That fear is still with us, as is evident in such stories as *The Matrix*, and *Terminator*, where machines have taken over important decision-making processes and have decided to run the world for their benefit, not that of humankind. It is also to be found in the classic *2001*, where the computer Hal becomes defensive and lethal. In Stanley Kubrick's film there is a famous jump-cut from the *clinamen* – the moment when human destiny changes on account of a small swerve in its development – when a proto-human picks up a bone to use as a weapon, the first tool: the tool being thrown in the air cuts to a space station revolving serenely in outer space – a later stage in the same process. The story that initiated this genre was *Frankenstein*, written by Mary Shelley in 1818. She was the daughter of two great political radicals, William Godwin and Mary Wollstonecraft, and eloped with the poet Shelley, marrying him after the suicide of his abandoned first wife. The story is well known from its film treatments, but they inevitably concentrate on the activity in the story – the running around, pursuits, murders – which in the original is very introspective and morally alert. Frankenstein (like Lucifer) oversteps the mark and puts himself on a par with God, but we are allowed to sympathize with his hopes for his creation of a creature that is designed to be beautiful and wonderful:

> No one can conceive the variety of feelings which bore me onwards, like a hurricane, in the first enthusiasm of success. Life and death appeared to me ideal bounds, which I should first break through, and pour a torrent of light into our dark world. A new species would bless me as its creator and source; many and excellent natures would owe their being to me. No father could claim the gratitude of his child so completely as I should deserve theirs. Pursuing these reflections, I thought, that if I could bestow animation upon lifeless matter, I might in process of time (although I now found it impossible) renew life where death had apparently devoted the body to corruption.[22]

It does not work out that way. A more precise precursor of Butler's vision of the natural machine, though, is *L'Homme machine*, by Julien Offray de La Mettrie, first published anonymously in 1748. This is an analysis of natural people in terms of machinic imagery, seeing them as naturally grown machines. He mentions for example crimes of passion – 'I believe that the wild girl of Châlons in Champagne repented her crime, if she truly did eat her sister. The same goes for all who commit crimes involuntarily or compulsively, such as Gaston d'Orleans who could not keep from stealing.'[23]

Section 3: Individual

> To be a machine, to feel, think, know good from evil like blue from yellow, in a word, to be born with intelligence and a sure instinct for morality, and yet to be only an animal, are things no more contradictory than to be an ape or parrot and know how to find sexual pleasure. And since the occasion presents itself for saying so, who would have ever divined *a priori* that shooting off a gob of sperm during copulation would make one feel such divine pleasure, and that from it would be born a tiny creature who one day, following certain laws, could enjoy the same delights? Thought is so far from being incompatible with organized matter that it seems to me to be just another of its properties, such as electricity, the motive faculty, impenetrability, extension, etc.[24]

In David Cronenberg's film *Existenz*, the narrative unfolds in a world where organisms and machinery are completely fused. Guns made from body parts can escape detection systems, which search for solid metal, so we find bony armatures that fire teeth instead of bullets. More crucially the plot revolves around sophisticated computers that have the appearance of being living creatures as they squirm about on the characters' laps. These machines can be wired directly to the spinal columns of their users, and their internal workings seem to have been composed by piecing together the internal organs of various genetically-modified creatures, developed for this very purpose. It is an uncomfortable but compelling vision, that has some relation to the real developing technologies of our day, just as Mary Shelley's monster bore some relation to the science of her day. It was not a practical possibility, but it did not seem impossibly remote. In today's science fiction, androids are routine, but the significant advances in intelligent machines are not usually given a humanizing form, which we might find disturbing. Machines do quite routinely talk to us however – on the telephone especially, but also in elevators, automobiles and on metro trains. And they talk to one another – even (using blue-tooth technology) telepathically. Who is to say that the day will never arrive when they could start to conspire? We continue to be worried that our machines, invented as tools to help us along, will end by taking over and running things, in the way that slaves have risen up in the past, and oppressed peoples have revolted. Nevertheless there are fortunes to be made from these technical advances, and although there are anxieties, somehow it seems unlikely that we will renounce future advances in the manner of the inhabitants of Erewhon.

If we look at ourselves as organisms plus habitat, then the unit of survival would include the house as part of the entity. The imagery involved is as much organic as it is mechanical – the two are conceptually fused. Le Corbusier's *machine à habiter*, with its industrial imagery, presented to the Anglophone world as a 'machine for living in' becomes rather a living-machine – an assemblage that makes possible a way of life. The challenge for the architect who has seen the way the mechanisms operate, is to find a way of giving appropriate expression to them. These machines do not have a human scale and a visible presence in the way that nineteenth-century machines did. There was no mistaking the power or the presence of a vapour engine, pounding and hissing as it powered a factory or thundered along rails. The sensors and engines that regulate our new machines are invisible to our unaided eyes, and have no inevitable expression, and it is this issue of expression that takes us away from the idea of the building as a utilitarian living machine to consider the ways in which it can produce feelings that belong to the realm of aesthetics; but as these feelings might themselves help the building to work, the separation is not altogether clear-cut. A building that seems introspective and unwelcoming, might fail as a public building; a house that really prompted the feelings of gloom and dread – as so many of them do in Gothic novels – might fail as a dwelling. 'Art,' said Deleuze in 1991, 'begins not with flesh but with the house. That is why architecture is the first of the arts.'[25] One feels less confident now about making that assertion, as body-artists have proliferated, and the art-world has been encouraging practices that mean that the term 'art' no longer means what it did.

The architecture-machine

With Deleuze the art-object, a building, a book, is encountered as a bloc of sensations that either produces an experience that we value, or else it does not. He remarked that 'the only question is "Does it work, and how does it work? How does it work for you?" If it doesn't work, if nothing comes through, you try another book.'[26] The point to be made here is that the book is a machine, but not the whole of the machine. In order for it to produce what it can produce, it needs to be connected to the sensory apparatus of the reader, it is the *agencement* 'book-plus-reader' that constitutes the machine, and the machine will only be productive if the reader is appropriately prepared. If we give a five-year-old a copy of *Ulysses*, or if we are faced with a book in a language which is unknown to us, then the machine will not be properly constituted and will not work – we look for another book. Similarly the house-plus-person will produce sets of states of mind that might be valuable or deplorable, depending on the state of the person's mind. Some parts of the response might be deep rooted, and be part of the most ancient reptilian inheritance of our genes, some parts might have been put in place only yesterday by looking at fashionable magazines, but our responses will seem to us to be immediate and visceral. If we follow John Dewey seeing art as experience, rather than as artefact,[27] then it makes perfectly straightforward sense to say that art is not a property of the art-object, but is produced when the art-object is brought into contact with an appropriately conditioned observer, and there is no sense in saying that one category of objects 'is' art while another isn't – 'a false concept,' says Deleuze, 'purely nominal'.[28] What we can legitimately say is that when we come into contact with this and that particular object then we have the type of experience which we call 'art'. Given that one person's life experiences have been different from another's, there is scope for disparity in these responses: an object may produce a powerful effect when I see it, and might leave you cold, or vice versa. I might find charming a well-kept thatched cottage with roses growing round the door, while you think it is nauseating *kitsch*. The reaction is genuine and visceral, but without prior experience and knowledge we would have no such reaction to notice. Given a degree of consensus in these matters and the fact that for reasons of politics and prestige some people's views carry more weight than others, we can go on from there to extrapolate a social theory of art. However the main point to be made here is that the cliché-system of our language does not reflect this state of affairs. We don't say: 'That building produced in me a powerful experience of beauty' (or terror, or well-being). What we say is 'That building is beautiful' (or terrifying, or comfortable), which has the effect of making the beauty seem to inhere in the building. In the same way it is convenient and socially normal 'to say that the sun rises, when everybody knows it's only a manner of speaking'; but, as Deleuze and Guattari say (with breathtaking irony) 'it's nice to talk like everybody else'.[29] Here we return to pragmatics, and the idea of redescription. We have different manners of speaking for different situations, and while there are times when it is appropriate to consider the earth as turning on its axis, at other times it would be socially odd to do so. We are always faced with some such problem whenever we are faced with a new concept. Its use means that we seem to be adopting an awkward or 'unnatural' way of speaking – to be speaking in a foreign language, which is often what happens when a writer tries to change an established set of views.[30] The bloc of sensations with which we engage when we visit or use or inhabit a building, remains more or less constant from one user to another. What varies is the prior life-experience (the conditioning) of the observer, and therefore different people can produce different architectures when they are brought into *agencement* with the building. Architecture is the experience that is produced by the architecture-machine, which is assembled when the inert building comes into contact with its users.

This improves on the traditional purely nominal formulation, most famously upheld by Nikolaus Pevsner: 'A bicycle shed is a building; Lincoln Cathedral is a work of architecture.'[31] We can remove the 'architecture' from the building-in-itself, and insist that it only comes into being when it is *experienced* (i.e. when there is someone experiencing it) we make it unproblematic to deal with cases where the status of buildings has shifted. The cottages of impoverished hill farmers were simply unenviable habitations, until Wordsworth saw stoic virtues and heroism in the lives of their occupants, and now there is no doubt that these cottages and farm buildings are vernacular architecture, and move us because they too seem to have the integrity and steadfastness of their builders. A cottage built from field-stones by someone fighting for survival might conceivably take the same form as a cottage built for the queen of France in the gardens of Versailles, but such a building would bring into play an entirely different range of emotional responses. Buildings are inert; architecture is volatile. We encounter buildings; architecture is experience.

This is true of our responses to place as well as to man-made buildings. One of Wordsworth's important themes was the heroic attachment to place in the face of the overwhelming indifference of nature, and this highly place-specific notion of dwelling informs Heidegger's consideration of the idea of dwelling. Deleuze, by contrast, valorized nomadism and the idea of flux and mobility. He cited Cézanne with approval: 'Look at the mountain, once it was fire.'[32] Wordsworth would never have said that – for him the mountains were fixed reference points and images of permanence. It is one thing to have these responses to places, and quite another to find ways of giving expression to them – whether through writing, painting, or in the buildings themselves and the uses to which we put them. From a pragmatic point of view the cottage that erupts from the field and attaches itself to the hillside like a barnacle to weather the winter storms, is a profoundly different entity from the same building used by someone with piped water, drainage, electricity, mobility and internet access. Its fabric has been taken up and made use of in two different machines (only two? – a proliferation of multiplicities of machines) that produce very different architecture, very different units of survival, very different identities. It remains useful to be able to talk about individual buildings, individual people and so on, but what we mean by the 'individual' – if we have been taking on the lessons of Deleuze and Guattari – is a group of habits, machines and connections, that might be stable for a while, but which might regroup and reconstitute, and produce unanticipated flows of desire, of capital, or of general well-being.

Notes

1. David Hume, *A Treatise of Human Nature*, in *Philosophical Works*, ed. Green and Grose, vol. 1, p. 505.
2. Thomas Jefferson, 'The Declaration of Independence' (1776) – 'We hold these truths to be self-evident: that all men are created equal; that they are endowed with certain inalienable rights; that among these are life, liberty, and the pursuit of happiness . . .'; Thomas Paine, Rights of Man: Being an Answer to Mr. Burke's attack on the French Revolution (London, 1791).
3. Michel Foucault, *Les mots et les choses* (Paris: Gallimard, 1966), trans. A. M. S. Smith, *The Order of Things: An Archaeology of the Human Sciences* (London: Tavistock, 1970), p. 387.
4. Pierre Manent, *La cité de l'homme* (Paris: Fayard, 1994) translated by Marc A. LePain, *The City of Man* (Princeton, New Jersey: Princeton University Press, 1998).
5. F. Scott Fitzgerald, 'The Crack-up' (1936) in *The Crack-up with other pieces and stories* (Harmondsworth: Penguin, 1965) p. 39. The piece is discussed in Gilles Deleuze and Félix Guattari, *Mille plateaux: capitalisme et schizophrénie 2* (Paris: Editions de Minuit, 1980) translated by Brian Massumi, *A Thousand Plateaus: Capitalism and Schizophrenia 2* (London: Athlone, 1987) pp. 198–200.
6. Ibid., p. 3,
7. Robert Louis Stevenson, 'The Strange Case of Dr. Jekyll and Mr. Hyde' (1886).
8. Marvin Minsky, *The Society of Mind* (London: Heinemann, 1987).
9. Félix Guattari, *Les trois ecologies* (Paris: Galilée, 1989) translated by Ian Pindar and Paul Sutton, *The Three Ecologies* (London: Athlone, 2000) p. 54; and see the translators' note 56, p. 93, referencing Gregory Bateson, *Steps to an Ecology of Mind* (New York: Chandler, 1972) p. 339, and pointing out that Guattari's 'quotation' is a paraphrase. See also Gary Genosko, *Félix Guattari: An Aberrant Introduction* (London: Continuum, 2002).
10. Gilles Deleuze and Félix Guattari, *L'Anti-Oedipe: capitalisme et schizophrénie 1* (Paris: Editions de Minuit, 1972) translated by Robert Hurley, Mark Seem and Helen R. Lane, *Anti-Oedipus: Capitalism and Schizophrenia 1* (New York: Viking, 1977) pp. 284–5.

Section 3: Individual

11. Ibid., p. 285.
12. Samuel Butler, *Erewhon* (1872) page references to Everyman Edition (London: Dent, 1965) p. 147.
13. Deleuze and Guattari, *Anti-Oedipus*, op. cit., p. 285.
14. Deleuze and Guattari, *Anti-Oedipus*, op. cit., p. 285-6.
15. Desiring machines: see *Anti-Oedipus*; op. cit., pp. 1–50. Potato: see below, p. 128.
16. Joseph Brent, *Charles Sanders Peirce: A Life* (Bloomington: Indiana University Press, 1998) p. 4.
17 Paul Feyerabend, *Against Method* (London: Verso, 1978).
18. Gilles Deleuze, *Difference et repetition* (Paris: Presses Universitaires de France, 1968) translated by Paul Patton, *Difference and Repetition* (London: Athlone, 1994) p. 75. The quotation is from Samuel Butler, *Life and Habit* (Jonathan Cape, 1910) p. 82.
19. See below, pp. 301–6.
20. See below, p. 120.
21. Slavoj Žižek argues that this is undesirable, but it is not nonsensical. See below, pp. 122–3.
22. Mary Shelley, *Frankenstein* (1818) (Oxford: Oxford University Press, 1994), p. 36.
23. Julien Offraye de la Mettrie, *l'Homme machine* (Paris: 1748), trans. G. Bussey, *Man a Machine* (New York: Open Court, 1977), p. 51.
24. Ibid, pp. 71–2.
25. Gilles Deleuze and Félix Guattari, *Qu'est-ce que la philosophie?* (Paris: Editions de Minuit, 1991) translated by Hugh Tomlinson and Graham Burchill, *What is Philosophy?* (London: Verso, 1994) p. 186.
26. Gilles Deleuze, 'Lettre à un critique sévère', in *Pourparlers* (Paris: Les Editions de Minuit, 1990) translated by Martin Joughin, 'Letter to a Harsh Critic', in *Negotiations* (New York: Columbia University Press, 1995) p. 8.
27. John Dewey, *Art as Experience* (1934) (New York: Puttnam, 1980).
28. Deleuze and Guattari, *Thousand Plateaus*, op. cit., p. 369.
29. Ibid., p. 3.
30. Marcel Proust, '*Les beaux livres sont écrits dans une sorte de langue étrangère*' ['Great books are written in a kind of foreign language']. In Marcel Proust, *Contre Sainte-Beuve*, translated by Sylvia Townsend Warner, *By Way of Sainte-Beuve* (London: Chatto and Windus, 1958) cited in Gilles Deleuze and Claire Parnet, *Dialogues* (Paris: Flammarion, 1977) translated by Hugh Tomlinson and Barbara Habberjam, Dialogues (London: Athlone, 1987) p. 5; also used as an epigraph to Gilles Deleuze, *Critique et clinique* (Paris: Editions de Minuit, 1993) translated by Daniel W. Smith and Michael A. Greco, *Essays Critical and Clinical* (Minneapolis: Minnesota University Press, 1997).
31. Nikolaus Pevsner, *An Outline of European Architecture* (1943). Page ref. to seventh edition (Harmondsworth: Penguin, 1968) p. 15.
32. Gilles Deleuze, *Cinéma 2, l'image-temps* (Paris: Editions de Minuit, 1985) translated by Hugh Tomlinson and Robert Galeta, *Cinema 2: The Time-Image* (London: Athlone Press, 1989) p. 328, n. 59.

Sigmund Freud, Julia Kristeva and Slavoj Žižek

The writers represented here are all instrumental in the development and exploration of psychoanalysis. Sigmund Freud is one of the great thinkers of the modern era, and has shaped much thought about how the mind works, finding evidence in his consultations with people suffering from mental illness. His ideas have been variously refined and repudiated in the field of psychiatry, but there is no doubt that the field remains indebted to his opening up of ways of thinking about the way the mind might work, such as the idea that primitive patterns of desire lie in the mind, ready to make themselves felt if they are triggered by the right stimulus. His invention or discovery of the Oedipus complex is now ingrained in a wide culture, and now every schoolboy knows that he wants to murder his father and sleep with his mother, but suppresses these ideas with his conscious mind because they are forbidden thoughts. Woody Allen has made a career in cinema by making jokes about Freudian psychoanalysis, which shows that there is a wide enough knowledge of some of these ideas to elicit a chuckle of recognition.

Psychoanalytic ideas are still in circulation, both in clinical application and in theory. The towering presence in French theoretical psychoanalysis has been Jacques Lacan (1901–81) the director of the Ecole Freudienne in Paris. He was the most prominent French Freudian, and the mentor of Félix Guattari and Luce Irigaray – both of whom he analysed, and both of whom repudiated and argued against his teachings in a way that the most amateur Freudian would easily suppose to be Oedipal. Guattari and Deleuze in *Anti-Oedipus* present the Freudian unconscious not as a universal statement about the human condition, but as a product of a particular set of social, economic and political relations. The presentation of the ideas is not set out as careful and systematic arguments, but as an episodic series of streams of consciousness, rather deliriously with moments of lucidity managing to convey a sense that Freud is to be overcome.[1] Irigaray's writing can have a similarly delirious quality, and invokes a range of specifically feminine images and strategies in an attempt to build an alternative to Freud's problematically phallocentric worldview.[2]

In *Civilization and its Discontents*, Freud made use of an extended metaphor comparing the city of Rome with the mind, or comparing the mind with the city of Rome. His point was that the comparison had its limits because the physical entity that is the city of Rome cannot in fact accommodate all the different buildings and urban projects that have been overlaid on the place during its long and complex history as a focus of power, civilization, culture and archaeological activity. By contrast the mind can accept new ideas and schemas without the old ones being entirely wiped out, and one finds them unexpectedly reasserting themselves. Freud's evocation of the city is compelling, and before drawing attention to the limitations of the metaphor, he establishes a strong idea of a rapport between this culturally-invested place and the mind.

Section 3: Individual

Sigmund Freud, from *Civilization and its Discontents*

Historians tell us that the oldest Rome was the *Roma Quadrata*, a fenced settlement on the Palatine. Then followed the phase of the *Septimontium*, a federation of the settlements on the different hills; after that came the city bounded by the Servian wall; and later still, after all the transformations during the periods of the republic and the early Caesars, the city which the Emperor Aurelian surrounded with his walls. We will not follow the changes which the city went through any further, but we will ask ourselves how much a visitor, whom we will suppose to be equipped with the most complete historical and topographical knowledge, may still find left of these early stages in the Rome of today. Except for a few gaps, he will see the wall of Aurelian almost unchanged. In some places he will be able to find sections of the Servian wall where they have been excavated and brought to light. If he knows enough – more than present-day archaeology does – he may perhaps be able to trace out in the plan of the city the whole course of that wall and the outline of the *Roma Quadrata*. Of the buildings which once occupied this ancient area he will find nothing, or only scant remains, for they exist no longer. The best information about Rome in the republican era would only enable him at the most to point out the sites where the temples and public buildings of the period stood. Their place is now taken by ruins, but not ruins of themselves but of later restorations made after fires or destruction. It is hardly necessary to remark that all these remains of ancient Rome are found dovetailed into the jumble of a great metropolis which has grown up in the last few centuries since the Renaissance. There is certainly not a little that is ancient still buried in the soil of the city or beneath its modern buildings. This is the manner in which the past is preserved in historical sites like Rome.

Now let us, by a flight of imagination, suppose that Rome is not a human habitation but a psychical entity with a similarly long and copious past – an entity, that is to say, in which nothing that has once come into existence will have passed away and all the earlier phases of development continue to exist alongside the latest one. This would mean that in Rome the palaces of the Caesars and the Septizonium of Septimius Severus would still be rising to their old height on the Palatine and the castle of S. Angelo would still be carrying on its battlements the beautiful statues which graced it until the siege by the Goths, and so on. But more than this. In the place occupied by the Palazzo Caffarelli would once more stand – without the Palazzo having to be removed – the Temple of Jupiter Capitolinus, and this not only in its latest shape, as the Romans of the Empire saw it, but also in its earliest one, when it still showed Etruscan forms and was ornamented with terracotta antefixes. Where the Coliseum now stands we could at the same time admire Nero's vanished Golden House. On the Piazza of the Pantheon we should find not only the Pantheon of today, as it was bequeathed to us by Hadrian, but, on the same site, the original edifice erected by Agrippa; indeed the same piece of ground would be supporting the church of Santa Maria Sopra Minerva and the ancient temple over which it was built. And the observer would perhaps only have to change the direction of his glance or his position in order to call up the one view or the other.³

Most of Freud's facts in this passage came from a chapter by Hugh Last in the *Cambridge Ancient History* of 1928 – a recent publication for Freud, who published the above passage in 1930, before Mussolini's interventions in and reinterpretations of the Roman fabric made the issues of archaeology, power and conservation all the more compelling.⁴ If Freud was concerned to draw attention to the limitations of Rome as an image of the mind, Julia Kristeva in *New Maladies of the Soul* suggests the idea of a rapport between modern mental health and the kind of city that we as a society make ourselves live in.

Julia Kristeva, from 'In Times Like These, Who Needs Pychoanalysts?'⁵

I am picturing a sprawling metropolis with glass and steel buildings that reach to the sky, reflect it, reflect each other, and reflect you – a city filled with people steeped in their own image who rush about with overdone make-up on and who are cloaked in gold, pearls, and fine leather, while in the next street over, heaps of filth abound and drugs accompany the sleep or the fury of the social outcasts. This city could be New York; it could be any future metropolis, even your own. What might one do in such a city? Nothing but buy and sell goods and images, which amounts to the same thing, since they both are dull, shallow symbols. Those who can or wish to preserve a lifestyle that downplays opulence as well as misery will need to create a space for an 'inner zone' – a secret garden, an intimate quarter, or more simply and ambitiously, a psychic life.

Yet that is where the story gets complicated. The West has been crafting this inner life since the beginning of the Christian era, when Plotinus transformed a Janus-faced Narcissus into two hands joined in prayer. Inner life has been reinforced by the spiritual path and carnival of the Middle Ages, and it has been shaped by Montaigne's fragile ego, Diderot's passions, and the meditations of Hegel and Kant. It has since become a psychic drama, a psychodrama.

Plotinus has degenerated into . . . Dallas. Indeed, the residents of this steel city are not in want of inner drama – in fact, they are as anxious, depressed, neurotic, and psychotic as the Freudian unconscious would wish them to be. If we believe, however, that we can escape from the surface value of our actions, we fall into the trap of psychology. Therefore, psychoanalysis has some work ahead of it, since Freud's doctrine seeks precisely to free us from this suppressed space of psychological ill-being.

The city that I chose as an image of contemporary life encourages us to include *social history* as one of the elements of organization and permanency that constitute psychic life. Using the terminology of our industrial society, one could say that psychoanalysis turns money into time and joins painful affect with language – language that may be listless or indecipherable, but that is always directed toward other people. Such an extraordinary metamorphosis, which goes against the tide of the market economy as well as the neurosis that it patterns, may also shed light on psychosis. Two thousand years of inner experience have built this prison of the soul, a prison that offers psychoanalysis an innocent vulnerability in which it can pierce a hole that will serve to resound the polyphony of our motives.

Proust has accorded us the finest summary of what is becoming (or will soon become) the Freudian psyche: 'Those who suffer feel closer to their soul'.[6] For even if we have the sensation of being always enveloped in, surrounded by our own soul, still it does not seem a fixed and immovable prison; rather do we seem to be borne away with it, and perpetually struggling to transcend it, to break out into the world, with a perpetual discouragement as we hear endlessly all around us that unvarying sound which is not an echo from without, but the resonance of a vibration from within.[7]

Proust's image of the soul here is an image that makes complex the idea of interior and exterior – the soul is around us, but somehow generated from within – making our own psychic space, which might be formed firmly or weakly, and be a refuge or a prison depending on our state of mental health. Kristeva's 'Dallas' is not only a Texan city, but also a television soap opera of the 1970s, the city as narrative. Kristeva refers to 'the current onslaught of psychological illness, which takes the form of "soap operas"',[8] saying that they seem to call out to psychoanalysis 'tell us the meaning of our inner turmoil, and show us a way out of it'. Psychoanalysis informs Adrian Stokes's rather mysterious essay 'The Impact of Architecture', written in 1961, which made use of illustrations of a dozen French Romanesque churches to discuss the general idea of how we relate to architecture. Here the architecture is the ostensible subject of the essay, but it manages to communicate very little about the buildings, and much more about Stokes's own sensibility. Of the church of Notre Dame du Port at Clermont-Ferrand for example he says:

> I attribute to the light here a quality like the smoothness of honey, to dark areas also. The little staccato accents of the chairs are out of place, incongruous as a butcher's shop in an attic. Being part of so noble an image of our internal organs, the chairs may be seen as ingesteds ardine-boxes, the statuary as exfoliations, excrescences, unlike the needed roughness of the columns' capitals. It seems birth would have been easy for such a body, lit, aerated and very strong, pounding in utter calm. The thickness, the height, the roundness everywhere seem spacious and gradually dominated by a permeating good, particularly in the barrel-vault that we will consider to be replenished with the circulatory darkness of a Rembrandt background. [. . .] we have . . . the sensation of a perfect fit for which contexts are likely to be many, mental as well as somatic; suggesting, in sum, the integrated psyche that we struggle to build amid a confusing scaffolding of psychological drives. A dome or head is the home of all our acts. Like perception, like an impact on the senses, light floods through the apse windows, within a mosaic of cellular indentations above the main arches.

> We look up open-mouthed, taking in a firm roundness that remains resilient and untouched by our attack. We are practising aggression and love, and their integration. [9]

In juxtaposing these passages from Stokes and Proust it is possible to suture them to make them seem to say that the harmonious sense that one has when contemplating a Romanesque interior can be felt to be a perfect fit with the psyche we aspire to have, as if the good part of ourselves, vibrating within, has resonated with stone and been made concrete around us. It suggests a mysterious but human reason for feeling good about the place (distinct from the mysterious and metaphysical claims that are sometimes made). If one way of working on architecture is to try to externalize the 'vibrations' coming from within, one can also work along this line in the opposite direction, working on the soul by internalizing the surroundings, and Kristeva seems to suggest some operation of cause and effect in the relation between urban surroundings and the troubled state of the contemporary soul; or possibly there are similar drives at work producing both the city and the individual, but certainly there is a rapport, and it is troubled, if not psychotic. Following on from Samuel Butler's way of thinking, one could see the city as a machine with its own collective soul dispersed among its buildings and its inhabitants. Could one begin, then, to psychoanalyse a city? The idea is not inconceivable, and Félix Guattari for one would not have hesitated to allow such a possibility, though he would have preferred to call it a schizoanalysis. On the other hand Slavoj Žižek recoils from the idea of allowing a group-identity to have claims of consciousness and to be understood as a 'subject' – which could have a point of view and maybe have rights. In making his argument he appeals not to the logic of the case, but to common sense, and thereby closes down a line of argument opened up by Guattari in *The Machinic Unconscious*, explored in *The Three Ecologies*, and *Chaosmosis*, and which is reflected in Deleuze's work on Spinoza.[10] It is also worth pointing to Rachel McCann's reading of John Dewey and Maurice Merleau-Ponty, from which she has developed an idea of 'wild being', with which to analyse architecture – an idea that supposes a hybridity of subject, including elements of creature and habitat in the entity (if 'entity' it is).[11]

Slavoj Žižek, from 'Of Cells and Selves'

> Let us begin with the inherent antagonism of today's 'Deep Ecology', discernible in its split into two main orientations: on the one hand, anti-anthropocentric Spinozan Deep Ecology, for which all forms of life are strictly equivalent, so that the rights of all elements of a biosphere, rivers and rocks included, have ultimately the same weight as the rights of man; on the other hand, New Age animist spiritualism, which conceives of the entire universe as a living organism whose development has culminated in man, its Omega-point, its steward-guardian (which is why references to *anima mundi* and the 'anthropic principle' abound here). According to this view we are today on the brink of a new cosmo-spiritual alteration which will deliver man from his narrow egoism and bring about a new solidarity of Life . . . . This inherent split of Deep Ecology is

Section 3: Individual

grounded in the ambivalent relationship of modern Cartesian science to so-called anthropocentrism: the non-anthropocentric and 'anti-humanist': that is, the moment Cartesian subjectivity is asserted, the pre-Cartesian humanist notions of man as the highest product of divine creativity, is done with . . .[12]

[. . .] This properly *psychotic* fantasy of leaving behind the level of subjectivity, with its contingent finitude, is one of the popular motifs of New Age techno-ideology: we are on the threshold of the transformation of human intelligence into something 'more than human', a higher-order Entity towards which we stand like animals (or even cells) stand to us.[13]

Žižek dismisses this idea, while asserting its currency. My view is that anthropocentrism is inescapable for anthropods, so it is not problematic when it is detected in our thought. However if we are working with a body-image based on the idea of flows and political interactions, then the idea of finding such a machine constructed across other entities and assemblages of entities is perfectly possible, and allows us to see a rapport between the schizo-analytic dispersed psyche and the elements of the outside world, that ceases to be entirely outside as it flows through and is involved in the body. If we allow ourselves to find a soul in ourselves, then by transferring the metaphor we can find one in the universe, a river, a city or a house. This may well be a psychotic fantasy (Deleuze and Guattari would embrace that idea, though they might insist on it being a real psychotic fact).[14] The mistake of New Age techno-ideology, as represented by Zizek, is not in wanting to give undue weight to this metaphor, but in supposing that it is something new, or that as a consequence of noticing it we are on the brink of previously unimagined possibilities. Firstly if the principle involved is anthropocentric then it can be seen as a continuation of the practice that turned natural forces into nymphs, naiads and dryads in ancient Greece,[15] or allowed Arthur Conan Doyle to imagine his fictional creation Professor Challenger make the Earth scream with pain, as he did in 1929.[16] In this story Professor Challenger makes the Earth notice him by exposing part of its sensitive core, and impaling it. The Earth is imagined as a living being that is rather more like a human than it really is. If we try to imagine other beings as having sensibilities radically different from our own, then it quickly becomes apparent that we cannot begin to empathize with them, so we tend to humanize everything we try to understand. Wittgenstein used a lion to make a point about language. He explained that even if he could use words of the lion's language, he would have no idea what they meant to the lion. There is an essay by Thomas Nagel called 'What is it Like to be a Bat?', which raises the question, considers the bat's sensory apparatus and ours, and concludes that we cannot know what it is like.[17] If this is the case for creatures which share so much genetic material with us, and have so many of the same needs – food and warmth, for example – then we are certainly impossibly remote from the types of entities made up by rivers and hills, and will not be able to see the world from their point of view or to make any sense of that view if by some chance we encounter it. There is a systematic attempt to explore this kind of territory in Deleuze and Guattari's 'Becoming Intense, Becoming Animal, Becoming Imperceptible', with its multiple viewpoints (albeit many of them human) including 'memories of a haecceity', 'memories of a molecule', 'becoming music',[18] and it is hinted at in Samuel Butler's 'Book of the Machines', where premonitions of consciousness are imagined in systems of levers and pistons.[19]

Notes

1. Gilles Deleuze and Félix Guattari, *L'Anti-Oedipe* (Paris: Editions de Minuit, 1972), translated by Robert Hurley, Mark Seem and Helen R. Lane, *Capitalism and Schizophrenia 1: Anti-Oedipus* (New York: Viking, 1977).
2. Luce Irigaray, *Amante marine* (Paris: Editions de Minuit, 1980), translated by Gillian C. Gill, *Marine Lover of Friedrich Nietzsche* (New York: Columbia University Press, 1991); Luce Irigaray, *Passions elementaire* (Paris: Editions de Minuit, 1982), translated by Joanne Collie and Judith Still, Elemental Passions (London: Athlone, 1992); Luce Irigaray, *L'Oubli de l'air chez Martin Heidegger* (Paris: Editions de Minuit, 1983), translated by Mary Beth Mader, *The Forgetting of Air in Martin Heidegger* (Austin: University of Texas, 1999).
3. Sigmund Freud, 'Civilization and its Discontents' in *The Penguin Freud Library*, vol. 12, pp. 256–8.
4. See for example Elizabeth Mae Marlowe, '"The Mutability of all Things": the Rise, Fall and Rise of the Meta Sudans Fountain in Rome' in *Architecture as Experience*, edited by Dana Arnold and Andrew Ballantyne (London: Routledge, 2004) pp. 36–56.
5. Julia Kristeva, *Les Nouvelles maladies de l'âme* (Paris: Fayard, 1993), translated by Ross Guberman, 'In Times Like These, Who Needs Pychoanalysts?', in *New Maladies of the Soul* (New York: Columbia University Press, 1995) pp. 27–45.
6. Marcel Proust, 'Les Plaisirs et les jours', in *Jean Santeuil* (Paris: Pléiade, 1971) p. 6; translated by Gerard Hopkins, 'Evenings at Saint-Germain', in *Jean Santeuil* (London: Weidenfeld and Nicolson, 1955) pp. 33–4.
7. Marcel Proust, *A la recherche de temps perdu*, translated by C. K. Scott Moncrieff and Terence Kilmartin, revised by D. J. Enright, *In Search of Lost Time* (London: Chatto and Windus, 1992) vol. 1, Swann's Way, pp. 101–102.
8. Julia Kristeva, *New Maladies of the Soul*, op. cit., p. 29.
9. Adrian Stokes, 'The Impact of Architecture' (1961) in *The Critical Writings of Adrian Stokes*, 3 vols (London: Thames and Hudson, 1978), vol. 3, p. 198.
10. Félix Guattari, *L'Inconscient machinique: essais de schizo-analyse* (Clamecy: Encres–Recherches, 1979); Félix Guattari, *Les trios écologies* (Paris: Galilée, 1989), translated by Ian Pindar and Paul Sutton, *The Three Ecologies* (London: Athlone, 2000); Félix Guattari, *Chaosmose* (Paris: Galilée, 1992), translated by Paul Bains and Julian Pefanis, *Chaosmosis: an Ethico-Aesthetic Paradigm* (Sydney: Power Publications, 1995); Gilles Deleuze, *Spinoza: philosophie pratique* (Paris: Presses Universitaire de France, 1970), translated by Robert Hurley, *Spinoza: Practical Philosophy* (San Francisco: City Lights, 1988).
11. Rachel McCann, 'Receptivity to the Sensuous: Architecture as "Wild Being"', in *Architecture and Civilization*, edited by Michael Mitias (Amsterdam: Rodopi, 1999) pp. 123–41.

Section 3: Individual

12. Žižek's note: A further antagonism exists between Deep Ecology and ecofeminism, which aims at replacing Deep Ecology's anti-anthropocentrism with anti-andocentrism and, consequently, reproaches Deep Ecology with retaining basic patriarchal premises.
13. Slavoj Žižek, 'Of Cells and Selves', in *The Žižek Reader*, edited by Elizabeth Wright and Edmond Wright (London: Blackwell, 1999) pp. 304–305.
14. Deleuze and Guattari, *Anti-Oedipus*, op. cit., opening pages.
15. Andrew Ballantyne, *Architecture, Landscape and Liberty* (Cambridge University Press, 1997) pp. 86–109.
16. Arthur Conan Doyle, 'When the Earth Screamed', in *The Complete Professor Challenger Stories* (London: Wordsworth, 1989) pp. 547–77.
17. Ludwig Wittgenstein, trans. G. E. M. Anscombe, *Philosophical Investigations* (Oxford: Blackwell, 1978) p. 223; Thomas Nagel, 'What is it Like to be a Bat?', in *The Philosophical Review*, 83, 4 (October 1974), pp. 435–50.
18. Gilles Deleuze and Félix Guattari, *Mille plateaux: capitalisme et schizophrénie 2* (Paris: Éditions de Minuit, 1980) translated by Brian Massumi, *A Thousand Plateaus: Capitalism and Schizophrenia 2* (Minnesota University Press, 1987) Chapter 10, 'Becoming Intense, Becoming Animal, Becoming Imperceptible', pp. 232–309.
19. Samuel Butler, *Erewhon*, pp. 143–4. See below, p. 126ff.

Samuel Butler

Butler's autobiographical memoir, *The Way of All Flesh* (1903) is a literary classic. Butler (1835–1902) devoted much intellectual energy to consideration of the idea of evolution, and his ideas on the topic are collected in a volume that is also in print: *Life and Habit* (1910). *Erewhon* (1872) was his most popular book during his lifetime. *The Way of All Flesh* made uncomfortable reading for people with the conventional attitudes of his own day, its later success attests to the fact that it resonated better with the attitudes of the middle years of the twentieth century. *Erewhon* is a fantasy, more a social fiction than science fiction, describing a visit to a country where industrial machinery has been abolished, not because of its immediate effects, but for fear of the consequences that would eventually follow. It is an adventure in thought, as Butler took the nineteenth-century enthusiasm for the machine and imagined where it might end. It is a brilliant speculation, made at a time when the steam engine was the closest thing to artifical intelligence that was practically available; but Butler foresaw the rise of the machines that still haunts the imagination of the audiences of popular cinematic apocalypses (such as *The Matrix*, and *Terminator* series). The key move in Butler's thought is to see machines not as isolated objects, but as assemblages of people and things, so that the steam engine (the vapour engine) is not just a mass of iron parts, but includes also its tracks and the man who stokes its boiler. The people involved in improving its design are part of its evolutionary process, and just where the volition in this assemblage is located becomes a matter of some uncertainty, because it seems to be dispersed among the various parts of the mechanism – organic and ferrous. Butler argues his points clearly and carefully, and only our established habits of thought will hold us back from accepting his conclusions. In our world these arguments against the machine were not found to be persuasive, and it continues to dwell among us and mediates our social interactions and political identities to an ever-increasing degree. At a time when the arguments should be much more compellingly persuasive than they were when they were framed, so we find ourselves so much a part of the machinery that it seems much too impractical to do anything about it. We accept our fate, which worries us nevertheless.

The Book of the Machines

The writer commences: 'There was a time when the earth was to all appearance utterly destitute both of animal and vegetable life, and when according to the opinion of our best philosophers it was simply a hot round ball with a crust gradually cooling. Now if a human being had existed while the earth was in this state and had been allowed to see it as though it were some other world with which he had no concern,

Section 3: Individual

and if at the same time he were entirely ignorant of all physical science, would he not have pronounced it impossible that creatures possessed of anything like consciousness should be evolved from the seeming cinder which he was beholding? Would he not have denied that it contained any potentiality of consciousness? Yet in the course of time consciousness came. Is it not possible then that there may be even yet new channels dug out for consciousness, though we can detect no signs of them at present?

'Again. Consciousness, in anything like the present acceptation of the term, having been once a new thing – a thing, as far as we can see, subsequent even to an individual centre of action and to a reproductive system (which we see existing in plants without apparent consciousness) – why may not there arise some new phase of mind which shall be as different from all present known phases as the mind of animals is from that of vegetables?

'It would be absurd to attempt to define such a mental state (or whatever it may be called); inasmuch as it must be something so foreign to man that his experience can give him no help towards conceiving its nature; but surely when we reflect upon the manifold phases of life and consciousness which have been evolved already, it would be rash to say that no others can be developed; and that animal life is the end of all things. There was a time when fire was the end of all things; another when rocks and water were so.'

The writer, after enlarging, on the above for several pages, proceeded to inquire whether traces of the approach of such a new phase of life could be perceived at present; whether we could see any tenements preparing which might in a remote futurity be adapted for it; whether, in fact, the primordial cell of such a kind of life could be now detected upon earth. In the course of his work he answered this question in the affirmative, and pointed to the higher machines.

'There is no security' – to quote his own words – 'against the ultimate development of mechanical consciousness, in the fact of machines possessing little consciousness now. A mollusc has not much consciousness. Reflect upon the extraordinary advance which machines have made during the last few hundred years, and note how slowly the animal and vegetable kingdoms are advancing. The more highly organized machines are creatures not so much of yesterday as of the last five minutes, so to speak, in comparison with past time. Assume for the sake of argument that conscious beings have existed for some twenty million years: see what strides machines have made in the last thousand! May not the world last twenty million years longer? If so, what will they not in the end become? Is it not safer to nip the mischief in the bud and to forbid them further progress?

'But who can say that the vapour engine has not a kind of consciousness? Where does consciousness begin, and where end? Who can draw the line? Who can draw any line? Is not everything interwoven with everything? Is not machinery linked with animal life in an infinite variety of ways? The shell of a hen's egg is made of a delicate white ware and is a machine as much as an egg-cup is; the shell is a device for holding the egg as much as the egg-cup for holding the shell: both are phases of the same function; the hen makes the shell in her inside, but it is pure pottery. She makes her nest outside of herself for convenience' sake, but the nest is not more of a machine than the egg-shell is. A "machine" is only a "device."'

Then returning to consciousness, and endeavouring to detect its earliest manifestations, the writer continued:

'There is a kind of plant that eats organic food with its flowers; when a fly settles upon the blossom, the petals close upon it and hold it fast till the plant has absorbed the insect into its system; but they will close on nothing but what is good to eat; of a drop of rain or a piece of stick they will take no notice. Curious that so unconscious a thing should have such a keen eye to its own interest! If this is unconsciousness, where is the use of consciousness?

'Shall we say that the plant does not know what it is doing merely because it has no eyes, or ears, or brains? If we say that it acts mechanically, and mechanically only, shall we not be forced to admit that sundry other and apparently very deliberate actions are also mechanical? If it seems to us that the plant kills and eats a fly mechanically, may it not seem to the plant that a man must kill and eat a sheep mechanically?

'But it may be said that the plant is void of reason, because the growth of a plant is an involuntary growth. Given earth, air, and due temperature, the plant must grow; it is like a clock, which being once wound up will go till it is stopped or run down; it is like the wind blowing on the sails of a ship – the ship must go when the wind blows it. But can a healthy boy help growing if he have good meat and drink and clothing? Can anything help going as long as it is wound up, or go on after it is run down? Is there not a winding-up process everywhere?

'Even a potato[1] in a dark cellar has a certain low cunning about him which serves him in excellent stead. He knows perfectly well what he wants and how to get it. He sees the light coming from the cellar window and sends his shoots crawling straight thereto; they will crawl along the floor and up the wall and out at the cellar window; if there be a little earth anywhere on the journey he will find it and use it for his own ends. What deliberation he may exercise in the matter of his roots when he is planted in the earth is a thing unknown to us; but we can imagine him saying, "I will have a tuber here and a tuber there, and I will suck whatsoever advantage I can from all my surroundings. This neighbour I will overshadow, and that I will undermine; and what I can do shall be the limit of what I will do. He that is stronger and better placed than I shall overcome me, and him that is weaker I will overcome."

'The potato says these things by doing them, which is the best of languages. What is consciousness if this is not consciousness ? We find it difficult to sympathize with the emotions of a potato; so we do with those of an oyster. Neither of these things makes a noise on being boiled or opened, and noise appeals to us more strongly than anything else because we make so much about our own sufferings. Since, then, they do not annoy us by any expression of pain we call them emotionless; and so *quâ* mankind they are; but mankind is not everybody.

'If it be urged that the action of the potato is chemical and mechanical only, and that it is due to the chemical and mechanical effects of light and heat, the answer would seem to lie in an inquiry whether every sensation is not chemical and mechanical in its operation? Whether those things which we deem most purely spiritual are anything but disturbances of equilibrium in an infinite series of levers, beginning with those that are too small for microscopic detection, and going up to the human arm and the appliances which it makes use of? Whether there be not a molecular

Section 3: Individual

action of thought, whence a dynamical theory of the passions shall be deducible? Whether, strictly speaking, we should not ask what kind of levers a man is made of rather than what is his temperament? How are they balanced? How much of such and such will it take to weigh them down so as to make him do so and so?'

The writer went on to say that he anticipated a time when it would be possible, by examining a single hair with a powerful microscope, to know whether its owner could be insulted with impunity. He then became more and more obscure, so that I was obliged to give up all attempt at translation; neither did I follow the drift of his argument. On coming to the next part which I could construe, I found that he had changed his ground.

'Either,' he proceeds, 'a great deal of action that has been called purely mechanical and unconscious must be admitted to contain more elements of consciousness than has been allowed hitherto (and in this case germs of consciousness will be found in many actions of the higher machines) – or (assuming the theory of evolution but at the same time denying the consciousness of vegetable and crystalline action) the race of man has descended from things which had no consciousness at all. In this case there is no *a priori* improbability in the descent of conscious (and more than conscious) machines from those which now exist, except that which is suggested by the apparent absence of anything like a reproductive system in the mechanical kingdom. This absence however is only apparent, as I shall presently show.

'Do not let me be misunderstood as living in fear of any actually existing machine; there is probably no known machine which is more than a prototype of future mechanical life. The present machines are to the future as the early Saurians to man. The largest of them will probably greatly diminish in size. Some of the lowest vertebrata attained a much greater bulk than has descended to their more highly organized living representatives, and in like manner a diminution in the size of machines has often attended their development and progress.

'Take the watch, for example; examine its beautiful structure; observe the intelligent play of the minute members which compose it; yet this little creature is but a development of the cumbrous clocks that preceded it; it is no deterioration from them. A day may come when clocks, which certainly at the present time are not diminishing in bulk, will be superseded owing to the universal use of watches, in which case they will become as extinct as ichthyosauri, while the watch, whose tendency has for some years been to decrease in size rather than the contrary, will remain the only existing type of an extinct race.

'But returning to the argument, I would repeat that I fear none of the existing machines; what I fear is the extraordinary rapidity with which they are becoming something very different to what they are at present. No class of beings have in any time past made so rapid a movement forward. Should not that movement be jealously watched, and checked while we can still check it? And is it not necessary for this end to destroy the more advanced of the machines which are in use at present, though it is admitted that they are in themselves harmless?

'As yet the machines receive their impressions through the agency of man's senses; one travelling machine calls to another in a shrill accent of alarm and the other instantly retires; but it is through the ears of the driver that the voice of the one has acted upon the other. Had there been no driver, the callee would have been deaf to the caller. There was a time when it must have seemed highly improbable that machines should learn to make their wants known by sound, even through the ears of man; may we not conceive, then, that a day will come when those ears will be no longer needed, and the hearing will be done by the delicacy of the machine's own construction – when its language shall have been developed from the cry of animals to a speech as intricate as our own?

'It is possible that by that time children will learn the differential calculus – as they learn now to speak – from their mothers and nurses, or that they may talk in the hypothetical language, and work rule of three sums, as soon as they are born; but this is not probable; we cannot calculate on any corresponding advance in man's intellectual or physical powers which shall be a set-off against the far greater development which seems in store for the machines. Some people may say that man's moral influence will suffice to rule them; but I cannot think it will ever be safe to repose much trust in the moral sense of any machine.

'Again, might not the glory of the machines consist in their being without this same boasted gift of language? "Silence," it has been said by one writer, "is a virtue which renders us agreeable to our fellow-creatures."'

Note

1. The root alluded to is not the potato of our own gardens, but a plant so near akin to it that I have ventured to translate it thus. Apropos of its intelligence, had the writer known Butler he would probably have said:
    'He knows what's what, and that's as high
    As metaphysic wit can fly.'
   [Note: the allusion is to Samuel Butler (1613–80), author of *Hudibras*, a celebrated comic verse.]

The Machines – *continued*

'But other questions come upon us. What is a man's eye but a machine for the little creature that sits behind in his brain to look through? A dead eye is nearly as good as a living one for some time after the man is dead. It is not the eye that cannot see, but the restless one that cannot see through it. Is it man's eyes, or is it the big seeing-engine which has revealed to us the existence of worlds beyond worlds into infinity? What has made man familiar with the scenery of the moon, the spots on the sun, or the geography of the planets? He is at the mercy of the seeing-engine for these things, and is powerless unless he tack it on to his own identity, and make it part and parcel of himself. Or, again, is it the eye, or the little see-engine, which has shown us the existence of infinitely minute organisms which swarm unsuspected around us?

'And take man's vaunted power of calculation. Have we not engines which can do all manner of sums more quickly and correctly than we can? What prizeman in Hypothetics at any of our Colleges of Unreason can compare with some of these machines in their own line? In fact, wherever precision is required man flies to the machine at once, as far preferable to himself. Our sum-engines never drop a figure, nor our looms a stitch; the machine is brisk and active, when the man is weary; it is clear-headed and collected, when the man is stupid and dull; it needs no slumber, when man must sleep or drop; ever at its post, ever ready for work, its alacrity never flags, its patience never gives in; its might is stronger than combined hundreds, and swifter than the flight of birds; it can burrow beneath the earth, and walk upon the largest rivers and sink not. This is the green tree; what then shall be done in the dry?

'Who shall say that a man does see or hear? He is such a hive and swarm of parasites that it is doubtful whether his body is not more theirs than his, and whether he is anything but another kind of ant-heap after all. May not man himself become a sort of parasite upon the machines ? An affectionate machine-tickling aphid?

'It is said by some that our blood is composed of infinite living agents which go up and down the highways and byways of our bodies as people in the streets of a city. When we look down from a high place upon crowded thoroughfares, is it possible not to think of corpuscles of blood travelling through veins and nourishing the heart of the town? No mention shall be made of sewers, nor of the hidden nerves which serve to communicate sensations from one part of the town's body to another; nor of the yawning jaws of the railway stations, whereby the circulation is carried directly into the heart – which receive the venous lines, and disgorge the arterial, with an eternal pulse of people. And the sleep of the town, how life-like! with its change in the circulation.'

Here the writer became again so hopelessly obscure that I was obliged to miss several pages. He resumed:

'It can be answered that even though machines should hear never so well and speak never so wisely, they will still always do the one or the other for our advantage, not their own; that man will be the ruling spirit and the machine the servant; that as soon as a machine fails to discharge the service which man expects from it, it is doomed to extinction; that the machines stand to man simply in the relation of lower animals, the vapour-engine itself being only a more economical kind of horse; so that instead of being likely to be developed into a higher kind of life than man's, they owe their very existence and progress to their power of ministering to human wants, and must therefore both now and ever be man's inferiors.

'This is all very well. But the servant glides by imperceptible approaches into the master; and we have come to such a pass that, even now, man must suffer terribly on ceasing to benefit the machines. If all machines were to be annihilated at one moment, so that not a knife nor lever nor rag of clothing nor anything whatsoever were left to man but his bare body alone that he was born with, and if all knowledge of mechanical laws were taken from him so that he could make no more machines, and all machine-made food destroyed so that the race of man should be left as it were naked upon a desert island, we should become extinct in six weeks. A few miserable individuals might linger, but even these in a year or two would become worse than monkeys. Man's very soul is due to the machines; it is a machine-made thing; he thinks as he thinks, and feels as he feels, through the work that machines have wrought upon him, and their existence is quite as much a *sine quâ non* for his, as his for theirs. This fact precludes us from proposing the complete annihilation of machinery, but surely it indicates that we should destroy as many of them as we can possibly dispense with, lest they should tyrannize over us even more completely.

'True, from a low materialistic point of view, it would seem that those thrive best who use machinery wherever its use is possible with profit; but this is the art of the machines – they serve that they may rule. They bear no malice towards man for destroying a whole race of them provided he creates a better instead; on the contrary, they reward him liberally for having hastened their development. It is for neglecting them that he incurs their wrath, or for using inferior machines, or for not making sufficient exertions to invent new ones, or for destroying them without replacing them; yet these are the very things we ought to do, and do quickly; for though our rebellion against their infant power will cause infinite suffering, what will not things come to, if that rebellion is delayed?

'They have preyed upon man's grovelling preference for his material over his spiritual interests, and have betrayed him into supplying that element of struggle and warfare without which no race can advance. The lower animals progress because they struggle with one another; the weaker die, the stronger breed and transmit their strength. The machines being of themselves unable to struggle, have got man to do their struggling for them; as long as he fulfils this function duly, all goes well with him – at least he thinks so; but the moment he fails to do his best for the advancement of machinery by encouraging the good and destroying the bad, he is left behind in the race of competition; and this means that he will be made uncomfortable in a variety of ways, and perhaps die.

'So that even now the machines will only serve on condition of being served, and that too upon their own terms; the moment their terms are not complied with, they jib, and either smash both themselves and all whom they can reach, or turn churlish and refuse to work at all. How many men at this hour are living in a state of bondage to the machines? How many spend their whole lives, from the cradle to the grave, in tending them by night and day? Is it not plain that the machines are gaining ground upon us, when we reflect on the increasing number of those who are bound down to them as slaves, and of those who devote their whole souls to the advancement of the mechanical kingdom?

'The vapour-engine must be fed with food and consume it by fire even as man consumes it; it supports its combustion by air as man supports it; it has a pulse and circulation as man has. It may be granted that man's body is as yet the more versatile of the two, but then man's body is an older thing; give the vapour-engine but half the time that man has had, give it also a continuance of our present infatuation, and what may it not ere long attain to?

'There are certain functions indeed of the vapour-engine which will probably remain unchanged for myriads of years – which in fact will perhaps survive when the use of vapour has been superseded; the piston and cylinder, the beam, the flywheel, and other parts of the machine will probably be permanent, just as we see that man and many of the lower animals share like modes of eating, drinking, and sleeping; thus they have hearts which beat as ours, veins and arteries, eyes, ears, and noses; they sigh even in their sleep, and weep and yawn; they are affected by their children; they feel pleasure and pain, hope, fear, anger, shame; they have memory and prescience; they know that if certain things happen to them they will die, and they fear death as much as we do; they communicate their thoughts to one another, and some of them deliberately act in concert. The comparison of similarities is endless; I only make it because some may say that since the vapour-engine is not likely to be improved in the main particulars, it is unlikely to be henceforward extensively modified at all. This is too good to be true; it will be modified and suited for an infinite variety of purposes, as much as man has been modified so as to exceed the brutes in skill.

'In the meantime the stoker is almost as much a cook for his engine as our own cooks for ourselves. Consider also the colliers and pitmen and coal merchants and coal trains, and the men who drive them, and the ships that carry coals – what an army of servants do the machines thus employ! Are there not probably more men engaged in tending machinery than in tending men? Do not machines eat as it were by mannery? Are we not ourselves creating our successors in the supremacy of the earth? daily adding to the beauty and delicacy of their organization, daily giving them greater skill and supplying more and more of that self-regulating, self-acting power which will be better than any intellect?

'What a new thing it is for a machine to feed at all! The plough, the spade, and the cart must eat through man's stomach; the fuel that sets them going must burn in the furnace of a man or of horses. Man must consume bread and meat or he cannot dig; the bread and meat are the fuel which drive the spade. If a plough be drawn by horses, the power is supplied by grass or beans or oats, which being burnt in the belly of the cattle give the power of working; without this fuel the work would cease, as an engine would stop if its furnaces were to go out.

'A man of science has demonstrated "that no animal has the power of originating mechanical energy, but that all the work done in its life by any animal, and all the heat that has been emitted from it, and the heat which would be obtained by burning the combustible matter which has been lost from its body during life, and by burning its body after death, make up altogether an exact equivalent to the heat which would be obtained by burning as much food as it has used during its life, and an amount of fuel which would generate as much heat as its body if burned immediately after death." I do not know how he has found this out, but he is a man of science – how then can it be objected against the future vitality of the machines that they are, in their present infancy, at the beck and call of beings who are themselves incapable of originating mechanical energy?

'The main point, however, to be observed as affording cause for alarm is, that whereas animals were formerly the only stomachs of the machines, there are now many which have stomachs of their own, and consume their food themselves. This is a great step towards their becoming, it not animate, yet something so near akin to it, as not to differ more widely from our own life than animals do from vegetables. And though man should remain, in some respects, the higher creature, is not this in accordance with the practice of nature, which allows superiority in some things to animals which have, on the whole, been long surpassed? Has she not allowed the ant and the bee to retain superiority over man in the organization of their communities and social arrangements, the bird in traversing the air, the fish in swimming, the horse in strength and fleetness, and the dog in self-sacrifice?

'It is said by some with whom I have conversed upon this subject, that the machines can never be developed into animate or quasi-animate existences, inasmuch as they have no reproductive system, nor seem ever likely to possess one. If this be taken to mean that they cannot marry, and that we are never likely to see a fertile union between two vapour-engines with the young ones playing about the door of the shed, however greatly we might desire to do so, I will readily grant it. But the objection is not a very profound one. No one expects that all the features of the now existing organizations will be absolutely repeated in an entirely new class of life. The reproductive system of animals differs widely from that of plants, but both are reproductive systems. Has nature exhausted her phases of this power?

'Surely if a machine is able to reproduce another machine systematically, we may say that it has a reproductive system. What is a reproductive system, if it be not a system for reproduction? And how few of the machines are there which have not been produced systematically by other machines? But it is man that makes them do so. Yes; but is it not insects that make many of the plants reproductive, and would not whole families of plants die out if their fertilization was not effected by a class of agents utterly foreign to themselves? Does any one say that the red clover has no reproductive system because the humble bee (and the humble bee only) must aid and abet it before it can reproduce? No one. The humble bee is a part of the reproductive system of the clover. Each one of ourselves has sprung from minute animalcules whose entity was entirely distinct from our own, and which acted after their kind with no thought or heed of what we might think about it. These little creatures are part of our own reproductive system; then why not we part of that of the machines?

'But the machines which reproduce machinery do not reproduce machines after their own kind. A thimble may be made by machinery, but it was not made by, neither will it ever make, a thimble. Here, again, if we turn to nature we shall find abundance of analogies which will teach us that a reproductive system may be in full force without the thing produced being of the same kind as that which produced it. Very few creatures reproduce after their own kind; they reproduce something which has the potentiality of becoming that which their parents were. Thus the butterfly lays an egg, which egg can become a caterpillar, which caterpillar can become a chrysalis, which chrysalis can become a butterfly; and though I freely grant that the machines cannot be said to have more than the germ of a true reproductive system at present, have we not just seen that they have only recently obtained the germs of a mouth and stomach? And may not some stride be made in the direction of true reproduction which shall be as great as that which has been recently taken in the direction of true feeding?

'It is possible that the system when developed may be in many cases a vicarious thing. Certain classes of machines may be alone fertile, while the rest discharge other functions in the mechanical system, just as the great majority of ants and bees have nothing to do with the continuation of their species, but get food and store it, without thought of breeding. One cannot expect the parallel to be complete or nearly so; certainly not now, and probably never; but is there not enough analogy existing at the present moment, to make us feel seriously uneasy about the future, and to render it our duty to check the evil while we can still do so? Machines can within certain limits beget machines of any class, no matter how different to themselves. Every class of machines will probably have its special mechanical breeders, and all the higher ones will owe their existence to a large number of parents and not to two only.

'We are misled by considering any complicated machine as a single thing; in truth it is a city or society, each member of which was bred truly after its kind. We see a machine as a whole, we call it by a name and individualize it; we look at our own limbs, and know that the combination forms an individual which springs from a single centre of reproductive action; we therefore assume that there can be no reproductive action which does not arise from a single centre; but this assumption is unscientific, and the bare fact that no vapour-engine was ever made entirely by another, or two others, of its own kind, is not sufficient to warrant us in saying that vapour-engines have no reproductive system. The truth is that each part of every vapour-engine is bred by its own special breeders, whose function it is to breed that part, and that only, while the combination of the parts into a whole forms another department of the mechanical reproductive system, which is at present exceedingly complex and difficult to see in its entirety.

'Complex now, but how much simpler and more intelligibly organized may it not become in another hundred thousand years? or in twenty thousand? For man at present believes that his interest lies in that direction; he spends an incalculable amount of labour and time and thought in making machines breed always better and better; he has already succeeded in effecting much that at one time appeared impossible, and there seem no limits to the results of accumulated improvements if they are allowed to descend with modification from generation to generation. It must always be remembered that man's body is what it is through having been moulded into its present shape by the chances and changes of many millions of years, but that his organization never advanced with anything like the rapidity with which that of the machines is advancing. This is the most alarming feature, in the case, and I must be pardoned for insisting on it so frequently.'

The Machines – *concluded*

Here followed a very long and untranslatable digression about the different races and families of the then existing machines. The writer attempted to support his theory by pointing out the similarities existing between many machines of a widely different character, which served to show descent from a common ancestor. He divided machines into their genera, subgenera, species, varieties, subvarieties, and so forth. He proved the existence of connecting links between machines that seemed to have very little in common, and showed that many more such links had existed, but had now perished. He pointed out tendencies to reversion, and the presence of rudimentary organs which existed in many machines feebly developed and perfectly useless, yet serving to mark descent from an ancestor to whom the function was actually useful.

I left the translation of this part of the treatise, which, by the way, was far longer than all that I have given here, for a later opportunity. Unfortunately, I left Erewhon before I could return to the subject; and though I saved my translation and other papers at the hazard of my life, I was obliged to sacrifice the original work. It went to my heart to do so; but I thus gained ten minutes of invaluable time, without which both Arowhena and myself must have certainly perished.

I remember one incident which bears upon this part of the treatise. The gentleman who gave it to me had asked to see my tobacco-pipe; he examined it carefully, and when he came to the little protuberance at the bottom of the bowl he seemed much delighted, and exclaimed that it must be rudimentary. I asked him what he meant.

'Sir,' he answered, 'this organ is identical with the rim at the bottom of a cup; it is but another form of the same function. Its purpose must have been to keep the heat of the pipe from marking the table upon which it rested. You would find, if you were to look up the history of tobacco-pipes, that in early specimens this protuberance was of a different shape to what it is now. It will have been broad at the bottom, and flat, so that while the pipe was being smoked the bowl might rest upon the table without marking it. Use and disuse must have come into play and reduced the function to its present rudimentary condition. I should not be surprised, sir,' he continued, 'if, in the course of time, it were to become modified still further, and to assume the form of an ornamental leaf or scroll, or even a butterfly, while, in some cases, it will become extinct.'

On my return to England I looked up the point, and found that my friend was right.

Returning, however, to the treatise, my translation recommences as follows:

'May we not fancy that if, in the remotest geological period, some early form of vegetable life had been endowed with the power of reflecting upon the dawning life of animals which was coming into existence alongside of its own, it would have thought itself exceedingly acute if it had surmised that animals would one day become real vegetables? Yet would this be more mistaken than it would be on our part to imagine that because the life of machines is a very different one to our own, there is therefore no higher possible development of life than ours; or that because mechanical life is a very different thing from ours, therefore that it is not life at all?

'But I have heard it said, "granted that this is so, and that the vapour-engine has a strength of its own, surely no one will say that it has a will of its own?" Alas! if we look more closely, we shall find that this does not make against the supposition that the vapour-engine is one of the germs of a new phase of life. What is there in this whole world, or in the worlds beyond it, which has a will of its own? The Unknown and Unknowable only!

'A man is the resultant and exponent of all the forces that have been brought to bear upon him, whether before his birth or afterwards. His action at any moment depends solely upon his constitution, and on the intensity and direction of the various agencies to which he is, and has been, subjected. Some of these will counteract each other; but as he is by nature, and as he has been acted on, and is now acted on from without, so will he do, as certainly and regularly as though he were a machine.

'We do not generally admit this, because we do not know the whole nature of any one, nor the whole of the forces that act upon him. We see but a part, and being thus unable to generalize human conduct, except very roughly, we deny that it is subject to any fixed laws at all, and ascribe much both of a man's character and actions to chance, or luck, or fortune; but these are only words whereby we escape the admission of our own ignorance; and a little reflection will teach us that the most daring flight of the imagination or the most subtle exercise of the reason is as much the thing that must arise, and the only thing that can by any possibility arise, at the moment of its arising, as the falling of a dead leaf when the wind shakes it from the tree.

'For the future depends upon the present, and the present (whose existence is only one of those minor compromises of which human life is full – for it lives only on sufferance of the past and future) depends upon the past, and the past is unalterable. The only reason why we cannot see the future as plainly as the past, is because we know too little of the actual past and actual present; these things are too great for us, otherwise the future, in its minutest details, would lie spread out before our eyes, and we should lose our sense of time present by reason of the clearness with which we should see the past and future; perhaps we should not be even able to distinguish time at all; but that is foreign. What we do know is, that the more the past and present are known, the more the future can be predicted; and that no one dreams of doubting the fixity of the future in cases where he is fully cognisant of both past and present, and has had experience of the consequences that followed from such a past and such a present on previous occasions. He perfectly well knows what will happen, and will stake his whole fortune thereon.

'And this is a great blessing; for it is the foundation on which morality and science are built. The assurance that the future is no arbitrary and changeable thing, but that like futures will invariably follow like presents, is the groundwork on which we lay all our plans – the faith on which we do every conscious action of our lives. If this were not so we should be without a guide; we should have no confidence in acting, and hence we should never act, for there would be no knowing that the results which will follow now will be the same as those which followed before.

'Who would plough or sow if he disbelieved in the fixity of the future? Who would throw water on a blazing house if the action of water upon fire were uncertain? Men will only do their utmost when they feel certain that the future will discover itself against them if their utmost has not been done. The feeling of such a certainty is a constituent part of the sum of the forces at work upon them, and will act most powerfully on the best and most moral men. Those who are most firmly persuaded that the future is immutably bound up with the present in which their work is lying, will best husband their present, and till it with the greatest care. The future must be a lottery to those who think that the same combinations can sometimes precede one set of results, and sometimes another. If their belief is sincere they will speculate instead of working; these ought to be the immoral men; the others have the strongest spur to exertion and morality, if their belief is a living one.

'The bearing of all this upon the machines is not immediately apparent, but will become so presently. In the meantime I must deal with friends who tell me that, though the future is fixed as regards inorganic matter, and in some respects with regard to man, yet that there are many ways in which it cannot be considered as fixed. Thus, they say that fire applied to dry shavings, and well fed with oxygen gas, will always produce a blaze, but that a coward brought into contact with a terrifying object will not always result in a man running away. Nevertheless, if there be two cowards perfectly similar in every respect, and if they be subjected in a perfectly similar way to two terrifying agents, which are themselves perfectly similar, there are few who will not expect a perfect similarity in the running away, even though a thousand years intervene between the original combination and its being repeated.

'The apparently greater regularity in the results of chemical than of human combinations arises from our inability to perceive the subtle differences in human combinations – combinations which are never identically repeated. Fire we know, and shavings we know, but no two men ever were or ever will be exactly alike; and the smallest difference may change the whole conditions of the problem. Our registry of results must be infinite before we could arrive at a full forecast of future combinations; the wonder is that there is as much certainty concerning human action as there is; and assuredly the older we grow the more certain we feel as to what such and such a kind of person will do in given circumstances; but this could never be the case unless human conduct were under the influence of laws with the working of which we become more and more familiar through experience.

'If the above is sound, it follows that the regularity with which machinery acts is no proof of the absence of vitality, or at least of germs which may be developed into a new phase of life. At first sight it would indeed appear that a vapour-engine cannot help going when set upon a line of rails with the steam up and the machinery in full play; whereas the man whose business it is to drive it can help doing so at any moment that he pleases; so that the first has no spontaneity, and is not possessed of any sort of free will, while the second has and is.

'This is true up to a certain point; the driver can stop the engine at any moment that he pleases, but he can only please to do so at certain points which have been fixed for him by others, or in the case of unexpected obstructions which force him to please to do so. His pleasure is not spontaneous; there is an unseen choir of influences around him, which make it impossible for him to act in any other way than

Section 3: Individual

one. It is known beforehand how much strength must be given to these influences, just as it is known beforehand how much coal and water are necessary for the vapour-engine itself; and curiously enough it will be found that the influences brought to bear upon the driver are of the same kind as those brought to bear upon the engine – that is to say, food and warmth. The driver is obedient to his masters, because he gets food and warmth from them, and if these are withheld or given in insufficient quantities he will cease to drive; in like manner the engine will cease to work if it is insufficiently fed. The only difference is, that the man is conscious about his wants, and the engine (beyond refusing to work) does not seem to be so; but this is temporary, and has been dealt with above.

'Accordingly, the requisite strength being given to the motives that are to drive the driver, there has never, or hardly ever, been an instance of a man stopping his engine through wantonness. But such a case might occur; yes, and it might occur that the engine should break down; but if the train is stopped from some trivial motive it will be found either that the strength of the necessary influences has been miscalculated, or that the man has been miscalculated, in the same way as an engine may break down from an unsuspected flaw; but even in such a case there will have been no spontaneity; the action will have had its true parental causes; spontaneity is only a term for man's ignorance of the gods.

'Is there, then, no spontaneity on the part of those who drive the driver?'

Here followed an obscure argument upon this subject, which I have thought it best to omit. The writer resumes: 'After all then it comes to this, that the difference between the life of a man and that of a machine is one rather of degree than of kind, though differences in kind are not wanting. An animal has more provision for emergency than a machine. The machine is less versatile; its range of action is narrow; its strength and accuracy in its own sphere are superhuman, but it shows badly in a dilemma; sometimes when its normal action is disturbed, it will lose its head, and go from bad to worse like a lunatic in a raging frenzy; but here, again, we are met by the same consideration as before, namely, that the machines are still in their infancy; they are mere skeletons without muscles and flesh.

'For how many emergencies is an oyster adapted? For as many as are likely to happen to it, and no more. So are the machines; and so is man himself. The list of casualties that daily occur to man through his want of adaptability is probably as great as that occurring to the machines; and every day gives them some greater provision for the unforeseen. Let any one examine the wonderful self-regulating and self-adjusting contrivances which are now incorporated with the vapour-engine; let him watch the way in which it supplies itself with oil; in which it indicates its wants to those who tend it; in which, by the governor, it regulates its application of its own strength: let him look at that store-house of inertia and momentum the fly-wheel, or at the buffers on a railway carriage; let him see how those improvements are being selected for perpetuity which contain provision against the emergencies that may arise to harass the machines, and then let him think of a hundred thousand years, and the accumulated progress which they will bring unless man can be awakened to a sense of his situation, and of the doom which he is preparing for himself.[1]

'The misery is that man has been blind so long already. In his reliance upon the use of steam he has been betrayed into increasing and multiplying. To withdraw steam power suddenly will not have the effect of reducing us to the state in which we were before its introduction; there will be a general break-up and time of anarchy such as has never been known; it will be as though our population were suddenly doubled, with no additional means of feeding the increased number. The air we breathe is hardly more necessary for our animal life than the use of any machine, on the strength of which we have increased our numbers, is to our civilization; it is the machines which act upon man and make him man, as much as man who has acted upon and made the machines; but we must choose between the alternative of undergoing much present suffering, or seeing ourselves gradually superseded by our own creatures, till we rank no higher in comparison with them than the beasts of the field with ourselves.

'Herein lies our danger. For many seem inclined to acquiesce in so dishonourable a future. They say that although man should become to the machines what the horse and dog are to us, yet that he will continue to exist, and will probably be better off in a state of domestication under the beneficent rule of the machines than in his present wild condition. We treat our domestic animals with much kindness. We give them whatever we believe to be the best for them; and there can be no doubt that our use of meat has increased their happiness rather than detracted from it. In like manner there is reason to hope that the machines will use us kindly, for their existence will be in a great measure dependent upon ours; they will rule us with a rod of iron, but they will not eat us; they will not only require our services in the reproduction and education of their young, but also in waiting upon them as servants; in gathering food for them, and feeding them; in restoring them to health when they are sick; and in either burying their dead or working up their deceased members into new forms of mechanical existence.

'The very nature of the motive power which works the advancement of the machines precludes the possibility of man's life being rendered miserable as well as enslaved. Slaves are tolerably happy if they have good masters, and the revolution will not occur in our time, nor hardly in ten thousand years, or ten times that. Is it wise to be uneasy about a contingency which is so remote? Man is not a sentimental animal where his material interests are concerned; and though here and there some ardent soul may look upon himself and curse his fate that he was not born a vapour-engine, yet the mass of mankind will acquiesce in any arrangement which gives them better food and clothing at a cheaper rate, and will refrain from yielding to unreasonable jealousy merely because there are other destinies more glorious than their own.

'The power of custom is enormous, and so gradual will be the change, that man's sense of what is due to himself will be at no time rudely shocked; our bondage will steal upon us noiselessly and by imperceptible approaches; nor will there ever be such a clashing of desires between man and the machines as will lead to an encounter between them. Among themselves the machines will war eternally, but they will still require man as the being through whose agency the struggle will be principally conducted. In point of fact there is no occasion for anxiety about the future happiness of man so long as he continues to be in any way profitable to the machines; he may become the inferior race, but he will be infinitely better off than he is now. Is it not then both absurd and unreasonable to be envious of our benefactors? And should we not be guilty of consummate folly if we were to reject advantages which we cannot obtain otherwise, merely because they involve a greater gain to others than to ourselves?

'With those who can argue in this way I have nothing in common. I shrink with as much horror from believing that my race can ever be superseded or surpassed, as I should do from believing that even at the remotest period my ancestors were other than human beings. Could I believe that ten hundred thousand years ago a single one of my ancestors was another kind of being to myself, I should lose all self-respect, and take no further pleasure or interest in life. I have the same feeling with regard to my descendants, and believe it to be one that will be felt so generally that the country will resolve upon putting an immediate stop to all further mechanical progress, and upon destroying all improvements that have been made for the last three hundred years. I would not urge more than this. We may trust ourselves to deal with those that remain, and though I should prefer to have seen the destruction include another two hundred years, I am aware of the necessity for compromising, and would so far sacrifice my own individual convictions as to be content with three hundred. Less than this will be insufficient.'

This was the conclusion of the attack which led to the destruction of machinery throughout Erewhon. There was only one serious attempt to answer it. Its author said that machines were to be regarded as a part of man's own physical nature, being really nothing but extra-corporeal limbs. Man, he said, was a machinate mammal. The lower animals keep all their limbs at home in their own bodies, but many of man's are loose, and lie about detached, now here and now there, in various parts of the world – some being kept always handy for contingent use, and others being occasionally hundreds of miles away. A machine is merely a supplementary limb; this is the be-all and end-all of machinery. We do not use our own limbs other than as machines; and a leg is only a much better wooden leg than any one can manufacture.

'Observe a man digging with a spade; his right forearm has become artificially lengthened, and his hand has become a joint. The handle of the spade is like the knob at the end of the humerus; the shaft is the additional bone, and the oblong iron plate is the new form of the hand which enables its possessor to disturb the earth in a way to which his original hand was unequal. Having thus modified himself, not as other animals are modified, by circumstances over which they have had not even the appearance of control, but having, as it were, taken forethought and added a cubit to his stature, civilization began to dawn upon the race, the social good offices, the genial companionship of friends, the art of unreason, and all those habits of mind which most elevate man above the lower animals, in the course of time ensued.

'Thus civilization and mechanical progress advanced hand in hand, each developing and being developed by the other, the earliest accidental use of the stick having set the ball rolling, and the prospect of advantage keeping it in motion. In fact, machines are to be regarded as the mode of development by which human organism is now especially advancing, every past invention being an addition to the resources of the human body. Even community of limbs is thus rendered possible to those who have so much community of soul as to own money enough to pay a railway fare; for a train is only a seven-leagued foot that five hundred may own at once.'

The one serious danger which this writer apprehended was that the machines would so equalize men's powers, and so lessen the severity of competition, that many persons of inferior physique would escape detection and transmit their inferiority to their descendants. He feared that the removal of the present pressure might cause a degeneracy of the human race, and indeed that the whole body might become purely rudimentary, the man himself being nothing but soul and mechanism, an intelligent but passionless principle of mechanical action.

'How greatly,' he wrote, 'do we not now live with our external limbs? We vary our physique with the seasons, with age, with advancing or decreasing wealth. If it is wet we are furnished with an organ commonly called an umbrella, and which is designed for the purpose of protecting our clothes or our skins from the injurious effects of rain. Man has now many extra-corporeal members, which are of more importance to him than a good deal of his hair, or at any rate than his whiskers. His memory goes in his pocket-book. He becomes more and more complex as he grows older; he will then be seen with see-engines, or perhaps with artificial teeth and hair; if he be a really well-developed specimen of his race, he will be furnished with a large box upon wheels, two horses, and a coachman.'

It was this writer who originated the custom of classifying men by their horse-power, and who divided them into genera, species, varieties, paid subvarieties, giving them names from the hypothetical language which expressed the number of limbs which they could command at any moment. He showed that men became more highly and delicately organized the more nearly they approached the summit of opulence, and that none but millionaires possessed the full complement of limbs with which mankind could become incorporate.

'Those mighty organisms' he continued, 'our leading bankers and merchants, speak to their congeners through the length and breadth of the land in a second of time; their rich and subtle souls can defy all material impediment, whereas the souls of the poor are clogged and hampered by matter, which sticks fast about them as treacle to the wings of a fly, or as one struggling in a quicksand; their dull ears must take days or weeks to hear what another would tell them from a distance, instead of hearing it in a second as is done by the more highly organized classes. Who shall deny that one who can tack on a special train to his identity, and go wheresoever he will whensoever he pleases, is more highly organized than he who, should he wish for the same power, might wish for the wings of a bird with an equal chance of getting them; and whose legs are his only means of locomotion? That old philosophic enemy, matter, the inherently and essentially evil, still hangs about the neck of the poor and strangles him; but to the rich, matter is immaterial; the elaborate organization of his extra-corporeal system has freed his soul.

'This is the secret of the homage which we see rich men receive from those who are poorer than themselves; it would be a grave error to suppose that this deference proceeds from motives which we need be ashamed of; it is the natural respect which all living creatures pay to those whom they recognize as higher than themselves in the scale of animal life, and is analogous to the veneration which a dog feels for man. Among savage races it is deemed highly honourable to be the possessor of a gun, and throughout all known time there has been a feeling that those who are worth most are the worthiest.'

Section 3: Individual

And so he went on at considerable length, attempting to show what changes in the distribution of animal and vegetable life throughout the kingdom had been caused by this and that of man's inventions, and in what way each was connected with the moral and intellectual development of the human species; he even allotted to some the share which they had had in the creation and modification of man's body, and that which they would hereafter have in its destruction; but the other writer was considered to have the best of it, and in the end succeeded in destroying all the inventions that had been discovered for the preceding 271 years, a period which was agreed upon by all parties after several years of wrangling as to whether a certain kind of mangle which was much in use among washerwomen should be saved or no. It was at last ruled to be dangerous, and was just excluded by the limit of 271 years. Then came the reactionary civil wars which nearly ruined the country, but which it would be beyond my present scope to describe.

Notes

1. Since my return to England, I have been told that those who are conversant about machines use many terms concerning them which show that their vitality is here recognized, and that a collection of expressions in use among those who attend on steam engines would be no less startling than instructive. I am also informed, that almost all machines have their own tricks and idiosyncrasies; that they know their drivers and keepers; and that they will play pranks upon a stranger. It is my intention, on a future occasion, to bring together examples both of the expressions in common use among mechanicians, and of any extraordinary exhibitions of mechanical sagacity and eccentricity that I can meet with – not as believing in the Erewhonian Professor's theory, but from the interest of the subject.

Donna Haraway

Susan Greenfield's book *Tomorrow's People* speculates about various conditions that might well be emerging as developing possibilities for the future. Of course predicting the future is always necessarily fraught with uncertainties, and if one looks back even thirty years at films that tried to predict what would be happening now, then all sorts of details are wildly wrong. The technical advances that have changed everyday facilities in the home, for example, are signalled by clumsy machinery, including anthropomorphic robots, and computers with lots of flashing lights and whirling tape spools. In the event our robots are highly specific and dispersed, so that sensors regulate invisibly, and computers are smaller and more powerful than anyone would have found plausible. The dramatic developments in nanotechnology have not yet led to the anticipated manufacture of self-replicating machines (nanobots) based on carbon rather than silicon, and the spectre of 'grey goo' – a mass of molecule-sized self-replicating machines that might form vast assemblages to become utterly alien 'organisms' – is still as firmly in the realm of fiction as Frankenstein's monster has always been; and yet we (as a society) are drawn to try to make these things happen, even as we scare ourselves with the possibility of them happening. Greenfield makes the point that 'ever since our ancestors had sufficient technology, money and time to choose wallpaper, hang up a photo or shift ornaments on the mantelpiece, we humans have seen our homes as extensions of ourselves'.[1] The only thing that sounds wrong with this is the timescale – for a futurologist perhaps the dawn of time is appropriately invoked by practices that go back perhaps to the eighteenth century – but the same impulses can be satisfied by other means, such as telling stories at a hearth (a function now routinely supplanted by television).[2] The house of the future might be a good deal more flexible than those we have at the moment, though the experience of movable partitioning systems in buildings to date has been that the additional expense of a special system is not matched by the desire to rearrange things on a regular basis, and relatively traditional building methods – plasterboard or blockwork walls, can be knocked down and rebuilt if there is a will to do it. At the moment most of us would not want to pay the increased costs involved in order to have bathrooms and kitchens that we could rearrange on a whim; however the technical possibility is there. The more significant aspect of such developments is the impact that they will have on such things as our sense of reality, and of ourselves. The digitally controlled environment in which one can call up moving wallpapers, sea breezes and music or sound effects, will not be within everyone's reach, but to grow up in such an environment, where a wish made is a wish come true, undermines something very basic about how we learn to relate to the world – especially if our experience of the environments created belongs entirely in this world of illusion without external reference points (such as an actual holiday on an actual beach).

Section 3: Individual

Greenfield observes that 'the pull of the virtual world will mean that, for better or worse, you are hardly ever truly alone. And as the boundaries smudge between yourself and the outside world, between you and your wishes, you yourself might become a vaguer phenomenon.'[3] If the technological detail of futurologists' speculations is often awry in important ways, it is more often the social formation and attitudes of the characters that fail to convince. Unconsidered aspects of life – those that have not been reinvented in the story because they are so completely ingrained in the author's or director's set of mental habits – that form the background to the story, rather than being the focus of it, are often the details that date the most. Donna Haraway's 'Cyborg Manifesto' analyses the underlying social conditions that inform a developing cyborg value-system (and a consequent world-view). It is a brilliant *tour de force*, and is often cited, arguing against an idea of the desirability of a sense of wholeness (which is found in the Bible and Plato) in favour of something altogether more dispersed and formless.

Notes

1. Susan Greenfield, *Tomorrow's People* (Harmondsworth: Allen Lane, 2003) p. 11.
2. Andrew Ballantyne, 'Spatiality of "the Box"', in *Television: Aesthetic Reflections*, edited by Ruth Lorand (New York: Peter Lang, 2002), pp. 127–38.
3. Susan Greenfield, *Tomorrow's People*, p. 13.

Donna Haraway, from *A Cyborg Manifesto: Science, Technology, and Socialist-Feminism in the Late Twentieth Century*

A cyborg is a cybernetic organism, a hybrid of machine and organism, a creature of social reality as well as a creature of fiction. Social reality is lived social relations, our most important political construction, a world-changing fiction. The international women's movements have constructed 'women's experience', as well as uncovered or discovered this crucial collective object. This experience is a fiction and fact of the most crucial, political kind. Liberation rests on the construction of the consciousness, the imaginative apprehension, of oppression, and so of possibility. The cyborg is a matter of fiction and lived experience that changes what counts as women's experience in the late twentieth century. This is a struggle over life and death, but the boundary between science fiction and social reality is an optical illusion.

Contemporary science fiction is full of cyborgs – creatures simultaneously animal and machine, who populate worlds ambiguously natural and crafted. Modern medicine is also full of cyborgs, of couplings between organism and machine, each conceived as coded devices, in an intimacy and with a power that was not generated in the history of sexuality. Cyborg 'sex' restores some of the lovely replicative baroque of ferns and invertebrates (such nice organic prophylactics against heterosexism). Cyborg replication is uncoupled from organic reproduction. Modern production seems like a dream of cyborg colonization work, a dream that makes the nightmare of Taylorism seem idyllic. And modern war is a cyber orgy, coded by C^3I, command–control–communication–intelligence, an \$84 billion item in 1984's US defence budget.[1] I am making an argument for the cyborg as a fiction mapping our social and bodily reality and as an imaginative resource suggesting some very fruitful couplings. Michel Foucault's biopolitics is a flaccid premonition of cyber politics, a very open field.

By the late twentieth century, our time, a mythic time, we are all chimeras, theorized and fabricated hybrids of machine and organism; in short, we are cyborgs. The cyborg is our ontology; it gives us our politics. The cyborg is a condensed image of both imagination and material reality, the two joined centres structuring any possibility of historical transformation. In the traditions of 'Western' science and politics – the tradition of racist, male-dominant capitalism; the tradition of progress; the tradition of the appropriation of nature as resource for the production of culture; the tradition of reproduction of the self from the reflections of the other – the relation between organism and machine has been a border war. The stakes in the border war have been the territories of production, reproduction, and imagination. This chapter is an argument for *pleasure* in the confusion of boundaries and for *responsibility* in their construction. It is also an effort to contribute to socialist-feminist culture and theory in a postmodernist, non-naturalist mode and in the utopian tradition of imagining a world without gender, which is perhaps a world without genesis, but

Section 3: Individual

maybe also a world without end. The cyborg incarnation is outside salvation history. Nor does it mark time on an oedipal calendar, attempting to heal the terrible cleavages of gender in an oral symbiotic utopia or post-oedipal apocalypse. As Zoe Sofoulis argues in her unpublished manuscript on Jacques Lacan, Melanie Klein, and nuclear culture, *Lacklein*, the most terrible and perhaps the most promising monsters in cyborg worlds are embodied in non-oedipal narratives with a different logic of repression, which we need to understand for our survival.

The cyborg is a creature in a post-gender world; it has no truck with bisexuality, pre-oedipal symbiosis, unalienated labour, or other seductions to organic wholeness through a final appropriation of all the powers of the parts into a higher unity. In a sense, the cyborg has no origin story in the Western sense – a 'final' irony since the cyborg is also the awful apocalyptic *telos* of the 'West's' escalating dominatioins of abstract individuation, an ultimate self untied at last from all dependency, a man in space. An origin story in the 'Western', humanist sense depends on the myth of original unity, fullness, bliss and terror, represented by the phallic mother from whom all humans must separate, the task of individual development and of history, the twin potent myths inscribed most powerfully for us in psychoanalysis and Marxism. Hilary Klein has argued that both Marxism and psychoanalysis, in their concepts of labour and of individuation and gender formation, depend on the plot of original unity out of which difference must be produced and enlisted in a drama of escalating domination of woman/nature. The cyborg skips the step of original unity, of identification with nature in the Western sense. This is its illegitimate promise that might lead to subversion of its teleology as star wars.

The cyborg is resolutely committed to partiality, irony, intimacy, and perversity. It is oppositional, utopian, and completely without innocence. No longer structured by the polarity of public and private, the cyborg defines a technological polis based partly on a revolution of social relations in the *oikos*, the household. Nature and culture are reworked; the one can no longer be the resource for appropriation or incorporation by the other. The relationships for forming wholes from parts, including those of polarity and hierarchical domination, are at issue in the cyborg world. Unlike the hopes of Frankenstein's monster, the cyborg does not expect its father to save it through a restoration of the garden; that is, through the fabrication of a heterosexual mate, through its completion in a finished whole, a city and cosmos. The cyborg does not dream of community on the model of the organic family, this time without the oedipal project. The cyborg would not recognize the Garden of Eden; it is not made of mud and cannot dream of returning to dust. Perhaps that is why I want to see if cyborgs can subvert the apocalypse or returning to nuclear dust in the manic compulsion to name the Enemy. Cyborgs are not reverent; they do not remember the cosmos. They are wary of holism, but needy for connection – they seem to have a natural feel for united front politics, but without the vanguard party. The main trouble with cyborgs, of course, is that they are the illegitimate offspring of militarism and patriarchal capitalism, not to mention state socialism. But illegitimate offspring are often exceedingly unfaithful to their origins. Their fathers, after all, are inessential.

[...]

Pre-cybernetic machines could be haunted; there was always the spectre of the ghost in the machine. This dualism structured the dialogue between materialism and idealism that was settled by a dialectical progeny, called spirit or history, according to taste. But basically machines were not self-moving, self-designing, autonomous. They could not achieve man's dream, only mock it. They were not man, an author to himself, but only a caricature of that masculinist reproductive dream. To think they were otherwise was paranoid. Now we are not so sure. Late twentieth-century machines have made thoroughly ambiguous the difference between natural and artificial, mind and body, self-developing and externally designed, and many other distinctions that apply to organisms and machines. Our machines are disturbingly lively, and we ourselves frighteningly inert.

[...]

So my cyborg myth is about transgressed boundaries, potent fusions, and dangerous possibilities which progressive people might explore as one part of needed political work. One of my premises is that most American socialists and feminists see deepened dualisms of mind and body, animal and machine, idealism and materialism in the social practices, symbolic formulations, and physical artefacts associated with 'high technology' and scientific culture. From *One-Dimensional Man* to *The Death of Nature*,[2] the analytic resources developed by progressives have insisted on the necessary domination of technics and recalled us to an imagined organic body to integrate our resistance. Another of my premises is that the need for unity of people trying to resist world-wide intensification of domination has never been more acute. But a slightly perverse shift of perspective might better enable us to contest for meanings, as well as for other forms of power and pleasure in technologically mediated societies.

From one perspective, a cyborg world is about the final imposition of a grid of control on the planet, about the final abstraction embodied in a Star Wars apocalypse waged in the name of defence, about the final appropriation of women's bodies in a masculinist orgy of war.[6] From another perspective, a cyborg world might be about lived social and bodily realities in which people are not afraid of their joint kinship with animals and machines, not afraid of permanently partial identities and contradictory standpoints. The political struggle to see from both perspectives at once because each reveals both dominations and possibilities unimaginable from the other vantage point. Single vision produces worse illusions than double vision or many-headed monsters. Cyborg unities are monstrous and illegitimate; in our present political circumstances, we could hardly hope for more potent myths for resistance and recoupling. I like to imagine LAG, the Livermore Action Group, as a kind of cyborg society, dedicated to realistically converting the laboratories that most fiercely embody and spew out the tools of technological apocalypse, and committed to

Section 3: Individual

building a polticial form that actually manages to hold together witches, engineers, elders, perverts, Christian, mothers, and Leninists long enough to disarm the state. Fission Impossible is the name of the affinity group in my town. (Affinity: related not by blood but by choice, the appeal of one chemical nuclear group for another, avidity.)[7]

Notes

1. In 1995–96 the estimated global expenditure on defence was $780 billion. www.osearth.com/resources/wwwproject/index.shtml.
2. Herbert Marcuse, *One-Dimensional Man: Studies in the Ideology of Advanced Industrial Society* (Boston: Beacon Press, 1964); Carolyn Merchant, *The Death of Nature: Women, Ecology and the Scientific Revolution* (New York: Harper and Row, 1980).
3. Zoe Sofia, 'Exterminating Fetuses: Abortion, Disarmament and the Sexo-Semiotics of Extra-Terrestrialism', in *Diacritics* (1984) 14 (2), pp. 47–59.
4. For ethnographic accounts and political evaluations, see Barbara Epstein, *Political Protest and Cultural Revolution: Nonviolent Direct Action in the Seventies and Eighties* (Berkeley: University of California Press, 1992), Noel Sturgeon, *Ecofeminist Natures: Race, Gender, Feminist Theory and Political Action* (London: Routledge, 1997). Without explicit irony, adopting the spaceship earth/whole earth logo of the planet photographed from space, set off by the slogan 'love your mother', the May 1987 Mothers and Others Day action at the nuclear weapons testing facility in Nevada nonetheless took account of the tragic contradictions of views of the earth. Demonstrators applied for official permits to be on the land from officers of the Western Shoshone tribe, whose territory was invaded by the US government when it built the nuclear weapons test ground in the 1950s. Arrested for trespassing, the demonstrators argued that the police and weapons facility personnel, without authorization from the proper officials, were the trespassers. One affinity group at the women's action called themselves the Surrogate Others; and in solidarity with the creatures forced to tunnel in the same ground with the bomb, they enacted a cyborgian emergence from the constructed body of a large, non-heterosexual desert worm.

Henry David Thoreau

Like Ralph Waldo Emerson, Henry David Thoreau (1817–62) lived in Concord, Massachusetts, and Emerson published a eulogy after Thoreau's death.[1] Thoreau's *Walden* is an account of the time he spent building and dwelling in a cabin a mile and a half from Concord, at Walden Pond. The document is a literary classic, stirringly written, and shot through with philosophical speculation and wisdom. The aim while there was to live a life of the utmost simplicity, as close to nature as possible, so as to be in touch with the sources of human needs and feelings, and to rethink the ways in which they were satisfied – or left unsatisfied – in polite society. Thoreau's hut has been adopted as an important reference point in American architectural culture, as a counterpart to the elitist and European Greek temple;[2] it was unpretentious and wholly American – quite pointedly so: Thoreau even moved into it on the fourth of July.[3] The contrasting attitudes to the commissioning of building in the cities of Athens and Sparta are neatly exemplified here – the splendid Greek temple acting as a model for those who aspire to magnificence in their buildings, while Thoreau himself cites Sparta as his ideal. He notices not only the fabric of the buildings but also their cost, measuring their cost as the quantity of life that has been consumed in making them and paying for them. He is constantly aware of the act of building as a process, and it is the process that is valued as good or bad, ethical or unethical. He is unable to see the finished building in isolation from this process, even when the process stopped long ago – as in the example that he gives of the Egyptian pyramids. Thoreau's way of looking at buildings is rigorously and uncomplicatedly moralistic, with no sense in his ethics of needing to find a balance between splendour on the one hand and modest utility on the other. For him the splendour is simply waste, and he is resolutely undazzled by it. Thoreau's appeal is austere and exacting, and it feels like an appeal to the best part of one's character. If this is not the way of the world, then so much the worse for the world.

Walden was not instantly greeted as the treasured work that is has become. Henry Abelove has pointed out that the initial reception of *Walden* was far from being uniformly warm. Thoreau was seen not so much as principled as eccentric; he had an 'odd twist in his brains', and the work would appeal 'to all fops, male and female'.[4] The particular problem that reviewers had was Thoreau's attitudes to domesticity, which failed to include romantic love, marriage, and any aspiration to a bourgeois family set-up; 'to transcend them is Walden's object, and if it fails fully to accomplish this transcending, the object remains'.[5] Abelove draws attention to a passage in which Thoreau entertains and seems to be trying to seduce a 28-year-old woodcutter, and suggests that his writing technique throughout the book is to position the reader as an object of homosexual seduction (though of course the readers are not all young men).[6] This 'queering' of Thoreau's text enables one to see the cabin as a queer space, but as it has been taken up and had so wide an influence on American culture, it is problematic to try to isolate it as a queer phenomenon. Indeed Abelove argues that one aspect of Emerson's eulogy of Thoreau was to neutralize the hints about the basis of Thoreau's 'eccentricity' by means of denials that there had been any affection in his dealings with the young men who gathered round him, and by sentimentalizing Thoreau's intellectual journey using resolutely heterosexual metaphors.[7] While it was arguably necessary to keep Thoreau's sexuality hidden from view in order for him to have widespread influence during the years since his death, it is now possible to draw attention to the fact that once again there is queer space at the heart of a well-established national institution.

Henry Thoreau, from *Walden*

As for a shelter, I will not deny that this is now a necessary of life, though there are instances of men having done without it for long periods in colder countries than this. Samuel Laing says that 'The Laplander in his skin dress, and in a skin bag which he puts over his head and shoulders, will sleep night after night on the snow – in a degree of cold which would extinguish the life of one exposed to it in any woollen clothing'. He had seen them asleep thus. Yet he adds, 'They are not hardier than other people'. But, probably, man did not live long on the earth without discovering the convenience which there is in a house, the domestic comforts, which phrase may have originally signified the satisfactions of the house more than of the family; though these must be extremely partial and occasional in those climates where the house is associated in our thoughts with winter or the rainy season chiefly, and two thirds of the year, except for a parasol, is unnecessary. In our climate, in the summer, it was formerly almost solely a covering at night. In the Indian gazettes a wigwam was the symbol of a day's march, and a row of them cut or painted on the bark of a tree signified that so many times they had camped. Man was not made so large limbed and robust but that he must seek to narrow his world, and wall in a space such as fitted him. He was at first bare and out of doors; but though this was pleasant enough in serene and warm weather, by daylight, the rainy season and the winter, to say nothing of the torrid sun, would perhaps have nipped his race in the bud if he had not made haste to clothe himself with the shelter of a house. Adam and Eve, according to the fable, wore the bower before other clothes. Man wanted a home, a place of warmth, or comfort, first of physical warmth, then the warmth of the affections.

We may imagine a time when, in the infancy of the human race, some enterprising mortal crept into a hollow in a rock for shelter. Every child begins the world again, to some extent, and loves to stay out doors, even in wet and cold. It plays house, as well as horse, having an instinct for it. Who does not remember the interest with which when young he looked at shelving rocks, or any approach to a cave? It was the natural yearning of that portion of our most primitive ancestor which still survived in us. From the cave we have advanced to roofs of palm leaves, of bark and boughs, of linen woven and stretched, of grass and straw, of boards and shingles, of stones and tiles. At last, we know not what it is to live in the open air, and our lives are domestic in more senses than we think. From the hearth to the field is a great distance. It would be well perhaps if we were to spend more of our days and nights without any obstruction between us and the celestial bodies, if the poet did not speak so much from under a roof, or the saint dwell there so long. Birds do not sing in caves, nor do doves cherish their innocence in dovecots.

However, if one designs to construct a dwelling house, it behoves him to exercise a little Yankee shrewdness, lest after all he find himself in a workhouse, a labyrinth without a clew, a museum, an almshouse, a prison, or a splendid mausoleum instead. Consider first how slight a shelter is absolutely necessary. I have seen Penebscot Indians, in this town, living in tents of thin cotton cloth, while the snow was nearly a foot deep around them, and I thought that they would be glad to have it deeper to keep out the wind. Formerly, when how to get my living honestly, with freedom left for my proper pursuits, was a question which vexed me even more than it does now, for unfortunately I am become somewhat callous. I used to see a large box by the railroad, six feet long by three wide, in which the laborers locked up their tools at night, and it suggested to me that every man who was hard pushed might get such a one for a dollar, and, having bored a few auger holes in it, to admit the air at least, get into it when it rained and at night, and hook down the lid, and so have freedom in his love, and in his soul be free. This did not appear the worst, nor by any means a despicable alternative. You could sit up as late as you pleased, and, whenever you got up, go abroad without any landlord or house-lord dogging you for rent. Many a man is harassed to death to pay the rent of a larger and more luxurious box who would not have frozen to death in such a box as this. I am far from jesting. Economy is a subject which admits of being treated with levity, but it cannot be disposed of.

[...]

Near the end of March, 1845, I borrowed an axe and went down to the woods by Walden Pond, nearest to where I intended to build my house, and began to cut down some tall arrowy white pines, still in their youth, for timber. [...] I hewed the main timbers six inches square, most of the studs on two sides only, and the rafters and floor timbers on one side, leaving the rest of the bark on, so that they were just as straight and much stronger than sawed ones. Each stick was carefully mortised or tenoned by its stump, for I had borrowed other tools by this time. [...]

By the middle of April, for I made no haste in my work, but rather made the most of it, my house was framed and ready for the raising. I had already bought the shanty of James Collins, an Irishman who worked on the Fitchburg Railroad, for boards. James Collins' shanty was considered an uncommonly fine one. When I called to see it he was not at home. I walked about the outside, at first unobserved from within, the window was so deep and high. It was of small dimensions, with a peaked cottage roof, and not much else to be seen, the dirt being raised five feet all around as if it were a compost heap. The roof was the soundest part, though a good deal warped and made brittle by the sun. Doorsill there was none, but a perennial passage for the hens under the door board. Mrs. C. came to the door and asked me to view it from the inside. The hens were driven in by my approach. It was dark, and had a dirt floor for the most part, dank, clammy, and aguish, only here a board and there a board which would not bear removal. She lighted a lamp to show me the inside of the roof

Section 3: Individual

and the walls, and also that the board floor extended under the bed, warning me not to step into the cellar, a sort of dust hole two feet deep. In her own words, they were 'good boards overhead, good boards all around, and a good window' [. . .]

I took down this dwelling . . . drawing the nails, and removed it to the pond side by small cartloads, spreading the boards on the grass there to bleach and warp them back again in the sun. [. . .] I began to occupy my house on the 4th of July, as soon as it was boarded and roofed, for the boards were carefully feather-edged and lapped, so that it was perfectly impervious to rain; but before boarding I laid the foundations of a chimney at one end, bringing two cartloads of stones up the hill from the pond in my arms. I built the chimney in the fall, before a fire became necessary for warmth. [. . .]

It would be worth the while to build still more deliberately than I did, considering, for instance, what foundations a door, a window, a cellar, a garret, have in the nature of man, and perchance never raising any superstructure until we found a better reason for it than our temporal necessities even. There is some of the same fitness in a man's building his own house that there is in a bird's building its own nest. Who knows but if men contstructed their dwellings with their own hands, and provided food for themselves and families simply and honestly enough, the poetic faculty would be universally developed, as birds universally sing when they are so engaged? But alas! we do like cowbirds and cuckoos, which lay their eggs in nests which other birds have built, and cheer no traveller with their chattering and unmusical notes. Shall we forever resign the pleasure of construction to the carpenter? What does architeture amount to in the experience of the mass of men? I never in all my walks came across a man engaged in so simple and natural an occupation as building his house. We belong to the community. It is not the tailor alone who is the ninth part of a man; it is as much the preacher, and the merchant, and the farmer. Where is this division of labor to end? and what object does it finally serve? No doubt another may also think for me; but it is not therefore desirable that he should do so to the exclusion of my thinking for myself.

True, there are architects so called in this country, and I have heard of one at least possessed with the idea of making architectural ornaments have a core of truth, a necessity, and hence a beauty, as if it were a revelation to him. All very well perhaps from his point of view, but only a little better than the common dilettantism. A sentimental reformer in architecture, he began at the cornice, not at the foundation. It was only how to put a core of truth within the ornaments, that every sugar plum in fact might have an almond or caraway seed in it, – though I hold that almonds are most wholesome without the sugar, – and not how the inhabitant, the indweller, might build truly within and without, and let the ornaments take care of themselves. What reasonable man ever supposed that ornaments were something outward and in the skin merely, – that the tortoise got his spotted shell, or the shellfish its mother-o'-pearl tints, by such a contract as the inhabitants of Broadway their Trinity Church? But a man has no more to do with the style of architecture of his house than a tortoise with that of its shell: nor need the soldier be so idle as to paint the precise color of his standard. The enemy will find it out. He may turn pale when the trial comes. This man seemed to me to lean over the cornice, and timidly whisper his half truth to the rude occupants who really knew it better than he. What of architectural beauty

I now see, I know has gradually grown from within outward, out of the necessities and character of the indweller, who is the only builder, – out of some unconscious truthfulness, and nobleness, without ever a thought for the appearance; and whatever additional beauty of this kind is destined to be produced will be preceded by a like unconscious beauty of life. The most interesting dwellings in this country, as the painter knows, are the most unpretending, humble log huts and cottages of the poor commonly; it is the life of the inhabitants whose shells they are, and not any peculiarity in their surfaces merely, which makes them *picturesque*; and equally interesting will be the citizen's suburban box, when his life shall be as simple and as agreeable to the imagination, and there is as little straining after effect in the style of his dwelling. A great proportion of architectural ornaments are literally hollow, and a September gale would strip them off, like borrowed plumes, without injury to the substantials. They can do without *architecture* who have no olives nor wines in the cellar. What if an equal ado were made about the ornaments of style in literature, and the architects of our bibles spent as much time about their cornices as the architects of our churches do? So are made the *belles-letters* and the *beaux-arts* and their professors. Much it concerns a man, forsooth, how a few sticks are slanted over him or under him, and what colors are daubed upon his box. It would signify somewhat, if, in any earnest sense *he* slanted them and daubed it; but the spirit having departed out of the tenant, it is of a piece with constructing his own coffin, – the architecture of the grave, and 'carpenter', is but another name for 'coffin-maker'. One man says, in his despair or indifference to life, take up a handful of the earth at your feet, and paint your house that color. Is he thinking of his last and narrow house? . . . better paint your house your own complexion; let it turn pale or blush for you. An enterprise to improve the style of cottage architecture! When you have got my ornaments ready I will wear them.

Before winter I built a chimney, and shingled the sides of my house, which were already impervious to rain, with imperfect and sappy shingles made of the first slice of the log, whose edges I was obliged to straighten with a plane.

I have thus a tight shingled and plastered house, ten feet wide by fifteen long, and eight-feet posts, with a garret and a closet, a large window on each side, two trap doors, one door at the end, and a brick fireplace opposite. The exact cost of my house, paying the usual price for such materials as I used, but not counting the work, all of which was done by myself was as follows [and here Thoreau included a table of materials, their costs totalling $28.12 1/2].

I intend to build me a house which will surpass any on the main street in Concord in grandeur and luxury, as soon as it pleases me as much and will cost me no more than my present one.

I thus found that the student who wishes for a shelter can obtain one for a life time at an expense not greater than the rent which he now pays annually.

[. . .]

Towers and temples are the luxury of princes. A simple and independent mind does not toil at the bidding of any prince. Genius is not a retainer to any emperor, nor is its material silver, or gold, or marble, except to a trifling extent. To what end, pray, is so much stone hammered? In Arcadia, when I was there, I did not see any hammering stone. Nations are possessed with an insane ambition to perpetuate the memory of themselves by the amount of hammered stone they leave. What if equal pains were taken to smooth and polish their manners? One piece of good sense would be more memorable than a monument as high as the moon. I love better to see stones in place. The grandeur of Thebes was a vulgar grandeur. More sensible is a rod of stone wall that bounds an honest man's field than a hundred-gated Thebes that has wandered farther from the true end of life. The religion and civilization which are barbaric and heathenish build splendid temples; but what you might call Christianity does not. Most of the stone a nation hammers goes toward its tomb only. It buries itself alive. As for the Pyramids, there is nothing to wonder at in them so much as the fact that so many men could be found degraded enough to spend their lives constructing a tomb for some ambitious booby, whom it would have been wiser and manlier to have drowned in the Nile, and then given his body to the dogs. I might possibly invent some excuse for them and him, but I have no time for it. As for the religion and love of art of the builders, it is much the same all the world over, whether the building be an Egyptian temple or the United States Bank. It costs more than it comes to. The mainspring is vanity, assisted by the love of garlic and bread and butter. Mr. Balcom, a promising young architect, designs it on the back of his Vitruvius, with hard pencil and ruler, and the job is let out to Dobson & Sons, stonecutters. When the thirty centuries begin to look down on it, man begins to look up to it. As for you high towers and monuments, there was a crazy fellow once in this town who undertook to dig through to China, and he got so far that, as he said, he heard the Chinese pots and kettles rattle; but I think that I shall not go out of my way to admire the hole which he made. Many are concerned about the monuments of the West and the East, – to know who built them. For my part, I should like to know who in those days did not build them, – who were above such trifling.

[...]

The only house I had been the owner of before, if I except a boat, was a tent, which I used occasionally when making excursions in the summer, and this is still rolled up in my garret; but the boat, after passing from hand to hand, has gone down the stream of time. With this more substantial shelter about me, I had made some progress toward settling in the world. This frame, so slightly clad, was a sort of crystallization around me, and reacted on the builder. It was suggestive somewhat as a picture in outlines. I did not need to go out doors to take the air, for the atmosphere within had lost none of its freshness. It was not so much within doors as behind a door where I sat, even in the rainiest weather. The Harivansa says, 'An abode without birds is like a meat without seasoning'. Such was not my abode, for I found myself suddenly neighbour to the birds; not by having imprisoned one, but having caged myself near them. I was not only nearer to some of those which frequent the garden and the orchard, but to those wilder and more thrilling songsters of the forest which never, or rarely, serenade a villager, – the wood-thrush, the veery, the scarlet tanager, the field-sparrow, the whippoorwill, and many others.

[...]

I went to the woods because I wished to live deliberately, to front only the essential facts of life, and see if I could not learn what it had to teach, and not, when I came to die, discover that I had not lived. I did not wish to live what was not life, living is so dear; nor did I wish to practise resignation, unless it was quite necessary. I wanted to live deep and suck out all the marrow of life, to live so sturdily and Spartan-like as to rout all that was not life, to cut a broad swath and shave close, to drive life into a corner, and reduce it to its lowest terms, and, if it proved to be mean, why then to get the whole and genuine meanness of it, and publish its meanness to the world; or if it were sublime, to know it by experience, and be able to give a true account of it in my next excursion. For most men, it appears to me, are in a strange uncertainty about it, whether it is of the devil or of God, and have *somewhat hastily* concluded that it is the chief end of man here to 'glorify God and enjoy him forever'.

Notes

1. Ralph Waldo Emerson, 'Thoreau', in *Atlantic Monthly*, August 1862; reprinted in Henry David Thoreau, *Walden and Civil Disobedience*, edited by Owen Thomas (New York: Norton, 1966) pp. 266–92.
2. W. Barksdale Maynard, Architecture in the United States, 1800–1850 (New Haven: Yale University Press, 2002); W. Barksdale Maynard, 'Thoreau's House at Walden' in *Art Bulletin*, 81, no 2 (June 1999) pp. 1–23; and W. Barksdale Maynard, *Walden Pond: A History* (New York: Oxford University Press, 2004).
3. Thoreau's own account has him moving in on the fourth of July, see below, p. 153.
4. Henry Abelove, 'From Thoreau to Queer Politics', in *Deep Gossip* (Minneapolis: Minnesota University Press, 2003) pp. 29–41; on this topic citing *Emerson and Thoreau: The Contemporary Reviews*, edited by Joel Myerson (Cambridge: Cambridge University Press, 1992) see Abelove, p. 29.
5. Abelove, p. 37.
6. Abelove, pp. 35–6.
7. Abelove, pp. 31–2.

Section 4
Pluralities

The other end of the telescope

Just as identities start to fall apart, and turn into complex interactions of interdependent parts, once we look closely at them, so crowds start to look unified and simple once we move further away from them. The behaviour of groups can be analysed as 'politics', if we want to draw attention to the role of the interactions between people, or as 'psychology' if we want to draw attention to the apparent unity of the group identity. Equally (and indifferently) it would be possible to continue with the image of the machine to describe the formation of the group-identity effects that are being produced. We can project the image of a person as easily into the disc of the full moon, as into the points of light and empty space that we recognize as Orion striding across the sky. Finding human form in ourselves is a special case, but projecting it elsewhere has the logically necessary but intuitively unexpected effect of changing our conception of ourselves. If the pattern of stars in the sky reminds me of a man, and I am a man, then in a strictly logical way I must be as much like the stars as the stars are like me. The identification with the house is more easily made, and is less unsettling in its implications, but what is a city but a large house, and what is a house but a small city?[1] And what about a nation state?

In 1651 Thomas Hobbes proposed an image of the nation as a large-scale individual – Leviathan – envisaging the whole population as an organism with the monarch at its head. There was an illustrated title page, which showed a colossal figure looming over a hilly landscape, with a city in the foreground, wearing a crown, holding a sword and a crozier. On closer inspection the body of this figure can be seen to be composed of the bodies of a vast crowd of more ordinary citizens. In the opening words of his Introduction Hobbes explained the image:

> Nature . . . is by the *Art* of man, as in so many other things, so in this also imitated, that it can make an Artifical Animal. For seeing life is but a motion of Limbs, the beginning whereof is in some principall part within; why may we not say, that all *Automata* . . . have an artificiall life. For what is the *Heart*, but a *Spring*; and the *Nerves*, but so many *Strings*; and the *Joynts*, but so many *Wheeles*, giving motion to the whole Body, such as was intended by the Artificer? *Art* goes yet further, imitating that Rationall and most excellent worke of Nature, *Man*. For by Art is created that great LEVIATHAN called a COMMON-WEALTH, or STATE, (in latine CIVITAS) which is but an Artificiall Man; though of greater stature and strength than the Naturall, for whose protection and defence it was intended; and in which, the *Sovereignty* is an Artificiall *Soul*, as giving life and motion to the whole body; The *Magistrates*,

and other *Officers* of Judicature and Execution, artificiall Joynts; *Reward* and *Punishment* (by which fastned to the seate of the Soveraignty, every joynt and member is moved to performe his duty) are the *Nerves*, that do the same in the Body Naturall; The *Wealth* and *Riches* of all the particular members, are the *Strength*; *Salus Populi* (the peoples safety) its *Buisnesse*; *Counsellors*, by whom all things needful for it to know, are suggested unto it, are the *Memory*; *Equity* and *Lawes*, an artificiall *Reason* and *Will*; *Concord, Health*; *Sedition, Sicknesse*; and *Civill war, Death*. Lastly, the *Pacts* and *Covenants*, by which the parts of this Body Politique were at first made, set together, and united, resemble that *Fiat*, or the *Let us make man*, pronounced by God in the Creation.[2]

The presentation of this idea is not so much that of an extended simile, but is a matter of proposing the metaphor as theory. Thinking about the body politic and its constitution will lead us better to understand the real state of affairs, and (Hobbes's purpose) will allow it to be well governed. The idea that a large group of people can have a collective will and psychology was closely scrutinized in an endlessly fascinating book by Elias Canetti, *Crowds and Power*, in which Canetti, tried to dissect the psychology of the crowd – its ability to form an identity, and to change character – as he had witnessed traumatically in Nazi Germany. The book is itself a crowd, as its observations – as polished as river pebbles – accumulate into something powerful and monumental. Elsewhere there is an essay by Canetti about the architecture of Albert Speer, analysed through the use of Canetti's own ideas about crowds, here particularly the crowd of the dead, which seeks its own inexorable increase.[3] But buildings do not just act as backdrops for the assembly of crowds of people, or represent a crowd's idea of itself. Buildings also can be crowds of stones.

> They are meant to be there for a long time, for a kind of eternity, and should never decrease but remain always as they are. They do not make their way into people's bellies, nor are they always lived in. In their oldest form each separate stone stands for the man who has contributed it to the heap. Later the size and weight of the individual stone increases and each can only be mastered by a number of men working together. Such monuments may represent different things, but each contains the concentrated effort of innumerable difficult journeys. Sometimes it is a mystery how they were erected at all, and the less they can be explained, and the more distant the origin of the stone, the greater the imagined number of their builders and the stronger the impression they make on later generations. They represent the rhythmic exertion of many men, of which nothing remains but indestructible monuments.[4]

The image is of a crowd acting in unison, as a dispersed body, but as a unitary machine. But as we have seen from the previous Section, each of the entities that makes up the dispersed body is already a crowd. In Marvin Minsky's 'society of mind', the mind is composed of thousands of parts, which do relatively simple things. It is when these parts are connected across with one another and act in collaboration that we can begin to do something like thinking.[5] If each of these elements in the mind is seen to be a machine, which can be incorporated into a larger more complex machine capable of doing more sophisticated things, then we have something like the idea of the mind in *Anti-Oedipus*, where Deleuze and Guattari draw a distinction between a paranoid and a schizoid state of mind. The paranoid is very coherent and systematic, and is highly inclined to perceive patterns and order – whether or not it is there. The schizoid mind by contrast works by having its various machines engage less strongly with one another, and act with greater autonomy. These categories do not correspond with those of psychiatrists, but are used freely nevertheless. The schizo taking a stroll at the beginning of Anti-Oedipus identifies with the environment more than with an inner 'self'.

> 'He thought that it must be a feeling of endless bliss to be in contact with the profound life of every form, to have a soul for rocks, metals, water, and plants, to take into himself, as in a dream, every element of nature, like flowers that breathe with the waxing and waning of the moon.' To be a chlorophyll- or photosynthesis-machine, or at least slip his body into such machines as one part among the others. Lenz has projected himself back to a time before the man–nature dichotomy, before all the co-ordinates based on this fundamental dichotomy have been laid down. He does not live nature as nature, but as a process of production. There is no such thing as either man or nature now, only a process that produces the one within the other and couples the machines together. Producing-machines, desiring-machines everywhere, schizophrenic machines, all species of life: the self and the non-self, outside and inside, no longer have any meaning whatsoever.[6]

In the Deleuze-and-Guattari-world the particular assemblage of machines that makes up an 'individual' is very fluid, as the multitude of machines come into contact with and engage with fresh stimuli and then move on. There is no significant change to be made in the description, if we move from the constitution of a personal or a group identity, as they are both effects of recognizing the group as an entity; it is just that we have different common-sense names for these things – a person, a crowd, a community, a nation – in the Deleuze-and-Guattari-world they are all equivalent, as they cohere through the effects of their various connections (transversals) but they operate at different scales. Every identity is a group identity.

Gangs of ancient Rome

Michel Serres' essay on the foundation of Rome, included here ('In the City: Agitated Multiplicity') is a presentation of a passage from the ancient historian Livy. The various bodies that are at work here are not so much individual people as gangs – multitudes, multiplicities – whose interplay shows how town planning and carnage are locked in a passionate embrace, describing a machine that consumes blood and produces the eternal city. It is a story that we have seen rehearsed more recently in Martin Scorsese's film *Gangs of New York*,[7] in which some individual people are presented as characters, but their behaviour and sense of destiny makes sense only when we see their behaviour in groups. Injuries are sustained not only by individuals, but also by gangs, and therefore there is a psychology of the crowd at work, in which the feelings that individuals have seem to take possession of them from outside, just as surely as a set of mechanisms propelled the wild girl of Châlons – mechanisms that she did not normally encounter or recognize, and over which she felt that she had no control. She could sincerely have felt herself to have been possessed by an alien spirit when one thing led to another and she ended up eating her sister. She did not normally engage with those mechanisms and had no idea how they would make her behave, how exhilarated they would make her feel, and how unable to hold back or to see her actions in those moments in the way that the world would see them in the cold light of day. In *Gangs of New York* the brutality of the street fighting is vividly depicted, and we see in the opening moments an uncomprehending child witness the group identity taking hold of people, bonding them together into a unified throng, which seems sullen until the action starts, at which point it is exhilarated to the point that individuals are prepared to die for the sake of the survival of the identity of the group. 'Foundation occurs when a multiplicity makes itself into a unity,' says Michel Serres, 'The multitude is formed around the unity of the corpse, around the place of the dead'.[8] There is an atmosphere of topology and physics about Serres' essay. 'Multiplicity' and 'singularity' are terms in Reimann's and Poincaré's mathematics (lucidly explained by Manuel Delanda)[9] and the crowds undergo various phase transitions, from a solid to a turbulent fluid state, or an evenly dispersed gas. Set theory is mentioned, and a threshold of crystallization or coagulation.[10] 'A bizarre mathematics or a bizarre chemistry.'[11] There is an idea that the city is formed from the action of these multiplicities – 'Does the built city harden the designs of heated, fluid multiplicities . . .?'[12] There is an allusion to the Situationist slogan 'beneath the paving slabs, the beach!', when Serres says 'underneath the conceptual pavement, lies the sandy myriad of the beach'.[13] But whereas for the Situationists the slogan was a clear invitation to shed cultural inhibitions, for Serres it is not clear that we would want to throw the paving slabs away – they are what the grains of sand, acting collectively have achieved. 'The multiple makes itself one by a change of phase'.[14] Serres seems to feel unclear whether he has found a useful metaphor here, or is describing a process that has real similarities with the transition from one physical state to another. My view is that if the metaphor is indeed useful, then we should use it, which is what Shelley would certainly have advised. If many people find it useful then in due course it will come to be seen as a self-evident truth, and will not be thought of as metaphor. If only a few of us use it then it will be an arcane secret. The 'ichnography' of urban architecture, to which Serres makes reference,[15] usually means its plan, but embedded in the word is the metaphor of its original coining. It derives from the Greek words ιχνος, which means a track or a trace, and γραφειν, to draw. It is closely related to the word 'ichnology', which is the study of fossil footprints. It implies (which is to say, literally, it 'folds in') a particular understanding of what the plan is – a marking out of traces that will be turned into walls – but also a predictive study of the tracks left by the occupants of the building, or those who pass through it. Ichnography is the tracing of the patterns of life, and it is life that will be shaped by the building once the building has solidified around this activity. In order that it be shaped sympathetically the life must be anticipated by the architect. Alternatively the life will invade the building and will find ways of thriving there despite anything that the architect might have imagined. The second of these is bound to happen whenever we are faced with an old building – and for our purposes here we could define an 'old' building as one whose envisaged purpose has fallen into obsolescence. Sometimes this shift is gentle, such as when a building continues in use as a house, but the pattern of use changes over time. Sometimes it is brutal, such as when a revolutionary change brings with it the destruction of the old iconographies. Sometimes it is just bizarre, such as when it is noticed that the cellular arrangement of a notorious prison would make it adapt easily into a luxurious hotel where celebrities aspire to stay.[16] The marking out of a plan therefore becomes a matter of the tracing of lives, or the fragments of lives that cross the threshold of the building. Some of these lives will be virtual – the possible lives of possible occupants imagined by the architect – others will be actual – the lives of the people who come into contact with the building. The gap, even when the building is new, can show, either because the architect made false assumptions about what kind of lives other people actually live,[17] or because perhaps it suits me for example to buy a standard sort of house designed for an imagined family life, and then adapt it to my own ends by putting up bookshelves and removing most of the doors.

Crowded house

As the 'individual' is already a micropolitical crowd, the household is always crowded. Just as Edgar Allen Poe's 'man of the crowd' engages with the various crowd-machines and becomes part of different mechanisms, thereby being possessed by different personae,[18] so the house can be overtaken by different sorts of crowds that make it work in different modes, and take on different characters at different times. The house when I am here alone, writing, preparing food, talking on the telephone, brings into play a set of machines that lie dormant when I am not engaged with them. A different set of machines is made when I entertain, and a group of visitors sit round talking to one another. More chairs are in use, the lighting is different, the apparatus in the kitchen is made to work to the limit of its capacity, and my attention is directed to the various people in the room, rather than focused on a text or a screen, or the view. I must behave as if I were in a less private place than my house usually is. It becomes a different kind of space, but it is the same building, just being used in a different way. Deleuze and Guattari, when they discuss the way in which people take on different *personae* introduce the idea of 'becoming' – in the sense that for example the wild girl of Châlons might be said to have 'become-wolf' when she attacked her sister, or to follow Deleuze and Guattari's usage more precisely, to have engaged with her 'wolf-becomings'.

> A becoming is not a correspondence between relations. But neither is it a resemblance, an imitation, or, at the limit, an identification. . . . Above all, becoming does not occur in the imagination, even when the imagination reaches the highest cosmic or dynamic level, as in Jung and Bachelard. Becomings-animal are neither dreams nor phantasies. They are perfectly real. But which reality is at issue here? For if becoming animal does not consist in playing animal or

imitating an animal, it is clear that the human being does not 'really' become an animal any more than the animal 'really' becomes something else.[19]

An example: Do not imitate a dog, but make your organism enter into composition with something else in such a way that the particles emitted from the aggregate thus composed will be canine as a function of the relation of movement and rest, or of molecular proximity, into which they enter.[20]

There are machines that we have in common with animals, and when they come into play then I do not want to say 'I decided to behave like a wolf', or 'I imitated a wolf', what I want to say is that I reacted instinctively to the situation, and I behaved in a wolf-like way, or to compress the image to say that I momentarily became wolf. This might sound too lurid and psychotic to be applicable in everyday circumstances, but surely it is only the most broken-spirited who are not at some point in touch with some undomesticated side of their nature. It is quite possible to read Hermann Hesse's *Steppenwolf* and understand the tensions involved, without being insane oneself. Deleuze and Guattari dismiss domesticated animals, pets who have learnt to behave like us are only sentimental attachments from which we can learn nothing but our own problems.[21] However the process of becoming-domestic is something that we all go through as we are inculcated into the ways of society. We turn ourselves into something like pets, so that we can live contentedly in our social groups, and need not be too surprised if from time to time a wild animal asserts its presence in domestic violence or crimes of passion. Nicolas Philibert's film *Être et avoir* shows in an accessible way the kinds of lessons that are learnt in early education, and how these lessons do not come naturally, but are direct and brutal in their non-negotiability, even when gently and considerately administered.[22] The most harrowing scene is one where a very small child has been left at the school for the first time, and he wants his mother. The piteous wails are heartbreaking, but the schoolteacher, who has seen this before, has endless patience. Gently, caringly, the child will be broken – it is inevitable – the outcome is not in question, no matter how determinedly the child rails against it. Le Corbusier, writing about the house, remarked that it is 'an object that interests both the beast and the head in us, because being inside it we submit to its constraint'.[23] The beast knows that it is to behave in a domesticated way when it is inside the house. This idea links back to Bataille's idea of architecture as the instrument of the expression of the order of the state, or of power. The great difference between Bataille and Le Corbusier is that Le Corbusier longed to become an instrument of the state, and did not much care which one, if it would commission his ideas for buildings. Le Corbusier had ideas, but by himself he was without the means to actualize them. As a means to this end he invented an architectural *persona*, to which he gave the name 'Le Corbusier' (which suggests an engagement in crow-becoming). He wrote:

> Le Corbusier is a pseudonym. Le Corbusier works exclusively in architecture. He pursues disinterested ideas. He has no right to compromise himself through betrayals and accommodations. He is an entity freed from the weight of the flesh. He must never (but will he manage to?) fall.

Ch. Édouard Jeanneret is the man of the flesh who has experienced all the adventures – whether thrilling or heartbreaking – of a rather eventful life.[24]

The benign but insignificant Charles Édouard Jeanneret, like Dr Jekyll, allowed an alternative *persona* into his life, and that character somehow had more vitality and energy than his creator, and after a few years took over altogether. The artificially constructed Le Corbusier is a mineral-becoming of Charles Édouard Jeanneret. He has identified himself with his buildings, and has become hard and inflexible. It was Le Corbusier who sang the eulogy of the right-angle, and loftily poured scorn on the donkey in its preference for the geometries of convenience – the non-orthogonal line that makes the shortest track across a space.[25] The buildings produced by animals testify to the generalization of this 'donkey geometry', whether it is birds, ants or beavers who are doing the building. The general principle involved is always different from the method of establishing axes that was taught at the École des Beaux Arts, or that of establishing a grid. The invention of that concept, the grid, as a way of composing cities was attributed in the ancient world to Hippodamus of Miletus – a Greek from Asia Minor – and in the modern world is most famously embodied in the street plan of the greater part of Manhattan – the capital of the twentieth century. By contrast the medieval citadel with its non-geometric mazes of street and alleyways was composed donkey-fashion, the roads taking the lines of least resistance up hills that were selected as settlement sites because they were defensible spots, and the rule of law was not to be taken for granted. The buildings of animals can have striking visual appeal, and when a selection is made with this aim in mind it can seem as if the animals have some kind of innate aesthetic sensibility,[26] but we are deceiving ourselves if we really think that that is the case. The animals' decisions are taken in relation to local circumstances, responding to the circumstances of the place, including the parts of the place that they themselves have built. When we respond positively to these buildings, it is because there is a feeling of an inner logic working its way through from within, related to the bodily needs of the occupants, and to the limitations – or more probably the unexpected possibilities – of the chosen building materials. So a nest is made of twigs that are selected from those available, and secured in high branches, working through to a down-lined bowl with a fine finish. The huge collective nests of the weaverbirds (*Philetairus socius*) for example seem to have the kind of discipline that one would find in a medieval village too small to have a church for the houses to cluster around.[27] Turning from these dwellings to the gridded right-angled city, it is as though we are so afraid of the animal-becomings in us, that we cauterize them out and make ourselves more or less autistic in the process. It was the mineral-hard uncompromising Le Corbusier that the twentieth-century world made into a hero, while the humane Charles Édouard Jeanneret was left in the shadow of his monster.

Colette's cat-becoming

Nobody has described better than Colette how our emotions take us off in directions that reason would argue against. She was often photographed with cats, and there is even a picture of her dressed as a cat. One might have taken her to be just sentimentally fond of animals, were it not for her novella *La Chatte* (The Cat) published in 1933. It is about a young man and woman, who marry and set up home together. It doesn't work. The domestic arrangements never quite fall into place, and they realize their incompatibility. The cat is at the heart of all this. The young wife would say – does say – that the husband (Alain) is too fond of his cat. But that is to miss the point – and she consistently does miss the point, we are not on her side in this narrative – the point being that the cat is the point of external contact that articulates Alain's cat-becoming, which is an important part of him. The wife (Camille) has no cat-becoming, or is not in contact with it, and she is presented as if she has no soul, despite having all the outward appearance of attractive qualities. Moreover Camille is at home in the modern world in a way that Alain is not. He is in touch with more primitive, even pre-human, instincts. In order to accommodate their new household in the house where Alain grew up, and where his mother still lives, various changes are being made, and one of the early signs that all will not be well is that Alain does not feel comfortable with them. Alain and the cat, Saha,

> inspected with equal hostility the pile of rubbish, a new French window, devoid of panes, inserted in a wall, various bathroom appliances, and some porcelain tiles.
>
> Equally offended, they calculated the damage done to their past and their present. An old yew had been torn up and was very slowly dying upside down, with its roots in the air. 'I ought never, never to have allowed that,' muttered Alain, 'It's a disgrace. You've only known it for three years Saha, that yew. But I...'
>
> At the bottom of the hole left by the yew, Saha sensed a mole whose image, or rather whose smell went to her head. For a minute she forgot herself to the point of frenzy, scratched like a fox-terrier and rolled over like a lizard. She jumped on all four paws like a frog, clutched a ball of earth between her thighs as a fieldmouse does with the egg it has stolen; escaped from the hole by a series of miracles, and found herself sitting on the grass, cold and prudish and recovering her breath.
>
> Alain stood gravely by, not moving. He knew how to keep a straight face when Saha's demons possessed her beyond her control. The admiration and understanding of cats was innate in him.[28]

The point about the cat, so far as this story is concerned, is that the lessons of domesticity do not quite stick, and the cat is really more at home stalking in the garden, where we first meet her, and on her first appearance inside the house she is climbing the brocade-covered wall, almost to the ceiling.[29] The cat-becoming is an element of Alain that finds no room for expression in the modernist apartment where he and Camille lodge temporarily while the building works are carried out. Instead of brocade there is sailcloth – sailcloth that will never be old like the brocade, because even though it is new it is already decaying from the sunlight that pours in superabundantly from large expanses of glass – and rooms that are either triangular or square. (Colette repeatedly mentions the triangularity, which becomes an index of the building's alienating character.) The apartment is on the ninth floor. There is a glass-topped dressing table. Camille likes this apartment, just as she likes driving the car. With her good teeth and bright eyes, she is the heartless representative of a mineral-based sensibility that the narrator seems to despise. She has to go, not just for the sake of Alain's relationship with his cat, but so that cat-becoming in him can survive.

Possible worlds

Nelson Goodman's *Ways of Worldmaking* is a short book that shows how few pages are needed to remake the world. It is represented here in a review by Paul Ricoeur, which summarizes its main arguments and makes it even shorter. The idea that I want to take up from it is the idea that different groups of people make use of different ideas for dealing with the world, and that these groups could be said to be living in different worlds, because the set of experiences of one group will not map directly on to the set of experiences of another. I would normally use the term 'cultures' to discuss these different groups, but in the current context one might as easily think of them as multiplicities or crowds, and the important thing about them is their plurality. One does not design a world, but one inhabits it. It will overlap with and engage with other people's worlds, but if we start trying to analyse where the ideas come from, and which social groups they belong to, then anyone engaged with anything other than the most parochial culture (and you, as a reader of this book, are certainly more exploratory than that) is bound to notice a degree of hybridity in their culture, and in their world, or in the worlds that they move between.

The range of cultural expectations, and our ideas about how it is proper to behave, will shift as we move from group to group, and our identity can shift also. We behave differently at home, at school, in the army, behind the steering wheel of a car, with new acquaintances, and if we had no idea of the different decorums that each role required, then we would at best find ourselves faced with social embarrassments and a limited circle of friends, and at worst would be arrested or killed. The same sort of thing happens to buildings, when different crowds assemble round them, identities multiply. To take a very well-known building as an example: the Villa Savoye is one of Le Corbusier's houses of the 1920s, and its image is well known to everyone with an architectural education. In the Le Corbusier-world, the world that was set apart from the full life of Charles Édouard Jeanneret, the Villa Savoye is found in company with various other villas and dwellings of the 1920s, and projects for cities as yet unrealized. The Villa Savoye in this grouping is normative. It looks as if it embodies clearly and in an exemplary fashion the principles that should guide the architecture of the future. It is in touch with the modern world, with modern construction methods, and embodies the five-point programme for architecture that Le Corbusier promoted so vigorously: the house lifted off the ground, with a garden on the roof, structural concrete, a free plan, and continuous long windows around the perimeter. It stands as an image of machinic perfection, its whiteness like that of an ocean liner, adrift in a field in the countryside not too far from Paris. In the Le Corbusier-world this is how all architecture should be.

In another grouping the identity is different. If we want to have an idea of what houses were like in the 1920s, then the Villa Savoye is a building we are very likely to find in the architectural history books, as it is one of the best-known buildings of that time; but actually it is highly unrepresentative of the mass of building output of the era. That was what made it special, and why we might want to single it out for particular attention, but its qualification to represent the times is highly suspect. Nearly all other houses were much more traditional in their layout and construction, and served their occupants well enough in the ways they expected. If we are trying to characterize the identity of 1920s housing then the Villa Savoye is so atypical as to fall outside our consideration, and so the building's identity in the 1920s building-world is marginal to the point of invisibility.

Another way to see the building is in terms of its micropolitics. The villa is so iconic an image of modernity, that it comes as a surprise when one examines the plans to find that there are rooms for servants, who have fallen out of the picture where all but the very richest homes are concerned in the twenty-first century, and few people now alive have any personal memory of living with servants in the house. The arrangements for a chauffeur and housekeeper therefore look oddly old fashioned. The dramatically open space of the main living room upstairs, that opens out on to a terrace, is glamorous and would make an outstandingly good venue for a party, but it is not a space for the whole year round, as the house was not supplied with insulation, and the means to heat such a space in winter would have been extraordinary. This is a villa to visit, not a house that would act as a family's main base, and it would only have been used during the warmer parts of the year. One reason that it was possible for it to be taken on as an extreme and uncompromising venture on the part of the owners was that it did not have to carry the full burden of identity-making. They could retreat into modernity for summer weekends, and perform modernity to astound their friends, but they did not have to live their modernity all the time. The pattern of life that this reveals has links back into a world of privilege and wealth, that found expression for example in Palladio's villas on the Veneto – and their proportioning system seems to have informed Le Corbusier's designs.[30] There is a world of social exclusivity here, which is never discussed in the books that treat architectural history as a story about the development of pure form, and yet it is a very important driving force in making people want to employ architects and in setting up expensive environments that carry social prestige whether because they are furnished in ways that display the trophies of power and acquisition, or because they show a sophisticated understanding of culture and of admired ways of living. The Villa Savoye had high social standing in the avant-garde art-world of the 1920s, but as it is no longer in private hands it has been taken out of that world, and is now visited for its cultural standing, which is the afterlife that some such architectural treasures enjoy.

The fact remains that in the world of cat-becoming, and indeed in the Colette-world more generally, the building would have low standing because it was never a good place to keep a cat, or to live as a cat. The house is removed from the natural garden, and contact with the earth, it has no deep shade, and no secrets. If the souls of the people who live here are to be saved, then it would be through their other house. This villa suppresses one's cat-becoming – makes it difficult or impossible to

Section 4: Pluralities

engage that side of one's unconscious – and therefore in the Colette-world such a building becomes murderous, as it turns the inhabitants into paler mineralized Le Corbusiers. They have to embrace the automobile to arrive here, and their pre-human becomings are either disconnected or annihilated. It becomes possible in such a building to murder a cat without ever quite noticing that one has done something wrong.[31] The attempted murder in Colette's story takes place on a triangular balcony with a door in its hypotenuse.[32] Grouped in such company, the Villa Savoye's identity turns into something more sinister, and to take up residence in it would imperil one's character. But notice how difficult it is to talk about such a subject. It is possible that it is important, but this discourse is easily set aside as madness or sentimentality. It is Camille, the unsuccessful murderer, whose mounting indignation brings her to say to Alain: '*You're* the monster'. And she is confident that she is right. And no protestation from the Colette-world would convince her otherwise. And the rhetoric of common-sense discourse is with Camille all the way. It is a testament to Colette's skill and the penetration of her insight that the story is told in such a way as to carry us along with it for as long as it does, before allowing the cold water of Camille's common sense to wake us from reverie.

Notes

1. Leon Battista Alberti, *De re aedificatoria in libri decem . . .* (1486) translated by Joseph Rykwert, Neil Leach and Robert Tavernor, *On the Art of Building in Ten Books* (Cambridge, Mass.: MIT, 1988) p. 23, see above, p. 7.
2. Thomas Hobbes, *Leviathan* (1651) Introduction [recent edition: Harmondsworth: Penguin, 1968, pp. 81–2].
3. Elias Canetti, 'Hitler According to Speer', in *Das Gaswissen der Worte*, translated by J. Neugroschel, *The Conscience of Words* (London: Seabury Press/André Deutsch, 1986).
4. Elias Canetti, translated by Carol Stewart, *Crowds and Power* (Harmondsworth: Penguin, 1973) p. 88.
5. Marvin Minsky, *The Society of Mind* (London: Heinemann, 1987). Cross refer to previous section.
6. Anti-Oedipus, p. 2. Quotation from Georg Büchner, *Lenz*, translated by Carl Richard Mueller in *Complete Plays and Prose* (New York: Hill and Wang, 1963) p. 141.
7. Herbert Asbury, *The Gangs of New York* (New York: Knopf, 1927); filmed by Martin Scorsese, 2002.
8. Michel Serres, *Rome: le livre des fondations* (Paris: Grasset, 1983) translated by Felicia McCarren, *Rome: the Book of Foundations* (Stanford, California: Stanford University Press, 1991) p. 232; 'In the City', included below, p. 183ff.
9. Manuel Delanda, *Intensive Science and Virtual Philosophy* (London: Continuum, 2002).
10. Michel Serres, *Rome*, op. cit., pp. 246, 249.
11. Ibid., p. 239.

12. Ibid., p. 243.
13. Ibid., p. 246.
14. Ibid., p. 251.
15. Ibid., p. 243.
16. These examples are taken from the essays by Laura Hollengreen and Zeynep Kezer. Chapters 4 and 10 respectively of *Architecture as Experience*, edited by Dana Arnold and Andrew Ballantyne (London: Routledge, 2004).
17. Russell Ellis and Dana Cuff, *Architects' People* (Oxford: Oxford University Press, 1989).
18. Edgar Allen Poe, 'The Man of the Crowd' – included below, p. 204.
19. Gilles Deleuze and Félix Guattari, *Mille plateaux: capitalisme et schizophrénie 2* (Paris: Editions de Minuit, 1980) translated by Brian Massumi, *A Thousand Plateaus: Capitalism and Schizophrenia 2* (London: Athlone, 1987) pp. 237–8.
20. Ibid., p. 274.
21. Ibid., p. 240.
22. Nicolas Philibert, *Être et avoir*, Maïa films, Arte France Cinéma, Les Films d'ici CNDP (2002).
23. Le Corbusier, *Une maison – un palais*, (Paris: G. Crès et Cie, 1928) p. 4; cited by Jean-Louis Cohen, 'Le Corbusier's Nietzschean Metaphors' in *Nietzsche and 'An Architecture of Our Minds'*, edited by Alexandre Kostka and Irving Wohlfarth (Los Angeles: Getty Research Institute, 1999) p. 320.
24. Le Corbusier (Charles Édouard Jeanneret) letter to Josef Červ, 18 January 1926, as cited by Patricia Seckler, 'Le Corbusier, Jeanneret, Patented Ideas and the Urbanistic Cell', La ville et l'urbanisme après Le Corbusier, Actes du colloque des 23–26 septembre 1987 (La Chaux-de-Fonds: Editions d'En Haut, 1993) p. 123; cited by Jean-Louis Cohen, 'Le Corbusier's Nietzschean Metaphors' in *Nietzsche and 'An Architecture of Our Minds'*, edited by Alexandre Kostka and Irving Wohlfarth (Los Angeles: Getty Research Institute, 1999) p. 318.
25. Le Corbusier, *La poème de l'angle droit* (Paris: 1955).
26. See for example Juhani Pallasmaa, *Animal Architecture* (Helsinki: Museum of Finnish Architecture, 2002).
27. Juhani Pallasmaa, *Animal Architecture* (Helsinki: Museum of Finnish Architecture, 2002) p. 3.
28. Colette, *La Chatte* (Paris: 1933); translated by Antonia White, 'The Cat', in *Gigi and The Cat* (London: Random House, 2001) p. 79. See also Judith Thurman, *Secrets of the Flesh: A Life of Colette* (New York: Knopf, 1999) and Julia Kristeva, Le Génie féminin, tome 3, *Colette* (Paris, Fayard, 2002), trans. by Jane Marie Todd (New York: Columbia University Press, 2004).
29. Colette, *The Cat*, op. cit., p. 69.
30. Colin Rowe, 'The Mathematics of the Ideal Villa', in *The Mathematics of the Ideal Villa and Other Essays* (Cambridge, Mass.: MIT, 1976) pp. 1–27.
31. Colette, *The Cat*, op. cit., p. 155.
32. Ibid., pp. 127–9.

Paul Ricoeur and Nelson Goodman

The essay here is by one philosopher, Paul Ricoeur (born 1913), reviewing a book by another, Nelson Goodman (1906–98). Both philosophers have done important work on metaphor and the review is less a critique than an exposition, as it is read from a very sympathetic point of view. Ricoeur's particular theme in his hermeneutic philosophy, is interpretation; while Goodman's was the construction of 'worlds' through symbolic structures. His point, with a nod to William James's *Pluralist Universe*, is that by deploying different conceptual frameworks – scientific, poetic, painterly or whatever – we generate different worlds of experience, and in them find different sorts of truths. There is no single world-view that can legitimately lay claim to generating the only correct view of the world, and this is not a problem, but something to celebrate. The content of Goodman's book, which is already short and clear, is set out in a highly disciplined way that makes it even shorter and clearer.[1] It is my contention that we design buildings that fit in with our understanding of what the world is, or what it is about it that matters, so where we have a plurality of worlds we have a plurality of approaches to design and of ways of dealing with buildings that are already built (which form a part of the world as given). In the Thoreau-world for example the means by which a building was built are very important, but that is not the case to nearly the same extent in the commercial world that finances speculative building projects. Ernst Cassirer (1874–1945) is mentioned in the text. He was a philosopher of culture, who saw the human being as 'the symbolizing animal'. Having fled the Nazis, in later life he wrote about political myths and irrational forces in the state.[2] Goodman's plurality is argued on philosophical rather than political grounds, but as in the work of John Dewey, or Richard Rorty, there is a feeling that each drives the other along.

Notes

1. Nelson Goodman, *Languages of Art: An Approach to a Theory of Symbols* (Indianapolis: Hackett, 1976); Nelson Goodman, *Ways of Worldmaking* (Indianapolis: Hackett, 1978); Nelson Goodman, 'How Buildings Mean' in *Critical Inquiry*, June 1978, pp. 642–53; Paul Ricoeur, *La métaphore vive* (Paris: Editions du Seuil, 1975), trans. by Robert Czerny, Kathleen McLaughlin and John Costello, *The Rule of Metaphor* (Toronto: University of Toronto Press, 1978).
2. Ernst Cassirer, *Philosophie der symbolischen Formen*, 3 vols (Berlin: Bruno Cassirer, 1923–9); translated by R. Mannheim, *The Philosophy of Symbolic Forms*, 3 vols (New Haven, Connecticut: Yale University Press, 1955–7); vol. 1: *Language*; vol. 2, *Mythical Thought*; vol. 3, *The Phenomenology of Knowledge*.

Review of Nelson Goodman's *Ways of Worldmaking*

The seven chapters which compose Goodman's new book will be no surprise for readers of *Fact, Fiction, and Forecast* and *Languages of Art*. But these readers will be confronted by the most radical and the most condensed exposition of the author's philosophy (plus some internal excursions, if I dare say so, which add the pleasure of discovery to that of recognition).

I

The thesis is simple, rigorous, and uncompromising. For the sake of didactic clarity, I analyse it in three partial theses:

1 / *We 'make' the world by construing symbolic systems* (in a sense of the word symbol akin to Ernst Cassirer's use of the term)[1] *which are numerous and equally legitimate: descriptive theories, perceptions, novels, paintings, musical scores, etc. (Thesis I)*

In order to help the reader to exercise the thesis, the author starts with a familiar example which implies only statements, but whose truth-claims are at odds with each other: 'The sun always moves,' 'The sun never moves.' We are ready to rewrite the two statements in such a way that the emphasis is shifted from what is described to systems of description: 'Under frame of reference A, the sun always moves, and under frame of reference B, the sun never moves.' A more difficult step is taken when we juxtapose and conjoin two pictures, say, a Van Gogh and a Canaletto, or a picture and a statement. All of them are equally versions or visions (I shall return in my critical part to this duplication of terms) of the world.

This first phase of the theory recalls Cassirer, but more strikingly radicalizes him. In the *Philosophy of Symbolic Forms*, linguistic forms, mythical and aesthetical forms, and scientific forms were indeed held as distinct and irreducible (in a cultural rather than transcendental sense of the term 'form'), but Cassirer's pluralism was still a mixed one to the extent that symbolic forms taken together constitute a teleological development ruled by the mind's thrust towards objectivity, i.e., scientific knowledge. In that sense the system of symbolic forms remains a hierarchical system. Unlike Cassirer, Goodman sees no such hierarchy obtaining between versions and visions. 'Just this, I think: that many different world-versions are of independent interest and importance, without any requirement or presumption of reducibility to a single base' (p. 4). In that sense, his pluralism is a radical pluralism.

Section 4: Pluralities

2 / *Each of these ways of world making is a world-version rather than a version of the world, in the sense that there is no world in itself before or beneath these versions. (Thesis II)*

This thesis is supported by the lack of any test that could allow us to compare a version to a world which would be neither described, nor perceived, nor depicted. Here, too, Goodman radicalizes a thesis that Cassirer had developed in *Function and Substance*, before writing his *Philosophy of Symbolic Forms*: by dissolving substance into function, Cassirer had completed the demolition of the thing in itself, insofar as the priority of the category of substance over that of causality among the triadic set of Kant's categories of relation could still offer a basis for reinstating the thing in itself. The same negative argument may be put in the following terms: there is no way of showing that two versions are of the *same* world, because the question 'same or not the same?' must be complemented by the addition of 'same what?' Then the use of the term *same* is always relative to a homogeneous kind. We may only say that versions differ in that not everything belonging to one belongs to the other, or that there is no more a unique world of worlds than there is a unique world (p. 17).

Therefore we must drop the idea that versions are versions of one and the same neutral and underlying world. As a corollary to this second stage of the thesis, we have to say that no version is the basic one and the others derivative, as physicalism does say of the physical world, phenomenalism of the perceptual world, and the man in the street of interpretations based on custom and prejudice. And if somebody asks out of what worlds are made, we have to answer: from other worlds, from worlds already on hand. The making is a remaking. In that way, the radical pluralism of the author is at the same time a radical relativism.

3 / *World versions other than the scientific one are neither true nor false. And yet some may be said to be right and others wrong. There must be therefore criteria to assign or to deny rightness to non-descriptive world versions. (Thesis III)*

This thesis first imposes a twofold limit to the concept of truth. First the question of truth makes sense only if a version is verbal and consists in statements. For non-verbal versions and verbal versions without statements, truth is irrelevant. Second, within these limits, truth cannot be defined or tested by agreements with the world, since one cannot compare a description to a non-described world. We can only say that 'a version is taken to be true when it offends no unyielding beliefs and none of its own precepts' (p. 17). '"The truth, the whole truth, and nothing but the truth" would thus be a perverse and paralyzing policy for any worldmaker' (p. 19). Now, what is *rightness* has still to be shown. But it is impossible to proceed farther without incorporating within the thesis some fundamental *rules of categorization* concerning the functioning of symbolic systems which are mainly imported from *Languages of Art*.

II

This reference to the scheme of organization governing symbolic systems proposed in *Languages of Art* requires from the reader of *Ways of Worldmaking* a rare mental effort. 'The pluralists' acceptance of versions other than physics implies no relaxation of rigor but a recognition that standards different from yet no less exacting than those applied in science are appropriate for appraising what is conveyed in perceptual or pictorial or literary versions' (p. 5). The difficulty is duplicated by the fact that this last book proceeds mainly by allusions and footnotes sending back to the appropriate chapters of *Languages of Art*. This is why it may be helpful to give at least a rough draft of this scheme.

The reader must take as a guideline the statement which closes the first chapter of *Ways of Worldmaking* that arts are *cognitive*: 'All the processes of world making I have discussed enter into knowing' (p. 22). Then he must learn to master the technical tools which allow us to ascribe reference and rightness to symbols which are neither verbal nor descriptive. The key distinctions occur within the framework of the *referential* function of all symbols, which implies nothing else and nothing more than that all symbolic systems are capable of making and remaking the world, of 'reorganizing the world in terms of works and works in terms of the world' (*Languages of Art*, p. 241). The key distinctions concern the appropriate use of such terms as denotation, description, depiction, exemplification, and expression, which together constitute the conceptual network of both books. Denotation defines the kind of referential function obtaining in the subclass of symbols which may be said to be *applied* to items. Exemplification, as we shall see, does something other than denoting, in spite of the fact that it refers in its own way. The two main kinds of denotation symbols are verbal descriptions and non-verbal depictions. Verbal descriptions apply 'labels' to occurrences. These 'labels' may be applied literally or metaphorically. Metaphors are merely unusual applications of 'labels,' i.e., applications of familiar labels (whose usage consequently has a past) to new objects: 'metaphor is an affair between a predicate with a past and an object that yields while protesting' (*Languages of Art*, p. 73). In that sense, we may speak of metaphorical truth, to the extent that we already speak of literal truth. Now the grouping of description and depiction under the same heading of denotation has as its aim to assimilate the relation between a picture and what it depicts to that between a predicate and that to which it is applied. At the same time, it says that representing (or depicting) is not imitating in the sense of resembling or copying. In that way, pictures are one of the ways through which nature becomes a product of discourse and of art. (By extension we may call 'labels' all symbols which denote: nouns, predicates, gestures, pictures.) We leave the subclass of denotative symbols when we introduce 'samples' and 'exemplifications.' Here, we no longer apply a given label to a something. We have the sample and we look for the property, the feature which is thus exemplified and which the sample 'possesses.' 'Samples' in that way refer too, but reference, here, runs in the opposite direction from denotation (i.e., description and depiction). 'Exemplification and expression, though running in the opposite direction from denotation – that is from the symbol to a literal or metaphorical feature of it instead of to something the symbol applies to – are no less symbolic referential functions and instruments of worldmaking' (*Ways of Worldmaking*, p. 12). What is most interesting for our discussion of *Ways of Worldmaking* is 1 / that such non-linguistic symbols as forms, feelings, affinities, contrasts may be exemplified; 2 / that exemplification, as well as application, may be literal or metaphorical, i.e., unusually extended or

Section 4: Pluralities

expanded. It is in that guise that we say that a painting 'expresses' sadness. Sadness is exemplified literally by human faces or gestures and expressed metaphorically by paintings, musical pieces, etc. Exemplification and expression are thus referential without being denotational. One may give a graphic sketch of this schema of categorization by saying that it proceeds by the way of a succession of extensions of the sphere of referentiality: 1 / starting from description (verbal symbol), 2 / adding metaphorical to literal description, 3 / then conjoining depiction (non-verbal symbol) to description, 4 / then adding metaphorical to literal depiction to complete the field of denotation, 5 / then complementing denotation by exemplification and expression. 'Worlds are made not only by what is said literally but also by what is said metaphorically, and not only by what is said either literally or metaphorically but also by what is exemplified and expressed – by what is shown as well as by what is said' (*Ways*, p. 18). 'A non-representational picture such as a Mondrian denotes nothing, pictures nothing, and is neither true nor false, but shows much. Nevertheless, showing or exemplifying, like denoting, is a referential function; and much the same considerations count for pictures as for the concepts or the predicates of a theory' (p. 19). This last extension is the most significant for our topic. It implies that abstract paintings and other works that have no subject nevertheless inform our worlds, through the feelings, rhythms, structures, and forms that they exemplify or express.

One may wonder whether this categorization of the system of symbols may be itself true or false. The answer is that it may be right or wrong, not true or false. We shall return to that sensible topic at the end of the present section.

This rough sketch allows me to give a brief account of the four studies that Goodman has, so to speak, interpolated between his first and two last broader studies. The author acknowledges in his foreword that 'this book does not run a straight course from beginning to end. It hunts ... And it counts not the kill but what is learned of the territory explored' (p. ix). This writer does not therefore need to be 'plus royaliste que le roi,' as we say in French. Nevertheless it is his task to find the unity underneath. This unity, we shall see, is provided by the conceptual network which we just described.

'The Status of Style' (chap. 2) has at its aim the delineation of the stylistic features of a work. If such distinctions as how and what, style and subject, style and feeling, extrinsic and intrinsic features are misleading oppositions, there remain two distinctive features. First, style functions like signature to identify an individual or a group as the 'place' of the work (in that way, Goodman denies that questions of authorship have nothing to do with the understanding of a work [p. 38]). Furthermore, style designates the symbolic function as such of the work, i.e., the kind of referential function that it assumes (description, depiction, exemplification, or expression). It is in that indirect way that the identification of the style of a work contributes to the understanding of its way of world-making. And this is not a secondary task, since nothing is more hidden than the actual stylistic traits of a work. 'Styles are normally accessible only to the knowing eye or ear, the tuned sensibility, the informed and inquisitive mind' (p. 39). The author may conclude his chapter by saying that 'the discernment of style is an integral aspect of the understanding of works of art and the worlds they present' (p. 40).

'Some Questions Concerning Quotation' (chap. 3) is, perhaps, a better sample of hunt than of kill. The main question is whether we may speak of quotation in non-verbal symbolic systems. If I am right, the question is relevant for the purpose of the present work to the extent that it gives an opportunity for testing the analogy between description and depiction. Furthermore, 'as ways of combining and constructing symbols, [pictorial and musical quotations] are among the instruments for world-making' (p. 56).

'When Is Art?' (chap. 4) is also linked to the main topic through indirect and tortuous links. Starting from the more classical question What is art? the author meets the purist (or formalist) thesis according to which any representational or expressive feature of a work is irrelevant to art criticism because it is external to the work. A dilemma confronts us here. Either 'we seem to be advocating lobotomy on many great works,' or 'we seem to be condoning impurity in art, emphasizing the extraneous' (p. 60). The solution to this dilemma is that the purist is both right and wrong – right in excluding everything which is extrinsic to the work, wrong in overlooking the kind of referential function inherent to the work. It is at that stage that our previous analysis of exemplification and expression becomes helpful: as any 'sample,' a work free of representation may still exemplify certain patterns of shape, colour, texture, that it shows forth and that contribute to world-making. 'Art without representation or expression or exemplification – yes; art without all three – no' (p. 66). But the confirmation of the referential thesis is not the only outcome of the analysis. The very initial question What is art? appears to be a wrong question. The functions of exemplifying symbols impose another more appropriate question: When is art? There is art *when* the 'symptoms' of what counts as art are there. Altogether they provide to a work of art a specific non-transparency which derives mainly from the integration and interaction of its multiple and complex references.[2]

The indirect contribution of this study to the overall undertaking of the book has now become quite clear. The way in which an object or event functions in certain circumstances as a work of art through certain modes of reference is a part of the way in which it contributes 'to a vision of – and to the making of – a world' (p. 70).

'A Puzzle about Perception' (chap. 5) seems to be more remote from the mainstream of the book. But it reminds us that perception, too, makes a world. We had learned that from Gombrich's analysis of perspective in *Art and Illusion*. Goodman adds here an argument borrowed from experimental psychology concerning the perception of apparent movement (apparent in the sense that it is 'not there' for the observer). Goodman does not only review some of the puzzles yielded by the experiments, but adds his own puzzle. Psychologists have only considered apparent changes in position, form, and size of moving objects and noticed that apparent transition in those cases is smooth. Goodman observes something new when we add colour to movement; for example, when a black square moves at moderate speed from left to right against a white background, at each moment, the left edge of the black flicks to white merging with the background (the same from black to white for the other edge), without passing through intermediate greys. This contrast between the smooth shape change and the colour-jumps *is* the puzzle. The puzzle evaporates, Goodman claims, when we consider that those jumps preserve the identity of the object in motion-perception. Object-identity, then, appears to be a construct, not a given.

Section 4: Pluralities

The example of motion-perception is not therefore marginal. It is rather a striking example 'of how perception makes its facts' (p. 89), in other words, of how the perceptual version of the world is *made*.

'The Fabrication of Facts' (chap. 6) is a kind of summary of the intermediary chapters and brings the reader back to the main thesis of chapter 1: 'worlds are made by making such versions with words, numerals, pictures, sounds, or other symbols of any kind in any medium; and the comparative study of these versions and visions and of their making is what I call a critique of worldmaking' (p. 94).

The main thing to say about this critique is that the *radical relativism* implied by the thesis allows no laxity. On the contrary, as in Kant and Cassirer, the task is to analyse with the utmost accuracy the *ways* of world-making proper to each kind of version. The technical examples selected above by Goodman show how demanding the task is. The most demanding cases are those belonging to versions that are not literal, not denotational, not verbal. Metaphors, exemplifications and expressions, pictures or sounds or gestures or other non-linguistic symbolic systems are the most difficult topics of the critique of world-making.

But the ultimate test of this critique is without any doubt the status of *rightness* of non-verbal versions. We gave above (at the end of the first part of this discussion) a first draft of the thesis that truth is relevant only for statements, but that there are criteria of lightness for non-verbal versions which are as cogent as those of truth for statements. Goodman returns to this thesis in the last chapter of his book, 'On Rightness of Rendering' (chap. 7), and supports it with the acquisitions made in the preceding parts of his book. Goodman resumes here the notion of *fitness* introduced in *Languages of Art* but brings it a bit farther. Two claims are made. First, truth is not even the only consideration in descriptive versions of the world. That choice among statements or versions requires some tests in *judging* truths already requires criteria of Tightness, such as utility or coherence, or better validity in deductive or inductive arguments, or still better *rightness of categorization*: 'Such rightness is one step farther removed from truth; for while deductive and inductive rightness still have to do with statements, which have truth-value, rightness of categorization attaches to categories or predicates – or systems thereof-which have no truth-value' (p. 127).

This thesis about rightness of categorization is all the more important since the whole critique of world-making falls under it, to the extent that this critique itself relies on the categorization of the symbolic systems. Therefore, Goodman has to apply to his own work what he says about categorial systems: 'For a categorial system, what needs to be shown is not that it is true but what it can do. Put crassly, what is called for in such cases is less arguing than selling' (p. 129).

Thus, it is the rightness of the whole proposed scheme of categorization which supports the very analysis of rightness of non-verbal versions. This can be shown in great detail. The test is fitness in exemplification. To the question: 'When is a sample right?' the only answer is nearly tautological: when it may be 'rightly projected to the pattern or mixture or other relevant feature of the whole or of further samples' (p. 135). Right projectability is fairness in exemplification. Yet, projectability is no mere equivalent of fairness, to the extent that to establish projectability is a quite demanding task; it depends upon conformity to good practice in interpreting samples, therefore, in the last resort, 'upon habit in continual revision under frustration and invention' (p. 137). Discovering what is exemplified requires taste, as Kant would say: 'what counts as success in achieving accord depends upon what our habits, progressively modified in the face of new encounters and new proposals, adopt as projectible kinds' (p. 137). In this arduous task we are no longer helped by arguments of universal and atemporal acceptability. To return to Kant, his criterion of the universality of the judgment of taste crumbles, since there is no universal and eternal acceptability. Test results are transient and what is once maximally acceptable may later be unacceptable. Nevertheless, we have to keep ultimate acceptability as what we mean by rightness, if rightness must remain parallel to truth. We are not that far from what Kant called 'aesthetic Ideas' in the third *Critique*, with the following pragmatic qualification: 'ultimate acceptability, though as inaccessible as absolute rightness would be, is thus nevertheless explicable in terms of the tests and their results' (p. 139).

Because of the circularity of the definition of rightness within a conceptual framework which cannot claim to be true but right, Goodman is *right* to conclude by these words: 'My readers could weaken that latter conviction [that any approach to universal accord on anything significant in artistic and even scientific judgment is exceptional] by agreeing unanimously with the foregoing somewhat tortuous and in a double sense trying course of thought' (p. 140). The last sentence of the book is more than a joke intended to capture the benevolence of the reader. Bordering the argument of the 'Liar,' it underscores the difficult epistemological status of a categorial system which unavoidably defines its own validity in the terms of the major category that the organizational scheme yields. We are therefore sent back to the aphorism: 'For a categorial system, what needs to be shown is not that it is true but what it can do' (p. 129).

III

My personal assessment of Goodman's work is a mixture of agreement and disagreement – but at different levels.

I have no hesitation in acknowledging that I heartily approve the daring attempt to go farther than Cassirer in the recognition of the plurality and irreducibility of world-versions. This thesis is not only liberal but liberating. To go farther than Cassirer, Goodman had to give up the still hierarchical conception of symbolic forms whose outcome was to put the scientific version at the top of the ascending scale of forms.

With an equal conviction I hold as plausible the organizational scheme of symbolic forms that Goodman transfers from *Languages of Art* to *Ways of Worldmaking*. I hold it not only as plausible, but as *right*, in the sense that the author ascribes to *rightness*. I adhere accordingly to the idea that a categorial system may be neither true nor false – in the sense of the term true that I shall discuss later – but right or wrong. Here, to be right means to *fit* with our current experience with symbols. And it fits to the extent that it provides guidelines for using such terms as 'description,' 'depiction,' 'denotation,' 'exemplification,' 'expression,' and so on, appropriately to the way we *already make sense* with statements or paintings, whether representational or not.

Section 4: Pluralities

In that sense, Goodman offers a modern version of what Kant called transcendental deduction, i.e., the justification (in the juridical sense) of the claim that the categorial network shows the condition of the possibility of meaningfulness in our use of symbolic structures. This transcendental deduction presupposes therefore that we have already recognized in a non-reflective way the variety of the referential modes of our world-versions. This previous recognition entails what we could call a spontaneous, i.e., non-reflective, phenomenology of the meaningfulness of statements and paintings. It is this spontaneous phenomenology of the universal and varied referentiality of all our symbols that justifies or warrants the construction of any organizational system of symbolic forms.

I should like now to inquire into this spontaneous phenomenology. It seems to me that it may entail some suggestions, even, some requirements other than those displayed by Goodman's *Ways of Worldmaking*.

Let us return to the three major theses which we commented on in our presentation of Goodman's book. It is within these theses that I find motives for both agreement and disagreement.

My praise of Goodman's pluralism seemed to endorse *Thesis I* without qualifications. Nevertheless my disagreement starts there. And it starts with the very expression world-*making*. On the one hand, Goodman makes a vibrant plea for the *cognitive* significance of works of art. His fights against the emotionalist and ornamental theory of metaphor – his defense of the referential capacity of non-representational painting – are the most striking examples of his declared intellectualism. Furthermore, he assumes M. Polanyi's use of the concept of understanding (p. 22). On the other hand, he transfers into the realm of knowledge categories which have their first use in the field of production. This transfer is not indeed wrong in all regards. Aristotle, speaking of the composition of a literary work such as epic and tragedy, applies to it the concept of *poiesis*, i.e., fabrication of something exterior to the maker, and the very expression 'work of art' witnesses to this right use of the term *making*. But, if the composition of a work (of discourse, of art, or whatever you have in the field of symbolic works) pertains to the order of making, is the referential aiming of the work itself fully characterized as making? What supports the partial identification between knowing and making is the description by Goodman of such *ways* of world-making as composition and decomposition, weighing, ordering, deletion and supplementation, deformation.[3] But these modes of construction do not exhaust the intentionality constitutive of the referentiality of symbols. The factor of otherness proper to this intentionality is overshadowed by the factor of fabrication proper to the ways of world-making described above.

My argument here is merely phenomenological. It intends to give an account of our dealing with symbols to which the symbolic system is supposed to be attuned. Does a painter like Cézanne make a version of the world in the same way as one makes a car? The deep thrust that moves him to paint, and which is the origin of that which Merleau-Ponty describes as 'Cézanne's Doubt' in a famous essay, seems to arise from a stubborn attempt to 'render' what he keeps calling Nature (with a capital N). Let us put aside for the moment the word *Nature*, and let us focus on the term '*render*.' Goodman too uses it. His last chapter is entitled 'On Rightness of Rendering.' My contention is that making and rendering are not substitutable terms

177

but form together a dynamical and dialectical pair at the phenomenological level. Tell a creator, say Van Gogh or Cezanne, that he is fabricating a world-version. He will not recognize himself in this account of what he is doing. And if by chance he accepted it, he would stop painting, because he would lose faith in the kind of constraint which makes his predicament. The painter – at least this kind of painter – understands himself as the servant – if not the slave – of that which has to be said, depicted, exemplified, expressed. Because a gap keeps recurring between *making* and *rendering*, he is never relieved from the duty of painting. Cézanne, facing 'la montagne sainte Victoire' or simply 'un compotier de pommes,' feels himself the bearer of an infinite debt as regards that which Merleau-Ponty calls the visibility of the visible. By the way, the English verb 'to render' displays a full array of potential meanings ranging from 'making' to 'giving in return or requital,' even to 'giving up' and 'surrendering.' The experience of the artist, it seems to me, encompasses the whole range of meanings from making to surrendering, through representing and interpreting.

At that point *Thesis II* (see above) awaits us. I hear Nelson Goodman telling me: In sum, you take my complete pluralism, but you claim to drop my radical relativism. This is impossible. You cannot get the one without paying the price of the other. I think, nevertheless, that there is something to say on behalf of a concept of world that would not fall under the blows of Goodman's critique. We could, in effect, wonder why Goodman does not get rid of the term *world* as the term common to all versions. Of course, he does not contradict when he substitutes world-versions for versions of the world. But is this substitution more than an artifice of writing? This way of speaking has not at all the same intent as in the case of such fictions as chimeras, for which it is perfectly right to say that the fiction *of* a chimera is a chimera-fiction, i.e., the member of a class of fictions. Here we speak within the framework of a theory of denotation, and the chimera is a case of null-denotation. But Goodman himself teaches us that denotation does not cover the whole field of referential symbols and that works of art with null-denotation – as is the case with non-representational paintings – keep referring in a non-denotational way, for example by exemplifying and expressing. What, then, compels Goodman to preserve reference at all costs, if not a dimension of experience entailed in the term *world* that he has not considered? The irreducible difference, it seems to me, between world-versions and versions of the world arises from the conviction that no version exhausts that which requires to be, literally or metaphorically, described, depicted, exemplified, or expressed. Otherwise why, throughout cultural changes, would men have wanted or needed to make new kinds of versions and new versions of the known kinds *again and again*? What are they after, what are they seeking for, by making new world-versions?

Here, Nelson Goodman would reply: either the world is apart from all versions and then you fall back to the absurd thesis of the *Ding an sich*, or you favour one version, most likely the phenomenist one, and then you make an arbitrary and imperialist claim.

I think that it is possible to escape this alternative choice. Contrary to the first alternative, the world may be more than each version without being apart from it. It is the very experience of making that yields that of discovering. And discovering is to confront the opacity of the world. The world is included – excluded as the horizon

Section 4: Pluralities

of each intentional aiming. It is not something to which versions refer, but that out of which, or against the background of which, versions refer. Contrary to the second alternative, the world is not either a phenomenon in the perceptual sense, although a phenomenology of perception, as well as that of the creative experience of painting alluded to above, is particularly suited to teach the difference between phenomenon and horizon. This capability of perception arises from the fact that our own body – as lived body – is implied in a unique way in perception. Now our body, as our own, is the basic medium of our being in the world as the place where we dwell. Dwelling, construing, and thinking, these are – according to the wonderful title of one of Heidegger's essays – human acts of an inexhaustible significance. To dwell is to be received as a guest. And construing is making, but in such a way that we do not make the world less worthy of dwelling in. Some kind of humility, accordingly, is entailed in the act of dwelling. This kind of humility in turn says something of the openness proper to perception. In that sense the significance of the world as horizon excludes any hypostasis of the phenomenist version.

The phenomenist version, as version, is exemplified by the perception of apparent movement so beautifully expounded by Goodman. It is only a version, in the sense that it is isolated by the artificial but necessary constraints of the experiment itself from the whole concrete context which makes observation inexhaustible, i.e., the interplay between all the perceptual fields, the movement of attention which expands or focuses alternately and the indefinite flight of the perceptual horizon. Whether we call this trait of perceptual experience inactuality or potentiality (Husserl), it makes the difference between world-version and version *of* the world. Deprived from the contextual feature, the perceived world becomes a phenomenon, in the Kantian sense of a 'representation' which abides in the mind. This reduction engenders the false problematics of the *Ding an sich*, to compensate, as it were, the phenomenist impoverishment of experience. Ultimately the old dichotomy, subject-object, has to be questioned, to the extent that the dichotomy phenomenon – *Ding an sich* – belongs to the same mistaken problematics of *Vorstellung*. For the same reason, the so-called realism of the *Ding an sich* is only and always the counterpart and the penalization of the idealism of *Vorstellung*. I find myself suddenly quite in agreement with this statement by Goodman: 'The realist will resist the conclusion that there is no world; the idealist will resist the conclusion that all conflicting versions describe different worlds. As for me, I find these views equally delightful and equally deplorable – for after all, the difference between them is purely conventional' (p. 119). *Bravo!*

A further reason not to hypostasize the perceptual version is that its own inexhaustibility, displayed by the experience of observing, makes possible the shift to other versions – among them, to the pictorial version. When Van Gogh depicts the furniture of his room and when he exemplifies by his painting some features, rhythms, moods, pertaining to his surroundings, does he not make visible certain textures and even certain non-Euclidean spatial structures that our usual perception, overloaded by traditions and prejudices (including the prejudice that the perceptual space is Euclidean), prevents us from seeing? In that sense the perceptual inexhaustibility of the world and its opacity are hints of, and clues to, the function of the world as horizon, as that which makes possible, suggests, and sometimes requires the transition from one version of the world to another. The possibility and the fact of such transitions are one more implication of the significance of the term 'world' without any regression to the logical concept of *sameness* that Goodman correctly excludes.

In conclusion, I should like to sketch a critical reflection on *Thesis III*. This thesis about the difference between rightness and truth is itself right as long as one decides to limit the meaning of the term *true* to the domain of denotations and among them to that of descriptions and finally of statements. Nevertheless, the duality rightness-truth seems to me to be a residue of the philosophy that the author condemns, i.e., the reduction of reference to denotation and to statements. By the same token, does he not remain captive of a verificationist (or falsificationist) prejudice that his whole philosophy of symbolic forms denies? If one gives back to the world its character of horizon, of inexhaustibility, and of opacity, has one not to question anew the concept of truth and to acknowledge that its amplitude is equal to that of world? Someone may say that the change is only of a semantic kind, to the extent that it entails merely the convention of including rightness in truth. I do not think that our contention bears merely on terminology. By calling rightness truth, we respond, I think, to a phenomenological requirement, namely to the same requirement which compelled us to distinguish between making and rendering.

I find in Nelson Goodman himself some symptoms of this requirement. First, his full respect for the cognitive function of the arts,[4] then his quasi-instinctive doubling of the term version by vision ('versions and visions,' pp. 2–5), then his right use of the term *rendering* when combined with rightness (would he say: rightness of making, with the same ... rightness?), and finally and above all, his fight on behalf of the reference of symbols in the absence of denotation. Why should this plea be so stubborn, if the search for truth were not, under the garment of rightness, the concern for doing justice to that which Hölderlin called *das Offene* – The Open – and which requires that we, literally or metaphorically, keep describing, depicting, exemplifying, and expressing *again and again*?

For my part, I have great difficulty in conceiving a philosophy of generalized reference which would not be stirred by the passionate concern for an equally generalized sense of truth.

Notes

1. The first chapter, 'Words, Works, Worlds,' was read at the University of Hamburg on the 101st anniversary of the birth of Ernst Cassirer.
2. To the four 'symptoms' dealt with in *Languages of Art* – syntactic density, semantic density, relative repleteness, exemplification – *Ways of Worldmaking* adds a fifth 'symptom,' that of 'multiple and complex reference, where a symbol performs several integrated and interacting referential functions' (p. 68).
3. One may notice that the expression 'ways of worldmaking,' taken in this more technical sense, becomes a subtitle within a chapter which bears the same title (pp. 7–17). See also pp. 101–2 in chapter 6, 'The Fabrication of Facts.'

Section 4: Pluralities

4. A major thesis of this book is that the arts must be taken no less seriously than the sciences as modes of discovery, creation, and enlargement of knowledge in the broad sense of advancement of understanding, and thus that the philosophy of art should be conceived as an integral part of metaphysics and epistemology' (p. 102).

Michel Serres

Michel Serres' writings exhibit an extraordinary hybridity of approach, drawn from areas of learning that we normally take care to separate in our educational systems and in our universities. Serres studied theory of science, but after the bombing of Hiroshima came to realize that scientific optimism needed to be informed by other aspects of life, and he moved across into the humanities.[1] His writing aims to fuse the various concerns together, so the work cannot be pigeon-holed neatly, and the scholarly apparatus is suppressed, so there are few footnotes and little indication of where the ideas are coming from – from literary criticism or from physics. The essay here is a case in point. It is a commentary on a text by the ancient historian Livy (Titus Livius, 59BC–17AD) about the foundation of Rome.[2] The action is configured in terms of the movements and interactions of crowds, which go through various types of behaviour. These are linked in Serres' commentary with the phase transitions that a material goes through in turning from solid to liquid, from liquid to gas – becoming more volatile as it melts and evaporates, becoming more unified as it condenses, flows, and freezes into a unified block. So although the text would make us want to file this essay under 'classics', the commentary does not draw at all on the culture of that discipline except for its raw material; a materials scientist would find the commentary more immediately comprehensible, but would not feel at home with the subject-matter. It is a model of interdisciplinarity, which should feel natural enough for architects who are familiar with the process of mediating between the cultures of engineers, builders, entrepreneurs and style-gurus; and with feeling misunderstood.

Note

1. Michel Serres and Bruno Latour, translated by Roxannne Lapidus, *Conversations on Science, Culture and Time* (Ann Arbor: University of Michigan Press, 1995) p. 15.
2. Specifically Livy, Book 2, 22–35; see Livy, trans. by Aubrey de Sélincourt, *The Early History of Rome* (Harmondsworth: Penguin, 1960), pp. 132–51.

In the City: Agitated Multiplicity

Let us return to the exact, earliest hour given for the founding of Rome. A little earlier, in the kingdom of Alba, enemy brothers are still killing each other. With the help of Remus, Numitor has just killed Amulius, his emulator. He quickly calls the people into assembly. From now on, watch the subtle movement of words or things, watch the recurrent movement: the multitude is forming. The murder has taken place; the assembly forms a council. In the middle of the council, the twins enter with their bands, who are anything but a council. In a united ensemble, the two groups intervene and hail Numitor as king. Then, unanimously, in a single voice, the multitude creates the king. The two bands accelerated the movement of union. Immediately after the murder, the multitude became a concourse and remains so around the king; the crowd opens before two different bands and consents again with a single voice. The multitude is assembled by the lynching, by the king, by the unanimity of suffrages.

The same movement begins again. By concourse Alba becomes a multitude once more; the population grows. The twins go off to the place where they were abandoned in order to found a new city. Each of them obviously still has his band, his group, his followers, his multitude. Two multiplicities do not make a city; six and twelve vultures do not make a single flight. That is the real question: each twin is surrounded by his vultures, and these vultures want a corpse, carrion. Yes, the auguries tell the truth; yes, the inauguration clearly precedes the foundation. The two teams come to blows; they form a mob in their undifferentiated, mixed sum. The crowd becomes a mob and the mob kills; the vultures finally make their move. So, we are told, the city is founded.

Foundation occurs when a multiplicity makes itself into a unity. The multitude is formed around the unity of the corpse, around the place of the dead.

This is the concept of Rome – its concept and its name.

The story relates the murder and its true or false motivations. And then it skips abruptly over the foundation. We did not see the foundation. We must believe that it is the murder itself. But if in addition we examine the names that are given to these groups, the foundation appears: the collective first is called multitude, then mob, then it is a city.

The same movement takes up again, everywhere recurrent. The city grows larger; Romulus peoples it through the wood of asylum. Who comes to this dark wood? The multitude. There the multitude again becomes an undifferentiated mob of freemen and slaves. The king frames it into a council.

In every case the dynamic goes from a multiple ensemble to a confused collective and from there, via some circumstance, arrives at unity. This circumstance is the murder of Amulius; it is the assassination of Remus by his brother or rather his lynching amid the mob; it is the shadow of the wood of asylum. Here obscure people hide their origins in the enclosure between two woods. So that Rome can hide what it has seen since its birth in Romulus. The place of asylum hides, it is closed off, protected by two woods, guarded by the sacred. The story hides as well; it would seem the foundation is completely different from what it is said to be.

The passage from multiplicity to concourse, by the mixture of the mob and lightning-bolt lynching, is a description of the social contract. It is not a contract – words must dissolve in the cries and the noise of the brawl; meaning returns to a murmur, relationships to quarrels, and the whole ensemble to chaos – no, it's not a contract, but it is nonetheless how the collective is founded, how a society begins. It never stops beginning this way.

Moreover, Livy displays a conceptual loyalty that philosophy forgets to practice. The place of asylum or the dark woods where people of obscure birth assemble, the dark cave of Cacus where the oxen bellow, the uneasy, symbolic addition of six and twelve vultures, the dark hollow where Numa secretly receives Egeria's counsel and from which an inexhaustible spring flows are better scenes than that of the contract. The philosophical concepts of origin are clearly presented, but they are obscure. Livy's objects carry their shadows with them – they are black boxes, a cavern, a wood, dark figures; they reveal our misunderstanding. They make us think without concepts. They make us see simultaneously the thing, the dynamic of the thing, and the misunderstanding in which our understanding of the thing is immersed. The light that does not admit its shadow is false; the chiaroscuro that makes it be seen is more honest and exact. We do not know our origins: an irreducible shadow prevents us from seeing them; something is behind us to which we will not turn back. We will not convert. The social sciences comprehend this shade. Legend makes it be seen and myth is accompanied by it, but the concept suppresses it and positive science eliminates it. A good theory of knowledge subtly negotiates its associated misunderstanding; a good theory of science knows what it can know, it knows the workings of the secret and the strict limits at which knowlege turns back into the unknown. Livy is sharper, more supple and subtle in the epistemology that his story implies than a philosophy or theory that plays at clear ideas. He shows us simultaneously the thing and its shadow: the origin, the murder, and its re-covering.

We have not adequately considered the flight and assembly of the people on the day of the Poplifugia. We looked at the Fathers closing in with their dense and bloody ring around the scattered limbs of the royal cadaver, but we gave less attention to the fluid ensemble calling out or throwing stones at one another; I shall return to it now. Much time has passed – the republic is founded; the twin consuls, often rivals, have replaced the expelled kings; the battle of Lake Regillus has made the usual carnage possible; and for the first time debts have become a problem. The people, irritated, agitated, come onto the scene. We could say that this scene slowly details the king's death and the people's flight; a multitude, which we will have to name, first surrounds a fantastical old man, a nameless character – nobody knows where he came from or where he will soon disappear to – and then surrounds the disagreeing senators. The people make a dense ring, and the Fathers scatter – an inversion.

I'm going to try to name this crowd. It is first of all the multitude, multiplicity. Since the adventure of this book began, since the adventure of our culture began, I

Section 4: Pluralities

have found only multiplicity. An ensemble of termites and bits of earth; the inaccessible ichnography of myth under the tracks of the herd of oxen; the two flights of vultures on the day of the foundation; the white surface of the Albula, a swelling of the innumerable to the incandescent in the kingdom of Alba; the ensemble of the pieces of empire and the limbs of the shredded body; the hail of stones, the blasts of voices, the rain of pennies – a sixth of an *as* per person – on the hero's body on the day of his funeral; the band, the groups, the wood of asylum, the assemblies, the mob, the army. Multiplicities. It is the moment to name them, to recognize them and make history of them. It is time to recognize that history is a processing of ensembles. That ensembles produce the time of history. Whence this book, whose stable object is multiplicity. Livy's book has the same object. Or, rather, the same subject. The continual effort consists in capturing it. It is sometimes so torrential, so turbulent that the concept itself cannot stop it, cover it over, subjugate it.

The multitude abruptly takes over the stage. It spreads through the city like the flames of a conflagration, one that smolders a long while in silence and then, when we're not watching, suddenly flares up. War is imminent; the Volsci are at Rome's gates. Civil war is also imminent, that of creditors against debtors; a revolt of plebeians is rumbling against the Fathers. The debtors are bound, immobilized, caught, chained. The enemy is less fearsome than those on the inside who reduce them to slavery. It is a second-generation war; that is, the war of foreign war against civil war. A violent mixture that breaks the chains and breaks free, released.

Mars engenders violence – war. Quirinus engenders violence – debts. Jupiter engenders violence – justice and sovereignty. Everyone at once is right and says the same thing. All these instances engender violence. But it is appeased, at the end of the scene, in the order of the camps. Mars dams up the violence; the war against the Volsci wins out over the revolution, at least temporarily. Quirinus appeases the violence; the questions of position, debt, and slavery are deferred somewhat. The sovereign Jupiter appeases violence; everyone turns toward the senate, and the consul pronounces a law that appeases the crowd. Money, we knew, puts a freeze on violence; the sacred, we learned, also freezes it; here we learn that a good war freezes it as well. The alignment of the camps is a peaceful order. The alignment of the front, a classical order, prohibits outbursts. If you want peace, make war. In a legion.

Each pole, each instance, each institution engenders and restrains violence, seems to produce and channel it, dams it and captures it with the participation of every other institution, with the help of the two other gods. And this is no doubt how each institution, each instance, each pole is founded and instituted. By fact and by right. By fact in the army as such, injustice, and in the circulation of money; and by right in theory. Each god, each social class is also a class of theory, a class of interpretation.

Livy recounts a story, real or legendary, a scene, a representation – it doesn't matter. You can find in it a philosophy of ordinary history, of economy and class struggle, *certamen ordinum*. You can find in it the lessons of power, Machiavellianism or Realpolitik, a strategy for the prince. You can uncover in it the traces of the three gods. And each person is right; the history or the scene includes their interpretations. And it is perhaps simply another foundation of Rome. It is the ichnography of our philosophies.

Money and economy envelop war and religion. Religion envelops war and economy, as well as law and sovereignty. War envelops economy and religion. Each term envelops or implies the others, is perhaps implied by each of the others. In the fact of the temple's durable wall, the camp, the tribunal, or the senate, in the fact and in the word, in the explanation we call theoretical, when he who speaks gets up and is understood to be right. He is always right. He commands. And he is content.

There are doubtless boxes so unyielding that we cannot play with their size and form. Rigid little boxes fit inside a big one, but the reverse isn't true. It is impossible to put the big one, rigid and inflexible, in any of the smaller ones. That's how it is. Now if there is a logic of boxes, perhaps there is a logic of sacks. A canvas or jute sack does not contain only wheat, flour, or cement. It can contain sacks as well. It is supple enough to be folded up in a sack with all the other folded sacks, even its former container. I believe that there is box-thought, the thought we call rigorous, like rigid, inflexible boxes, and sack-thought, like systems of fabric. Our philosophy lacks a good organum of fabrics; I often dream of it. If we had one, many tricks would no longer be possible, but reason would be spared much inflexibility. There are conditions prior to implication that forbid its turning back. They are not always adhered to. Elasticity is not always a sin against straightforward reason. It is so only if it hides itself. Our multiplicities are like gases – they can expand over Rome, its forum, its streets, its public spaces; they can contract in the camps. The concepts that capture them are as fluid as they are; they imply each other reciprocally – what a scandal. Let us learn to negotiate soft logics. They are only crazy if we do not understand them. Let us finally laugh about those who called rigorous what was precisely their soft discourse. And let us no longer scorn what is soft – fluid ensembles.

The question of the ichnography is solved right away. Establishing it was no waste of time. The certitude arises that all interpretations succeed one another as scenographies in the face of the multitude. It remains only to consider the multitude as such.

It forms a fluctuating field buffeted among these three poles that are poles only in appearance or, rather, only according to violence. It is formed by these forces, and that is exactly what Livy's narrative says. Our theories lack this fluctuating field, this moving ensemble, and most of all the multiple that moves or rushes there. It is always captured. The multiple is captured. Captured by the single, it is concept and synthesis; captured by one or several individuals, it is power, as well as representation, tragedy, political assembly. All of Livy's stories recount the capture of the multiple by the single. This history is one of capture; this capture is itself our history. The multiple rushes along, then is trapped by the single. Whether that is called theory or practice, power or representation, it leads back to this primary and constant operation. Thus we have to search for the single king, hero, master, slave, someone or other, the standard or most recent situation onto which this operation projects the multiple. Theoretical representation or social practice or political astuteness or the historical narrative project onto a singleton the ensemble as such. Thus we must first of all pay attention to this ensemble.

Question: in this narrative, what does the author call the crowd? A series of names is itself worth many theories. Livy is crafty with multiplicity. He names it in multiple ways.

Section 4: Pluralities

The Volsci, the plebs, the Fathers. The ensembles are there, united separately and disjointed. The forces are present, as they say. As is customary, they come in threes: Saint George, the dragon, the heap of corpses. The fire can break out, is going to break out; external or internal war is imminent, lance against armor, dismemberment.

For the violence to flame high, it takes a spark; let us watch this singularity carefully.

The singleton, extracted from order or projected outside of it, is full of fury. He burns and flames. No, he is not simply a warrior. No, the question does not reduce itself to the premises of combat, to the initiations of warring societies; it touches the deepest foundations of social order and group conflict, even the foundations of Rome.

An opportunity is what it takes – a spark. I repeat, let us watch this singularity carefully. Perhaps the hero is going to be born; perhaps we will witness the origin of tragedy. The origin of the concept, the capture of the multiple.

Insignis unius calamitas, the marked suffering of a single one ignited hatred. I should specify that this hatred in Latin is called malevolence – *invidia*, the evil eye or what is seen with the evil eye. We will have to specify what division means, from the same point of view. What fans violence is the marked suffering of a single one. *Insignis* means marked, remarkable; this singular person bears distinctive marks, signs. Here they are.

They are signs of old age, suffering, exhaustion, disease, combat, torture. There is not a mark on his oppressed body that does not reveal the nearness of death – age, scars, or the recent stripes of the whip. He stirs up horror, anger, and pity; he is no mediocre tragic hero but one who bears on his person the scope of tragedy. He bears the signs of battle, the chest scars of the glorious centurion he once was, the marks of Mars; he bears the signs of the plebeian's struggle against the Fathers, the traces of whips, of chains, of torture for his debts. His squalor and emaciation are evidence of prison, poverty, servitude; he is a victim of Jupiter's sovereignty, a miserable victim of Quirinus's fortune. But his age and his air are those of a commander. Who is the singleton? You have recognized him even though he is unknown; the Romans recognized him in a flash. He bears all the signs of the victim. He is the intersection of the ensembles present. He is the intersection of the enemy Volsci, the Fathers' prison, the plebs's poverty. He is the intersection of three functions: the centurion in his glorious hour of service; the peasant farmer ruined by debts and taxes; the imposing old man with silver head and beard – a strange and charismatic apparition of authority. His body, covered with signs, is already carved up: one part for the soldiers, one for the farmers, one for the tribunal. He is precisely the joker; he carries all signs, all values. The sum of signs or their union, the intersection of groups and their convergence in one divided individual. The union and intersection of the subgroups present.

He is alone; yet the separate groups touch at this point, like tangents. In this great, withered old man, contingency appears. And the geometry or logic of contingency is no trifle. We are in the habit of scorning it excessively. It is not the absence of law but the local accumulation of refined little laws. The joker, positioned in a sequence, neighboring one value on one side and another on the other side, makes the sequence bifurcate. Through him it jumps from war to debt, for example, or inversely, from the potential to the act; it does not jump from one state to another without him. In this point of contingency, two unrelated variations are tangential; that is the role of the old man, the joker. Here, through him, in him – depending on the circumstance, or what happens locally around him – history will hesitate; it will take, or could take, a certain direction or meaning. Contingency is precisely this place of bifurcation. The old singleton is a singularity, like Cleopatra's nose;[1] he is the projection of given multiplicities. I suppose that the famous nose of the Egyptian queen was a sign as legible to the multiple as the signs on the joker's body are visible.

Old man singularity, the bearer of traces and marks, is capable – capable in the geometrical sense, as a segment is capable of a thousand angles under which we see it – of the ensembles that concern it. The soldiers see him as a centurion; the debtors see him as someone whipped or bound, and thus they conspire with the former warriors. This capacity has the same name as potency; it is potentiality. This potency is power. Whoever holds power is capable of angles, views, ensembles; thus he can only be a motley joker or a white-headed man, white as the sum of all possible colors. He bears all signs. He is already completely carved up. The old joker bears on himself, in himself, the vestiges of all possible violence. Thus he is seen and read by the *invidia*, the hatred that sees with its evil eye. He is carved up, torn up, divided. He is seen by the mixed gaze of divided multiplicities. The *invidia* of the *divisio*.

A bizarre mathematics or a bizarre chemistry. The body is well marked with a precise, decomposed, legible formula. Now it enters into the melange. It is drowned in contingency. It is absorbed by the crowd, by the text, and will never come out; it will never be mentioned again. Annihilated, dissolved. Like the god Tiberinus in the waters of the white river. Expelled. Expelled from the text like a king.

On the contrary – will it reappear?

Around him is the crowd. Look closely at the crowd's denominations now. As I said, they form an impressive series equal to all theories. With each fluctuation, each transformation, the crowd changes names. With each reaction it changes formulas.

First, *turba circumfusa* – the crowd spreads out, liquid, in fusion. It surrounds the old man like a turbulent whirlwind. *Turba, turbo*. The crowd spills out around him; we could almost call it a popular assembly – *contio*, a convention. He speaks and it speaks, saying to itself, among its members, that it recognizes this singleton. It rushes toward him and reads him.

There amid the *turba*, in its turbulence, is an old man close to death, his body covered with scars – a hero who has been at death's door, a farmer, a peasant financially ruined and in debt, beaten, whipped, emaciated, haggard, starving, with long hair and a savage look, with no name – like an abstract operator. Nameless, substitutable. On death's doorstep.

Everyone looks at him, interrogates him, recognizes him. A joker, he has all values. A catalyst, he precipitates, makes the entire process possible; he is its condition.

He tells a story. He tells the story of populations. Not in the usual sense but the pillage of pillagers. *Populari* means to ravage, devastate, depopulate. The population moves toward this singleton, pillages his farm, steals his harvest, drives off his cattle. Next the state, another population, moves toward the land of his father and grandfather, demanding taxes and obliging him to borrow; the old man is entirely a

Section 4: Pluralities

subject. What difference does it make if it's a matter of Sabines and not Volsci and not the *turba*? It is, for the moment, population. That is how it occupies space. The crowd listening to him can become a population.

How does it occupy space and hold onto it?

A solid cannot invade an expanse; it remains local. Determined, defined, decided, it is restrained; it has rigid limits – one cut is catastrophe. Liquid has none; it spreads, spills, is diffused. Vaper flies through a volume, sometimes turning, turbulent. Fluids fill up the potential by their inundation; they abound. The crowd is fluid. An institution is stable, solid. The foundation solidifies the crowd. Cools it down, freezes it, restrains it spatially. Now defined, it has limits; it becomes reasonable, rational. Thus Romulus's trench is that of a decided society, and Remus's leap is that of the labile crowd. The liquid multitude exceeds all limits. The ditch's function is the evacuation of water. In Rome it is a *cloaca*, a sewer. The ordinary solid history of gold or bronze or polished stone defines liquid history or the ages of water. It stops them. Foundation. It evacuates them.

The ravage of destruction takes over space, devastation advances on the vast plain without limitation. The conqueror expands by the fire that spreads or the iron that brings everything down to a fine dust; this is population. Population pillages. Occupies the world by destroying it. Violence invades the expanse without constraint. Violence invades the pillagers as well. Violence stops violence. Foundation. It limits it. Ditch. The sacred that depends on violence, in Girard, creates the sacred that depends on limits, in Eliade; this is the foundation of civil society, in Rousseau – to delimit a field. But the intelligent Rousseau asked only for fools. That is not sufficient.

Sickness and contagion invade the space – germs spread, the plague contaminates the expanse; its former occupants are now only carriers of the epidemic, the epizootic, the plague. Plague kills its carriers. Stop. The dynamic of the conquest is that of its limitation.

The sound of clamor invades the space, and tumult takes up its expanse. There is an inundation, a deluge. There is destruction, violence, and war. There are illnesses, tabes, or plague. Here, now, is the hubbub. These are the images of the multitude. These are the avatars or apparitions of population. These are its performances as well. Foundation, then, is the passage from water to stone, the transition of phases; let us not forget the first waters. It is the passage or transformation of violence into the sacred; let us not forget populations. The passage of the plague to its own destruction; the group is immunized by exposure, vaccinated. But it is now the passage, the same passage, the transition of phases or the transformation, from nonsensical clamors to language, from barbarous language to human language, from noise to the voice, from cacophony to sense, from the sound of the sea to harmony, from background noise to music, from white noise to information, from the hubbub to the contract. The clamor of the multiple makes noise; it suddenly takes form as hope or deception; it achieves harmony, and this harmony is the contract. Before the unanimous cry comes noise.

We forget the nature of the phenomenon that precedes foundation. Whether it be fluid or flood, violence or pillage, plague or clamor, it is always a process that spreads, that expands in space and occupies its volume. The pure multitude expands. It spills, spreads, invades the expanse and holds it; it swells. It sacks and scatters. The multiple multiplies itself, or perseveres in its being. And that is the essential; that is the secret of its names.

Before the real or figurative contract, noise holds the space.

Here first of all is the plague, *tabes*, rotting and contagion. The war escalates; debts, deluge, and violence mount; the plague gains ground. The old man is overwhelmed by this growth – no more farm, no more land, no more worldly goods, no more family, and, since he is bound, no more body. The violence of Jupiter's justice and power, the violence of Mars's Sabine war, the violence of Quirinus's exchange and debt. The sickness spreads, it slips in everywhere.

Facing the crowd in the forum, the old man tells the story of population. A crowd here; a crowd there. This is representation: the current relation of the single to the multiple is articulated in the recollection of a relation of the multiple to the single.

Thus *clamor ingens, tumultus* – noise is born in the square, it swells, rises, fills the forum, slips in everywhere, seizes the city. It accompanies the multiple and it is the multiple.

Sedition clamors; noise makes a ruckus.

Sedition indicates a coming-and-going, a fluctuation. *Itus et reditus, itio et seditio*, departure and return, going and coming. The *turba circumfusa* of a minute ago, the diffuse mob, is rather the cloudy or overflowing chaos – we hear its hubbub; sedition, in its local comings-and-goings separated by Brownian movement, is the Poplifugia, this flight of the people in which they call out and meet up. The people's flight is their sedition; they withdraw to the Sacred Mount.

Screaming bands run toward the forum: 'multis ... agminibus per omnes vias cum clamore in forum curritur'; the multiple gallops in little pockets through the streets toward the center, amid the clamors. The sound of screams and cries has seized the city; there is no longer a single place in Rome where some volunteer isn't joining the revolt. There is no longer a soundproof box; that is the law of propagation. Plague: not all will die, but all will be attacked. Clamor: not everyone approves or participates, but all, even if they don't repeat it, at least hear it. A phenomenon of expansion that knows no obstacle, whose law knows no exception. By taking over the space, multiplicity mounts to totality. Rome is seized; Rome is taken; Rome is Rome. All the streets are invaded – all. All, then, run toward the forum. The centered diagram of the star, fluid in the case of the crowd, rocky in the diagram of lapidation – Tarpeia or the women of the Poplifugia – is here constructed in earth or stone, sketched out in the ichnography of urban architecture. Does the built city harden the designs of heated, fluid multiplicities or, on the contrary, channel them? Does a river dig out its valley or choose it?

Everything rests on the question of bonds. The debtors, bound and tied, under bodily constraint, are free, unbound, when they are solvent. An unbound multiplicity moves and rushes – the people in flight. We remember that atoms bind or not in the turbulence that attaches and constructs things, that they unbind and detach themselves in the same turbulence that wears away and destroys. Are you speaking of the world or of man? The parallel simply uses an ancient figure from physics. Clearly; but why do we say free energy or bound energy? The language of energy was often, and still is, a simple or complicated account of exchange and debt. The question of indebtedness thus freezes or liberates a formidable social energy.

Section 4: Pluralities

Economy frees or freezes violence. The accounts of gifts accompany the accounts of damage. Quirinus has the same sort of weapons as Mars. But Quirinus's weapons are more refined than those of Mars. Economic violence will end up as war. The bond of debt will be removed so that the debtors can gird on the sword. Warfare or civil violence ends up, somewhere else, as the sacred. The three gods are not on the same level. Quirinus is deeper, more hidden, more powerful, more recent than the other two. Economy is a strategy, a stratagem, underneath those of Mars. More refined. It is a theology, a jurisdiction, underneath those of Jupiter. More refined. More implacable. Economic tyranny succeeds the first two and has preserved their lessons. Money procures arms or monstrances; the economist is a master as well as a warrior, he capitalizes on the other functions. History is not forgetful. Tarquinius knows how to make war; he faces the fortune-tellers. Money hits lower than fetishes and arms; it digs out a steeper slope; it recruits more.

Indeed, we are going to be very unhappy. Our ancestors knew sacred tyranny. Those who followed suffered military power. We know the oppression of calculus and money. It is more implacable than the other two. It moves more easily toward the universal, leaves nothing lacking, and knows no opposition. The tyranny of information succeeds it, even more terrible. To the point where, like the Roman plebeians, our contemporaries seek refuge in war. Mars seems less formidable to them. Jupiter, the sacred, seems kind and old-fashioned.

Freed energy is, again, the *turba* of the origin. The peril was great for those senators who found themselves in the forum. The crowd floats, and now it seems that the old man is no longer there, that he has been absorbed by or into the pure multitude. The assembly has come undone; the energy tied to the singleton comes untied; the crowd floats, coming, going, *seditio*, from senator to senator, without being fixed.

Is the senator who is now endangered the same old man who has just lit the fire?

Suddenly the multitude spills over. It is turning – turning away, inflecting its course, diverted, *multitudo versa* – toward the two consuls. It exactly retraces the history of Rome – it has left the victim, the narrative forgets him; Rome has expelled the king; the crowd surrounds the consuls, surrounds the curia. The overturned chaos, liquid or clouded, versatile, turns. The cloud turns to a turbulent whirlwind because it is centered. Social physics. The crowd turns away from the old man toward the senators, then toward the consuls. A game of substitutions. The joker begins to be identifiable – he had no name; he only bore signs. Then they had no name; they just bore a title. Now they do have names, two names: Claudius and Servilius, the servile and the lame. The old man was an intersection full of signs. The consuls create an intersection by their names: one is on the side of the plebs, and the other on the side of inequality. In any case each is marked at his site; marked by the old man's signs, maked by some sign of victimization, marked enough to substitute for the first joker. The old man's intersection becomes double; it becomes, by the substitution of the two opposing consuls – one from the plebeian slaves, the other from the nobles – opposed like classes or parties, yet twin in its function. Here are Romulus and Remus; we are in fact in a primitive scene, I mean one of a foundation. History advances by means of substitutions. That is how, through the joker, it bifurcates.

Around the curia the people grumble; *iras hominum*, Livy writes – the anger of men. The senate is divided, like Rome itself, into partisans of each of the consuls;

each twin has his flight of vultures, each little leader has his lobby. The multiple of men, the heated multiple of angry men, surrounds like a crown this curious, almost empty place. The senators are few and rather in disorder; the majority is absent. Attention: the plebs are close to power, approaching the empty space as the Fathers formerly approached the throne of the apotheosis. Servilius wants to deflect this powerful movement, not break it: 'concitatos animos flecti quam frangi.' This deflection is an inclination; we still hear the physics of Lucretius, but the consul fears fracture, fragmentation, fracas; he is afraid of the suffrages. So much so that for the first time the rising is called communal; so much so that the movement, the action, moves under the prefix of harmony – the multiple is no longer named for its separation and disorder. We have to decide between liquid and solid. What is liquid is neither cut nor broken, nor does it decide; it deflects.

We are at the summit. Then, in the tumult, the host of Volsci arrives at a gallop in this form, in formation. Only another multiplicity can undo what is being made here or divert what is born from a first multiple.

Back to the people rumbling around the divided senate in the curia and the enemy rumbling around the divided city of Rome. These images are fundamental. The public rumbles around the stage where Curiatius meets Horatius. Weapons rumble in the theater of war where the king will meet the dictator. The crowd in fusion, seemingly chaotic, surrounds the rivalry of classes, people, individuals, kings, heroes, nations. Everything is always played out in this relation between the multiple, fluid crowd and the single in one-on-one combat, in this relation between the multitude and the rarity. History, philosophy, the philosophy of history – in short, theory – and narrative set the only stage; that is, the hero, the twins, the struggle, the rivals, but rarely the cloud of chaotic energy that surrounds them. As if the author of the text or the concept, taking his place on the stage, always brought the scene back; as if the concept, by capturing the multiple, always brought back unity. What is to be said, then, about multiplicities? They float; they change names. Horatius will have the name Horatius, and Servilius, Servilius, but the cloudy mass, which cannot be a concept, will take the name of mob, pillaging population, plague, sound, clamor, tumult, multitude; since it escapes unity, it is without representation or concept. Like chaos, like heat.

The figure is the one I called a star, or the relation between the single and the multiple. We can see from the point of view of the single – the side of the concept, of science, of the actor, and of representation; we must also see from the point of view of the multiple, and this reversal is not common. It is useful to place persons, masks, heroes, and prosopopoeia back in ensembles and crowds, in the logic of sets. Important here is population, in the categorical sense as in a concrete sense – it fluctuates and evolves; energy is displaced; the singleton is only there to stop, freeze, and bind this energy, to reveal the stable ensemble. He captures the force of the multiple. Thus the keen concept is formed. Romulus kills Remus in the first version; but in the second version Remus falls dead amid the crowd's blows. The second version goes a little farther from the scene. It is useful to introduce set theory into political theory and history. Underneath concepts, underneath the conceptual pavement, lies the sandy myriad of the beach. The crowd is absent in the traditional duel between the twin brothers. Now I hear more clearly the clamoring around the combat of Horatius and Curiatius, the silent sounds in history since Abel, since Cain.

Section 4: Pluralities

Those we have tried to reduce to silence by force, exploitation, and elimination are not the only silent ones. Silence is the zone that surrounds concepts, theories, orders in general, because they are theories, classes, or concepts. History itself, by the very fact that it is told, announced, or recounted, produces this deafness. The multiple clamors noisily; the capture of the multiple is tacit.

Thus the host of Volsci gallops into the narrative. Listen to the thundering hooves, the Latin cavalry announcing the enemy. The diagram does not change form; it only changes locations. The two rivals, Remus and Romulus – no, Servilius and Claudius – are surrounded by the heated mob, and now the two subgroups are surrounded by the heated enemy. No, it is never the work of the negative that transforms things; it is the work of multiplicities.

Suddenly the bonds shift, the knots shift, the energy moves from Quirinus to Mars; debts are remitted for the time of combat. The logic of the gift shows its face under the profile of a logic of damage. The plebeian ensemble, multiply named, moves from the prison, which it was coming out of, to a military role, which it enters into – from chains to oaths, from *concitatos animos* to *concursus*. It is now a concourse in the public square, taking an oath.

The consul Servilius stands alone before the people, who are assembled, an assembly, *contio*. The consul speechifies about classes and subgroups. Concepts are quickly formed when danger nears. The ensemble becomes an assembly; the assembly becomes a concourse under enemy fire, under the pressure of another crowd, under the new work of another multiplicity. Just as the senate reaches a decision quickly under the pressure of the screaming people around the curia. The plebs was about to achieve unanimity, its unity, its totalization; the story ends by speaking of men and their communal bonds. Barely has this accord been reached when the concourse is displaced by the surrounding Volsci. From the political to the military, from civil war to external war, from class struggle to armed conflict. The breathless narrative rushes to pile up the new names of the multitude, which is finally penned in, finally reduced to unity: conscripted men form a body, *manus*; but why call it a body, when they form a hand? The consul controls these forces, *copias*, enclosing them in a camp, *castra*. This is the end of the story, but we dare not call it its point. The public tumult falls silent in the concentration of the camp. War captures violence; Mars appeases violence, although he appears to be launching it. Mars, to speak theologically – or struggle, war, combat, duel, strategy, or dialectic, to speak historically – transforms the work of the multiple into the work of the negative, transforms the real into representation.

Effort wasted after effort won, the Roman people, after the victory, will secede on the Sacred Mount. War commands violence; appearing to liberate it, it negotiates or domesticates it. The crazed clamoring of the multiple is projected onto the hero, who capitalizes on its fury – that is the barbaric solution; or it is concentrated into the squarely framed camp or the formation of lines and columns – that is the Roman solution. They are not so opposite. The multiple is ordered by the single, in the first case, and unified by order in the second. The multiple is brought back to unity, to order, by either a star or a quadrille, by a polarized space or a Cartesian space, but it is always an order. And it is always a representation. Isn't there either a centurion, a general, or a cavalry leader in the camps? What is essential is to erase multiplicity. And that is how Mars tames violence, while appearing to release it.

The multiple takes refuge on the Sacred Mount. The sacred, then, will be the domain where violence again becomes civilized. In the same way this negotiation will see the passage from the multiple to the single. We will soon get to that.

A brief account of these multiple names for the multiple. *Turba* first, the turbulent crowd. *Prope in contionis modum*, something like an assembly. *Populatio*, a pillaging band. It is not uninteresting that a given space peoples itself by ransacking; the multiple rushes headlong, making in space this clean slate that elsewhere I called a blank domino. The turbulence passes like a devastating storm. *Tabes*, plague or contagious illness. The whirlwind moves through the city of Athens, leaving piles of bodies. *Clamor, tumultus*, sound and clamors. The crowd passes, whirling and screaming. The swarm passes, buzzing. *Seditio* – this is the revolt, the multiple movement of the multiple and its nonunified fluctuations, everyone running in every direction, each element going off its own way, separately. Sedition at first is not the negative, the mass rising against a force; sedition is first of all like the Brownian movement of elements in an ensemble – it is Poplifugia, the flight of the multiple. Sedition considered as an uprising is the work of the negative, but sedition in the radical sense, fluctuating movements, is the work of the multiple – that is to say, the displacement of each force in the multiplicity, a force different in every point, a different movement for each difference. The work of the multiple has not been imagined or directly evaluated, but everything goes on as though it were primitive. Can it really be evaluated? *Agminibus cum clamore*, the screaming bands run down every street to the forum. Sedition is channeled by the paths of urban planning, by the topography of places. Little grouped pockets converge toward the unity of the assembly. Subgroups appear amid the clamors. In the sound emerges direction, then meaning. The mechanism here described is the polarization of sedition, its inclination. Each group is on its own side; suddenly they all move toward the same single point.

Multitude versa – the crowd then turns around. It seems that here it has arrived at a point, a threshold of crystallization or coagulation, because its movements are oriented, inflected toward the forum, around the senator, in the direction of someone or other passing by or posted there; this is the polarized space I was talking about. We do not really know what to call these phenomena; we only have abstract words for them, physical images, all metaphors. Why does this man alone, an old man, a consul, hero, soldier, orator, suppliant, actor, dictator, or victim, make the multitude turn? Is it enough to say that he bears on his body the marks of the ensemble? What is this process of identification? What is this unleashed fury? Why does this singleton make the multitude swerve, spill out, circle? Why and how does he make the turbulent mob come about-face? How does he make the whirlwind spin, inflect, evolve? Why and how does he sow revolt or revolution? Why these well-chosen words, these well-formed phenomena? Let's admit that we know nothing about this. All we know is that the language speaks of a turning movement that happens swiftly, immediately after disorder. After the chaos of sedition, the little pockets form and the multitude overturns. Revolt and revolution, considered as uprising, do the work of the negative; but in the radical sense, as in the sense of a birth, revolt is the turning movement of the mob, the turbulent crowd – its first ordered movement, the first global result of the work of the multiple. The multiple then is displaced as a compact mass. Brownian sedition makes the turbulent revolt. The first is scattered and the second overturns. Integrating force is born in it; we don't really know how. Synthesis is born in it, the synthesis of the multiple. What is this mobile, floating unity?

What is impressive here is the fidelity to the physical model. It would be impressive if our models of physics – hardening, cooled liquids, crystallization, formation in cells and spirals – could be induced from what we know of social processes. I don't know where to draw the line; who does? We are even less capable of doing so since it is also the idea we create for ourselves of the formation of ideas, or of representation – the synthesis of the multiple. As if we had a representation of representation. Suddenly devoid of the means of thought, we are going to lose heart. No doubt a sign that there is much here to be thought about.

The multiple is primitive. It is differentiated everywhere, floating, fluctuating, chaotic. Yes, chaos is primitive, and our myths have always said so. The mass is not reducible to the state – this sentence has a physical meaning and a social meaning. The multiple is anterior to all formation and all synthesis; all formation and all synthesis are its derivative, its declension. In Rome, when the multitude becomes a concourse it deviates, migrates toward the troop, the army corps, the camp. The force of the camp, the force of order – this force that rests in the consul's hands, against the enemy, and tomorrow will rest in the tribune's hands against the consul – issues from the sudden integration of the multiple. The troop is a crowd that has lost its differentiation, its seditious variegation. The big problem is this loss or this forgetting. The mixed ensemble becomes homogeneous. How, once again, does the multiple make itself one? How does the whole crowd let itself go toward the singleton? It is true, Livy's old man already bore on his shoulders the suffering of everyone else.

The multiple makes itself one by a change of phase. We must be attentive to the intermediary states; it is true that our sciences of the collective often stop at states – that is, at equilibriums, institutions, classes, subclasses – in short, at statics even, and above all, when they hide these statics in the discourse of dynamism. The collective changes phases, however; it knows intermediary states, turbulent states that do not merit the name of states. No, I am not projecting one language onto another, physics onto history, an exact science onto a social science; I am simply trying to speak in several voices. I am trying to imagine multiplicity in its difference and its fluctuations. I am lost, displaced, right in the middle of the Northwest Passage, in an intermediary state between the sciences, in the fractal and multiple distribution of lands, water, thin ice, and ice floes. I mean that I am trying to remain without a specialty in the rather large desert between the exact sciences and the social sciences, outside of the very precisely divided space of classification. I believe that this place is one of the places for philosophy today. I am trying to imagine the intermediary state there, whatever and wherever it might be, in the vicinity upstream from the formation, before synthesis, as close as possible to integration. I am trying to imagine nature in the sense of birth, when newness is created, is going to be created, or unexpectedly appears. I am trying to imagine the margin that separates the multiple from the ordered, the moment when the solid is at the point of setting, in agitated crystals, when turbulence spins in its whirlwind, when life is connected, liberated, awakened, organized, when the message makes sense in the clamorous tide of the charivari, when the music raises its voice over the scattered sounds, when the first hallelujah surfaces amid the stammering, when the concept defines an exactitude on the fertile field that precedes the intuitive dawn. Everything at first is in the work of multiplicities. It is still hard to imagine, as though repressed, and negatively named – nonsense, chance, or disorder. Take heart – the multiple arrives, from every direction, in every science.

A word on this intermediary place without a place, where I find myself. It is a place of collection; by this I mean that in this place I collect the voices issuing from elsewhere, at almost equal intensity. The intense division of knowledge defines sites, the places from which to speak. From there one speaks above all of the site itself. Places impose words; they are mouthpieces. An inhabitant speaks his language and defends his culture. Have you ever heard a specialist praise the neighboring specialty? This external word is unheard of. The division of the sciences creates the conflict of the faculties; inversely, this war creates the partition. The new thing would be – the truth? – the external word; I will no longer believe anything but citations from outside of the lobby. Everything else is only publicity, only war and concurrence. If philosophy adopts the language or metalanguage of a chosen place, it just adds to the conflict of the faculties – redundant redundancy. Thus we often see discourses shaped with the unique purpose of showing the nonvalidity of the neighboring discourse. That is strictly a political discourse, a straw man's discourse on the neighboring straw man. This speech is, alas, empty of speech; it reveals nothing more than the hatred nourished in one place for the neighboring places. The space resounds with squabble or noise; nothing moves, because this is the most deeply rooted conservatism since the dawn of time; knowledge and novelty dissolve. The work of the negative always freezes a state in its state; it is conservative. The philosopher, then, must rally his forces to avoid being from a physical, social, or ideal place; he must put all his effort into trying to avoid any speciality and all his passion into not being from any group. He avoids redundancy, the discourse that duplicates place; avoids the polemical freeze of the pillar of salt. He puts all his strength into hearing specialities. Certainly he thereby suffers grave losses, loses his listening post and other amenities and accumulates all disadvantages, but he gains in mobility and truth by his detachment. He listens in what I have called an equal intensity; he can attempt to speak a language of multiple voices. He is the man of the multiple, he who tries to imagine the multiple. He leaves the single at its own command. He watches it shut up the multiple into camps, concentrated between four trenches. He watches it divide it from within and apportion it into sites. Military discipline where the plebeians fall, scientific discipline where thought can cave in, technical languages crisscrossed by bonds.

The military solution is worn out. The people retreat; they have distanced themselves in the strict sense – they have fled. And we are told in fact that they fled in calling out to one another. They follow, however, the customs they have been given; on the Aventine hill or the Sacred Mount – it makes no difference, so I will opt for the Sacred Mount – on the mountain to which they withdraw they establish a camp, a post, ditches, a stockade. A camp with no enemy. A camp for civil war? There, peacefully, amid their provisions, they eat and wait. And they know that they form a body. A military body in its camp, formed by maniples, limbs, and hands.

Thus Menenius or Valerius – it makes no difference – comes there to talk about the body. About the body and eating, about the belly. He retells the old apologue of

Section 4: Pluralities

the body, the limbs, and the belly. The noble patrician speaks to the illiterate people in a language that they can understand – such scornful abuse was already current then. That is important, as is this: that he speaks, alone, before the mass of plebs. Let the limbs understand, he is saying, that the stomach is also a limb.

Amid the scattered members, does one of them make a group on its own? Let us redraw the archaic biological model of the group in the good old Latin that we had lost. Menenius, the popular orator, is speaking.

'Today the body forms a harmony,' he says. The Latin says *omnia in unum*, which I read as *all in one*. Traditions and translations have volunteered that all the organs, all the limbs, consent, *consentiant*, in a harmonious whole. Distributively, they all move toward a global accord, *omnia in totum*; separately, they all move toward a unitary whole. That is not what is written here; what Livy actually writes is *omnia in unum*, all in one. I am not sure of this *one* or of this *in*. All consent in a single one; this is how it is written, I can do nothing about that.

So it is today. But there was a time when each one of the organs singularly had its opinion and its own discourse. Each one had its *consilium*, whereas now all arrive at *consensus*. At that time, then, everyone deliberated. On his own and for himself, *cuique*. Sudden indignation. Which organs were indignant? The rest, precisely – *reliquas paries*. Which rest? Those left in the account, left to account for themselves. Which account? Precisely that of all but one. This one is well-placed, *in medio*; the belly is in the middle. Quiet, in repose, with neither work nor care, he enjoys a luxurious sinecure afforded by the work and the ministry of others, the rest. And the rest are indignant at having to work for him, having to work together and separately for him alone in the middle. I like the word indignation: dignity is decency, one is indignant then at that which is not fitting. Because it is contrary to harmony.

Horror. Hypocrisy. Is Menenius joking?

Hypocrisy – the rest, all but one, work for the one at the center. Exactly – *omnia in unum*. Now this is how the orator defined harmony. Thus the problem is already resolved, even before it is posed; there is no gap between the time of this fable and today's accord. All agree, in some fashion, because each one on his own forms this all-but-one – that is to say, this remainder that is at work for the one situated at the very center. The *omnia in unum* is invariable through time, whatever catastrophes there might be.

Hypocrisy. Each one does his job, his work, takes care, accomplishes his ministry. I like the word *ministry*, even if I hate administration. A master, *magister* – that is, a great one, *major* – is surrounded by ministers, little ones, *minus*. All these little ones work for the great one they surround, like Lilliputians swarming around the mountainous stomach of a reclining Gulliver with cables, ladders, and cranes. All these minimals are ministers.

Since there is time, I will invent another apologue along the way, for another time. Look at hypocrisy: the master with the round stomach, wishing to make the minimals forget his enormity and their tininess, subtly takes their name. The great one will call himself minister. Or secretary, or servant. The great calls himself little. The strong one takes everything from the weak, including their name. Gulliver moves on to the land of giants; now he is minister. The wolf has himself called a lamb; the minister, although a master, a grand personage, takes the name of the slave – the *major* plays the *minus*, and the powerful, famous dialectic is thwarted. Then everyone sees that the little minister accomplishes his ministry, his servitude. Hypocrisy.

I have finished the demonstration; I have finished my work, my ministry; the proof is that I am amusing myself by talking about the little minister. The demonstration was closed from the beginning. If the goal is *omnia in unum*, then all the rest work for the one, and the problem is resolved. If necessary, for the rest to be really all, it is enough to minimize the one, to make it a minister. The gap that is left cannot be seen, or can barely be seen. No, I can no longer see the fabled delay between that time and now; time and history, the time and the evolution from state to state are annulled or wiped out, comparison disappears, as does the narrative, as does the apologue, the model, organic or otherwise, fades away, and there remains the bleak repetition of the relationship between the several and the single, the silent plebs with Valerius orating in their midst, *in medio*; there remains the bundle of the multiple and the single, *omnia in unum*, the star. I am not very sure about this *in*. But the one – then or now, long ago or not long ago – is Valerius or the stomach, it does not matter which; what is essential is his site, at the intersection. Low or high, on the periphery, at the center, in the middle, *in medio* – the essential is not the quality of the site but the fact that in this place intersection takes place.

Whence the giant and minimal fraud, the fraud of revolution, at the time of illusions; I mean the fraud at this illusory time when we believe we are changing. The apologue repeats and varies, as that which we learn under the category of history repeats and varies. The bleak iteration of the star, of the diagram of one-all. We change it and it always comes back. Horatius alone with the Curiatii. Or the warring heroes and the army that faces them.

Whence conspiracy. *Conspirasse*. Now *consensus*, formerly *consilium*, and in the interim, *conspiratio*. That is all well and good. But perhaps we should see in it 'sensation' or 'respiration' – the primitive organic models that are hidden – to sense, to respire. As if an organic model were exposed by means of hidden organic models.

Before eating, together or separately, one must breathe in or smell. Or think. Just as the star is invariable through its apparent changes, the harmonious body is invariable through the variation of its functions. The demonstration on digestion assumes the experience of other demonstrations on respiration or sensation.

If they conspired, it is because they still agreed. They were in agreement against. All against one. All against the stomach, all against Valerius. From now on, understand the value of *in* – *omnia in unum*. The genius of the Latin language is to say in this one word both the pro and the con. Only our geometry has the same capacity; the star's bouquet moves toward its intersection, toward the fixed and central point of the spray – or the cone or the circle, it doesn't matter – and that movement does not prejudice what passes through its lines. To work for or to conspire against is always to repeat *omnia in unum*, the multiple-single star, the diagram of power, representation, or concept. The plebeians served Valerius and conspired against him; but that makes no difference to Valerius, since he did not change sites. Victim or despot, sacrificial king or Oriental-style tyrant, Louis XVI decapitated, Robespierre guillotined, Napoleon on Saint Helena or elected president – what remains invariable is being at the center of the star. By speechifying, Valerius handsomely occupies the place of power. Or Menenius does, or another orator. The apologue repeats indefinitely the scene that it establishes and plays.

The conspiracy, it is said, goes badly. The body falls ill. *Tabes*, putrefaction, epidemic, contagious malady. The plague – they all have the plague. *Una*, each one, *totumque corpus*, the whole body; it never ceases. They are always agreed, let us say, by contagion. They will not all die, but all are struck – all. In agreement by opinion, in agreement by conspiracy, in agreement by contagion, in agreement by consensus. Nothing new under the sun but this star.

Of course the plague is violent, as the conspiracy was violent, as the work of all for one alone was by violence. How can we remove ourselves from this plague? The apologue removes itself, because it doesn't move.

Apparuisse. It appears. It becomes manifest. We remove ourselves by understanding. The only solution to this problem is to understand. To understand well what is going on and not to hide it. Even as he shows the plebs what has to be understood, Valerius the patrician hides it. He hides the *divisum pariter*, the redistribution.

It appears to everyone that all work for one, the belly, and that the belly, a member, works for all. The diagram has not moved an inch; *omnia in unum*, whatever the sense of this *in* – for, toward, against, in the direction of the center or the periphery – and no matter what travels along its paths; be it food, hatred, words, plague, blood. Veins lead toward the stomach and away from it. We have known since the death of Romulus that the blood flows from the crowd to unity or from unity to the crowd. Is this an organic model or a violent or religious one? The flow of blood, of sound, of words, of meaning, the flow of hatred, noise, germs of the plague, a flow of harmony – it is in fact the flow that changes in a bundle that itself does not change. The fable of the stomach takes the diagram and beats it down, takes it up again, inside out, then right side out, folding it over on itself, as the baker does his dough. You think you are feeding me, and it is I who feed you.

Now, for the first time, I am stupefied to read here the word *division* – *divisum pariter*. Division is precisely the vision departing from the starred center. The vision that the single can have of the multiple is named division. And the division of labor is this very vision. Divide in order to conquer: a tautology, the bleak iteration of the same diagram; conquering consists in occupying the place from which one sees by division. I, Valerius, the stomach, am speaking to you, and I see you according to the thousand veins of my gaze; I distribute words like food among you, I distribute blood. This is my blood. He who distributes, who allocates, who divides is the master, *magisterium, ministerium* – he is at the central point of the star, the exchanger, the turntable; he has, all alone, a relation to all. A minister by the smallness of the site, a magistrate by its capacity. *Omnia in unum* – that could be said, in elementary arithmetic, to posit a division. That could be said, as well, in Greek: *diasparagmos*, eucharist. Because it can be read one way or another.

This entire misery of history and this whole trap can essentially be understood. We do not know what 'all' really means. *Omnia* and *totus* escape us. Society and groups are black boxes. Our general will remains dark, as do our contracts. What remains dark is the act of uniting ourselves. Union is a dark operation. Hard to imagine, hard to direct, hard to realize.

Hypocrisy consists in imagining or positioning the intersection in the place of union, in practicing one as a substitute for the other, in building this one and never that. But perhaps I am too severe; perhaps this hypocrisy is only impotence. The intersection seems clear, distinct, immediately recognizable; it is imaginable, it functions comfortably. The union appears dark, chaotic, dangerous; the crowd rushes. It is the crowd that rushes toward *diasparagmos*, toward intersection. Intersection is an operation in set theory that bears the name *diasparagmos*.

Fear seems to choose between tyranny and the crowd in fusion. Between intersection and union, our culture and our history seem to choose – while often hiding it – the first over the second.

Unions. I'm summarizing the story. Everyone once had his *consilium*. They then proceeded to *conspiratio*. Crisis spread *contagio* in their midst. And the evil ended in *consensus*. That's it for the body. Stability replaces history.

The discourse of the father was the comparison, *comparando*. Then came *concordia*, harmony. Livy shows it in good measure: 'de concordia coeptum, concessumque in condiciones.' He accumulates these words of unity. We observe, in passing, that foundation is one of these words. *Ab urbe condita*. Foundation is a condition. The condition is union – that which is situated or put together, stored away, held in reserve, locked up in a safe place, and thus hidden from the gaze, beyond understanding.

Everything I have said since the beginning is only the explanation of foundation itself. *Ab urbe condita* – since the union of the city. This condition is buried, hidden. This union is hidden. Indeed, we don't know what union is. Thus we never stop founding the city, founding Rome, here. All these words of concord and conspiracy, contagion and counsel, are terms of condition, infinite variations on the same act of foundation. We vary by not knowing.

Alas, it all starts over again. Concord simply creates the same pattern again. Intersection. Thus the plebs' tribunes were named. In place of Valerius or Menenius, consuls or patricians, are Gaius Licinius and Lucius Albinus, tribunes. A new relation between the multiple and the single; that is to say, the same one. And the star returns. What does it matter if they are leaders or the leaders of non-leaders, since it is always a question of leaders? Masters of masters or of slaves, what difference does it make? What difference does it make for the union of slaves? The law of history is substitution.

Union produces intersection. Can we say such a thing? It founds it, I believe; at least language says so.

In any case, I am pleased that the first tribune bears the same name as the man in the chariot, the vestals' rescuer when Rome is in the hands of the barbarous Gauls, the man of the white jar and the black jar and divine vision – Lucius Albinus, the white light.

Apparuisse. They had understood. Perhaps we must understand history's simple and bleak law. Because everything is in comprehension, because the one explains to all who try to understand and try to change by having understood the comparison. Thus the consuls go to fight the tribunes, delegates against delegates; the little leaders, out of their class, out of the battle lines, go make a spectacle before the masses united to watch them. Intersection, the all-one diagram, begins again. And it is called politics. Horatius, with or without his brothers, leaves the ranks. Across from

Section 4: Pluralities

him Curiatius has left his, and they fight with swords of equal length, on a stage; union is voided because everyone, in unity, watches them. They do not watch their contract, but they blank it out while realizing it. Horatius or the consul, the tribune or Curiatius – what is the difference?

Leibniz said it very well: representation is the single-multiple diagram itself.

I'm stopping for a moment.

The plebeians withdraw to the Sacred Mount, pitch camp, dig a trench. Why didn't they found a new city? Because they did not kill Valerius, who crossed the trench to enter into talks with them.

If they had put Valerius to death, they would again have drawn the diagram of intersection, by *diasparagmos*, in blood. That did not happen; they were on the Sacred Mount. They wanted to massacre but did not do so; they were bound by oath or sacrament. They withdrew onto the Sacred Mount.

They dig a trench. They draw a closed circle. They unite within it. Ensemble. Union.

Valerius arrives and makes a speech. All who have revolted against him watch him, lend him their ear; but they will later delegate a tribune of the plebs. They all hold lines of the network that go toward him, toward the one. Intersection.

All? Not all, says the fable, but *reliquas partes* – the rest; all minus one. Singleton, remnant, subtraction.

Seen from the singleton's point of view, the rest is divided. Valerius, the stomach, the tribune, the consul – no matter – sees the union along the lines of the network, in the cone of vision. Division. I'll stop.

The whole process simply adopts, at each step, an elementary operation of set theory or of arithmetic. Better yet, the process makes us understand them better. It is true that I had never understood the word union so well – concept, conspiracy, contagion, consensus, or concord. Nor had I understood the operation of intersection well or the term *division* at all. Put another way, exact science awakens the apologue; both the fable of the limbs and the history that dramatizes it receive from it an undeniable clarity. But reciprocally, the social and political process wakes exact science and makes its first steps easier to see, perhaps. Add in inclusion, exclusion, the excluded third, membership – all charged with hate.

Here one will ask for decision, but decision is absurd. Is it the genesis of understanding, a genealogy of operations, a famous episode of the prehistory of science; would there be, at the origin, a social set theory? Perhaps. Is it an explanation of social processes by an operational method? Is the mathematical model the best to help us understand? They understood; and we have finally understood that they did not understand and let themselves be deceived. A paradox: both the apparent organic model and the latent organic model disappear, leaving room for the arithmetic model of sets, valid both for the body and the social body. And, in effect, we must think *totus*, the whole, and *omnia*, the distributive whole. Perhaps. Is there some isomorphism between an event issuing from the fabled depths of our cultural history and the categories of reason taught today to children in school – the blind mathematical education of the Roman people, the blind Roman education of the calculus class? Perhaps.

The first hypothesis is evolutive. But we can engender the operations of calculus by means of little pebbles. And Rome never invented what the Hellenes invented. The second hypothesis is epistemological, after the theory of models. Yes, models are useful, and we change ours every day, for usefulness. The last is structural, adventurous. Why choose? And what if we had crossed three times in one the Northwest Passage? We have, simply, understood a bit better. Every theory would like to hold the facts, all the facts, in its hand – its own, unique hand, *omnia in unum*. Not so here. Here we remain with multiplicities.

But why didn't they found a second city? Their stockades were high, their ditches had been dug; another Rome was ready to be born. But like soldiers, they built only a sort of camp.

They understood, we are told. They first understood that it was necessary to fight. They understood the relations of force. By fighting, they failed to establish. It is necessary to leave in order to found somewhere else, not to keep aside – on the side of one's brother, one's city, or one's enemies; on the side of discipline or of familiar or habitual thought. In fighting, they did not see the singleton capture their forces. They were trapped by class struggle. The only real trap is war, hatred, the polemic.

They understood – white light. They understood and they did not kill. Murder is transformed into spectacle. The thing is transformed into fable. Into words.

Romulus left. Romulus is excluded. He takes to the woods. He does not understand. Romulus buries his thought at the bottom of the ditch. They understood. And they did not establish. They form an unfounded city within the founded city.

Notes

1. The subject of one of Pascal's *Pensées*. [Cleopatra's nose: had it been shorter, the whole aspect of the world would have been altered.]

Edgar Allen Poe

Poe (1809–49) was a prolific writer of stories and poems. His parents were travelling actors, he spent a year at the University of Virginia as a student, enlisted in the US army, from which he was dishonourably discharged, married a thirteen-year-old cousin, and died feverishly from the combined effects of alcohol, heart failure and epilepsy. His life was beset by problems with money, gambling and debt; and there is no doubt that he knew about life from many points of view. His writings were popular and inventive. He is best remembered for his horror stories, including *The Fall of the House of Usher*, which Debussy was going to set as an opera, which is testimony to the fact that he was adopted as an enthusiasm by the artistic avant-garde at the end of the nineteenth century.[1] There were lurid and loose adaptations of Poe stories among the works of the film-maker Roger Corman during the 1960s, but Poe deserves to be read – and he is read. He does not always make the flesh creep. 'The Man of the Crowd' is far from being a horror story, but it is difficult to say just what sort of story it is. It is included here because it helps to consolidate the theme of group identities, but Poe's treatment of the idea is idiosyncratic, imagining the crowd's identity being condensed into the identifiable figure of a visible person – who is far from pleasant – 'the type and genius of deep crime'. It is an intuition of the psychology of the crowd that precedes the particular wickednesses of crowds during the twentieth century (as analysed by Canetti and Cassirer) and is all the more striking for that. There is a story by Henry James, 'The Private Life' (1892) where one of the characters, Lord Mellifont, is discovered to disappear when there are no other people around. His personality and his very existence are generated only in relation to others. The man of the crowd seems to be such a person – an emergent property of the crowd, not an individual with the possibility of an independent existence. The 'Hortus Animae' mentioned in the final sentence of the story is *The Little Garden of the Soul*, a prayer-book that had a great popularity in the early sixteenth century. Poe's point seems to be that it is unreadable – even more unreadable than the human heart – and it is a mercy that the heart cannot be read. Gorgias, the sophist philosopher mentioned near the beginning, is now known only through Plato's version of an encounter between him and Sophocles, in which Sophocles, as ever, wins. Sophistical reasoning has had a bad name ever since this version of Sophist teaching became the means by which we learn about it.

Notes

1. Debussy never completed the work.

The Man of the Crowd

Ce grand malheur, de ne pouvoir être seul. – LA BRUYERE

It was well said of a certain German book that *'er lasst sich nicht lesen'* – it does not permit itself to be read. There are some secrets which do not permit themselves to be told. Men die nightly in their beds, wringing the hands of ghostly confessors, and looking them piteously in the eyes – die with despair of heart and convulsion of throat, on account of the hideousness of mysteries which will not *suffer themselves* to be revealed. Now and then, alas, the conscience of man takes up a burden so heavy in horror that it can be thrown down only into the grave. And thus the essence of all crime is undivulged.

Not long ago, about the closing in of an evening in autumn, I sat at the large bow-window of the D – Coffee-House in London. For some months I had been ill in health, but was now convalescent, and, with returning strength, found myself in one of those happy moods which are so precisely the converse of *ennui* – moods of the keenest appetency, when the film from the mental vision departs – the αχλυζ οζ πριν επηεν – and the intellect, electrified, surpasses as greatly its every-day condition, as does the vivid yet candid reason of Leibnitz, the mad and flimsy rhetoric of Gorgias. Merely to breathe was enjoyment; and I derived positive pleasure even from many of the legitimate sources of pain. I felt a calm but inquisitive interest in every thing. With a cigar in my mouth and a newspaper in my lap, I had been amusing myself for the greater part of the afternoon, now in poring over advertisements, now in observing the promiscuous company in the room, and now in peering through the smoky panes into the street.

This latter is one of the principal thoroughfares of the city, and had been very much crowded during the whole day. But, as the darkness came on, the throng momently increased; and, by the time the lamps were well lighted, two dense and continuous tides of population were rushing past the door. At this particular period of the evening I had never before been in a similar situation, and the tumultuous sea of human heads filled me, therefore, with a delicious novelty of emotion. I gave up, at length, all care of things within the hotel, and became absorbed in contemplation of the scene without.

At first my observations took an abstract and generalizing turn. I looked at the passengers in masses, and thought of them in their aggregate relations. Soon, however, I descended to details, and regarded with minute interest the innumerable varieties of figure, dress, air, gait, visage, and expression of countenance.

By far the greater number of those who went by had a satisfied, business-like demeanor, and seemed to be thinking only of making their way through the press. Their brows were knit, and their eyes rolled quickly; when pushed against by fellow-wayfarers they evinced no symptom of impatience, but adjusted their clothes and hurried on. Others, still a numerous class, were restless in their movements, had flushed faces, and talked and gesticulated to themselves, as if feeling in solitude on account of the very denseness of the company around. When impeded in their progress, these people suddenly ceased muttering, but redoubled their gesticulations, and awaited, with an absent and overdone smile upon the lips, the course of the persons impeding them. If jostled, they bowed profusely to the jostlers, and appeared overwhelmed with confusion. – There was nothing very distinctive about these two large classes beyond what I have noted. Their habiliments belonged to that order which is pointedly termed the decent. They were undoubtedly noblemen, merchants, attorneys, tradesmen, stock-jobbers – the Eupatrids and the common-places of society – men of leisure and men actively engaged in affairs of their own – conducting business upon its own responsibility. They did not greatly excite my attention.

The tribe of clerks was an obvious one; and here I discerned two remarkable divisions. There were the junior clerks of flash houses – young gentlemen with tight coats, bright boots, well-oiled hair, and supercilious lips. Setting aside a certain dapperness of carriage, which may be termed *deskism* for want of a better word, the manner of these persons seemed to be an exact facsimile of what had been the perfection of *bon ton* about twelve or eighteen months before. They wore the cast-off graces of the gentry; – and this, I believe, involves the best definition of the class.

The division of the upper clerks of staunch firms, or of the 'steady old fellows,' it was not possible to mistake. These were known by their coats and pantaloons of black or brown, made to sit comfortably, with white cravats and waistcoats, broad solid-looking shoes, and thick hose or gaiters. They had all slightly bald heads, from which the right ears, long used to pen-holding, had an odd habit of standing off on end. I observed that they always removed or settled their hats with both hands, and wore watches, with short gold chains of a substantial and ancient pattern. Theirs was the affectation of respectability – if indeed there be an affectation so honorable.

There were many individuals of dashing appearance, whom I easily understood as belonging to the race of swell pick-pockets, with which all great cities are infested. I watched these gentry with much inquisitiveness, and found it difficult to imagine how they should ever be mistaken for gentlemen by gentlemen themselves. Their voluminousness of wristband, with an air of excessive frankness, should betray them at once.

The gamblers, of whom I descried not a few, were still more easily recognizable. They wore every variety of dress, from that of the desperate thimble-rig bully, with velvet waistcoat, fancy neckerchief, gilt chains, and filigreed buttons, to that of the scrupulously inornate clergyman, than which nothing could be less liable to suspicion. Still all were distinguished by a certain sodden swarthiness of complexion, a filmy dimness of eye, and pallor and compression of lip. There were two other traits, moreover, by which I could always detect them: a guarded low-ness of tone in conversation, and a more than ordinary extension of the thumb in a direction at right angles with the fingers. Very often, in company with these sharpers, I observed an order of men somewhat different in habits, but still birds of a kindred feather. They may be defined as the gentlemen who live by their wits. They seem to prey upon the public in two battalions – that of the dandies and that of the military men. Of the first grade the leading features are long locks and smiles; of the second, frogged coats and frowns.

Descending in the scale of what is termed gentility, I found darker and deeper themes for speculation. I saw Jew peddlers, with hawk eyes flashing from countenances whose every other feature wore only an expression of abject humility; sturdy professional street beggars scowling upon mendicants of a better stamp, whom despair alone had driven forth into the night for charity; feeble and ghastly invalids, upon whom death had placed a sure hand, and who sidled and tottered through the mob, looking every one beseechingly in the face, as if in search of some chance consolation, some lost hope; modest young girls returning from long and late labor to a cheerless home, and shrinking more tearfully than indignantly from the glances of ruffians, whose direct contact, even, could not be avoided; women of the town of all kinds and of all ages – the unequivocal beauty in the prime of her womanhood, putting one in mind of the statue in Lucian, with the surface of Parian marble, and the interior filled with filth – the loathsome and utterly lost leper in rags – the wrinkled, bejewelled, and paint-begrimed beldame, making a last effort at youth – the mere child of immature form, yet, from long association, an adept in the dreadful coquetries of her trade, and burning with a rabid ambition to be ranked the equal of her elders in vice; drunkards innumerable and indescribable – some in shreds and patches, reeling, inarticulate, with bruised visage and lack-lustre eyes – some in whole although filthy garments, with a slightly unsteady swagger, thick sensual lips, and hearty-looking rubicund faces – others clothed in materials which had once been good, and which even now were scrupulously well brushed – men who walked with a more than naturally firm and springy step, but whose countenances were fearfully pale, whose eyes were hideously wild and red, and who clutched with quivering fingers, as they strode through the crowd, at every object which came within their reach; beside these, piemen, porters, coal-heavers, sweeps; organ-grinders, monkey-exhibitors, and ballad-mongers, those who vended with those who sang; ragged artizans and exhausted laborers of every description, and all full of a noisy and inordinate vivacity which jarred discordantly upon the ear, and gave an aching sensation to the eye.

As the night deepened, so deepened to me the interest of the scene; for not only did the general character of the crowd materially alter (its gentler features retiring in the gradual withdrawal of the more orderly portion of the people, and its harsher ones coming out into bolder relief, as the late hour brought forth every species of infamy from its den), but the rays of the gas-lamps, feeble at first in their struggle with the dying day, had now at length gained ascendancy, and threw over every thing a fitful and garish lustre. All was dark yet splendid – as that ebony to which has been likened the style of Tertullian.

The wild effects of the light enchained me to an examination of individual faces; and although the rapidity with which the world of light flitted before the window prevented me from casting more than a glance upon each visage, still it seemed that, in my then peculiar mental state, I could frequently read, even in that brief interval of a glance, the history of long years.

With my brow to the glass, I was thus occupied in scrutinizing the mob, when suddenly there came into view a countenance (that of a decrepid old man, some sixty-five or seventy years of age) – a countenance which at once arrested and absorbed my whole attention, on account of the absolute idiosyncrasy of its expression. Any thing even remotely resembling that expression I had never seen before. I well remember that my first thought, upon beholding it, was that Retzch, had he viewed it, would have greatly preferred it to his own pictural incarnations of the fiend. As I endeavored, during the brief minute of my original survey, to form some analysis of the meaning conveyed, there arose confusedly and paradoxically within my mind, the ideas of vast mental power, of caution, of penuriousness, of avarice, of coolness, of malice, of blood-thirstiness, of triumph, of merriment, of excessive terror, of intense – of supreme despair. I felt singularly aroused, startled, fascinated. 'How wild a history,' I said to myself, 'is written within that bosom!' Then came a craving desire to keep the man in view – to know more of him. Hurriedly putting on an overcoat, and seizing my hat and cane, I made my way into the street, and pushed through the crowd in the direction which I had seen him take; for he had already disappeared. With some little difficulty I at length came within sight of him, approached, and followed him closely, yet cautiously, so as not to attract his attention.

I had now a good opportunity of examining his person. He was short in stature, very thin, and apparently very feeble. His clothes, generally, were filthy and ragged; but as he came, now and then, within the strong glare of a lamp, I perceived that his linen, although dirty, was of beautiful texture; and my vision deceived me, or, through a rent in a closely-buttoned and evidently second-handed *roquelaire* which enveloped him, I caught a glimpse both of a diamond and of a dagger. These observations heightened my curiosity, and I resolved to follow the stranger whithersoever he should go.

It was now fully night-fall, and a thick humid fog hung over the city, soon ending in a settled and heavy rain. This change of weather had an odd effect upon the crowd, the whole of which was at once put into new commotion, and overshadowed by a world of umbrellas. The waver, the jostle, and the hum increased in a tenfold degree. For my own part I did not much regard the rain – the lurking of an old fever in my system rendering the moisture somewhat too dangerously pleasant. Tying a handkerchief about my mouth, I kept on. For half an hour the old man held his way with difficulty along the great thoroughfare; and I here walked close at his elbow through fear of losing sight of him. Never once turning his head to look back, he did not observe me. By and by he passed into a cross street, which, although densely filled with people, was not quite so much thronged as the main one he had quitted. Here a change in his demeanor became evident. He walked more slowly and with less object than before – more hesitatingly. He crossed and re-crossed the way repeatedly, without apparent aim; and the press was still so thick, that, at every such movement, I was obliged to follow him closely. The street was a narrow and long one, and his course lay within it for nearly an hour, during which the passengers had gradually diminished to about that number which is ordinarily seen at noon on Broadway near the park – so vast a difference is there between a London populace and that of the most frequented American city. A second turn brought us into a square, brilliantly lighted, and overflowing with life. The old manner of the stranger re-appeared. His chin fell upon his breast, while his eyes rolled wildly from under his knit brows, in every direction, upon those who hemmed him in. He urged his way steadily and perseveringly. I was surprised, however, to find, upon his having made the circuit of the square, that he turned and retraced his steps. Still more was I astonished to see him repeat the same walk several times – once nearly detecting me as he came round with a sudden movement.

In this exercise he spent another hour, at the end of which we met with far less interruption from passengers than at first. The rain fell fast; the air grew cool; and the people were retiring to their homes. With a gesture of impatience, the wanderer passed into a by-street comparatively deserted. Down this, some quarter of a mile long, he rushed with an activity I could not have dreamed of seeing in one so aged, and which put me to much trouble in pursuit. A few minutes brought us to a large and busy bazaar, with the localities of which the stranger appeared well acquainted, and where his original demeanor again became apparent, as he forced his way to and fro, without aim, among the host of buyers and sellers.

During the hour and a half, or thereabouts, which we passed in this place, it required much caution on my part to keep him within reach without attracting his observation. Luckily I wore a pair of caoutchouc overshoes, and could move about in perfect silence. At no moment did he see that I watched him. He entered shop after shop, priced nothing, spoke no word, and looked at all objects with a wild and vacant stare. I was now utterly amazed at his behavior, and firmly resolved that we should not part until I had satisfied myself in some measure respecting him.

A loud-toned clock struck eleven, and the company were fast deserting the bazaar. A shop-keeper, in putting up a shutter, jostled the old man, and at the instant I saw a strong shudder come over his frame. He hurried into the street, looked anxiously around him for an instant, and then ran with incredible swiftness through many crooked and peopleless lanes, until we emerged once more upon the great thoroughfare whence we had started – the street of the D – Hotel. It no longer wore, however, the same aspect. It was still brilliant with gas; but the rain fell fiercely, and there were few persons to be seen. The stranger grew pale. He walked moodily some paces up the once populous avenue, then, with a heavy sigh, turned in the direction of the river, and, plunging through a great variety of devious ways, came out, at length, in view of one of the principal theatres. It was about being closed, and the audience were thronging from the doors. I saw the old man gasp as if for breath while he threw himself amid the crowd; but I thought that the intense agony of his countenance had, in some measure, abated. His head again fell upon his breast; he appeared as I had seen him at first. I observed that he now took the course in which had gone the greater number of the audience – but, upon the whole, I was at a loss to comprehend the waywardness of his actions.

As he proceeded, the company grew more scattered, and his old uneasiness and vacillation were resumed. For some time he followed closely a party of some ten or twelve roisterers; but from this number one by one dropped off, until three only remained together, in a narrow and gloomy lane, little frequented. The stranger paused, and, for a moment, seemed lost in thought; then, with every mark of agitation, pursued rapidly a route which brought us to the verge of the city, amid regions very different from those we had hitherto traversed. It was the most noisome quarter of London, where every thing wore the worst impress of the most deplorable poverty, and of the most desperate crime. By the dim light of an accidental lamp, tall, antique, worm-eaten, wooden tenements were seen tottering to their fall, in directions so many and capricious, that scarce the semblance of a passage was discernible between them. The paving-stones lay at random, displaced from their beds by the rankly-growing grass. Horrible filth festered in the dammed-up gutters. The whole atmosphere teemed with desolation. Yet, as we proceeded, the sounds of human life revived by sure degrees, and at length large bands of the most abandoned of a London populace were seen reeling to and fro. The spirits of the old man again flickered up, as a lamp which is near its death-hour. Once more he strode onward with elastic tread. Suddenly a corner was turned, a blaze of light burst upon our sight, and we stood before one of the huge suburban temples of Intemperance – one of the palaces of the fiend, Gin.

It was now nearly daybreak; but a number of wretched inebriates still pressed in and out of the flaunting entrance. With a half shriek of joy the old man forced a passage within, resumed at once his original bearing, and stalked backward and forward, without apparent object, among the throng. He had not been thus long occupied, however, before a rush to the doors gave token that the host was closing them for the night. It was something even more intense than despair that I then observed upon the countenance of the singular being whom I had watched so pertinaciously. Yet he did not hesitate in his career, but, with a mad energy, retraced his steps at once, to the heart of the mighty London. Long and swiftly he fled, while I followed him in the wildest amazement, resolute not to abandon a scrutiny in which I now felt an interest all-absorbing. The sun arose while we proceeded, and, when we had once again reached that most thronged mart of the populous town, the street of the D – Hotel, it presented an appearance of human bustle and activity scarcely inferior to what I had seen on the evening before. And here, long, amid the momently increasing confusion, did I persist in my pursuit of the stranger. But, as usual, he walked to and fro, and during the day did not pass from out the turmoil of that street. And, as the shades of the second evening came on, I grew wearied unto death, and, stopping fully in front of the wanderer, gazed at him steadfastly in the face. He noticed me not, but resumed his solemn walk while I, ceasing to follow, remained absorbed in contemplation. 'This old man,' I said at length, 'is the type and the genius of deep crime. He refuses to be alone. *He is the man of the crowd.* It will be in vain to follow; for I shall learn no more of him, nor of his deeds. The worst heart of the world is a grosser book than the "Hortulus Animæ,"[1] and perhaps it is but one of the great mercies of God that *"er lasst sich nicht lessen."'*

Notes

1. '*The Hortulus Animæ cum Oratiunculis Aliquibus Superadditis*' of Grünninger.

Mabel O. Wilson and Le Corbusier

Mabel Wilson's essay here revisits Le Corbusier's 'radiant city' (*la ville radieuse*) and draws attention to the role of black people in it. Le Corbusier's utopian ideas for urban living have had a profound effect on the way cities were thought about in the mid-twentieth century. He presented his ideas using techniques drawn from advertising, deploying startling juxtapositions of images and declamatory slogans. These writings can be read now not as the instructions for practical actions, but as historical documents that explain why it was that architects found his instructions so compelling. Behind the polemic there were arguments, based on sets of assumptions that either reflected the common sense of the day, or that were kept well hidden. There is an air of rationality about the writing, but their real appeal is not to the faculty of reasoning but to something much more instinctive – a feeling that one should follow orders. Le Corbusier's rhetoric is a mixture of appealing metaphors and *mots d'ordres* – slogans – the 'order words' of a disciplinary society.[1] Le Corbusier's hidden agendas have been studied for example in discussing his ideas about proportion, Nietzschean metaphysics, nature and Orphism.[2] Simon Richards has been piecing together the idea of the self that acts as a grounding presupposition in Le Corbusier's thought, and which Le Corbusier himself thought was 'the keystone of the whole structure' of the Ville Radieuse:

> The present neglect, apparent in all spheres of life, seems to me to lead to the simple question: *Who am I?*
> Revision.
> Affirmation of the individual.
> Recasting of the social structure.[3]

In order to design, Le Corbusier needed 'a definition of modern consciousness. Without it we cannot keep any clear image of the man for whom we are building the modern home.' Such a perception is of course the generative impulse for the present collection of essays, and is the fulcrum about which the architecture-world turns, whether or not we pay attention to it. Mabel Wilson's essay here draws out race issues from Le Corbusier's writings about his imagined city of the future. He was intending to write about architecture, not about these issues, but the sets of ideas are inextricably caught up together as Wilson's analysis shows, and as Le Corbusier himself would have had to affirm, had he thought about it. The article makes the point that buildings are involved in identity-politics, and in a plurality of perspectives, or worlds. Aspects of the Radiant City that were incidental for Le Corbusier are made central here, and there is no arguing with the fact that Wilson's fresh perspective has legitimacy. In the radiant modernist heyday, aesthetic ideals included geometric purity and utilitarian rationalism. Le Corbusier imagined that the apartments of the radiant city might be stacked up anywhere in the world, as if humanity's cultural universals were of greater significance than cultural differences. Today this looks like a clumsy attempt to bend the whole world to his will, while we escape in all directions, finding ways to flourish without needing his permission to do so.

Notes

1. See the essay included below, Gilles Deleuze, 'Postscript on Control Societies'.
2. Colin Rowe, 'The Mathematics of the Ideal Villa' in *The Mathematics of the Ideal Villa and Other Essays* (Cambridge, Mass.: MIT, 1976) pp. 1–27; Charles Jencks, *Le Corbusier and the Tragic View of Architecture* (Harmondsworth: Penguin, 1987); Sarah Menin and Flora Samuel, *Nature and Space: Aalto and Le Corbusier* (London: Routledge, 2003); Flora Samuel, Le Corbusier: Architect and Feminist (London: Wiley-Academy, 2004).
3. Le Corbusier, *La ville radieuse: elements d'une doctrine d'urbanisme pour l'équipement de la civilisation machiniste* (Paris: Voncent Fréal, 1964) translated by Pamela Knight, *The Radiant City: Elements of a Doctrine of Urbanism to be Used as the Basis of our Machine-Age Civilization* (London: Faber, 1967) p. 97; quoted by Simon Richards, *Le Corbusier and the Concept of Self* (New Haven: Yale University Press, 2003) p. 47.

Dancing in the Dark

The inscription of blackness in Le Corbusier's Radiant City

>This picture is not symbolic. It is a large painting composed in 1930, at the same time as the plates for the Radiant City were being worked on in our studio. It is possible that there is a relationship between these works despite their wholly different intentions. The human creative work stands midway between the two poles of the objective and the subjective, a fusion of matter and spirit.
>
>(Le Corbusier[1])

>Black slavery enriched the country's creative possibilities. For in that construction of blackness and enslavement could be found not only the not-free but also, with the dramatic polarity created by skin color, the projection of the not-me. The result was a playground for the imagination.
>
>(Toni Morrison[2])

Architects imagine and create buildings through the scribing of drawings, treatises, manifestos, and theoretical texts. Given these disciplinary and professional practices, architecture is a discourse and thereby situated within social spheres informed by racial categories, institutions, and beliefs known as racial formations. The articulation of racial formations within architectural discourse, however, is often difficult to discern. In methodologies similar to the objectification of the text in modern literary criticism, architects, historians, and critics, for example, often limit their analysis to intrinsic qualities of architectural form – typologic relationships, qualities of light, and internal organizational concepts such as axialities, figure/ground relationships, and so forth.[3] These methods of evaluation privilege the building as the locus of critical inquiry and divorce it from key generative processes: theorization, techniques of representation and production, and those social, political, and economic factors which also contribute to the making of architecture. To expose how racial formations operate within architecture we must sift through a variety of ways in which architects realize ideas and forms as well as how people receive and live through these architectural creations.

Section 4: Pluralities

In *Playing in the Dark: Whiteness and the Literary Imagination*, novelist Toni Morrison offers a useful critique of how racial formations, in this instance articulated through literature, come to serve the formation of America's socio-cultural beliefs, practices, and national identity. In particular, Morrison posits that colonial Euro-Americans meditated upon the modalities of enslaved Africans in order to imagine their democratic nation, a supposedly enlightened socio-political body whose founding principles of individual freedom and liberty would guide the destiny of their new civilization. In this process the cultural hegemony of this white identity, one steeped in individualism, is established by writers who strategically situate within their prose and poetry an 'Africanist' presence – a character, an event, or locale – metaphorically connoted by blackness to represent black identity. American novelists Edgar Allan Poe, Willa Cather, Mark Twain, and Ernest Hemingway conjure up in their narratives images of whiteness when by itself as 'empty,' 'mute,' and 'vacuous.' These flat, singular images often representing an individual's search for affirmation and wholeness, acquire complexity and depth, signifying self realization, through an encounter with blackness. The presence of blackness unleashes 'self-contradictory concepts of the self' that are complexly 'evil *and* provocative, rebellious *and* forgiving, fearful *and* desirable'[4]. These now canonic literary works carefully deploy metaphors of blackness, 'Africanisms,' that shuttle between dialectical pairings of images and concepts to construct and stabilize white identity. Significantly, it was through the fervid imagination of both author and audience, according to Morrison, that the writing and reading of these novels constituted a white American identity.

Morrison's understanding of whiteness on the level of literary representation proves extremely useful in examining how these same socio-cultural forces of identity formation operate spatially and are thus underpinned by architecture and architectural discourse. In order to discern in architecture an Africanist presence, connoted by metaphors of 'blackness,' we must sift through a variety of ways in which architectural ideas and forms are conceptualized and circulated through writing and drawing, as well as through building.[5]

I shall focus on the work of modern architect Le Corbusier whose prolific career spans over fifty years. As the Father of the international style, his abstract, white forms represent the core of modernism's Utopian impulse. His *œuvre* includes numerous commissions, speculative designs, polemical books, and a significant body of paintings and sculptures. But while historians and architects often foreground the design of his buildings, ostensibly a vast and rich source for inquiry, it is crucial to consider how these buildings are positioned within a web of creative and conceptual endeavors that include writings, paintings, and sculpture. Whether he is critiquing the ostentatiousness and impracticality of domestic wares in *Decorative Arts of Today* (1925), or designing a modern domicile such as the Villa Savoye (1929–31), Le Corbusier experiments in each genre with new theories, forms, or techniques of construction. In fact, Le Corbusier was keenly aware of the interrelation between these various modes of theoretical and aesthetic experimentation; he wrote in the frontispiece of the *Radiant City*: 'it is possible that there is a relationship between these works [urban theory and painting] despite their wholly different intentions'.[6] Corbusier 1967 [1933]: frontispiece).

Le Corbusier's experimentation with urbanism commences with the reformulation of garden city planning tenets in his design of the Ville Contemporaine of 1922 and reaches its apex with the monumental master plan and designs for India's new administrative capitol in the Punjab at Chandigarh, begun in 1951. I focus on the period of the late 1920s and 1930s, because it is at this moment Le Corbusier, observing of the effects of industrialization on European cities and populations, theorizes a new city – a Taylorized urban form where industrial production organizes social and political life. His theories on contemporary urban design evolve accordingly through a plethora of written works: journal articles, pamphlets, books, and visionary urban schemes.[7] In 1933 many of these writings were compiled into a complex opus entitled *The Radiant City* featuring designs for an ideal city of the same name.

In order to disseminate his ideas and rally financial backing to realize his vision of a modern metropolis, Swiss-born Le Corbusier left Paris and traveled to New York, Buenos Aries, Rio de Janeiro, Sao Paulo, Moscow, Geneva, Antwerp, Stockholm, Rome, Barcelona, and several cities in French colonial Algeria. During these forays into Western and colonial capitals, exuberant followers who had been won over by his widely circulated Utopian manifestoes invited Le Corbusier to lecture. At venues crowded with eager architects, urban planners, and students, Le Corbusier gave animated performances highlighted by the telling of anecdotes and the constant jotting of sketches and diagrams. Typically, these lectures culminated in the application of Radiant City planning techniques and forms to an area of the host city. Often during these visits, Le Corbusier met with local authorities – mayors, municipal officials, and venture capitalists – and challenged them to realize his vision of a modern metropolis. He implored them to implement his plans for modernizing their cities to avert devastating physical and social collapse caused by the poor condition of the urban infrastructure: dilapidated housing stock, streets ill-suited for high-speed vehicular traffic, and sparse green spaces and parkland.

An account of a 1935 US junket, a lecture tour sponsored by the Museum of Modern Art, is recorded in the travelogue *When the Cathedrals Were White* (1936).[8] Over a four-month period Le Corbusier visited universities and museums in the northeastern and midwestern United States. In the book Le Corbusier recounts in a sometimes jocular tone, a myriad of adventures, from delivering a radio broadcast from deep inside the towers of Rockefeller Center to a delightful automobile excursion through the suburban parkways of Connecticut. He describes a colorful but restrained masquerade ball in Manhattan and relates the social nuances of a haughty business lunch at the Plaza Hotel in Manhattan. These events and others confirm his opinion that Manhattan's culture, nurtured by America's international economic prowess exudes a raw physical energy that should interest the culturally stagnant French. Yet the brilliance of American economics pales in comparison to the 'timidity' and 'puerility' he observes pervading American society. In America Le Corbusier detects an ominous blackness permeating the cavernous winding streets of New York City, he senses its presence in the 'roaring cadence' of Negro jazz, and discerns it in his encounters with 'Amazon-like' society matrons who roam Manhattan's cocktail party circuit. To the European eyes of Le Corbusier, Manhattan is in its infancy, merely twenty years old. Manhattan was born in the first decade of the twentieth century with the erection of its imperial architecture – its skyscrapers. This young, metaphorically black and primitive America awaits a renaissance in which its culture will come into fruition. In contradistinction to America, Le Corbusier reminds his French readers that France has had skyscrapers for centuries, grand gothic cathedrals, majestic monuments to rational building techniques. France, according to Le Corbusier, teeters on the brink of a second Renaissance in which French arts, music, and architecture, cultivated and refined over many centuries will lead the vanguard in the salvation of Western culture. In this tumultuous period of rebirth, Le Corbusier's urban plan to erect a new metropolis composed of crystalline, 'white' cathedrals of glass and steel will rescue French cities from imminent destruction brought on by decades of poor planning and neglect.

Imagining racial patriarchies

Significantly, three key elements: trees, mannequins, and blackness encodes racialized metaphors of American life into the narrative of *When the Cathedrals Were White*. These metaphors underwrite a social order which architecturally and spatially structures the Radiant City. Crucial to Le Corbusier's analysis of America is that an overarching metaphoric 'blackness' incites complex dialectical pairs sometimes described as demonic *and* playful, desirable *and* fearful, or spiritual *and* material. In his narrative blackness registers upon the bodies of the unfettered American woman and the Negro, both of whom fulfill a requisite position in America's social and economic order as laboring bodies. The work of these bodies not only reproduces the racial stock and produces capital, but also accords freedom from physical work and power to those who assume roles of intellectual labor. When underwriting a social hierarchy defined by racial categories, this metaphysical distinction between mind and body becomes a racial patriarchy.

As a social order, racial patriarchy privileges and accords power to dominant racial groups who monopolize education and intellectual labor, while leaving subordinate groups to carry out physical labor[9]. In *Bordering on the Body*, literary theorist Laura Doyle writes that racial patriarchy is 'an inherently metaphysical social formation – one that rests on the metaphysical distinction between a ruling "head" and a laboring "body" and one that genders and racializes this distinction'[10].

Concepts of racial patriarchy are rooted in the nineteenth century. During this period science ascribed to certain peoples, particularly those biologically linked through spurious racial classifications, various physical attributes: diminutive bodies, hulking physiques, and other deformities. Substantiated by data accrued through cranial measurements, for instance, it was widely accepted that certain racial groups had a limited intellectual capacity and were therefore in need of supervision and governance. A cadre of scientists and those who avidly ascribed to Social Darwinism rationalized that these racial groups were biologically equipped for physical labor. Many of these notions, disseminated in part through eugenics, gained currency in America's burgeoning industrial society and continued in popularity well into the twentieth century. Scientific hierarchies of biological difference were neatly overlaid onto the ideology of capitalism's striated work force of owners, managers, and laborers. The result: a new American social order in which those in possession of valued intellectual faculties, now corroborated by scientific research, assumed positions of power and wealth and those with less legitimate abilities became laboring bodies – blacks, women, ethnic immigrants and poor whites.

Returning to Le Corbusier's *When the Cathedrals Were White*, we find intertwined in his urban adventures a racial – patriarchal schema inscribed through a dynamic, invigorating, yet threatening blackness. These concepts underwrite a critique of the area surrounding Manhattan's Empire State building. Le Corbusier proclaims:

> And once again this: *that black* and *those mannequins*: Aeschylus. Once more this: there are *no trees* in the city![11]
>
> Le Corbusier

Since the implications of these metaphors will be more fully elaborated upon later in my argument, I will briefly mention here that the phrase 'that black' alludes to both the ebony marble interiors of the Empire State Building and jazz, the 'frenzied' music and dance of Harlem, whose dangerous explosive energy must be harnessed to erect Le Corbusier's transcendent white cathedrals. 'Those mannequins' refers to both the statuesque mannequins poised in the shop windows around 34th Street and the domineering bourgeios white women who threaten to depose, in Le Corbusier's eyes, the patriarchal order of America society. And finally 'trees' whose ubiquitous absence in Manhattan is duly noted by most visitors, in Le Corbusier's narrative their scarcity reveals an imbalance in the natural order, whose stability is key to nurturing the proliferation of the white race.

While seeking an American society founded upon and organized by a racial patriarchy, Le Corbusier instead discovers a culture churning with racialized bodies and unbridled feminine figures. As the cure, he presents his Radiant City as an urban and architectural mechanism that socio-spatially enforces and guarantees racial patriarchal order. Le Corbusier's skyscrapers, contemporary 'white cathedrals,' symbolize the restoration of a Western culture that transcends and masters filth, the infiltration of 'blackness,' and the materiality of the body. Aspiring to stem off an ideological upheaval and revolution ignited by the destructive forces of a heretofore mismanaged industrialism, Le Corbusier made plans, architectural plans for a Radiant City. His new metropolis would be a panacea for the current ills of modern urban life. Ironically, Le Corbusier's theories and architecture for a gleaming white metropolis and ideal society depends upon a controlled blackness; a blackness transposed onto bodies not only to racialize them, but to articulate normative heterosexual ideals of family and motherhood.

No trees in the city

> There are no trees in the city! That is the way it is.
> Trees are the friends of man, symbols of every organic creation; a tree is an image of a complete construction.

Section 4: Pluralities

> Sun, Space, and trees are the fundamental materials of city planning, the bearers of the 'essential joys.' Considering them thus, I wish to restore urban man to the very heart of his natural setting, to his fundamental emotion.
>
> Le Corbusier[12]

When theorizing the geographic context for his city in the *Radiant City*, Le Corbusier stipulates that it should be located within what he terms 'natural regions,' areas possessing 'permanent elements that dominate the machine-age adventure: climate, topography, geography, race'[13]. In other words these raw elements: soil, topography, and climate of a 'natural region' nurture biologically specific races or groups which share physiognomic features. Additionally, a natural region fosters a social order that begins at the micro-scale of the family, the 'cell of society,' next spirals outward to the tribe or the race, and finally moves outward to the macro-scale of the region. Besides the specific racial character of a natural region, its topography also forms a 'natural frontier.' Since these natural frontiers or boundaries are underwritten by racial difference, they would supplant what Le Corbusier asserts are the arbitrary borders of nation-states. By planning new cities, Radiant Cities, within these specified topographic natural regions, conflict and war, the outcomes of different racial groups cohabiting in the 'unnatural' regions of nation-states, could be thwarted.[14]

Notions such as natural regions and frontiers, illustrates the degree to which Le Corbusier's new architectural metropolis is predicated upon reified conceptions of nature. Le Corbusier believed that a dense richly planted landscape would bring modern man, overwhelmed by the grim-laden, disorderly industrial city, physically and psychologically back into alignment with nature's order. The triad 'sun, space and trees,' emblematic of nature in the text of *The Radiant City*, are base elements with which to build the green city. His seventeen illustrations of the Radiant City depict a lush verdant Utopia. Broad carpets of greenery stretch below elevated blocks of housing units, skyscrapers, and highways. Trees are plentiful. Wide swathes of grass are dotted intermittently with gardens and athletic facilities. Rooftop gardens and artificial beaches for sun bathing and recreation cap residential units, housing 1000 inhabitants per hectare. Each building is also equipped with 'exact respiration' or conditioned air, a novelty in the 1930's, providing for clean, mechanically controlled breathing for inhabitants. Collectively, these planned amenities not only aimed to improve the physique of the residents, but also attempted to restore their 'fundamental emotion' and psychological well-being.

Beliefs such as Le Corbusier's in the necessity of physical vitality for intellectual acuity, reflect ideals first propounded in the nineteenth century. The doctrines of scientists Comte de Gobineau, Karl Pearson, and Francis Galton often invoked soil/tree metaphors and

> take on more than local significance in the light of an emerging, if still infant, science of national or racial character. Although thinkers and scientists ... were beginning to explore the genetic transmission of racial characteristics, the predominant secular explanation in this period was still the climatic theory, namely, that racial features were shaped by the soil and climate of a country.[15]

These tracts of the founders of eugenics inferred that racial superiority was discernible in certain physiognomic characteristics. Interpreting Darwin's theories of natural selection toward their own ends – justifying a racially segregated capitalist society – Eugenicists postulated that the highest intellectual capabilities would certainly be an attribute of the dominant racial group. They theorized that European and Euro-Americans were intellectually superior and thus the guardians of history and the forebears of progress.[16]

At the other end of the eugenics scale were racial groups positioned lower on the Social-Darwinian chart of biological, social, and cultural evolution. These groups – ethnic immigrants, working classes, peasants, and newly emancipated slaves – were thought to be biologically best suited for physical labor and predestined to ill-health. As Doyle concurs:

> Dominant kin groups associate themselves with mind or spirit and associate subordinate groups with body or matter. The conflated kin and metaphysical distinctions in turn justify a division of power and labor by which hand workers serve brainworkers.[17]

These conceptions of racial difference had profound effects upon social divisions and urban development. Surfacing among middle- and upper-class white urban populations during this period, for instance, was an alarming fear of miscegenation in which 'good blood' when mixed with 'bad blood' would eventuate in the debilitating traits of feeblemindedness and degeneracy. Biologistically racialized and classed bodies were thereby sorted out and maintained under the strictest of controls. Under the sway of these ideas, racially inferior groups or those seen as socially deviant and dangerous, were forced to live at some distance from bourgeois whites. In the service of elite interests, municipal authorities eventually zoned and planned cities so that bourgeois and upper-class whites, safe within suburban enclaves abounding with sun and verdure, were far from the threatening unsanitary slums of racially inferior groups. Under this misconception, those factors such as inadequate wages and squalid housing conditions: consequences of social inequalities affecting these marginalized groups, could be and were for a long time ignored.

Returning to the narrative unfolding in *When the Cathedrals Were White*, Le Corbusier asserts in New York City there are 'no trees.' Trees, a key indicator of a thriving 'natural region,' are noticeably absent. By pointing out their scarcity a vigilant Le Corbusier wants to alert his reader (remember this book was originally addressed to a French audience), that something in the natural order of America has gone amiss.

Those mannequins

> The wax mannequins in the windows of the smart dress shops on Fifth Avenue make women masters, with conquering smiles. Square shoulders, incisive features, sharp coiffure – red hair and green dress, metallic blond hair and ultramarine blue dress, black hair and red dress.

Section 4: Pluralities

> The mannequins in the windows have the heads of Delphic goddesses. Green, lamp-black, red hair. ... Polychromy. When polychromy appears it means that life is breaking out.
> Next door I note the funereal entrances of the Empire State Building.
>
> And once again this; that black and those mannequins: Aeschylus. Once more this: there are no trees in the city!
>
> Le Corbusier[18]

While the natural order of society may be predicated on geographic and climatic specificity, stabilized through racial homogeneity, it is women, precisely because they reproduce and nurture the family, who become the guardians of the racial and natural order. In *When the Cathedrals Were White*, Le Corbusier puts forth a 'dangerous hypothesis:' the death of the American family, and it is the white bourgeois woman, as Mother, who is held accountable for its murder.

In a section entitled 'Searching and Manifestations of the Spirit,' white American women, typically middle and upper class, appear to Le Corbusier in one of two guises: either desirous or threatening. While visiting the Connecticut countryside to lecture at the women's college of Vassar, a delighted Le Corbusier tells us of its learned, privileged, and desirable coeds: 'they are in overalls or in bathing suits. I enjoy looking at these beautiful bodies, made healthy and trim by physical training' (Le Corbusier 1967: 136). A few passages later, a harried Le Corbusier informs us that following his lecture these attractive coeds metamorphosed into aggressive 'Amazons,' greedily grasping to retrieve a shred of his sketches as a souvenir. Both alluring *and* ominous these women are an indication to the discerning eye of Le Corbusier that America's natural order, in this instance a biological one, is in disarray.

A similar assessment of American women can be ascertained from Le Corbusier's kaleidoscopic description of the fashion displays in the shop windows near the Empire State Building. The unnatural wax figurines outfitted in resplendent, shapely Delphic sheaths, remind him of Clytemnestra, Aeschylus' infamous Greek murderess. In brief Aeschylus' classic *Oresteian Trilogy* tells a tragedy in which adultery, patricide, and matricide destroy the royal family of King Agamemnon. A firestorm of destruction is unleashed by the machinations of the all-too-powerful Mother, Queen Clytemnestra. This strong-willed Matriarch, whose 'words are like a man's,' murders her husband King Agamemnon to usurp the throne.[19] Clytemnestra frantically racing to escape detection of her deed, enwraps the King's lifeless body in a luxuriant purple silk robe soaked in crimson blood. Aeschylus' vivid prose captures the tumultuous events, reckless deeds, and uncontrolled passions of this domestic tragedy.

Along Manhattan's 34th Street a modern Oresteian tragedy is evoked the omnipotent posture of its mannequins and the polychromatic setting. Le Corbusier spies in the shop windows, similar phantasmagoric hues of the 'lamp-black,' 'green,' 'red,' and 'metallic blond' hair and exaggerated artifice of the 'Delphic dresses' sheathing 'those mannequins.' This urban drama culminates in its own funereal spirit, set against a vertical shaft of blackness: the Empire State Building. If 'those mannequins,' like

Clytemnestra, is a metaphor for defiant American women, then how do they imperil the natural order of America's racial patriarchy?

Historically ascribed as the primary biological reproducers of the race, women's bodies have been regulated through social practices and codes of morality in order to guard against the infiltration of the genetic traits of inferior races. Beginning in the mid-nineteenth century, the editor and writers of women's magazines and leaders of bourgeios women's associations circulated notions of feminine propriety and motherhood. Mothers were advised as to how to provide for the moral education of their children. Wives were instructed on methods of maintaining a fastidious, healthy, domestic environment. Many women were led to believe that they should not undertake professional employment. Nor should they profess an interest in politics, economics, theater, or any subject matter that might be the purview of their spouses. On the contrary, women were persuaded to direct their energies into their reproductive duties[20]. Such disciplining practices associated with motherhood not only focused women's labor toward replenishing the racial stock, but also aided in the maintenance of its purity. The vaunted white Mother became the guardian of the racial patriarchy. Doyle compellingly argues

> This metaphysical division [between matter/mind and spirit/body] further determines the function of the dominant group mother: she sorts out bodies not only into kin and non-kin but also into brainworkers and handworkers.[21]

In other words, the bourgeois white maternal body sat precariously at the border between the dominant race group who were the intellectual elites and all others who were the physical laborers. Following this logic of racial division, if a daughter or wife gave birth to child by a man of a lesser racial group, she ruptured and polluted the family's bloodline. Not accorded status of Mother, the 'fallen' woman and her child were cast out of the family and exiled from the Father's house. Therefore, to avoid enticements that would lead to shame and degradation, women were kept busy at home with their wifely duties. Rigorous regimens of housework popularized by ladies magazines and facilitated through the mass production of household equipment, ensconced bourgeois white women in domestic spheres far away from the 'dangers' of urban life. Tucked away from the dark, foreboding metropolis teeming with lesser races, the white Mother was secure from possible rape, impregnation, and ruin.

Given that for Le Corbusier American women represent nature's equilibrium gone awry, then what would be the fate of America's natural order, an order in which it is imperative that men determine the discourse of family life and women work to maintain the family and household? To verify the death of the American family, Le Corbusier's 'dangerous hypothesis,' he tells a parable entitled 'The Family Divided.' In it he describes the daily regimen of a typical middle-class Euro-American household. Leading separate lives the husband works in the city and the wife remains at home in the suburb. The husband commutes via rail to his place of employment in the central city, where he arduously labors, as Le Corbusier quips, to 'shower her with attention – money, jewels, furnishings'.[22] But while the husband toils, his wife cultivates her intellect through reading, attending lectures, and socializing with her circle of friends. From these events, Le Corbusier deduces: 'the husband is intimidated, thwarted. The wife dominates'.²³ This reversal in the natural order where man is now equated with the body and woman equated with the mind, precipitates the death of the family.

Le Corbusier concludes that American men, overshadowed by these shrewd Clytemnestra-like women, possess unremarkable intellects. The poignant comedic performances of Charlie Chaplin and Buster Keaton reflect this denigrated, lackluster American male spirit. Le Corbusier speaks of these cinematic characterizations as representing:

> The simple man ..., a good fellow full of friendly and altruistic thoughts which are often puerile. Around him an overwhelming situation of inhuman dimensions. That disproportion is the rule in the USA: *an abyss opens up ...* at every step.²⁴

While searching for 'manifestations of the Spirit,' Le Corbusier comes upon an 'abyss' of unfathomable blackness. An aftermath of the death of the family and the Father caused by the domineering Matriarch, a deep melancholic spirit envelops everyone and everything. A dark abyss swallows the 'funeral' cloaked shaft of the Empire State building. An abyss erupts in the geography of the city separating downtown from uptown, white Manhattan from black Harlem. In the dynamic 'mongrel metropolis' (to borrow historian Ann Douglas' phrase) however, mobile white bodies travel across these racial and spatial borders to the phantasmal nightlife of Harlem's clubs, theaters, and dancehalls. However, to be sure, such a journey into Black Manhattan exposes white bodies to the constant threat of corruption and contamination.

That black

> On the stage of Armstrong's night club a series of dances follow each other, supported by the music and stimulating the body to frenzied gesticulation. Savagery is constantly present, particularly in the frightful murder scene which leaves you terrified; these naked Negroes, formidable black athletes, seem as if they were imported directly from Africa where there are still tom-toms, massacres, and the complete destruction of villages or tribes. Is it possible that such memories could survive through a century of being uprooted? It would seem that only butchery and agony could call forth such cries, gasps, roars.
> Le Corbusier²⁵

As brilliant stage performers, efficient porters and slum-dwelling social outcasts, African Americans appear in a myriad of incarnations throughout Le Corbusier's travel narrative. Observing African Americans exclusively in servile guises, Le Corbusier overlooks Harlem's diverse social milieu that included various ethnicities and classes, as well as an established community of intellectuals and artists. Those Negroes (I employ his term here,) Le Corbusier does encounter are 'good-natured, cordial, and companionable.' He believes they pose a thorny question to white

Americans, a question that cannot be resolved 'in a superficial manner'.[26] Beyond their affable character, Le Corbusier observes that many Negroes reside in horrid, squalid communities hidden from more prosperous white New Yorkers who 'if they knew the slums, it would make them sick at heart and they would make new city plans.' Negroes are social 'pariahs,' who resettle areas abandoned by whites; and in these 'former paradises' they 'sow a spirit of death' – again a metaphor of blackness.[27] Despite recognizing the unbearable living conditions and racial injustices to Blacks in America, Le Corbusier nevertheless imagines his white city, his Radiant City through tropes of blackness.

Over the course of his stay, Le Corbusier visited some of the popular haunts of Jazz Age Manhattan, including those within and associated with Harlem such as the raucous Savoy Ballroom and the downtown incarnation of Harlem's famous Connie's Inn at Broadway and 49th Street where he saw Louis Armstrong headlining a show called 'the Hot Chocolates of 1936.' These experiences are retold in the chapter 'The Spirit of the Machine and Negroes in the USA' which strategically follows the tale of the death of the family. Louis Armstrong takes center stage. Le Corbusier benights Armstrong:

> the black Titan of the cry, the apostrophe, of the burst of laughter, of thunder. He sings, he guffaws, he makes his silver trumpet spurt. He is mathematics, equilibrium on a tightrope ... with Armstrong, the exactitude leads to an unearthly suavity, broken by a blow like a flash of lightning.[28]

Clearly in admiration of Armstrong's brilliance and artistry, Le Corbusier identifies a regal composure: 'he is in turn demonic, playful, massive, from one second to another, in accordance with an astounding fantasy. The man is extravagantly skillful; he is king'.[29] During the performance Armstrong incarnates brute physicality – emitting a fierce heat that combines with the driving rhythm of the drums and blare of the horns. Imbued with a sublime spirit, Armstrong's 'voice is as deep as an *abyss*, it is a *black* cave'.[30] Paradoxically Armstrong radiates a spirit of a material sort – a kind of black ore, raw matter, that fuels the machines of the modern age. In his prose Le Corbusier simultaneously envies and dreads the 'demonic' *and* 'playful' Armstrong. In a complex association, Armstrong's corporeal and metaphoric blackness is emblematic of the primitive, a modality which in turn engenders the modern.

As a telltale sign of the primitive, acts of savagery are ever-present in the description of the performers of the floor show at Connie's Inn. In his reverie, Le Corbusier evokes the typical tropes of blackness – primitive, rhythmic, frenzied, abysmal, frightful, murderous, and explosive – to characterize the performance. As he is entertained by a dance review choreographed to the syncopation of jazz, he senses 'savagery is constantly present, particularly in the frightful murder scene'.[31] To Le Corbusier these black bodies, like those ravenous Vassar coeds, are athletic *and* savage, incarnating imminent death, and posing a threat to racial patriarchal order. A similar eruption of primitivism infuses the passages about Lindy Hoppers at the Savoy Ballroom where 'ordinary colored people join each other in very nearly savage rights'.[32] The ethereal environs of the dance hall envelop Le Corbusier. With the architecture of the hall receding in the glow of the flickering projector, the kinetic twists and turns of the dancers apparently evoke memories of his journey to French colonial Africa. He remembers a similar phenomenon in the fierce eroding winds that batter the peaks of the Atlas Mountains. Observing from the bird's-eye view of an airplane, the winds unfold into a primeval scene of nature, a 'geological drama,' where one seeks shelter against the 'tumult' of the 'unfathomable march of the elements.' The eroding mountains elide with the dancing black bodies to create a sublime performance witnessed by the rational disembodied eye of the architect.

Ironically, while Le Corbusier fears abysmal blackness, it nonetheless deliriously intoxicates and spiritually envelops him; therefore, he desires it as part of his Radiant City. Dancing across the text, dynamic, kinetic black bodies of African Americans exude the energy and spirit of the machine age: 'new sounds, of everything and from everywhere, perhaps ugly or horrible: the grinding of the streetcars, the unchained madness of the subway, the pounding of machines in factories'.[33] He couples the precise rhythm of black tap dancers with the exactitude of machines – sewing machines – producing the raw material to sustain industrial capitalism. These black bodies provide the labor to erect the 'foundations of cathedrals of sound which are already rising.' As a complex duality indicative of Africanisms, 'blackness' is both spirit *and* matter.

In this very primitivism Le Corbusier discovers a rationality and regularity that counters the confusion and unpredictability of the chaotic industrialization of the twentieth century. He aligns the art of the Negro with the art of the engineer, 'the old rhythmic instinct of the virgin African forest has learned the lesson of the machine.' These performing black bodies are machines: the rhythmic 'tap-tap-rap-tap-tap' of dancers are 'as mechanical as a sewing machine' and the jazz band's tempo is a 'smoothly running turbine.' Together they create a symphony of production,

> The Negro orchestra is impeccable, flawless, regular, playing ceaselessly in an ascending rhythm: the trumpet is piercing, strident, screaming over the stamping of feet. It is the equivalent of a beautiful turbine running in the midst of human conversations. Hot jazz.[34]

Le Corbusier exalts and desires these black bodies because he finds flourishing in them a primal human spirit; it is an essential spirit lacking in the European soul dampened by the chaotic industrialization of the twentieth century. The cacophony of sound and energy emitted by these black bodies and/as pulsing machines are the base elements of a modern world over which nevertheless, Euro-American and European men, must be masters. From the performances of the machines/nature/black bodies Le Corbusier composes an opus, a great symphony for a modern society – a plan for a Radiant City.

This alluring 'blackness' however is not confined to Harlem's dance halls and nightclubs, it invades the space of Manhattan where a 'vast nocturnal festival … spreads out.' As with the black entertainers, Le Corbusier admires the raw performative energy of the skyscrapers, noting that 'Manhattan is hot jazz in stone and steel.' Both jazz and skyscrapers are events, gestures, bursts of activity. For Le Corbusier neither jazz nor a skyscraper is a 'deliberately conceived creation,' he continues 'if architecture were at the point reached by jazz, it would be an incredible spectacle. I repeat: Manhattan is hot jazz in stone and steel'.[35] In the end, Le Corbusier informs his reader that black culture, jazz, and the American skyscraper are a folk tune of emotion, not a symphony of rationality.[6] Despite his fascination with their energetic expression, Le Corbusier's sees them as an inefficient use of their verticality, exclaiming in a *New York Times* interview 'They are too small!' Although he admires the masterful engineering of Manhattan's high-rises, Le Corbusier observes, in an ominous tone, that the streets of Manhattan are clogged with automobile and pedestrian traffic, there is a proliferation of slums, and the migration of middle-class white populations to garden city suburbs erodes the vitality of the city. The city dies. This spirit of death cloaks the skyscrapers. A funereal spirit connoted, once again, by blackness – 'the black polished stones, the walls faced with dark gleaming slabs' enwraps the art deco edifice of the Empire State and overwhelms the city.

White cathedrals and black bodies

Thus far, I've illustrated how Le Corbusier metaphorically scripts 'blackness' as an uncontrollable force threatening to depose the order of a racialized patriarchy. But it is important also to consider how these metaphors constitute conceptions of whiteness, which similarly spatialize and structure his desired racialized society. What then are the operative metaphors of whiteness within *When the Cathedrals Were White*?

Following his metaphoric drama of the death of the family, the kinetic black bodies of Harlem, and those phantasmal mannequins, Le Corbusier unveils plans to transform Manhattan into a Radiant city of pristine white skyscrapers. In a sobering chapter entitled the 'Necessity of Communal Plans and Enterprises,' Le Corbusier's lament ensues: 'When the cathedrals were white, spirit was triumphant. But today the cathedrals of France are black and the spirit is bruised.' Unsurprisingly, he longs for the era of the glorious Gothic cathedrals in which the world was 'white, limpid, joyous, clean, clear.' The architecture produced an orderly society whose culture manifested 'itself in fresh color, white linen and clean art.' Here, whiteness metaphorically evokes purity and cleanliness. I concur with architectural theorist Mark Wigley, who asserts that Le Corbusier's architectural whiteness works as a thin opaque layer of whitewash to master and stabilize the architectural and corporeal body in order to liberate the mind.[37] Whiteness as a necessary structural element appears in a variety of modes: as a racialized concept ordering the narrative of *When the Cathedrals Were White*, as a thin coat of white paint ordering the modern facade, as starched white undergarments ordering clothes, and as white skin ordering the surface of the body. Yet, lurking menacingly below the stable surface of whiteness is blackness. Blackness manifested as death, dirt, and lawlessness – posing a persistent threat to the natural order and necessitating containment and control.

This articulation of whiteness ordering a dynamic and unstable blackness also characterizes the socio-cultural relationship between France and America. Towards the end of the chapter on Negro culture, Le Corbusier compares it to his own folkloric cultural heritage. Upon return from America, his wife, Yvonne:

puts on the record 'Fifine', a Parisian java ... here I am in the presence of the real originality of the java; I find in it mathematical France, precise, exact; I find in it the masses of Paris, a society worthy of interest, so measured, precise, and supple in its thought. A controlled sensuality, a severe ethics.[38]

Reinforcing the racialized maternal ideal, it is his wife – the bearer of his racial heritage – who dutifully brings him this pleasurable snippet of folkloric culture 'the Java.'[39] In Le Corbusier's house in Paris, we are assured that all is in order. In contrast to America's inchoate culture, superior French culture is refined, mathematical, and most importantly 'controlled sensuality.' Paris, but more importantly France, home of the majestic gothic cathedrals, is the patriarch of fledgling America.

As a tourist, Le Corbusier peruses America's socio-cultural spectrum and imagines through a metaphorically black America what his beloved France is not. From his journey, he concludes that the society, preferably France, that transcends blackness will achieve the order and harmony necessary to erect the 'bright whitewashed,' 'radiant filigreed white-cathedrals' of his modern metropolis. The architecture of Le Corbusier's cathedrals will herald a new heroic period, one that echoes a mythic past in which 'an international language reigned wherever the white race was, favoring the exchange of ideas and the transfer of culture'.[40]

But how will his imaginary society come into being? How is a racial – patriarchal social order reliant on the rift between physical and intellectual labor configured into the design of the Radiant City? And where is Le Corbusier in the scheme of things?

The plans for the Radiant City harbor the promise of an orderly society and city, transcending chaotic infrastructure and grime-laden edifices. To achieve this end, Le Corbusier invents a meticulously functioning urban machine. Enamored by modern production theories such as Taylorism, Le Corbusier designs an urban standard, an '*objet type*,' based upon a set of criteria that allow for a variety of possible iterations. As an ideal form, the elements can be modified when applied to a given topography, in this instance, New York City. The layout of the elements of the Radiant City resembles a body: as legs – warehouses, heavy industry, factories; as the torso – housing, cultural institutions, hotels, embassies; as the neck – rail and air terminals; as the head – the business center; as a network of arteries weaving across the entire city – highways and railways. The productive forces of the economic base warehouses and industries, are the legs that carry the load of the social body housing, cultural amenities, business, commercial and government buildings. Building vertically by elevating each mass onto '*pilotis*' or columns, achieves the desired population density. And also frees the ground from congestion allowing for ample coverage of park space and recreational facilities. So that mothers (remember they are the custodians of the racial order) would be near their children, the plans include nurseries, kindergartens, and schools within each housing block. A worker would no longer waste valuable productive time traveling by train from garden suburbs to his job in the city, in the Radiant City he could drive his automobile along the extensive network of highways to nearby offices and manufacturing facilities. To maximize exposure to sunlight and air, necessary to sustain the natural order, the entire city would be oriented on a 'heliothermic axis' determined by local climatic conditions.

The city's distribution of elements and functions also reflects what Le Corbusier labels in the *Radiant City* as the 'pyramid of natural hierarchies.' The pyramid, a socio-political order structured according to a resident's occupation, is based upon theories espoused by a French labor movement known as Syndicalism to which Le Corbusier had affiliations in the 1930s.[41] The Syndicalists, in brief, proposed the reorganization of French society and politics away from Republican ideals of citizenry and participatory government and toward a ruling ethos emphasizing industrial production and governance by worker's guilds or 'metiers.' In this planned economy, at the bottom of the pyramidal order would be workers' groups organized into trades that form 'metiers.' At the next level are the leaders from these groups making up an inter-union council who would deliberate and resolve inner disputes between trades, as well as implement economic policy stabilizing production and distribution. At the top of this social order is the 'extra metier,' the grand chiefs, or the supreme authorities who would be 'free from all problems stemming from technical insufficiencies. This group of intellectual elites is at liberty to concentrate on the country's higher purposes.' The supreme authority – a body of men, not engaged in corporal labor and entrusted with the future of Western civilization would be housed in a grid pattern of 'Cartesian skyscrapers' located in the business district at top of the city. The behemoth steel and glass towers, maximizing exposure to light and air, would be a phenomenal feat of ingenuity created by the marriage of engineering and architecture. The Radiant City's political order fits neatly into the schema of a racial patriarchy, since these men would be those with the highest intellectual acuity, biologically predestined to be free from physical work. These Cartesian skyscrapers, translucent white cathedrals 'at' and 'as' the head the Radiant City, project the gaze of the supreme authority, and ultimately the gaze of Le Corbusier, outward to survey the neatly ordered city of light, sun, space, and trees.

White place, black face

Throughout his narrative Le Corbusier envisions himself outside worldly materiality, transcending the body – a pure mind. Yet, the act of writing itself deceives him by leaving traces of his corporeality. His inscriptions tie him bodily to the text and conversely the political effects of his texts draw them into the world of things. In fact, *When the Cathedrals Were White* teems with passages that reveal Le Corbusier's uneasiness about his own and others' bodily presence. In an amusing story centered around the events of a masquerade ball at the Waldorf Astoria, Le Corbusier remarks of his physique: 'Not being a handsome fellow, I keep my anatomy out of sight'.[42] During the festivities, outfitted in simple blue and white attire, whilst others are adorned in colorful, brilliantly plumed and brocaded costumes, Le Corbusier relates his disdain at the conspicuousness of his body, 'I was neither mad nor clownish, I was a sore thumb. I was out of place'.[43] His rational discerning character conveyed through the severity of his dress is lost, displaced by the phantasmal whirlwind of color, costume, and corporeality.

Continually traveling within Le Corbusier's gaze over the course of his journey to America are the bodies of 'those mannequins' and 'that black.' It is their corporeality whether maternal or racialized, which consistently disrupts his much-desired patriarchal order. Uncontrolled, women and Blacks impinge upon the smooth architectural and socio-political workings of his Radiant City. Yet, as much as Le Corbusier privileges the mind as the ultimate measure of civilization's progress, the body returns as a specter – to dance with Le Corbusier in his text and in his city – forever haunting his crystalline vision.

My reassessment of Le Corbusier's urban theories and architecture illustrates that architecture although material in nature, nevertheless is conceived, constructed, and lived through a multitude of social formations – practices, institutions, cultural beliefs, political affiliations and so forth. Perhaps it is because of its supposed ideological bent toward universality that Le Corbusier's urban theories, along with those of other modern architects, enjoined quite smoothly with the aspirations of twentieth century colonialism and imperialism. Significantly we find most of the international style of architecture built not in the Western countries, but instead in so-called 'third world' nations and enclaves. In former colonial outposts such as Brazil, India, Zimbabwe, and elsewhere, monumental modern architectural projects cater to the economic, political, and social aims of ruling elites, who were formerly backed by powerful colonial empires and are now supported by influential Western nations and transnational corporations.

In America, similar sites of experimentation with the tenets of modernism can be found in segregated and impoverished communities such as Harlem, Newark, Detroit and Chicago – cities that bore the brunt of state-funded social housing beginning in the 1930s. Forsaking Le Corbusier's utopian vision of a gleaming white metropolis, large numbers of bourgeois Whites and those various groups of immigrants and blue-collar workers who garnered the 'wages of whiteness,' moved out of central cities (a migration subsidized by government agencies promoting the growth of suburbs) after the Second World War. Those who remained in cities, Blacks and Latinos, the poor and the underclasses – those disempowered in the American sociopolitical system – were shuttled into towering housing blocks whose designs reflected the then prevailing theories in modern architecture. In the end, these edifices were quite different from those sprouting across the verdant landscape of Radiant City. In Le Corbusier's heroic white towers, the gaze of the supreme authority oriented outward. Ironically in these American reiterations of his skyscrapers, the gaze – a panoptic one of the State and dominant white society – pierced dauntingly inward.

Notes

> I am grateful to Mark Wigley, Paul Kariouk, Wallis J. Miller, Ernest Pascucci and Jerzy Rozenberg who offered helpful comments to various drafts of this chapter. I also want to thank Steve Pile for his thoughtful suggestions and Heidi J. Nast for her inspiration, as well as her patience and tenacity in coaxing this endeavour out of me.

1. Le Corbusier, (1933) trans. by D. Coltman, *The Radiant City* (New York: Orion, 1967) frontispiece.
2. Toni Morrison, *Playing in the Dark: Whiteness and the Literary Imagination* (New York: Vintage Books, 1992), p. 38.

3. These methods of analysis, emerging in the 1960s and 1970s, are commonly taught as part of the curriculum in many architecture programs. These techniques of formal analysis are found for example in Francis Ching, *Architecture: Form, Space and Order* (London: Wiley, 1995), a popular book assigned in many beginning design courses. But one can also find these categories which parallel high-modernist conceptions of aesthetic quality utilized in many scholarly articles and books.
4. Morrison, op. cit., p. 59.
5. A recent issue (number 16) of the architecture magazine *Any*, 'White Forms, Forms of Whiteness' explores the myriad of social and formal interpretations of the term 'whiteness' and architecture. Drawing out the complex incarnations of whiteness in architectural discourse editor Ernest Pascucci observes in his introduction to the issue: 'Whiteness is sometimes as dumb as a colour, "an achromatic colour of maximum lightness" whose dictionary definition is cannot help but enter into a complementary if antagonistic relationship with black. In a psychoanalytic sense, white envelops the most beautifully dumb substitute objects, on to which fantasies of pure form and good democracy (or is it good form and pure democracy?) are projected and acted out. And sometimes white acts as a visual blocker concealing a disavowed racial unconscious, especially when opposed to grey, thus leaving black, metaphorically and otherwise, out of the picture'.
6. Le Corbusier, *Radiant City*, op. cit., frontispiece.
7. Prior to the publication of the *Radiant City* in 1933, Le Corbusier wrote a number of books outlining his urban theory; these included *The City of Tomorrow*, *Precisions* and *Towards a New Architecture*. Architect Rem Koolhaas in *Delirious New York* (London: Thames and Hudson, 1978) devotes a chapter to Le Corbusier's critique of Manhattan. For ideological critique of his work see Manfredo Tafuri, *Architecture and Utopia* (Cambridge, MA: MIT Press, 1979); for critics of gender and sexuality in Le Corbusier's urbanism and architecture see Beatriz Colomina, *Privacy and Publicity: Modern Architecture as Mass Media* (Cambridge, MA: MIT Press, 1996) and Zeynep Celik, 'Le Corbusier, Orientalism, Colonialism' in *Assemblage* 17 (1992), pp. 58–77.
8. Le Corbusier arrives in the fall of 1935 and departs in the winter of 1936. Le Corbusier, trans. by F. Hyslop, *When the Cathedrals Were White* (New York: McGraw Hill, 1947).
9. Laura Doyle, *Bordering on the Body* (New York: Oxford University Press, 1994), p. 6.
10. Ibid., p. 20.
11. My emphasis. Le Corbusier, *Cathedrals*, op. cit., p. 188.
12. Ibid., p. 71.
13. Le Corbusier, *Radiant City*, op. cit., p. 193.
14. Ibid., p. 193.
15. Doyle, op. cit., p. 43.
16. Recent scholarship on racial science examines the political, economic and social investment made in the name of research by those in power. For further reading see Daniel J. Kevles, *In the Name of Eugenics* (New York: Knopf,

1985); Laura Ann Stoler, *Race and the Education of Desire* (Durham, NC: Duke University Press, 1996); William H. Tucker, *The Science and Politics of Racial Research* (Chicago: University of Illinois Press, 1996); Robin Wiegman, *American Anatomies: Theorizing Race and Gender* (Durham, NC: Duke University Press, 1995).
17. Doyle, op. cit., p. 28.
18. Le Corbusier, *Radiant City*, op. cit., p. 165.
19. Aeschylus, trans. by P. Vellacott, *The Oresteian Trilogy* (Harmondsworth: Penguin, 1956) p. 55.
20. Carolyn Merchant, *Ecological Revolutions* (Chapel Hill: University of North Carolina Press, 1989) p. 163.
21. Doyle, op. cit., p. 28.
22. Le Corbusier, *Cathedrals*, op. cit., p. 154.
23. Ibid., p. 154.
24. Ibid., my emphasis, p. 157.
25. Ibid., p. 160.
26. Ibid., p. 87.
27. Ibid., p. 86.
28. Ibid., p. 159.
29. Ibid., p. 159.
30. Ibid., my emphasis, p. 159.
31. Ibid., p. 160.
32. Ibid., p. 161.
33. Ibid., p. 161.
34. Ibid., p. 161.
35. ibid., p. 161.
36. Blackness is configured not only as a threat but also as the site of desire. America's blacks and their musical innovation, jazz, become the locus of Le Corbusier's yearnings, remarking 'if architecture were at the point reached by jazz, it would be an incredible spectacle'. Through their sensuality he can free himself from the chains of the past and conceive, reflexively, his new heric city of white cathedrals. In *White Walls, Designer Dresses*, Mark Wigley thoroughly unpacks the sexual implications of Le Corbusier's remarks, writing 'an architecture that releases the sensual potential of the machine age would, like jazz, contain the pre-machine past as well as the present, putting "dynamism into the whole body by putting people in touch with the irreducibly sensual origins of humanity"' Mark Wigley, *White Walls, Designer Dresses* (Cambridge, MA: MIT Press, 2001), p. 294.
37. Mark Wigley, 'Architecture After Philosophy: Le Corbusier and the Emperor's New Paint', in *Architectural Design* (1989) Philosophy and Architecture, pp. 84–95; p. 85.
38. Le Corbusier, *Cathedrals*, op. cit., p. 163.
39. The implications of sexuality underlying this passage were brought to my attention by Mark Wigley. *White Walls, Designer Dresses*, op. cit., examines the banishment of color and ornament in the design of modern buildings. This examination of repression parallels discussions of clothing, fashion and the

body, now sexualized and racialized, in architectural discourse in the first half of the twentieth century.
40. Le Corbusier, *Radiant City*, op. cit., p. 4.
41. Mary McLeod, *Urbanism and Utopia: Le Corbusier From Regional Syndicalism to Vichy* (Michigan: UMI, unpublished dissertation, 1985).
42. Le Corbusier, *Cathedrals*, op. cit., p. 150.
43. Ibid., p. 150.

Section 5
Relations

Tools

In a pragmatist frame of mind, one stops asking 'what is it?' and instead asks 'what does it do?' Ideas become tools, and with any sort of tools we don't feel inclined to say that they're right or wrong in themselves, just that they're not the right tool for the job, or unhelpful just now. There are some tools that are blunt and powerful, others that are highly specific and delicate, and they are not interchangeable. It is possible to crack open nuts by using a sledgehammer, but proverbially there are more appropriate tools to use. There can be many different ways to achieve the desired result, and which ones seem most convenient will probably depend on our prior habits, as it will be easier to adapt a well-established skill than to learn a whole new set of them. A pragmatist outlook is highly pluralistic. As soon as anything is investigated, it proliferates and multiplies, spreading out unanswered questions in every direction, as Emerson described in his essay 'Circles'.[1] We don't have to have answers to all these questions before we can act; indeed if we did have to have the answers then we would never be able to act. There are questions that could be called 'metaphysical' so far as the matter in hand is concerned. There are some thinkers who would want to rule out all discussion of metaphysics, and others who would want on occasion to be able to pursue it. The pragmatic way to think about it is to say that the results of that discussion would not have a material bearing on the questions that are being addressed here and now, and therefore we do not need a resolution of the discussion – it can continue in its own time, for as long as anyone wants, but it need not detain us here.[2] One of the things that complicates the question so far as architecture is concerned is that one of the things that architecture has repeatedly tried to do over the centuries is to give expression to the metaphysics of the age, and architects have shown themselves to be highly inclined to be drawn into arcane discussion where they are well out of their depth. This need not be a worry. If the point of the exercise is to design buildings that are seen to embody the values of the people who commission them, or some other agenda of the architect's own, then perhaps all we need are a few symbols here and there that give the right signals, and the quality of the actual understanding of the metaphysics can seem insignificant. The builders of the Gothic cathedrals took specialist advice about the symbols they made visible. More to the point perhaps, they did not properly understand gravity, but their ingenuity in exploiting it can still be admired after more than one revolution in our understanding of it. From a pragmatist standpoint, one tries to equip oneself with a good range of tools, intellectual and practical tools, so that one can address the problems that can be anticipated, and perhaps have a good many to spare – the various tools that one learnt when training that have never in fact been put to use, but which would still be there if the need arose, and a variety of things that have been learnt in the course of a life, some of which might already have been useful, some of which merely seem promising or in some indefinable way 'compelling', so that one would hope to see them put to use in future. These are the tools that one has, and that one uses in making designs.

Another set of tools comes into use when the building has been built, and people come and use it, or look at it, or whatever. A sophisticated reader of buildings, such as Mabel Wilson or Ian Buchanan (see above and below) will certainly be able to see in the building qualities that the architect did not intend when it was designed. This does not invalidate their readings, nor imply that the architect should have known more. The building is now engaged in a different machine, and the architecture that it produces can be different. It could also (incidentally) be substantially the same, if the designer and the observer have been through a similar educational process, and it is on those occasions (when the architectural profession speaks to itself, and validates its own worth in its own eyes) that it generates its own culture. However the various ways in which buildings are construed by the people who make use of them, are of more crucial importance in the lives of the buildings themselves and of the communities that develop around them. For example a jewellery shop in a local high street was denied permission to remove its fine early twentieth-century windows, because they were of historic interest. The reason that the proprietor of the shop wanted to remove them was that people in the street assumed that because of the fine quality of the windows, the jewellery on display was also of high quality, and that therefore they would not be able to afford it. They noticed the small glittering objects on display, thought well of them, and kept on walking. The building was being understood in a completely sympathetic way by the general public, but in a way that undermined the effective working of the shop, which was trying to reach the general public with inexpensive low-grade paste.

Buildings are tools, which may be well or badly adapted to the jobs that we ask them to do for us. As with any tool, we can supplement it with others, and we can find new ways to use it. To take a small and reductive example: I have a number of polypropylene boxes that I bought at the local supermarket. They are very simple but ingeniously designed, so that they sit inside one another, or put the other way round they stack on top of one another. I have been finding them useful, for taking bottles to the recycling bins, for taking washing to the line, for storing books – especially the books that have to travel (they can be stacked into provisional bookshelves, or can be separated and put in the back of the car) – and then if turned upside down it is possible to sit on them, as makeshift stools, and one has been pressed into service as a temporary bedside table. The box remains the same box, but it is used in different ways. In pragmatic terms it is not clear what the box is when it isn't being used for anything – one wonders if perhaps it just fades from consideration and might as well have ceased to exist. In Deleuze's terms the box-not-in-use is 'virtually' all the things that it could be used for, and is actualized as a seat, a washing basket, a carrier or a table when it is actually in use. So if I am sitting on it, I have actualized its seat-becoming, while its other uses remain virtual. The box itself is easily described to a manufacturer, and is cheaply made, unproblematically. The manufacturer does not necessarily know all the uses to which the box will be put, but certainly has an idea

Section 5: Relations

that it will be useful. One way of maximizing the sales of the box would be to put an illustrated label on it, so that potential buyers could be put in mind of the box's potential. We could see the box multiplied: neatly stored, or stacked up high, being used in a variety of ways. At the point of purchase, the box is not being used in any way, and what actually changes hands for the money is a dream of utility – a nest of virtualities, that will be actualized one way or another, in due course. This set of virtualities is Deleuze's 'multiplicity' – in theory endlessly multidimensional, as each usage calls a different dimension into play, and opens into a different 'world', or becomes part of a different machine. Moving up an order of magnitude or two from the portable box to a building, the multiplicity is more complex because it engages in a wider range of becomings. A house does much more than shelter, and when I purchase one, then unless I am very rich or very reckless I will have in mind a range of concerns – I will consider how it will perform in various different machines – some in a very clear way ('will I be able to survive here?', 'would I be able to entertain my friends here?') others being left at an ambiguous intuitive or instinctive level ('it doesn't feel right'). There will be questions of identity ('it's a perfectly good house, but it just isn't "me"'), of the likelihood that it will be possible to sell it again in a few years' time, that the neighbours will be congenial (or at least not hostile or criminal), that the purchase will enhance rather than diminish my social standing, etc., etc. Each of these dimensions involves a different way of looking at the building and the way it will perform. What I am buying is a set of virtualities, some of which will, in due course, be actualized. A persuasive salesman will be able to point out to me the potential, so that I can see the value before I agree the price. Some of the potentialities however will not become apparent until later, some of them will escape me altogether and be noticed (and maybe even actualized) by a later occupier of the property. In the Deleuze-world all these potentialities are dimensions of the multiplicity at its heart.

The house shifts its role and what we ask it to do, according to what is going on at the time. At night it gives us a secure place to sleep. Before meals when the kitchen is in use various little machines are brought into play – flows of water, electricity, heat, food, drink are released – and linked with an assemblage of consumption that may include visitors and special forms of behaviour that helps to reinforce links into one community or another. If there are several people in the house, each with a degree of autonomy, then there will be a complex interweaving of patterns of actualization and assemblage, as people come and go and engage with flows of information from television sets, newspapers, computers and books, flows of other kinds in the bathroom. Somehow there is a flow of income into the household – though this is rather metaphysical, as the flow is likely to be into bank accounts, which are regulated remotely and the sets of digits that pass between our employers, the banks, the credit card companies, and the suppliers of goods and services seem to be remarkably abstract. Nevertheless these abstract flows have very concrete effects on the ways in which we can live our lives and run our households. In addition to the flows of information and supplies into and out of the house, there is a flow of material, energy and information that went into the building, and which has to continue being put into it if the building is not to deteriorate and become useless. On a geological timescale the lives of buildings have been negligibly short. Few have survived over a thousand years. But the materials and energy that have made the buildings have left scars that may last longer. Once we start to look at buildings as sets of activities and processes, then they turn into interconnected machines with wide ramifications.

As with all tools, we tend to call our buildings names that draw attention to their functions – houses are there to house. We have some idea of the kinds of things that go on in offices, and that they're different from the kinds of things that go on in stations. In fact we give our buildings names according to their virtual functions, and don't have a separate word for a house that has stopped housing because its dwellers have gone out for the day. In fact it probably carries on being called a house even if it has been abandoned altogether; but if at some point it is sold, and then comes back into use as the club-house of a golf course, then somewhere along the way it stopped being a dwelling and became a club. Logically one would want to say that the house stopped being a house when no one was housed there, such as when no one was actually in it, but it would be confusing to do so in company, and we name the virtual dwelling that still lingers about the former house. Similarly a cave becomes a dwelling at the point when people start living in it. The thing-in-itself (the building) considered remotely from any possible human engagement, is real enough, but is pure virtuality. Always when we experience it we do so through sets of stimuli that engage with our perceptual and cognitive processes, some of which may be instinctive, some culturally produced, and an aspect of the building is thereby actualized as we engage it whether as an object of barely-noticed aesthetic interest, or as a dwelling for the rest of our lives. Architecture is gesture made with buildings, and it therefore always has a cultural element in it.[3] There is no architecture that is independent of experience, as it is only through encounters with buildings that their gestures could ever be inferred.

What it is that buildings seem to be, will depend on what we are using them to do. Houses can be particularly charged with meaning because we spend so much time imaginatively involved with them, as they shelter us, and we look after them by cleaning, painting, decorating and so on. They allow us to live the lives that we do live, and send out helpful or unhelpful messages about our social standing. We can identify closely with these buildings, which seem to be part of ourselves. Eileen Gray, for example, wrote in the 1930s rejecting Le Corbusier's conception of the house as a machine, saying 'a house is not a *"machine à habiter"*. It is man's shell, his continuation, his spreading out, his spiritual emanation. Not only its sculptural harmony, but its whole organization, every aspect of the whole work combined, come together to make it human in the most profound sense.'[4] This image of the house as a shell puts her in tune with Bachelard's perceptions, but not in this instance with Le Corbusier's. Samuel Butler would have accepted the shell as a machine, where Gray used the shell as a contrast with the machine. Given that she had this particular conception of the house, it is particularly painful to find that Le Corbusier broke into her house at Cap Martin (which she had designed herself) and painted large murals on eight of the walls. It was a violation that had apparently been encouraged by her partner Jean Badovici, who dealt in works of art and would have seen this as opportunity to have works of art at no cost. However it is not surprising to find that the relationship between Gray and Badovici broke apart, more surprising that it did not happen sooner, as Gray certainly resented the act, but she admired and did not efface the intrusive works, and Le Corbusier continued to visit the house.[5] One set of values stood in opposition to the other – the personal hurt, versus the art-world approval – and the cool public continuation of civilities makes it seem as though the treachery were too disgraceful to acknowledge. My general point here is that meaning is generated by the uses to which we put things, and this is an example of a house being put to an unanticipated use, which generated powerful and unwelcome meaning, doing violence against the house's soul.

Edges

Le Corbusier pointed out that a city is a tool.[6] It is a huge complicated tool, made up of thousands upon thousands of smaller tools, multiplicities and assemblages – swarms of machines. He illustrated the tools that the Baron Haussmann's workmen had at their disposal when they built the magnificent boulevards of Paris.[7] Individually the tools are small and simple: spade, pickaxe, ladder, wheelbarrow, winch; but they were used in great swarms, and therefore were able to achieve great and complex things. What is a city but a large house? And what is a house, but an extension of the person? And what is a person but a swarm of desiring-machines? We reduce our pluralities to identities to simplify things, so that we have a way of dealing with the world. If we start to see things in terms of flows of consumption and production, and see 'things' as the sum of what they can do, then we are in a world of networks and connections, rather than a world of neatly identifiable objects.[8]

There is a strong nostalgia for cities to have edges. In the pre-modern world this used to happen as a matter of course. Cities depended on a food supply from an agricultural base, and transport involved either walking or being drawn along by horses at their pace. Only in exceptional circumstances (Rome, Constantinople) did cities reach any great size. Usually the edge of the city would be defined by the need to fortify. Defensive ramparts would be built, and the area outside them would be kept clear of buildings, for the sake of the defences working properly. The citadel, within which the city's main institutions would all operate, had a high degree of visual definition and coherence. Even here, though, the autonomy was less than complete. The city was dependent on the surrounding farmland, and would offer protection to the villagers who tended the land. In times of war they might move inside the city walls on a temporary basis, along with their animals, so the walls do not mark the edge of the city as a functioning organism. Looked at as one of Samuel Butler's machines, the city in times of crisis withdrew into its shell in the same way that a tortoise might. If the city were not an independent city-state, but answered to a national power, then another scale of external connection could be involved, if for example the citadel had a strategic significance. Such was the case for example with Besançon, close to France's eastern border, and therefore the recipient of fortifications to Vauban's designs. The visual effect of the city as walled and self-contained is produced by the fortifications, and is not a reflection of the functional networks that tied the city into larger structures of power and influence, that here found visual expression only in the roadways. The linkages back to the sources of power were direct, but remained unexpressed, except in the scale of the fortification work, which nevertheless presents a visual idea of an edge rather than its real but invisible connection back to the strategic decision-making at Versailles and Bazoches.

We are now in quite a different position. The railways exploded the visual coherence of cities in the nineteenth century, making it possible for people to travel much greater distances into work. The relations of commerce have replaced those of feudalism.[9] Where we once had cities that could be traversed with a fifteen-minute walk, we now have hundred-mile cities, and global cities.[10] Fewer people work on the land. More people derive their income from the cities, whether or not they actually live within the city boundary. We can no longer defend the city by building walls around it, and no one builds city walls any more. This leaves the city free to spread, and modern transportation and patterns of work make it possible to spread much further than before. Most places that look like villages now operate as places for city-workers to sleep – the money spent in the village comes from the city, and it is probably spent on goods that have been made and distributed by way of a city (even the vegetables in the local grocer's shop are likely to have been grown in another country). The village is therefore totally dependent on there being a city nearby, and functionally the village is part of that city – they are part of the same organism, the same machine. Where villages are beyond the reach of cities, the countryside depopulates. We tend still to have an image of the city as a contained space with countryside around it, and we maintain this image by way of legislation (green belts) when it does not happen 'naturally'. Actually what we have is networks of intensity, that are more concentrated in some places, and more dispersed in others. The city is more like a gravitational field that decreases its influence with distance; 'inside' and 'outside' no longer have any meaning, the point is to be connected or disconnected. If we try to find a way of giving expression to this conception of the city, it is not clear what the result will be, but it will not be the sort of city that has a well-defined edge condition, that articulates a threshold of passage from the rusticity of the countryside to the rule of civilization in the city. The threshold states will be something more like phase transitions, as the dispersed gaseous particles of settlement are found with increasingly regularity, forming a viscous liquid in the suburbs, and solidifying as densely packed crystals downtown; perhaps imploding – when infrastructures are overstretched – to make sporadic inner-city black holes.

This image of the city has its appeal, and is to be seen compellingly in New York, where the threshold transition is articulated by the rivers around Manhattan Island, giving the island a visual autonomy that means that it photographs well from across the water and looks like a unified whole, despite the multifarious links, some of them visible, some of them invisible, that mean that the island does not function autonomously. Its water supply, its electricity, many of its workers are brought from off the island, by various means of transport, and the various forms of telecommunications and networking are densely packed. When a road-surface is broken into so that pipes can be repaired or installed, it looks as if the city is built not on bedrock but on an amazingly complex and densely packed stratification of services. There was a recent news report that a woman had been electrocuted by standing blamelessly on a steel manhole cover near Central Park, which is a reminder that the city services are close at hand – sometimes too close. By contrast Los Angeles works without the intense build-up of density at its centre. There is a downtown area, and it is visually striking to see the tall buildings erupting up from the diffuse urban grid, but the tall buildings are not really an expression of a build-up of intensity, as of the feeling that the city should have a downtown like everyone else's.[11] It actually works as a series of overlaid networks, that allow a great deal of connectivity from one part to another, and as there is a fairly free flow in a broadly featureless landscape, there is no need for an intense centralization, and the city can operate highly effectively without the need for a traditional city centre. As a model for a utopian steady-state city, it is seriously flawed, as the ways in which the city are used are such as to produce social groups that tend not to come into contact with one another, and when they do come into contact the results can be catastrophic rather than stimulating. The ability to be selective about one's networked connections, and the ability to move easily within this network without needing to engage with other networks, simplifies one's own life, and makes it more efficient, but also allows for the development of high levels of ignorance across from one network to another, and consequently high levels of mistrust and paranoia. It is a place where ideas are acted upon and are highly developed more quickly than elsewhere. The fact that it brings together so many elements of the ideal and the calamitous, gives it an air of impermanence, as if we are witnessing the last days: the ideal climate, but prone to earthquakes; the unparalleled glamour of the movie stars' lives, but the Rodney King riots.

L.A. is moving.
It's moving, of course, all the time, round-the-clock in cars on its lethally-interconnected empire of freeways. It's moving in the sky, in helicopters, jets, Goodyear blimps bearing one-liners out over the basin. Its weather is moving, jumpy as context in video-cam reportage. As Joan Didion observed a while back, the weather of Los Angeles is not resort-like, it is apocalyptic. We have fires, floods, Med-fly plagues, tidal waves, strange low-pressure cells, fog, lost satellites and insistent UFOs.[12]

If Hollywood is still 'the dream factory', it reflects our dreams back to us, reshaping them along the way. It knows that we dream about places other than Los Angeles, and fabricates other worlds, making itself invisible. It may be the capital of the twenty-first century, but we might not notice it, as we are entranced with its images of New York. Los Angeles, like ancient Sparta, is not a place that is defined by its monuments, but by what can be done there. Thucydides remarked that anyone coming on the ruins of Sparta would think that it had been no more than a collection of villages, and would never infer what a powerful state it had been.[13] What made it powerful was its culture and organization. It had no need of a city wall because its army was so lethal it annihilated any enemy that came near. It did not petrify its institutions in monuments, but kept them as dynamic forces, assembling, dispersing, wild energy, always on the move. Architects have always responded more warmly to the Athenians' tendency to spend huge sums of money on monuments – a tendency that eventually choked the Athenian Agora – but Winckelmann's conception of stylistic unity across the arts was rooted in a vision of the ancient world that was light on its feet.[14] We need not be weighed down by history, nor by an oppressive weight of monumental building, if we are not mesmerized by it, as Bataille clearly was. His neighbour Eileen Gray by contrast made her modest incursions into the architecture-world with a strong idea that architecture was there to support the practices of life, not to commemorate the dead or to ossify the living.[15] There is a grace about her work that is made all the more evident in her preparedness to move on from it, and to see it as something that was bound up in a relationship with a place, a time and a person from which and whom she had dissolved her links. The Eameses' house had a similar delicacy – an air of lightness and disposability – without any of the stuffiness that an ancestral monument might have brought with it. Los Angeles has seen large-scale building projects, but so far they have avoided the oppressive qualities that Bataille felt when confronted by monuments. Los Angeles has grown by colonizing the desert, and even when a development is not the first on a site, there is no build-up of historical complexity. Whole areas can be bulldozed for the sake of a new project, and any real memory of what was there before seems to have been completely obliterated. An urban historian can retrieve information and can piece together a picture of what has happened, but it is not part of the lived experience of the place, in the way that it is in an old European town, where the urban fabric is sedimented over centuries.[16] It is possible to live in L.A. without feeling the need to go into the downtown area on a regular basis. Activities are dispersed in the suburbs – which are no longer quite 'sub-urbs' because they constitute the 'urbs', the city itself. As the centre has been abolished, there is no theoretical limit to growth, and the city is already the size of Denmark. France is still 'the hexagon', its seventeenth-century shape, but Los Angeles has no shape, no edge, no limits – that isn't the point – it is *informe*. Its identity comes from its networks and connections. The city has become a machinic assemblage without monumental presence – just enough fabric to keep everything working, with occasional displays of personal or corporate extravagance in the form of spectacular buildings, but none of them individually necessary to sustain the working of the city as an entity. The Agora is in the airwaves. The cathedrals are in the suburbs. The freeways are in the soul.

The reason that this is of compelling interest is that all our settlements are turning into Los Angeles, or 'edge city', as this pattern of settlement-without-edges has become known.[17] It is what the free-market economy produces in the twenty-first century. We can't necessarily tell by looking at the fabric of the older established cities, but they have changed the way in which they function, so even if the historic town centre still looks very much the way it did, it is no longer working in the way that made it take shape. An example in Burgundy: the place to go for routine shopping near here is Avallon. It is a very picturesque town, sited on a crag over the Cousin river, with ramparts, turrets, cobbled streets, a fine collegial church dating from the twelfth century, strangely poetic street names (la rue de Bel-Air, la rue Masquée) and a large farmers' market on Saturday mornings. It could not look more settled and traditional. However this town of 8620 inhabitants has an out-of-town shopping mall,[18] with a huge supermarket, and a row of smaller shops including a restaurant, France Telecom, dry cleaning, key-cutting, hairdressing, photographic supplies, clothes for men and women, shoes, a newsagent, etc. At close hand as part of the same strip there is a large do-it-yourself store, a pharmacy, a garage and petrol station; and a McDonald's. This strip is used by people from miles around. It is necessary to have a car to reach it, but there is ample parking and if one has a car then it is more convenient than going into the town and finding a parking place. There are two other smaller supermarkets in the town, with substantial car parks. So although smaller shops in the Grand Rue are the more pleasant alternative, they are used more by those for whom shopping is a valued leisure activity, and less by people who think of it as a utilitarian exercise or who are pressed for time. The forces that are shaping the new building in and around the town are making it function more like Los Angeles, even though for other reasons – cultural reasons – the built fabric of the town centre is being well maintained and old appearances conserved.

Tectonics Generalized

It has been a theme of the discussion in this book to trace the ways in which metaphors have been carried across from one order of magnitude to another, transferred from person to building, machine to building, person to machine, escalating from the confined room to the outer reaches of the night sky. Another theme has been to notice the effects of swarms – multitudes – whether they be molecules multiplied up to the molar scale of human experience, or crowds of people. At any scale we learn about the character or the crowd by learning about the political relations – the kinds of bonds at work. We have different common-sense names for these bonds at different scales of operation. We know that marble has properties that make it different from timber, so we do not use these materials interchangeably. The materials have different properties because of what is going on at the molecular scale, but we know from experience only at a much larger scale. If we were the same size as molecules then we might intuitively think of the materials as being caught up in different sorts of political relations. Similarly we can think of different parts of society as having a different grain, so some types of behaviour can be managed, while others will never happen. At the level of buildings, the sympathetic handling of materials to produce architectural effects – building construction, artistically considered – is known as 'tectonics', deriving from the old Greek word for a carpenter, or form-giver, *tekton*, which survives in the last syllable of the name 'architect'. The design of buildings is an art of relations: relations of people with one another, as they are brought together and kept apart by walls and spaces, relations of crowds of stones and timbers as they co-operate in holding together an assembly of many parts that we perceive as some kind of unity, contractual relations as the flow of money and labour makes this assembly, and the volatile relations between the building and the metaphor-producing cultures that come into contact with it. It does not matter which element we start with in these sets of relations; in the end they will all have their say. Traditionally in recent years architects have learnt about building materials and what they can sympathetically do. Gottfried Semper visited the Crystal Palace in London in 1851, and came away with a lasting impression of a Caribbean hut he had seen there, from considering which he elaborated principles that might apply to architecture in general. There was a solid base, made from earth or closely packed cut stone; there was a timber frame, generating a regularly proportioned grid up above; there was a hearth in the floor, generating the idea of home; and there was a fabric covering of some kind to make the walls. These were his four elements of architecture.[19] The approach that Semper sketched out can be extended to cover a wide range of architecture that is informed by a consideration of building materials and their expressive use.[20] This does not include all architecture, because some has always made an attempt to suppress the constructional aspect of building design. For example Adolf Loos's ideas about architecture were framed in a way that stood self-consciously against Semper; and much 'popular' building – the mass of commercial housing, and home improvements – deals with insubstantial signifiers that are not rooted in any sense of constructional integrity or expressivity. The important relations here are between the consumers' imaginations and the signs that they are given to work on: so a Corinthian column on each side of the front door can act as a means to signify quality and tradition without being connected into the constructional logic of the building (which generally goes unnoticed). In a market where such signs are valued and the costs of having them are minimized – the costs of effort, as well as the price – the result is *kitsch*: the buildings laying claim to symbols of a status that they aspire to have, but which they do not embody.

Architecture is an art of relations, just as music and politics are arts of relations, and once we start to generalize the point we can see that every art is an art of relations: between one pigment and another, between the art-object and the viewer's memory and imagination, between the art-object and other art-objects, and indeed between the viewer and the viewer's cultural circle – desire is produced not in isolation but sociably, which is to say politically (I want what my friends want – mimetic desire).[21] The idea that we interact with things, and with others, in a responsive and considered way could be seen as a generalized metaphorical transfer of the idea of tectonics. Moving from Saint Bernard listening to the trees in the forests around Fontenay in the twelfth century, to Louis Kahn's conversation with a brick in the twentieth (the brick says 'I like an arch') there is a long tradition of inferring ideas from mute matter, and feeling that one has learnt something profound by doing so. This tradition is continued and revitalized in Félix Guattari's ecologies,[22] where habitats (or organisms plus habitats) start to acquire identities and rights. If this is read alongside Richard Rorty's model of philosophical discourse as a conversation,[23] then we have a way to see the *informe* as being taken up in relation to our particular (and changing) interests and purposes, and being given instrumental value in the process. There is no underlying 'truth' in the material, but a multiplicity of virtual instruments that are actualized when they are put in relation with one machine or another. The 'conversation' here is a negotiation with the instrument, trying to see what it can be asked to do (what is its potential); and if that conversation is to follow Rorty's model, then it is not just a matter of projecting into the dumb instrument the prejudgements and clichés that we bring to the table, but of making a life-changing exchange with them. The language that is used to describe such an encounter might be exotic or mundane, depending on the circumstances and the scale of operations. In politics it has the vocabulary of democracy and human rights, of the obligation to accommodate various perspectives and points of view. In philosophy it has the vocabulary of perspectivism. In building it has the craftsman's traditional respect for materials, alongside the architect wondering what it is like to be a brick.

Section 5: Relations

Atmospheres

We move from experience to conjecture, the particular to the abstract, from the familiar to the strange, from the near to the distant. We start from ourselves, and project ourselves on to the world, which we see in relation to what we are trying to do. It is only later, when I am more familiar with the world's indifference to my personal fate, that I can begin to see that I am peripheral and contingent. We are highly inclined to see human form in non-human things, but what kind of form is it that we see? Man the miracle of creation, as a perfectly proportioned reflection of divinity, whose limbs and lineaments could be measured and embodied in buildings, has been replaced by man the sport of evolution, a machine that consumes and produces. Our metaphors, with habit and repetition, turn into clichés, our clichés turn into truisms, and our truisms into the self-evident premises on which we can all agree. The small things under my control are symptomatic of larger things that aren't, and it gives me some satisfaction to see my actions in a larger frame, as it gives meaning and significance to what I can do. Moving from the molecular to the molar, multiplying my little actions by thousands of millions, gives me, if not quite a sense of power then at least a sense that my good intentions are not altogether futile. Market forces have taken their place alongside gravity as forces of nature, and globalization means that I would be implicated in the destruction of the Amazonian rainforests on the other side of the world, if I specified the cheapest hardwood for my doors. So, it is worth spending the extra money in order to know that I have done the right thing? If it's just me, then the effect is insignificant, and I might as well economize, but if it's a matter of principle, multiplied up a thousand million times, then it is worth doing. But then, what if I am working for a client, should I insist that the extra money must be spent? (What if I lose the commission in consequence? What if the client really can't afford the difference?) The answers to such questions will tell me what my values really are, if I am put in these positions. I know the answers that I am supposed to give, and therefore the questions are less pressing on the page than they are when we face them in life, when the alternatives can each seem compelling to different parts of our minds. The most telling piece of information that we can have about a building is how much it cost – how much effort, how costly the materials, how large the project? The particular approach of the architect, which is under the architect's control, is of a lower order of magnitude in significance, but as it is all that the architect can influence it tends – in the architect's perspective – to seem all-encompassing and the architect all-powerful. Bataille's reading of the architect as the servant of power is more accurate, but unflattering. In the eyes of those with power architects are either toadies or eccentrics who seem intriguing and should perhaps be indulged. If they become annoying they soon after become invisible. The architect's task is to deploy a selection from all the little machines that are available for use, and to marshal them in order, so that together they make a grand machine that mobilizes images and practical utilities, producing responses that work together so as to be able to produce a building, which if it works properly will be an aid to sustaining a good life, a spectacle, a sequence of pleasures, an image of the order of the world.

Whether the architect has any awareness of it or not, it will be a product of the forces operating in the building's world, and will embody the values of the society in which it is produced. If it is a large or a costly building, or if it is a small part of a larger grouping, then we can infer something from it that touches on issues that are more significant than a personal whim, and that is why buildings as artefacts are of such interest to archaeologists. We need to have some information in order to contextualize the individual building-performances, but if we can do that then the buildings, whatever their merits, can tell us a great deal. The great unknown in all this is the part of the machinery that is in the minds of the people who come into contact with the building. If I were to design a building that made sense only in terms of this week's news, then it would be obsolete long before it was built. Therefore we must look for a slower-moving culture to which the building can relate. Hence the range of material included in the present volume, much of which is pre-architectural in its content – taking us back to a place before there is a building, and asking not what shape it is to be, but what would be the forces that could be in play in affecting its reception. The point is to understand the emerging view of the world and how we can conduct ourselves in it, and then find ways of making buildings reflect that view. As architects in moments of intensity we can crystallize a molecular fragment of the world as it is now, and which might, by spreading like a crystal, structure the world to come. The buildings will embody some such view, whether we will it or not, and as a writer I can express the view that as bodies, machines and cities become diffuse and dispersed, it is only to be expected that our buildings will do the same. I can even assert that it is already going on all around us, and has been for thousands of years. But it is the work of an architect to find ways of persuading buildings to make gestures that are expressive of this state of affairs. There has been much freakish novelty that has caught the attention of architects, but such things pass in moments. A building is inevitably the embodiment of the forces that brought it into being, and the convincing architectural gesture will give expression to some of those forces. Sometimes it has happened unselfconsciously, but now – like the dancer in Kleists's essay included below – we need to work to recapture that grace. The most traditional task of the architect has been to make settings that show us that we are at home in the world, but the world that we are in keeps changing as our state of knowledge changes. To be able to make such settings convincingly, without affectation or self-consciousness, demands wide knowledge, confidence, practice and playful spontaneity in making the decisions; and stern discipline and unrelenting tenacity in seeing them through.

Notes

1. Ralph Waldo Emerson, 'Circles', above, p. 30ff.
2. See William James above, p. 49ff.
3. Andrew Ballantyne, *What is Architecture?* (London: Routledge, 2002).
4. Peter Adam, *Eileen Gray: Architect/Designer* (New York: Abrams, 1987, revised 2000) p. 309. I have retranslated the French original.
5. Ibid, p. 311. Caroline Constant, *Eileen Gray* (New York: Phaidon, 2000) pp. 122–5.
6. Le Corbusier, *Urbanisme*, translated by John Rodker, *The City of Tomorrow and its Planning* (London: Architectural Press, 1929) p. xxi.

Section 5: Relations

7. Ibid., p. 155.
8. Deleuze and Guattari's concept 'the rhizome' is pertinent here, but I have not felt the need to explain it because the idea of non-centred dispersed networks has become so very widespread with the rise of the internet that I imagine readers will not need to be persuaded on this point. The specific provenance of the idea is unimportant, but see Deleuze and Guattari, *Thousand Plateaus*, op. cit., pp. 3–25.
9. Though the two may be more closely linked than we like to admit. See Umberto Eco, translated by William Weaver, 'The Return of the Middle Ages', in *Faith in Fakes* (London: Secker and Warburg, 1986) [retitled *Travels in Hyper-Reality* for the paperback edition] pp. 59–85.
10. Deyan Sudjic, *The 100-Mile City* (San Diego: Harcourt Brace, 1992); Joel Garreau, *Edge City: Life on the New Frontier* (New York: Doubleday, 1991); Stephen Graham and Simon Marvin, *Splintering Urbanism: Networked Infrastructures, Technological Mobilities and the Urban Condition* (London: Routledge, 2001).
11. Reyner Banham, *Los Angeles: the Architecture of Four Ecologies* (Harmondsworth: Penguin, 1971).
12. Carol Muske Dukes, introduction to *Absolute Disaster: Fiction from Los Angeles*, edited by Lee Montgomery (Los Angeles: Santa Monica Review, 1996) unnumbered page.
13. Thucydides, translated by Rex Warner, *History of the Peloponnesian War* (Harmondsworth: Penguin, 1954) p. 41.
14. Andrew Ballantyne, 'Space, Grace and Stylistic Conformity: *Spätrömische Kunstindustrie* and Architecture' in *Framing Formalism: Riegl's Work*, edited by Richard Woodfield (New York: G and B Arts International, 2001) pp. 83–106.
15. Eileen Gray and Georges Bataille both lived in Vézelay, but I am being fanciful in calling them neighbours because they lived there at different times. Bataille from 1943 in the rue de l'Hôtel de Ville, Gray about a hundred metres away in the rue de l'Argenterie, which runs into the rue de l'Hôtel de Ville at one end, obliquely, so the road seems to take a turn rather than go round a sharply defined corner. However she had left by about 1940. Michel Surya, *Georges Bataille, la mort à l'oeuvre* (Paris: Gallimard, 1992) translated by Krzysztof Fijalkowski and Michael Richardson, *Georges Bataille: An Intellectual Biography* (London: Verso, 2002) p. 399. Peter Adam, op. cit, p. 257; Caroline Constant, op. cit., pp. 82–6.
16. Dana Cuff, *The Provisional City: Los Angeles Stories of Architecture and Urbanism* (Cambridge, Mass: MIT Press, 200).
17. Joel Garreau, *Edge City*, op. cit.
18. The population figure is that given by Ian Ousby, *Blue Guide: Burgundy* (London: A & C Black, 1992).
19. Gottfried Semper, *Der Stil in den technischen und tektonischen Künsten*, 2 vols (1860 and 1863); see Gottfried Semper, translated and edited by Harry Mallgrave and Wolfgang Herrmann, *The Four Elements of Architecture and Other Writings* (Cambridge: Cambridge University Press, 1989).
20. Kenneth Frampton, *Studies in Tectonic Culture: the Poetics of Construction in*

Nineteenth and Twentieth-Century Architecture (Cambridge, Mass.: MIT, 1995); Demetri Porphyrios, 'From *Techne* to Tectonics' in *What is Architecture?* edited by Andrew Ballantyne (London: Routledge, 2002) pp. 129–37.
21. Rene Girard, *Mensonge romantique et vérité romanesque* (Paris: Grasset, 1961) translated by Yvonne Freccero, *Deceit, Desire and the Novel: Self and Other in Literary Struture* (Baltimore, Maryland: Johns Hopkins University Press, 1966).
22. See above, pp. 35–6.
23. Richard Rorty, *Philosophy and the Mirror of Nature* (Princeton, N.J.: Princeton University Press, 1980) pp. 389–94: the section headed 'Philosophy in the Conversation of Mankind', which alludes to Michael Oakeshott, 'The Voice of Poetry in the Conversation of Mankind', in *Rationalism and Politics* (New York: 1975).

Gilles Deleuze

Given Deleuze's pervasive presence in the commentary in this collection, he probably needs no introduction at this point. However Deleuze (1925–95) was Professor of Philosophy at the University of Paris VIII, at Vincennes, his anti-authoritarian manner ensuring that he was seen to be continuing a project that had links with the student revolts of 1968. He published regularly, right up to his suicide, and his influence seems to be growing steadily, as people engage with his texts. His best-known works are his collaborations with Félix Guattari (1930–92): creative work that defies conventional categorization. Many of Deleuze's books however were studies of the work of individual philosophers (such as Hume, Nietzsche, Bergson, Spinoza, Leibniz, Kant). These were never the standard texts that their titles seemed to propose, but spun away from the texts of their subjects to produce new ideas and ways of thinking, developed from an analysis of concepts drawn from the writing of the philosopher under discussion. The article included here was first published in *L'Autre Journal*, and is at the more accessible end of Deleuze's spectrum of writing styles. Two metaphors do need explaining though: the mole and the snake. 'Money's old moles are the animals you get in places of confinement', says Deleuze, and this image conveys an idea of money as something held underground in confined spaces – buried treasure in a bank vault, the traditional wealth of gold ingots, rather than the vaporized money of electronic digital media. Martin Joughin, Deleuze's translator here, points out that a *vieille taupe* (which translates literally as 'old mole') is a disagreeable old woman – who lets you know what she doesn't like about you.[1] However the old mole has another life in Marxist literature, with which this passage certainly resonates. It alludes to a mataphor in a passage in Marx, where Marx images the revolution, currently invisible, as a mole, at work out of sight underground.[2] Antonio Negri (a friend of Deleuze and Guattari) in his book *Empire* glosses this as a reference to this image in Marx.[3] Rosa Luxemburg used the mole as an image of history, or historical processes: 'History, old mole, you've done good work!'[4] Bataille offered a polarity 'old mole' versus 'soaring eagle':

> Revolutionary idealism tends to make of the revolution an eagle above eagles, a *supereagle* striking down authoritarian imperialism, an idea as radiant as an adolescent eloquently seizing power for the benefit of utopian enlightenment. This detour naturally leads to the failure of the revolution and, with the help of military fascism, the satisfaction of the elevated need for idealism. The Napoleonic epic represents its least ridiculous development: the castration of an Icarian revolution, shameless imperialism exploiting the revolutionary urge.
>
> Meanwhile, brought back to the subterranean action of economic

facts, the 'old-mole' revolution hollows out chambers in a decomposed soil repugnant to the delicate nose of the utopians. 'Old mole,' Marx's resounding expression for the complete satisfaction of the revolutionary outburst of the masses, must be understood in relation to the notion of a geological uprising as expressed in the *Communist Manifesto*. Marx's point of departure has nothing to do with the heavens, preferred station of the imperialist eagle as of Christian or revolutionary utopias. He begins in the bowels of the earth, as in the materialist bowels of proletarians.[5]

Although Deleuze's image is distinct from these, as it is specifically an image of money, it nevertheless resonates with them, caught up in an old-fashioned view of hoarded wealth and revolutionary activity. The snake by contrast is unconfined. As a metaphor it is much less complex and can easily be pinned down. Before the Euro was introduced as a common currency across much of Europe, the nations of the European Union held their currencies in a fixed relation to one another, in a mechanism that was known as 'the snake' because of the shape of the line on a graph that could act as a diagram of the process. The snake is as elusive as the mole, but for different reasons. In Deleuze's French there is a significant play on words as money forsakes its mole-becoming for its snake-becoming: we move from a world controlled by slogans, to one controlled by passwords. The slogans shouted by revolutionaries in the street – including Rosa Luxemburg – would be called *'mots d'ordre'* (literally 'order-words', which might mean 'commands'); while 'passwords' are *'mots de passe'*; so we slide from a world controlled by *mots d'ordre*, to one controlled by *mots de passe* – from commands to permissions – and the world restructures itself around us. In fact there have always been controls of this latter type, which would allow some doors to open to people with power, privilege or money; the novelty is rather their invisibility, as footmen have been replaced by turnstiles, and then by smartcards and microtechnologies that regulate our access to places and information without our being aware that we are being regulated at all, unless we are in a position to compare our experiences with those of other people from different groups, who turn out to live in different worlds.

Notes

1. Martin Jouchin, in Gilles Deleuze, *Pourparlers* (Paris: Éditions de Minuit, 1990) translated by Martin Jouchin *Negotiations* (New York: Columbia University Press, 1995) p. 203.
2. Karl Marx, 'The Eighteenth Brumaire of Louis Bonaparte', in *Karl Marx: Selected Writings*, edited by David McLellan (Oxford: Oxford University Press, 1977) p. 316: 'But the revolution is thoroughgoing. It is still journeying through purgatory. It does its work methodically. By 2 December 1851, it had completed one half of its preparatory work; it is now completing the other half. First it perfected the parliamentary power, in order to be able to overthrow it. Now that it has attained this, it perfects the executive power, reduces it to its purest expression, isolates it, sets it up against itself as the sole

Section 5: Relations

  target, in order to concentrate all its forces of destruction against it. And when it has done this second half of its preliminary work, Europe will leap from its seat and exultantly exclaim: Well grubbed, old mole!'

3. Antonio Negri and Michael Hardt, *Empire* (Cambridge, Mass.: Harvard University Press, 200) p. 57 – with reference to the Deleuze essay discussed here – 'We suspect that Marx's old mole has finally died'; but note that Deleuze is imaging money, not Marx's revolution, as an old mole.
4. Rosa Luxemburg, *Spartakusbriefe* no. 5, May 1917; concluding paragraph: '*Histoire, vieille taupe, tu as fait du bon travail! En cet instant retentit sur le prolétariat international, sur le prolétariat allemand le mot d'ordre, l'appel que seule peut faire jaillir l'heure grandiose d'un tournant mondial: Impérialisme ou socialisme. Guerre ou révolution, il n'y a pas d'autre alternative!*'
5. Georges Bataille, 1929–30, first published *Tel Quel* 34 (Summer 1968); in volume 2 of Georges Bataille, *Oeuvres complètes*, edited by Denis Hollier (Paris: Pléiade, 1970) pp. 93–109; translated by Donald M. Leslie Jr, 'The "Old Mole" and the Prefix *Sur* in the Words *Surhomme* [Superman] and *Surrealist*', in *Visions of Excess: Selected Writings 1927–1939*, edited by Alan Stoekl (Minneapolis: University of Minnesota Press, 1985) pp. 34–5.

Postscript on Control Societies

History

Foucault associated *disciplinary societies* with the eighteenth and nineteenth centuries; they reach their apogee at the beginning of the twentieth century. They operate by organizing major sites of confinement. Individuals are always going from one closed site to another, each with its own laws: first of all the family, then school ('you're not at home, you know'), then the barracks ('you're not at school, you know'), then the factory, hospital from time to time, maybe prison, the model site of confinement. Prison provides a model for the others: thus the heroine in *Europa 51*, on seeing the workers, cries out: 'I thought they were convicts ...' Foucault has thoroughly analyzed the ideal behind sites of confinement, clearly seen in the factory: bringing everything together, giving each thing its place, organizing time, setting up in this space-time a force of production greater than the sum of component forces. But Foucault also knew how short-lived this model was: it succeeded *sovereign societies* with an altogether different aim and operation (taking a cut of production instead of organizing it, condemning to death instead of ordering life); the transition took place gradually, and Napoleon seems to have effected the overall transformation from one kind of society into the other. But discipline would in its turn begin to break down as new forces moved slowly into place, then made rapid advances after the Second World War: we were no longer in disciplinary societies, we were leaving them behind.

We're in the midst of a general breakdown of all sites of confinement – prisons, hospitals, factories, schools, the family. The family is an 'interior' that's breaking down like all other interiors – educational, professional, and so on. The appropriate ministers have constantly been announcing supposedly appropriate reforms. Educational reforms, industrial reforms, hospital, army, prison reforms; but everyone knows these institutions are in more or less terminal decline. It's simply a matter of nursing them through their death throes and keeping people busy until the new forces knocking at the door take over. *Control societies* are taking over from disciplinary societies. 'Control' is the name proposed by Burroughs to characterize the new monster, and Foucault sees it fast approaching. Paul Virilio too is constantly analyzing the ultrarapid forms of apparently free-floating control that are taking over from the old disciplines at work within the time scales of closed systems. It's not a question of amazing pharmaceutical products, nuclear technology, and genetic engineering, even though these will play their part in the new process. It's not a question of asking whether the old or new system is harsher or more bearable, because there's a conflict in each between the ways they free and enslave us. With the breakdown of the hospital as a site of confinement, for instance, community psychiatry, day hospitals, and home care initially presented new freedoms, while at the same time contributing to mechanisms of control as rigorous as the harshest confinement. It's not a question of worrying or of hoping for the best, but of finding new weapons.

Logic

The various placements or sites of confinement through which individuals pass are independent variables: we're supposed to start all over again each time, and although all these sites have a common language, it's *analogical*. The various forms of control, on the other hand, are inseparable variations, forming a system of varying geometry whose language is *digital* (though not necessarily binary). Confinements are *molds*, different moldings, while controls are a *modulation*, like a self-transmuting[1] molding continually changing from one moment to the next, or like a sieve whose mesh varies from one point to another. This comes out well in the matter of wages: the factory was a body of men whose internal forces reached an equilibrium between the highest possible production and the lowest possible wages; but in a control society businesses take over from factories, and a business is a soul, a gas. There were of course bonus systems in factories, but businesses strive to introduce a deeper level of modulation into all wages, bringing them into a state of constant metastability punctuated by ludicrous challenges, competitions, and seminars. If the stupidest TV game shows are so successful, it's because they're a perfect reflection of the way businesses are run. Factories formed individuals into a body of men for the joint convenience of a management that could monitor each component in this mass, and trade unions that could mobilize mass resistance; but businesses are constantly introducing an inexorable rivalry presented as healthy competition, a wonderful motivation that sets individuals against one another and sets itself up in each of them, dividing each within himself. Even the state education system has been looking at the principle of 'getting paid for results': in fact, just as businesses are replacing factories, *school* is being replaced by *continuing education* and exams by continuous assessment.[2] It's the surest way of turning education into a business.

    In disciplinary societies you were always starting all over again (as you went from school to barracks, from barracks to factory), while in control societies you never finish anything – business, training, and military service being coexisting metastable states of a single modulation, a sort of universal transmutation. Kafka, already standing at the point of transition between the two kinds of society, described in *The Trial* their most ominous judicial expressions: *apparent acquittal* (between two confinements) in disciplinary societies, and *endless post-ponement* in (constantly changing) control societies are two very different ways of doing things, and if our legal system is vacillating, is itself breaking down, it's because we're going from one to the other. Disciplinary societies have two poles: signatures standing for *individuals*, and numbers or places in a register standing for their position in a *mass*. Disciplines see no incompatibility at all between these two aspects, and their power both amasses and individuates, that is, it fashions those over whom it's exerted into a body of people and molds the individuality of each member of that body (Foucault saw the origin of this twin concern in the priest's pastoral power over his flock and over each separate animal, and saw civil power subsequently establishing itself by different means as a lay 'pastor'). In control societies, on the other hand, the key thing is no longer a signature or number but a code: codes are *passwords*, whereas disciplinary societies are ruled (when it comes to integration or resistance) by *precepts*.[3] The digital language of control is made up of codes indicating whether access to some information should be allowed or denied. We're no longer dealing with a duality of mass and individual. Individuals become '*dividuals*,' and masses become samples, data, markets, or '*banks*.' Money, perhaps, best expresses the difference between the two kinds of society, since discipline was always related to molded currencies containing gold as a numerical standard, whereas control is based on floating exchange rates, modulations depending on a code setting sample percentages for various currencies. If money's old moles are the animals you get in places of confinement, then control societies have their snakes.[4] We've gone from one animal to the other, from moles to snakes, not just in the system we live under but in the way we live and in our relations with other people too. Disciplinary man produced energy in discrete amounts, while control man undulates, moving among a continuous range of different orbits. *Surfing* has taken over from all the old *sports*.

It's easy to set up a correspondence between any society and some kind of machine, which isn't to say that their machines determine different kinds of society but that they express the social forms capable of producing them and making use of them. The old sovereign societies worked with simple machines, levers, pulleys, clocks; but recent disciplinary societies were equipped with thermodynamic machines presenting the passive danger of entropy and the active danger of sabotage; control societies function with a third generation of machines, with information technology and computers, where the passive danger is noise and the active, piracy and viral contamination. This technological development is more deeply rooted in a mutation of capitalism. The mutation has been widely recognized and can be summarized as follows: nineteenth-century capitalism was concentrative, directed toward production, and proprietorial. Thus it made the factory into a site of confinement, with the capitalist owning the means of production and perhaps owning other similarly organized sites (worker's homes, schools). As for markets, they were won either through specialization, through colonization, or through reducing the costs of production. But capitalism in its present form is no longer directed toward production, which is often transferred to remote parts of the Third World, even in the case of complex operations like textile plants, steelworks, and oil refineries. It's directed toward metaproduction. It no longer buys raw materials and no longer sells finished products: it buys finished products or assembles them from parts. What it seeks to sell is services, and what it seeks to buy, activities. It's a capitalism no longer directed toward production but toward products, that is, toward sales or markets. Thus it's essentially dispersive, with factories giving way to businesses. Family, school, army, and factory are no longer so many analogous but different sites converging in an owner, whether the state or some private power, but transmutable or transformable coded configurations of a single business where the only people left are administrators. Even art has moved away from closed sites and into the open circuits of banking. Markets are won by taking control rather than by establishing a discipline, by fixing rates rather than by reducing costs, by transforming products rather than by specializing production. Corruption here takes on a new power. The sales department becomes a business center or 'soul.' We're told businesses have souls, which is surely the most terrifying news in the world. Marketing is now the instrument of social control and produces the arrogant breed who are our masters. Control is short-term and rapidly shifting, but at the same time continuous and unbounded, whereas discipline was long-term, infinite, and discontinuous. A man is no longer a man confined but a man in debt. One thing, it's true, hasn't changed – capitalism still keeps three quarters of humanity in extreme poverty, too poor to have debts and too numerous to be confined: control will have to deal not only with vanishing frontiers, but with mushrooming shantytowns and ghettos.

Program

We don't have to stray into science fiction to find a control mechanism that can fix the position of any element at any given moment – an animal in a game reserve, a man in a business (electronic tagging). Félix Guattari has imagined a town where anyone can leave their flat, their street, their neighborhood, using their (dividual) electronic card that opens this or that barrier; but the card may also be rejected on a particular day, or between certain times of day; it doesn't depend on the barrier but on the computer that is making sure everyone is in a permissible place, and effecting a universal modulation.

> We ought to establish the basic sociotechnological principles of control mechanisms as their age dawns, and describe in these terms what is already taking the place of the disciplinary sites of confinement that everyone says are breaking down. It may be that older means of control, borrowed from the old sovereign societies, will come back into play, adapted as necessary. The key thing is that we're at the beginning of something new. In the *prison system*: the attempt to find 'alternatives' to custody, at least for minor offenses, and the use of electronic tagging to force offenders to stay at home between certain hours. In the *school system*: forms of continuous assessment, the impact of continuing education on schools, and the related move away from any research in universities, 'business' being brought into education at every level. In the *hospital system*: the new medicine 'without doctors or patients' that identifies potential cases and subjects at risk and is nothing to do with any progress toward individualizing treatment, which is how it's presented, but is the substitution for individual or numbered bodies of coded 'dividual' matter to be controlled. In the *business system*: new ways of manipulating money, products, and men, no longer channeled through the old factory system. This is a fairly limited range of examples, but enough to convey what it means to talk of institutions breaking down: the widespread progressive introduction of a new system of domination. One of the most important questions is whether trade unions still have any role: linked throughout their history to the struggle against disciplines, in sites of confinement, can they adapt, or will they give way to new forms of resistance against control societies? Can one already glimpse the outlines of these future forms of

resistance, capable of standing up to marketing's blandishments? Many young people have a strange craving to be 'motivated,' they're always asking for special courses and continuing education; it's their job to discover whose ends these serve, just as older people discovered, with considerable difficulty, who was benefiting from disciplines. A snake's coils are even more intricate than a mole's burrow.

L'AutreJournal 1 (May 1990)

Notes

1. *Une* modulation, *comme un moulage auto-déformant*: a *moule* is a mold, *moulage* the process of molding, while 'modulation' as *auto-déformant* is a process of 'remolding' that itself has no extrinsic pattern or mold (cf. 'On *The Movement-Image*, n. 6). The French *déformation* is an essentially 'neutral' reshaping or change of form, while 'deformation' in English has a resonance of departing from a true or proper form, and although it is used at one point below as equivalent to 'transformation,' the latter word is also used in many other contexts, and I have had to use 'transmutation' here and below as the least bad alternative to render *déformation*.
2. *Contrôle continu*: literally 'continuous control'. The French verb *contrôler* also has the sense of 'monitoring,' 'checking' (and this sense is often present at various points where I have used the word 'control').
3. *Mots d'ordre* as 'watchwords,' maxims, universal 'directives' – literally 'ordering' words or phrases – are here contrasted with the *mots de passe* that regulate a system of individual moves.
4. A *vielle taupe*, literally an 'old mole,' is also a nasty old woman, an old crone or hag; the European Community/Union 'Exchange Rate Mechanism,' in which currencies are allowed to vary in value or 'float' within limits set by their notional rate against a weighted basket of other participating currencies, was commonly called 'the snake.'

Brian Massumi

Brian Massumi translated *A Thousand Plateaus*, and is the author of *A User's Guide to Capitalism and Schizophrenia: Deviations from Deleuze and Guattari* (1992). The essay that follows is an argument taken from *Parables of the Virtual: Movement, Affect, Sensation* (2002) – one section of chapter 8, 'Strange Horizon'. It discusses the body image with reference to topology, and connects with the theme of the essays gathered in this section in considering the generation of form from within – or rather the dissolving of traditional ways of describing form by transferring attention to alternatives to the Euclidean geometries of well-defined regular shapes such as squares and circles – the forms that the Renaissance artists inscribed around the body. The chapter is divided up into a sequence of arguments for seeing a correlation between the body and the novel architectural forms generated by computers and a sophisticated understanding of topology – the branch of mathematics that deals with the properties of shapes that remain the same even when the figures are twisted, stretched and folded (the corners of a triangle no longer add up to 180°, for example, but there is a bounded space of variable form and extent). In architecture the result has been the generation of convoluted 'blobs' of ever-increasing complexity and sophistication.[1] The final section, which follows, describes the body as a folded membrane – taking up the theme of the fold from Deleuze's book on Leibniz, and the theme of the permeable body from *Anti-Oedipus*.[2] 'Mitochondria' incidentally are of molecular scale. They are found in large numbers in the cytoplasm of cells (where they store and release energy).

Notes

1. Greg Lynn, *Folds, Bodies and Blobs* (Brussels: La Lettre Volée, 1998).
2. Gilles Deleuze, *Le Pli: Leibniz et le baroque* (Paris: Editions de Minuit, 1988) translated by Tom Conley, *The Fold: Leibniz and the Baroque*; (London: Athlone, 1993); cross reference.

The Argument from Inner Space

The body is composed of a branching network, decreasing in size right down to the level of molecular tubes at the mitochondrial scale. Geometrically, a body is a 'space-filling fractal' of a 'fourth' dimensionality, between a two-dimensional plane and a three-dimensional volume.[1] 'Our skin obeys the laws of three dimensions ... but our internal anatomy and physiology is living in a four-dimensional spatial world' (the three of enveloping Euclidean space plus the 'fourth' fractal dimension of internal branching).[2] A body lives in three dimensions only at the envelope of the skin. The 'Euclidean' space of the body is a *membrane*.

The membrane isn't closed. It folds in at the mouth, ears, nostrils, eyes, anus, urethra, vagina, and pores. The mouth connects through the stomach and intestines to fold back out the anus. This is one leaky 'box.' It's closer to a Klein bottle: a two-dimensional topological figure. Even the skin isn't really three-dimensional. It just acts as if it were. It creates a three-dimensional closure effect by regulating movements into and out of the space-filling fractal it twistedly envelops. Biologically, it's all an act, a complex nutritive, excretive act: circus of the body. We do not live in Euclidean space. We live *between* dimensions.

Might it still be argued that even if we do not live in Euclidean space, we certainly build in it? Fair enough: we build in Euclidean space in the same sense that we eat in it. To build is to produce a closure-effect by regulating movements in and out (and fractally all around). A building is a membrane.

Regulating movements is a question of scale and speed. An architect or engineer is not concerned with the swarming micromovements of matter occurring in insane velocity at the molecular level of the materials used in construction. All that concerns her is that at a certain level those unpredictable movements settle into a dependable patterning. It is the undependable movements' *aggregation* that can be depended upon: their manner of massing. The solidity of a brick is a mass mannerism, a crowd phenomenon: a *molar* relational effect.

When you place a brick against a brick, you are not rubbing hard matter up against hard matter. The electrons and nuclear particles making up the molecular aggregates are separated by voids many orders of magnitudes larger than they are. A brick is as sparse as a little universe. Nothing actually touches. The brick's 'surface' is pitted by emptiness. Nor is there anything solid within each atom. Subatomic innards are a quantum soup of intense, virtual events, some occurring faster than the speed of light (quantum tunneling), some enjoying experimentally verified recursive causality (complementarity). The effective stability of the brick emerges from the interrelation of those intensive, incorporeal movements. The quality of hardness is a surface-effect defined by what the holding-together of the brick's fused elementary constituents lets pass, captures, or blocks. It is a regulated regime of movement. The 'surface' itself

Section 5: Relations

is nothing other than this relational effect of hardness, or regime of passage. The effect is relative to the nature of the movement that comes to pass, its scale, and speed (a gamma ray would neither find it hard nor treat it as a surface to bounce off).

When you place a brick next to another brick you are not placing matter against matter. You are placing effect against effect, *relation against relation*. You are building a conglomerate economy of movement. You are hinging molar stabilities to build larger molar stability. What we think of as Euclidean space is a mutual holding in relational stability of incorporeal event-spaces, relative to kind of movement, scale, and speed. Incorporeal: abstract. Euclidean space is the *relative concreteness of the abstract*. It is a certain kind of abstract-surface hinge-effect.

When you place bricks together to build four walls and then put a body inside, something similar is happening. The memories, habits, and tropisms the body carries with it in the associated, intensive event space of incorporeal or abstract movement evoked repeatedly in this essay, constitute an aggregate of relation. All the goings-on and passings-by around the building constitute another aggregate of relation: a sea of movements, each of which has a potential effect on the body, capable of modulating which determinate threads are pulled from the relational continuum it carries. Which threads the body reexpresses is regulated by the modulatory sense-interferences that the walls, doors, and windows – not to mention screens and speakers – let pass. Certain tendential headings, perceptions, and cognitions are backgrounded, peripheralized, or blended out by the synesthetic economy of movement-across that is regulated by the architectural regime.

A building is a technology of movement – a technology of transposition – in direct membranic connection with virtual event spaces. It functions topologically, folding relational continua into and out of each other to selective, productive effect. It functions abstract-concretely to inflect determinations of potential experience. A building is an experiential supermodulator device: a modulator of modulations. It is a way of placing relation against relation, toward inflected variation. Its three-dimensional closure effect is a regulated coupling between virtual sea's of relation, swarming and smudgeable. We build in Euclidean space when we design the kind of aggregate hinge-effects between swarmings and smudgings of experience that shake out in favor of maximum stability of cognitive result ('there's nothing like home': recognition). To build in Euclidean space is to build in predictability.

Is it possible, in addition, to build for newness, for the emergence of unforeseen experiential form and configuration, inflected by chance? We know that it is possible to design topologically. This essay has argued that we live topologically. But can we also build topologically?

To build topologically would be to accept that the body's ultimate innards are as effectively incorporeal, as really abstract, as the atom's. The body's innards are not just the stomach and intestines. As vitally as food, a life feeds on habits, memories, and tropisms. The living body's 'ultimate' innards are the proprioceptive habits on a level with muscle fiber. They are the microsocial skills on a level with a single visual neuron. They are enculturated memories lying at the crossroads of sense channels coursing through the flesh. They are the pattern of preferential headings hinging on all of the above, which we somewhat grandly call our 'personality.' The body *is* the holding-together of these virtual innards as they fold out, recursive-durationally, in the loopy present, in determinate form and configuration, always provisional because always in becoming.

The arguments presented in this essay all make the same point: that the life of the body, its lived experience, cannot be understood without reference to abstract-real processual dimensions. These cannot be contained in Euclidean space and linear time. They must be topologically described, using an array of concepts specially honed for the task: continuous variation, intensive movement, transpositionality, event, durational space, recursive-duration, modulation, qualitative effect, biogram, and feedback of higher functions, to name just a few.

This is not to say that there is one topological figure, or even a specific formal non-Euclidean geometry, that corresponds to the body's space-time of experience or some general 'shape' of existence. Topologies, like Euclidean geometry, are modeling tools. Each echoes an aspect of the world's dynamism (and share of stability). Each repeats, on screen or in thought, an intensive mode of movement that is really of this world. Each is capable of bringing to formal expression certain dimensions of the infinitely twisted life of the body and the cosmos. No one model can lay claim to a final 'reflection' of or 'correspondence' to reality. It is simply not about reflection or correspondence. It is about *participation*. Differential participation. In what way does a given geometry's effective resonance with intensive movements in the world allow us to extend them, in our orientations, memories, and brain-lagged awareness, toward their (and our) creative variation? How can geometry make a qualitative difference in the world?

Once again, these are pragmatic rather than critical issues. It's a question of appropriate technology. Choosing a geometry to design with is to choose potential modulations not only of the designed form but, through its device, of people's lives. It was not the purpose of this essay to suggest particular design methods, aesthetics, or 'ideal' end effects. It was only to suggest that new paths might be found by letting go of the sterile opposition between the abstract and the concrete and its fellow-traveler, the subjective and objective. To do this, it is necessary to take another look at perception and lived experience and even broach such tired topics as consciousness. The fear that this will inevitably fall into a domesticating, self-satisfied subjectivism-in-spite-of-itself, like that preached by phenomenological architecture, is not justified. All you need to do to avoid that path is, quoting Deleuze and Guattari: *look only at the movements*.[3] It has been suggested that extending the concept of the diagram into the biogram might be a vector worth pursuing. Formal topologies are not enough. The biogram is a *lived* topological event. It is *onto-topological*. It is the event of experience folding back on itself for its own furtherance, its continuing becoming. Onto-topological means *ontogenetic*. The biogram is experience reaccessing its powers of emergence, for more effect. It is the existential equivalent of lifting oneself up by the bootstraps: ontogenetic and *autopoietic*.

Look only at the movements – and they will bring you to matter. The perspective suggested here displays a tropism toward realist materialism (without reflection: especially not 'pre-'). At virtually every turn in the discussion, dynamics that seemed 'subjective' to the extreme made a literal end run back to impersonal matter. The end run of mindedness back to matter always somehow coincided with its emergence from it, the exemplary case being Libet's feedback loop between the dawning of

Section 5: Relations

perceptual awareness and the ever-present previousness of movements of brain matter capable of coloring experience without themselves becoming aware. Accepting this insistence of the material and impersonal (the 'involuntary') *in* bootstrapped personal experience distinguishes the current account most sharply from phenomenological approaches. Its claims both to realism and materialism paradoxically depend on it – paradoxically, because the 'backdating' of matter-driven consciousness is also an argument that there is no essential difference between perception, cognition, and hallucination. This is a realist materialism with a paradoxically creative edge, summed up in the mantra: involuntary *and* elicited. The involuntary and elicited no-difference between perception, cognition, and hallucination can in turn be summed up in a single word: *imagination*.

This is also where topological architecture is carnally challenged and proves inadequately abstract. It does well with the involuntary, in the form of chance variations programmed into the topological form-generating software. It does much less well with the elicited. Putting the two together is necessary for grasping the minded body's mode of reality, which can be evoked by any number of necessary oxymorons: modulated self-decision, creative receptivity, induced self-activity, laboriously orienting autopilot, ever-present lapse. Use your imagination: no single logic, geometric or otherwise, is flexible enough to encompass the concrete abstractness of experience in all its ins and outs. Just as the body lives between dimensions, designing for it requires operating between logics. To be sufficiently abstract, topological architecture needs to welcome the translogical. A translogic is different from a metalogic. It doesn't stand back and describe the way multiple logics and the operative levels they model hold together. It *enters* the relations and tweaks as many as it can to get a sense of what may come. It is pragmatic. It imaginatively enters the fabric of transition and pulls as many strands as it can to see what emerges. It is effective. Rather than metalogical, it is supermodulatory.

It is not that architecture does not already go about its business like this, in a certain regulatory manner, if not always fully cognizant of the strange horizon of that relational fact, and at times even in outright denial of it (as when it proudly deconstructs positively absent structures, or privileges determinations of history over potential becomings, or cutely cites when it could be effectively tweaking, or boringly domiciles the world in its own supposed prereflection). If architecture pursues extending diagrams into biograms it will become more what it has always been: a materialist art of qualitative body modulation, a translogical engineering of matter gone mindful. Its buildings will also be more what they are. More modulatory. More flexibly membranic. More intensely lived between more relational dimensions brought concretely into abstract-surface proximity. How such an onto-topological architecture will develop, if it does, certainly cannot be prereflected. It will unfold experimentally. Or not.

To be determined.

Notes

1. Geoffrey B. West, James H. Brown, and Brian J. Enquist, 'A General Model for the Origin of Allometric Scaling Laws in Biology,' *Science* 276 (4 April 1997): pp. 122–6. In all organisms 'essential materials are transported through space-filling fractal networks of branching tubes', p. 122.
2. Geoffrey West, quoted in Roger Lewin, 'Ruling Passions,' *New Scientist*, 3 April 1999, 39.
3. Gilles Deleuze and Félix Guattari, *Mille plateaux* (Paris: Minuit, 1980) translated by Brian Massumi, *A Thousand Plateaus* (London: Athlone, 1987), p. 281.

Patsy Healey

Healey is a theorist of urban planning, and has developed ways of thinking about the formulation of urban policy that involve consultation and feedback from social groups that might otherwise be excluded from the planning process in one way or another. The essay included here 'Planning in Relational Space' suggests that there is a way of thinking about cities (in relation to running them) that involves a range of the concepts and metaphors that we have seen in other essays collected here. The city is as much a body as is the Bonaventure Hotel in Ian Buchanan's essay, and it configured in terms of its internal and external relations, not with reference to a geometric (or other) form. This is the *informe* at urban scale, networked into the space of flows, with a multiplicity of 'worlds' (in Nelson Goodman's sense) overlaid through one another – 'transecting' is the word used here. The old images of centralized power are displaced into something more fluid and vaporous, with responsive mechanisms that are influenced by forces acting from within or without (indifferently). The body-image that we need for such an organism is the body of the Anti-Oedipus, and a city so conceived becomes a city in human form, which thus miraculated, fades away and radiates into the *informe*. The role of metaphor in configuring the imagination, and therefore in shaping our lived experience of reality, is strongly in evidence here, though the language draws its vocabulary from the social sciences rather than from Shelley.

Planning in Relational Space and Time: Responding to New Urban Realities

Urbanists and planners often tell a familiar story about cities in the modern age, to account for the rise of the twentieth-century planning idea. The appearance of big urban agglomerations, whether through the industrialization of nineteenth-century Western cities, or the explosive development of the cities of the developing world in the second part of the twentieth century, generates images of chaotic disorder, characterized by appalling living conditions and damaging social, environmental, and economic conditions. The challenge for urban governance was to sort all this out, and produce a harmonious 'order', smoothing out conflicts, and creating a framework for improved quality of life, business efficiency and conserving environmental assets. The 'planning idea' seemed to provide the answer.[1] Planners brought to this task a conceptual equipment which mixed a designer's imagination with a regional geographer's conception of integrated spatial orders based on analyses of prevailing European settlement patterns of the early twentieth century. Cities were relationally self-contained, pivoting around the city centre, and spreading out across a rural region for which they acted as key markets and sites for relations with the outside world. Land uses in the city were to be separated, to reduce adverse impacts on each other. They were ordered hierarchically in terms of land value, in relation to access to the key location, the city centre. Relations with the 'outside world' were conducted through the industries which provided the 'driver' for this integrated urban system.[2]

These days, so the story goes, the conception of the self-contained, internally integrated, 'uniplex' city is no longer believable, in a world of multiplex and globalized relationships. Cities are referred to as fragmented, in bits and pieces, divided, disorganized, chaotic.[3] Urban governance capacity, once assumed to be located in the municipal office, has now been 'distributed', undermined by competition with other sources of power.[4] Municipalities and their planners have little leverage over the flow of events through which the socioplastic relations of cities are actively being constructed. The planning practices of the 'ordering imetus' have become part of the problem. Embedded in routine governance practices, planning has been criticized by analysts as class-driven, dominatory, the mode of action of a rationalizing social ordering project.[5] The planning idea, in one ending to this story, is a relic of the 'command and control' welfare state, and of the modernist conceptual equipment of positivist science and utilitarian rationalism which went with it.[6] The analytical task is then to research urban governance practices, and 'excavate' and critique these old ideas as they live on in governance routines.[7]

Yet this ending does not seem to fit with another observable reality, the expanding public and political concern, with the quality and 'sustainability' of urban conditions. Most people in the world now live in cities. Many of them take what opportunities become available to assert their concerns in public arenas. In some countries, and notably in Britain, the apparatus of planning systems has become a key institutional site for an increasingly complex dialectics of environmental contestation.[8] The neoliberal strategy (as developed in, for example, Britain and New Zealand) is to seek to transform planning systems into quasi-market regulatory mechanisms for dealing with conflict mediation over complex spatially manifest environmental disputes.[9] But this strategy fails to attend to the multiplicity of relationships which transects places and the complex ways thay intersect in the assertion of place qualities. In particular, it 'splits up' into separate issues people's daily life experiences and their sense of qualities of particular places. Rejecting planners' conceptions of self-contained, integrated sociospatial systems, it assumes that the spatiality of relations and the meaning of places are unimportant dimensions in cities. It ignored the role of the assertion of 'place identity' in counteracting the sense of explosive expansion and fragmentation of the relations which used to bind people and firms together in internally integrated urban systems. Places, to the extent that they are of any relevance to contemporary life, are in this conception made and unmade by the forces of market relation.

Such an approach privileges economic and material dimensions of existence over cultural, environmental, and political ones. But this is not the only storyline for cities. There is another, arising from cultural studies, the 'new' institutionalism, and the environmental movement, which emphasizes the importance of a politics of place-making. This other storyline explicitly recognizes the multiple relationships which transect the space–time of cities and locales within them, a politics and governance practice which seeks to shape those relationships in order to cultivate their interrelationships, reduce the harm they cause to each other and actively shape place identities. Is there a new 'planning imagination' which can be harnessed to this task, to help generate new practices and refurbish old ones?

In this chapter, I argue that there is such an emerging imagination. It is based in an explicit recognition of the multiple relational webs which transect cities, each with their own time horizons and spatial reach, each 'creating', through their conceptions and activities, an imagined city and a socially and physically concrete one. It emphasizes that 'making places' is achieved not by the imposition of a technical order by the state, but by the active social construction of place-focused frameworks and through efforts to cultivate a strategic imagination through which key attributes of a 'place' can become identified and 'owned' by the many stakeholders in the 'place' of a city. In this way, 'permanences' are created in the dynamic relational dialectics of urban life.[10]

The planning idea emerges, in this story, as a form of governance, which is open, driven by inclusionary perspectives on what makes for human flourishing in the urban context, rather than the generalized ideologies of politicians or the self-interest of elites.[11] Such a planning focuses on developing qualities of 'habitus', the places of daily life, of commercial endeavour, or social exchange, and the public realm. It involves asserting the qualities of places, to be promoted and maintained, against forces pushing in different directions. It involves practices which develop strategies, shape investment programmes and frame regulatory judgements in open, visible forms, confronting the forces encouraging behind-the-scenes manipulation and subversion of publicly agreed policy directions. If successful in the struggle for power with competing governance forms, this kind of planning has the capacity to develop sufficient discursive strength to generate the political leverage to assert a broadly shared and 'multiplex' 'place identity'. It then has the capacity to shape market opportunities and influence sociocultural evolutions.

Facing the Challenge of Multiplex Systems: Into the Finegrain of Practice[12]

I return to this normative planning idea at the end of the chapter. Some have argued that it is an ideal without any roots in contemporary planning practices from which it could grow and develop.[13] Certainly British planning practice has been heavily moulded in recent years by neoliberal influences.[14] However, policy systems and practices are not static, but are pushed and pulled to respond to different situations. In this section, I illustrate such evolutions through an examination of two areas of English planning practice. Both cases are from England, with its distinctive governance and legal context for planning systems and their practices.[15] One shows the work of regulatory permitting, focusing on the negotiation of developers' contributions to ameliorating adverse impacts ('development control' and 'planning gain/planning obligations' in British planning jargon). The other is of strategic spatial plan-making (the 'structure plan' level of 'development plans' in the British context). In both cases, models of integrated urban systems, with their two-dimensional 'Euclidean' space and linear time, have decayed, to be replaced by conceptions of complex, open relations emerging in new discourses about impacts and about strategy. But these new ideas are developing hesitantly, without a coherent conceptual imagination and discourse to drive across the practice landscape. This creates a conceptual vacuum into which a despatialized neoliberal policy discourse has established itself. The dialectical struggle is now not merely between 'uniplex' versus 'multiplex' conceptions of urban sociospatial relations. It is overlain by another struggle between 'place-blind' and 'people-diminishing' urban policy versus 'place-aware' and 'people-sensitive' approaches.

The impacts of development projects

Many webs of relations are affected by development projects. These could potentially encompass the networks of, and relations between, landowners, developers, financiers, end-users, various third parties, different actors of central and local government, local politics, national politics, pressure groups of all kinds. Some planning systems attempt to define the universe of potential impacts in advance and convert these into rules to apply to any development project that comes along. The British planning system, characterized by the exercise of administrative-political judgement in determining whether a permit should be given, in contrast provides a flexible formal structure in which new ideas about what impacts can emerge.[16] The system structures the making of judgements so that planning officers pay attention to national statements of planning policy, local statements (primarily embedded in the 'development plan') and other considerations specific to the case.[17] Most discussion of the impacts of development traditionally focused on the qualities of the site, or on local impacts, and, in particular, on adjacent impacts. The primary concern was to 'fit' a new project into the existing 'jigsaw' landscape of buildings and open spaces and deal with the additional loads on infrastructure caused by a development. Wider impacts were assumed to be addressed by the policy framework. The 'development plan' was supposed to specify broadly the amounts of development which might be expected in an area, the general locations where such developments might happen, and the time periods over which developments might take place. But when a project actually arrives for the regulatory judgement, it comes with a whole nexus of potential relations of its own, which affect its viability and political acceptability. As it 'lands' on a particular site at a particular time, it has impacts along all kinds of relations in which the site and the project have significance.

Until the 1980s, the implicit urban model used in assessing development impacts was the hierarchically integrated 'uniplex' city. The land-use patter was taken as a proxy for the social processes. The relations of the activities were assumed to be structured by propinquity and utilitarian rationality. The city was presented as a kind of 'jigsaw', the separate pieces making up a hierarchically ordered pattern. People went to work in the nearest business. They shopped at the nearest foodstore. They went to the city centre for their durable shopping and cultural recreation. They were assumed to care most about what happened nearest to them. The focus of the assessment of development impacts was on 'neighbourhood' effects, adjacent to the site in question. Propinquity was the dominant principle and 'planning gain' negotiations focused on honing the development project so it fitted better into its 'jigsaw' space. By the 1980s, however, the conception of impacts widened out. For example, a large residential development upstream could damage downstream water flows. Agreements might be negotiated for actions and financial contributions which linked the stage of the building process and the state of the housing market to phased investment in a system of temporary and permanent balancing lakes and run-off channels across the drainage basin. In such a case, the flow dynamics of a hydrological system and the dynamic relations of a particular market supplement consideration of impacts were based on simple propinquity.[18]

In some situations, local residents organize to demand some compensation for adverse impacts. This may lead to agreements not only for contributions to highway and drainage infrastructure, but to provision of schools and playing fields, recreational and amenity open space, and landscaping features. In one case, a developer of a project of 1000 dwellings provided half a million pounds to a local parish council for recreational and community purposes. Here, propinquity gave special bargaining power to a particular and visible affected group.[19] This raises questions of legitimacy. Why do adjacent impacts get such consideration compared to more distant ones?

When disputes enter the legal arena, a more relational emphasis opens up, in the legal language of a 'reasonable relationship'.[20] In the division of labour between law and policy in the British planning system, it is left to planners to articulate what is a 'reasonable' relationship. In principle, this allows the variable space–time linkages of a multiplex world to be brought into play. But these shifts are not underpinned by coherent conceptualizations. In the arenas of government policy, in local negotiations, in public inquiries, and the courts, planners struggle to articulate principles to govern the decisions they make. The pressures of local politics, and national pressure groups promoting conflicting objectives, are pushing them along. This privileges the circuitry of the vocal and powerful. Impacts on those without the power and resources to speak up, and on those distant in space and time, are neglected. This helps governance elites mediate conflicts in the short term. But many stakeholders and many relationships are not represented in these mediations. In a governance context where power is increasingly widely distributed, excluded considerations have a habit of popping up to disturb the apparent consensus and challenge the legitimacy of planning decisions and frameworks.

From development plans to local 'visions'

Changing conceptualizations of space and time are more obvious in the arena of plan-making. British development-plan practice in the second part of the twentieth century may be crudely divided into three phases, reflecting the 'master narrative' outlined above: the 'blueprint' land-use plans of the early postwar years, the strategic spatial plans grounded in conceptions of regional sociospatial systems, and the sectoralized policy plans of more recent years. The blueprint style arose in part from a conception that planners could control spatial change, rather than merely shape the flow of processes of change. The plan delineated what was to be built where, in five-year periods, assuming that the complex relations of multiple development processes could be co-ordinated in a common schedule. This managerial viewpoint was attached to a 'uniplex' conception of the city, translated into a hierarchical spatial order. Activities and their relationships could be 'read off' from the land-use pattern. The classic British spatial plan associated with Patrick Abercrombie and others envisaged a city which combined the patterns of Iasrdian central place theory with the notions of self-contained *gemeinschaft* communities.[21]

This approach was heavily criticized in the 1960s for its failure to appreciate the dynamics of regional development. Drawing on a more sophisticated geography and ecology, and much influenced by S.J. Chapin, British planning theorists sought to imagine the city in relational terms.[22] The focus of attention shifted from spatial patterns *per se*, to the dynamics of the regional economic system and the urban communications system, both in terms of transport and information flows. Drawing heavily on economic base theory and the behavioural urban ecology of the Chicago sociologists, the ambition was to build dynamic 'systems' models of the economic and social relations of settlements, and translate these into spatial patterns. Such models, it was hoped, would not only allow the exploration of alternative sociospatial scenarios (primarily to manage the relations between land needs for growth and infrastructure investment); they could also be used in regulatory practice, to allow the impacts of a development to be assessed by checking them out against the relational assumptions in the model, a kind of systematized environmental appraisal.[23] These 'systems models', which dominated the technical planning literature in Britain and the US in the late 1960s and early 1970s, underpinned early British attempts at producing the new kinds of 'structre plan' introduced in the 1970s.[24] However, while more dynamic and relational than their predecessors, these models were still underpinned by hierarchically integrated, 'uniplex', conceptions of the city.

A pioneering example in Britain was the South Hampshire Structure Plan.[25] This involved an elaborate exercise in modelling existing relationships, forecasting growth and then exploring different development location scenarios. The conceptions underlying the model were very simple: 'Three activities and uses (i.e. land uses) are of particular strategic importance . . . – employment, homes and shopping'.[26] Activities are seen to occur on sites connected by movement channels. Drawing on the classic Abercrombie tradition, the urban 'structure' is set within a 'rural framework' which provides resources of agriculture and recreation opportunities for the urban inhabitants.[27] This 'largely self-contained city region' is conceived in terms of a hierarchy of central places, but with a polynodal rather than a uninodal structure.[28]

In the model, the dynamic of regional growth is perceived as largely internal to the area. External inputs are confined to migration flows from the rest of the South-East Region. The language of analysis deals in aggregates rather than differentiated dynamics. There is no comment on the relational dynamics or locational preferences of the various firms which are 'growing'. The plan nevertheless presents a striking attempt to develop an overarching conception of the regional economy. The problem lies in its closure, and in the way it considers internal system relationships. It sets up the regional dynamics of the area as a closed system with internal feedback loops, on the lines of Forrester's conception of urban dynamics.[29] This assumes equilibrium-seeking systems rather than evolutionary systems.[30] It treats space as Euclidean and time as linear. In retrospect, the approach not only failed to identify the contingencies of the South Hampshire economy, which became obvious as recession and restructuring set in during the 1970s and 1980s, it also failed to consider the political, institutional, and resource context in which the regulation and promotion of development would take place. South Hampshire was treated as an 'object' to which strategies were applied, rather than a dynamic *mélange* of social relations within which planning actions would be variously articulated and intertwined.

Despite serious economic difficulties in some sections of the regional economy, South Hampshire has continued to grow and the political problems of allocating sites for new development has become increasingly acute for both local and national politicians. By the 1990s, Hampshire County Council was locked in battles with central government over how much of the regional demand for housing in South East England as a whole would be accommodated in the county. Structure-plan practice evolved in the 1980s to reflect the institutional context. The presentation of a spatial territory into which development would be fitted (the spatial 'jigsaw') was replaced by an 'institutional territory' in terms of which projects had to be legitimated (the institutional 'jigsaw'). This recognized the power of agency in structuring space, but at the cost of losing the sense of space and place. The plan was no longer even a two-dimensional map. Instead, it became a record of sites and zones affected by particular policy considerations.

The Hampshire County Council Structure Plan of 1994 was still concerned with accommodating growth and maintaining the discreteness of urban settlements: 'a central theme of the Plan is to preserve the distinction between town and country as two different kinds of environment'.[31] 'Strategic gaps' of landscape are to be retained between settlements, to sustain the illusion of self-contained settlements. Apart from these 'inherited' spatial principles, the plan divides its material into a series of topics, each being discussed largely in isolation from the others. By 1996, however, a new concern with place and identity appears in the plan. The elements of the spatial order remain the same. However, 'suburban development has tended to reduce local distinctiveness and sense of place in many parts of the County . . . community identity, a sense of place and belonging, which is part of this heritage, also needs to be defended'.[32]

The notion of community identity has political attractions in a county where the politics of the defence of place against further growth became acute in the 1990s. The 1996 Plan attempts a more coherent overview of the county as a place, using the marketing language of 'vision' and the environmental language of 'systainability'. The idea of a 'Vision', borrowed from the business-marketing arena and from practices around urban regeneration projects, promotes the qualities of a place. It also potentially offers an 'integrative conception' to bind the many, potentially conflicting, parties into a shared approach and/or programme of actions.[33] But Hampshire's 'vision' is not developed into a reconception of the sociospatial dynamics of change in the subregion, nor is there any recognition of the multiplex times and places which are evolving in the county area. The topic chapters of the plan provide policy criteria, in the neoliberal mode, intended to be used in assessing actual development projects, at the point where the institutional and spatial 'jigsaw' interact. This evolution of the Hampshire Structure Plan illustrates well how the uniplex strategic conception of the

1960s and 1970s decayed into a highly generalized conception of the 'space' of the county, with the policy dynamic of the plan structured not by technical analyses of sociospatial dynamics, but by the politics of institutional interactions. In these interactions, multiplex space–time perspectives are consolidated through the voices of powerful local players and the regulatory vocabulary of national planning policy.[34]

Reconceptualizing Planning in Relational Time and Space

In both these examples, simple models of sociospatial relations have been largely abandoned, though they live on in techniques (such as transport modelling and retail appraisal) in regulatory practices (the continued preoccupation with adjacent or site-based impacts) and in notions of the local community and its needs. But there is no coherent reconceptualization of the urban region in multiplex space and time. Instead, strands of understanding from contemporary urban and regional geography filter into analyses of economic issues, and ecosystemic ideas from the environmental sciences flow into policy with respect to the natural environment. Instead of being allowed to intertwine and develop innovatively, they are being forced into the straitjacket of despatialized policy criteria, which limit the relations which are considered and which ignore considerations of place identity. As a consequence, urban planning practice in Britain has become peculiarly unprepared for attention to the qualities of places.

Two evolutions are counteracting this narrowing of the thought-worlds of English planning practice. The first focuses on developing a new 'place imagination', the second emphasizes more inclusive practices for policy development and discussion, through which multiple perceptions can find voice and contribute to the active construction of new conceptions of 'place identity'.

The resources for new conceptions of urban dynamics and place qualities can be found in the exploding international social science literature on the city, urban economies, societies, environments, and governance. They can also be found in rich encounters with 'local knowledge' about place relations.[35] The 'postmodern' turn enabled analysts and policy actors to perceive the diversity and openness of urban relations, which had been drowned out by the holistic simplifications of modernist urban analysis. It gave full play to particularity, complexity, and contingency. But in its extreme forms, too little attention was given to relations and processes, and the interweaving of continuities and innovations in evolving urban dynamics. The new poststructuralist thinking, evident in many strands of analysis,[36] takes a dynamic relational view of urban life. Its focus is on relations and processes, not objects. It emphasizes dynamics not statics, and the complex interactions between local continuities and 'social capital' and innovative potential. It 'sees' multiple relations transecting the space of the city, each 'driven' and 'shaped' by different forces, interacting with each other in different ways, bypassing, conflicting, co-ordinating in complex trajectories. It recognizes that these social relationships, although shaped by powerful forces, often outside the space of a particular urban area, are actively socially constructed. In the social processes of defining meanings and identities and in the routine ways of living in the city, people make the multiplex times and places, its differentiations, cohesions and exclusions, and its power dynamics. The quality of the 'places' of the urban lies in both the social resources – in the range and intersections of the relational resources available to people and firms, in the balance between security/stability and creative tention/innovation, in the capacity for collective development of 'place quality' – and in the spatial manifestations of places: the key sites of public interaction, the symbolic reference points, the design of both 'neighbourhoods' and 'nodal areas' in the urban fabric. The governance of 'places' then has a key role in the development of these qualities, in the way governance processes intertwine with the complexity of intersecting relationships, helping to maintain and build meanings and relationships. Such governance can also help to 'fix' and transmit place quality and identity in a multivocal context.[37]

This turns the spotlight on the quality of governance practices themselves. It is here that the alternative planning imagination outlined at the start of this chapter comes into play. It requires a governance dynamics and culture which encourages officials to move outside the city hall, to work interactively with the multiple relational webs which transect the urban. It involves combining formal analysis with 'local knowledge' and popular imaginations, to identify the key qualities of places which people want to maintain, develop, enhance, and create. It draws on 'conversations' between different relational worlds, through which some kind of shared ownership of strategies and regulatory and investment actions can develop, imbued with recognition of the inherent struggles, tensions, and conflicts which are manifest in any multivocal urban context. The developments within planning theory on communicative, collaborative planning processes provide rich resources for such a reconstruction of planning processes,[38] while the practice of partnership and 'enabling governance' had generated an array of practical experience and 'local knowledge' in many western cities.[39]

But these practices also show that interactive governance and collaborative planning initiatives come in several forms. In some instances, such processes get hijacked as a way of re-establishing the hegemony of powerful groups. Specifically, they provide an opportunity for the re-entry of local business elites into local governance in situations where they have been pushed aside by the ideological politics of the welfare state which set the 'public' interest against 'private' interests. This potential for takeover puts a premium on an inclusionary ethics, a commitment by those in governance positions to attend to the range of relations through which people and firms, in diverse ways, 'inhabit' and give meaning to the urban. It demands that planners develop skills in facilitating encounters between different groups.[40] And bringing in voices currently on the margins of governance.[41] Such an inclusionary ethics needs to permeate the processes for building strategies and frameworks through which to promote particular place qualities. It needs to infuse not only the regulatory practices and investment programmes through which material resources and opportunities are distributed, but also the way relational resources are developed. It needs to be grounded in broadly distributed rights to challenge governance actions on the grounds of inclusionary failures and in obligations to demonstrate inclusionary intentions.[42] Such an inclusionary ethics is not just needed to keep alive the idea of social justice in a world where the relations of injustice and domination are multiple and often invisible. They are also needed as a continual challenge to the embedding of a narrow and inflexible imagination as an inward-looking response to the dynamic dialectics of a multiplex world.

In many parts of the world, governance elites are trying to write new stories for their cities, to inscribe these stories in the identities of the key players upon whose actions the core relations of a city depend and to incorporate them into the practices of an urban governance which stretches beyond the town hall to a wide range of people involved in governance in one way or another.[43] The challenge for planners is to reconstruct their own ways of thinking and acting to provide creative resources for critiquing and facilitating this work of story-writing. In this role, some of the evangelism of past generations of planners needs to be rediscovered. The planners of the mid-century believed in their imagination for the city and what its values should be. This included a deep commitment to quality of life for 'ordinary people', and to a more just distribution of life opportunities in the urban environment.[44] Of course their ideas about urban form, social organization and their power to influence events have all proved in retrospect erroneous and often damaging to these values. But it is not the values which were the problem. It was rather the belief that knowledge resides only with experts and that urban form is the prime determinant of the quality of urban life. A multiplex urban imagination among those who become the expert facilitators in urban governance, along with a commitment to an inclusionary ethic, could make a real difference to the future qualities of urban life. But this imagination needs to be informed by a rich and dynamic appreciation of the diverse everyday experiences and symbolic significances of our contemporary multiplex cities.

Notes

1. M. Christine Boyer, *Dreaming the Rational City* (Boston, Mass.: MIT, 1983); S. Ward, *Planning and Urban Change* (London: Paul Chapman, 1994).
2. B. McLoughlin, *Urban and Regional Planning: A Systems Approach* (London: Faber, 1969); J. Forrester, Urban Dynamics (Boston, Mass.: MIT, 1969).
3. William Mitchell, *City of Bits* (Cambridge, Mass.: MIT, 1995); David Byrne, 'Chaotic Places of Complex Places', in *Imagining Cities*, edited by S. Westwood and J. Williams (London: Routledge, 1996); Mike Davis, *City of Quartz* (London: Verso, 1990).
4. D. King and G. Stoker, *Re-inventing Local Democracy* (London: Macmillan, 1996).
5. Manuel Castells, *The Urban Question* (London: Edward Arnold, 1977); Boyer, *op. cit.*; O. Yiftachel, 'Planning and Social Control: Exploring the Dark Side', *Journal of Planning Literature*, 12, 1998 (4), pp. 395–406.
6. M. Dear, 'Prolegomena for a Postmodern Urbanism' in *Managing Cities*, edited by Patsy Healey *et al.* (London: Wiley, 1995).
7. M. Huxley, 'Planning as a Framework of Power: Utilitarian Reform, Enlightenment Logic and the Control of Space', in *Beasts of Suburbs: Reinterpreting Culture in Australian Suburbs*, edited by S. Ferber, C. Healey and C. McAuliffe (Melbourne: Melbourne University Press, 1994); P. Healey, 'Sites, Jobs and Portfolios: Economic Development Discourses in the

Planning System', in *Urban Studies* (1999) 56 (1) pp. 27—42; G. Vigar, P. Healey, A. Hull and S. Davoudi, *Planning, Governance and Spatial Strategy in Britain* (London: Macmillan, 2000).

8. R. Grove-White, 'Land, the Law and Environment', in *Journal of Law and Society* (1991) 18 (1) pp. 32—47; S. Owens, 'The Abercrombie Lecture: "Giants in the Path": Planning Sustainability and Environmental Values', in *Town Planning Review* (1997) 68 (3) pp. 293—304.
9. P. Healey, 'Collaborative Planning in a Stakeholder Society', in *Town Planning Review* (1998) 69 (1) pp. 537—57; B. Gleeson and K.J. Grundy, 'New Zealand's Planning Revolution Five Years On: a Preliminary Assessment', in *Journal of Environmental Planning and Management* (1997) 40 (3) pp. 293—314.
10. D. Harvey, *Justice, Nature and the Geography of Difference* (Oxford: Blackwell, 1996).
11. P. Healey, *Collaborative Planning: Shaping Places in Fragments Societies* (London: Macmillan, 1997); L. Sandercock, *Towards Cosmopolis* (London: Wiley, 1998).
12. This section is substantially a revised version of S. Graham and P. Healey, 'Relational Concepts of Place and Space: Issues for Planning Theory and Practice', in *European Planning Studies* (1999) 7 (15) pp. 623—46.
13. M. Tewdr-Jones and P. Allmendinger, 'Deconstructing Communicative Rationality: a Critique of Habermasian Collaborative Planning', in *Environment and Planning A* (1998) 30 pp. 1979—89.
14. A. Thornley, *Urban Planning Under Thatcherism* (London: Routledge, 1991); Healey, 'Collaborative Planning', op. cit..
15. Commission the European Communities (CEC), *The EU Compendium of Spatial Planning Systems and Policies* (Brussels: European Communities, 1997)
16. Ibid.; H. Davis, D. Edwards, A. Hooper and J. Punter, *Planning Control in Western Europe* (London: HMSO, 1989); P. Booth, *Controlling Development* (London: UCL Press, 1996).
17. J.B. Cullingworth and V. Nadin, *Town and Country Planning in Britain* (London: Routledge, 1994); M. Tewdr-Jones, 'Plans, Policies and Inter-Governmental Relations: Assessing the Role of National Planning Guidance in England and Wales', in *Urban Studies* (1997) 34 (10) pp. 141—62.
18. P. Healey, M. Purdue and F. Ennis, *Negotiating Development* (London: Spon, 1995).
19. Such payments are actually very rare and much frowned on in British planning practice. Ibid.
20. Ibid.
21. A. Ravetz, *Remaking Cities* (London: Croom Helm, 1980); P. Hall, H. Gracey, R. Drewett and R. Thomas, *The Containment of Urban England* (London: Allen and Unwin, 1973).
22. S.J. Chapin, *Urban Land-Use Planning* (Urbana: University of Illinois Press, 1965); B. McLoughlin, *Urban and Regional Planning: A Systems Approach* (London: Faber, 1969).
23. Chapin, op. cit.; McLoughlin, *Urban and Regional Planning*, op. cit.; B. McLoughlin, *Control and Urban Planning* (London: Faber, 1973).

24. T. Cowling and G. Steeley, *Sub-Regional Planning Studies: an Evauation* (Oxford: Pergamon, 1973).
25. South Hampshire Structure Plan Advisory Committee, *South Hampshire Structure Plan* (Winchester: Hampshire County Council, 1972).
26. Ibid., para 4.8, p. 19.
27. Ibid., p. 21.
28. Ibid., para 2.28, p. 10.
29. J. Forrester, *Urban Dynamics* (Boston: MIT Press, 1969).
30. S.W. Hwang, 'The Implications of the Nonlinear Paradigm for Integrated Environmental Design and Planning', in *Journal of Planning Literature* (1996) 11 (2) pp. 167—80.
31. Hampshire County Council, *Hampshire County Structure Plan (Approved)* (Winchester: Hampshire County Council, 1994) para 27, p. 10.
32. Hampshire County Council, *Hampshire County Structure Plan 1996-2011 (Review) Deposit Version* (Winchester: Hampshire County Council, 1996) para 21, p. 6.
33. M. Neuman, 'Images as Institution Builders: Metropolitan Planning in Madrid', in *European Planning Studies* (1996) 4 (3) pp. 293—312; P. Healey, A. Khakee, A. Motte and B. Needham, *Making Strategic Spatial Plans: Innovation in Europe* (London: UCL Press, 1997); D. Stevenson, 'Values, Vision and Governance in East London' in Rising East: the Journal of East London Studies (1998) 1 (1) pp. 15—35.
34. Tewdr-Jones, op. cit.; Healey, 'Collaborative Planning' op. cit.
35. See for example J. Bishop, 'Reinventing Planning 3: Collaboration and Consensus', in *Town and Country Planning* (1998) 67 (3) pp. 111—13.; P. Burton, *Community Visioning* (Bristol: Policy Press, 1997).
36. A. Amin and S. Graham, 'The Ordinary City', in *Transactions of the Institute of British Geographers* (1998) 22, pp. 411—29; P. Healey, *Collaborative Planning*, op. cit.; Sandercock, op. cit.; N. Thrift, *Spatial Formations* (London: Sage, 1996); A. Amin and N. Thrift, 'Globalization, Socioeconomics, Territoriality', in *Geographies of Economies*, edited by R. Lee and J. Wills (London: Arnold, 1997) pp. 147—57; M. Castells, *The Rise of the Network Society* (Oxford: Blackwell, 1996); G. Dematteis, 'Global Networks, Local Cities', in *Flux* (1994) 15, pp. 17—24; R. King, *Emancipating Space: Geography, Architecture and Urban Design* (London: Guildford, 1996); M. Storper, 'Regional Economies as Relational Assets', in *Geographies of Economies*, op. cit., pp. 248—58; J. Friedman, 'Towards a Non-Euclidean Mode of Planning', in *Journal of the American Planning Association* (1993) 59 (4) pp. 482—4; Hwang, op. cit.
37. Sandercock, op. cit.; and thereby generating the kinds of stable meanings and 'permanences' which are captures in notions of urban regimes (cf. Harvey, op. cit.; *Reconstructing Urban Regime Theory*, edited by M. Lauria (London: Sage, 1997).
38. J. Forrester, *Critical Theory, Public Policy and Planning Practice* (New York: SUNY, 1993); *The Argumetative Turn in Policy Analysis and Planning*, edited by F. Fischer and J. Forrester (London: UCL Press, 1993); T. Sager,

Section 5: Relations

Communicative Planning Theory (Aldershot: Avebury, 1994); J. Innes, 'Planning Theory's Emerging Paradigm', in Journal of Planning Education and Research (1995) 14 (3) pp. 183—90; Healey, *Collaborative Planning*, op. cit.; P. Healey, C. Hoch, M. Lauria and M. Feldman, Planning Theory, Political Economy and the Interpretive Turn: the Debate Continues', in *Planning Theory* (1997) 17 summer (special issue); Sandercock, op. cit.

39. See *Cities for Citizens*, edited by M. Douglass and J. Friedmann (London: Wiley, 1998).
40. Healey, *Collaborative Planning*, op. cit.
41. Sandercock, op. cit
42. Healey, *Collaborative Planning*, op. cit.
43. The distinction between inscription and incorporation comes from P. Connerton, *How Societies Remember* (Cambridge: Cambridge University Press, 1989) but it parallels my own in distinguishing between ways of thinking and ways of acting. Healey, *Collaborative Planning*, op. cit.
44. P. Hall, *Cities of Tomorrow* (Oxford: Blackwell, 1998); P. Hall, 'Bringing Abercrombie Back From The Shades', in *Town Planning Review* (1995) 66 (3) pp. 227—42; S. Ward, *Planning and Urban Change* (London: Paul Chapman, 1994).

Ian Buchanan and Fredric Jameson

Ian Buchanan's essay here is a commentary on a passage in *Postmodernism: or, the Cultural Logic of Late Capitalism*, by Fredric Jameson.[1] It analysed the Bonaventure Hotel in Los Angeles, designed by John Portman, the architect responsible now for many spectacular hotels. Their characteristic feature is a huge atrium space, usually with wall-climbing lifts with glass enclosures. At the Bonaventure Hotel they are particularly spectacular as they climb up the outside of the building to reach the rooms. On the downward journey there is a moment of crisis as the expansive and vertiginous views suddenly change into views across a complex lobby space with multiple symmetries, that Jameson found disorienting, and quintessentially postmodern. No one now lays claim to being postmodern – the term had its heyday in the 1980s, and was importantly discussed by Charles Jencks in his *The Language of Post-Modern Architecture* of 1977.[2] Jencks's discussion was important for Jameson, who saw architecture as leading the way in defining the new paradigm. However Portman's building did not make use of the historical references and paraphernalia that are particularly characteristic of Jencks's architectural postmodernism, and Jameson's misprision of it took off in a different direction, making the experience of the building (rather than any architect's intentions) the postmodern aspect of the place. It is Jameson's contention that here, postmodern hyperspace – whatever that is –

> has finally succeeded in transcending the capacities of the individual human body to locate itself, to organize its immediate surroundings perceptually, and cognitively map its position in a mappable external world. It may now be suggested that this alarming disjunction between the body and its built environment – which is to the initial bewilderment of the older modernism as the velocities of spacecraft to those of the automobile – can itself stand as the symbol and analogon of that even sharper dilemma which is the incapacity of our minds, at least at present, to map the great global multinational and decentered communicational network in which we find ourselves caught as individual subjects.[3]

It is just such decentred networks and no-longer-individual 'subjects' that are set up as the basis of understanding by Deleuze and Guattari; and making them our starting-points makes it possible to dissolve Jameson's problems, as Buchanan shows in his essay. This essay revisits some important themes introduced earlier in the volume, including importantly the focus on function (practice) rather than form (being) and it helps to emphasize the pragmatics-based aspect of Deleuze's thinking. There is also an anthropomorphism based around a functional rather than formal image of the body, as the hotel is imaged as a body engaging with flows of people and capital.

Section 5: Relations

We are indeed in the realm of the *informe* (it is impossible to guess simply from reading this essay what the form of the building might be) and we find our way round it by establishing relations between signs, within the building and beyond it. My own memory of this hotel lobby is of going there to hire a car. I thought I would take it for a turn round the block to get the feel of the unfamiliar controls, before trying to orientate myself with a map. However the route round the block was more nuanced than I had realized, and in moments I was on a freeway spinning out to goodness knows where, evocative place names on the road signs, and nothing for it but to go with the flow.

Notes

1. Fredric Jameson, *Postmodernism: or, the Cultural Logic of Late Capitalism* (London: Verso, 1991) pp. 38–45.
2. Charles Jencks, *The Language of Post-Modern Architecture* (London: Academy, 1977).
3. Jameson, *op. cit.*, p. 44.

Schizophrenic Utopianism

> Perhaps today, where the triumph of more Utopian theories of mass culture seems complete and virtually hegemonic, we need the corrective of some new theory of manipulation...
>
> (Fredric Jameson, *Late Marxism*)

Within walking distance of the space where some of the best scenes in *Blade Runner* occur, namely the Bradbury Building on Broadway – that archetype of high modernism, which today is preserved like a museum piece amidst an inner-city reproduction of a third-world shanty town, its refurbished rusticity belying its pretence at being a functioning commercial centre – is the stage for a very different kind of drama: the ongoing metacritique of postmodernity. I am of course talking about the Westin Bonaventure Hotel, which, as Derek Gregory has rightly observed, has become the very topoi of postmodernism.[1] (The essay which propelled this literally remarkable building into the spotlight, Jameson's 'Postmodernism, or, the Cultural Logic of Late Capitalism', is correspondingly one of the most written about and commented on pieces of writing produced in the last two decades.[2]) Today, though, to approach the Bonaventure from this direction, up either Fourth St or Third St to Flower St, is to discover straightaway that one of the cornerstones of Jameson's argument (the lack of a traditional marquee entrance, and the consequent closed-face the hotel seemed to present to the city at street level) has been chipped away. There is now a marquee entrance on Flower St replete with all the bunting and embossed livery one would expect, which establishes a direct relation between the building and the street so that one can now enter the building on the same level as the lobby and check-in is situated. Is this just good business, or do we need to change our theory too?

According to Sean Homer, Jameson's reading of the Bonaventure 'was initially one of the most persuasive aspects of his analysis of postmodernism but has subsequently been subjected to a great deal of critical analysis'.[3] This is simply a polite way of saying that in recent years Jameson's argument has been repudiated more often than it has been affirmed. What is interesting about this, besides the intensity of the felt need to denounce *this* reading of *this* building (why not his reading of *Lord Jim* too?), is the fact that such denouncements tend to be made following field trips to the Bonaventure. Upon finding it far less astonishing and disorienting than Jameson depicts it, critics seem to need to write back in anger, and bolstered by their own experience of the building (which they take as objective proof of their point) they feel justified in doing so.[4] It appears, then, that the reason *this* reading of *this* building is

Section 5: Relations

such a frequent target is its apparent ease of invalidation: one can say Jameson got it wrong simply by visiting the hotel and failing to be impressed by it, whereas it takes a great deal more work and perspicacity to put oneself in the position of being able to say the same of his interpretation of Conrad. But besides bad faith, what such arguments really prove is how satisfying the illusion of reference is, as well as how difficult it is to think in fact the loss of referentiality that postmodernity is supposed to entail, because what they all rely on is the assumption that the Bonaventure itself can be used to falsify Jameson's claims.

What such an assumption misses, because it glosses it too quickly I suppose, is the fact that the argument against Jameson, as well as Jameson's own, is based on the experience of the Bonaventure, not the building itself as objective referent (it has more to do with noesis than noema, if I may be permitted an artificial disjunction). Both responses are in fact completely subjective, and, what is more, self-consciously so – it being just as subjective to fail to be amazed as it is to be dizzied by it, though for some reason the sober response is allowed to see itself as objective and somehow scientific. In other words, what this particular debate exposes, and the reason why it interests me so much, is the incommensurability of the gap between perception and conceptualisation. Such an inquiry is exceedingly pertinent to Deleuze because many of his claims are far wilder than Jameson's quite reasonable (and by comparison, modest) assertion that he found the idiosyncratic arrangement of entrances and exits disorienting and that his reaction might serve as a figure for the larger fact that postmodernity itself, understood as an epochal convulsion if not a genuine shift, is giddying. For instance, how might one apprehend the very strange claim that Amsterdam is a city 'entirely without roots' except as a concept, when to treat it as a percept is to try to connect it to an expressive image, and that straightaway leads to all kinds of confusions?[5] As I've tried to show in the previous chapters, what is at stake here is a process I have found it useful to call conceptualisation, namely the properly philosophical process of converting intuitions into concepts.

One of the greatest sources of confusion concerning Jameson's own process of conceptualisation with regards to the Bonaventure is the fact that he really isn't trying to offer a reading of the hotel space so much as use his intuited impressions of it as evidence of a peculiar cultural turn he identifies with postmodernity. Therefore, it is the epoch that he is conceptualising, not the hotel's architecture (the Bonaventure is a symptom of postmodernism, not an agent or cause of it). If we were to critique his reading, then, we would have to start from this fact. There would then be a range of questions we could usefully ask: does he convert the hotel into an expression of postmodernity?; or, alternatively, does he treat it as a representation of it? As we shall see, strictly speaking, neither is the case. My purpose, though, is not so much to critique Jameson's account as to offer my own differently conceived reading. What I will try to do, which because Jameson does not, often puts me in a position of disagreement with him, is offer a conceptualised reading of the hotel itself. Such a reading, I will argue, should attempt to define the building's mechanisms of manipulation because insofar as it is a business that must finally be what is primarily at issue. How does it draw people to itself? What kind of a libidinal apparatus, if it is one, is it? If anything is actually missing from Jameson's account, that he missed something being the most common objection to his reading of the

Bonaventure, then I would say it is a consideration of the Bonaventure's manipulative capacities.[6]

I want to suggest, then, following Deleuze, that a very different reading could be given of both the Bonaventure itself and more generally of postmodern styles of architecture with respect to late capitalism than the one offered by Jameson simply by taking into account its day-to-day commercial operations – its associated flows of money and people. It is true, Jameson does not ignore the fact that the Bonaventure is a business. He notes that it is part of the renaissance of the downtown, by which he means, though without ever putting it in so many words, nothing other than property speculation (a topic he gets around to discussing a decade or so later); he also notes that the businesses within the hotel complex itself seem to have suffered in consequence of its strange design, pointing to tell-tale shop vacancies.[7] Beyond that, though, there is no consideration of its day-to-day operation, the sheer fact in other words that it is a hotel. Now, by the same token, it must be admitted that Deleuze does not dwell on architecture all that often. He keeps even his remarks on the Gothic architecture so pertinent to his conception of the Baroque to a bare minimum. Yet in that he often has recourse to spatial figures such an extension of his work seems both possible and desirable. And indeed such work has already begun, and my aim here is to extend that work further.[8] My argument, though, will be somewhat different from the current trend in that I will insist that any attempt to use Deleuze to discuss spatiality must be done in tandem with his discussion of the operations of capitalism.

Our first task will be to get behind representation to the real production of desire. According to Deleuze, as we've already seen, if we want to apprehend desire for itself we have to look on the reverse side of any representation we are confronted with, whether that is a book, a dream, or a building. To get to that reverse side, though, we first of all need to seek out dark precursors, those minute and myriad indices of connections, disjunctions and conjunctions, in short, all the flows and their schizzes, which all but imperceptibly dot the surface of a text.[9] In the end, it comes down to this: flows and their schizzes.[10] One can already imagine that Deleuze would want to call the Bonaventure a rhizome because it does indeed seem to be constructed according to principles that counter architecture's usual hierarchies: it can effectively be reduced to the connections and blockages it creates with respect to the flows of people and the associative flow of money, these being our dark precursors. To begin with, internally it consists of a number of deliberate obstacles to movement up and down that tend to foreground the lateral in a way one is unaccustomed to in a building that from the street at least would seem to be governed by conditions of verticality: some levels of the mezzanine are connected only by stairs while others can be reached only by elevators, and not all lifts stop at all floors so if you get on the wrong one you are bound to overshoot your mark (they are at least colour-coded so you can figure out which lifts go to which range of levels).[11]

Yet, this very emphasis on the lateral has the effect of introducing a new order of verticality into this sector of the downtown because it is possible to enter the building from the fourth and sixth floors as well as the first and ground. It has the effect of stratifying the city, enabling its flows of people to conduct themselves on several levels besides that of the street. Indeed, the street falls into redundancy because of the two upper entrances, which face on to potted garden plateaus that branch directly into adjacent office buildings, thereby cutting a swathe across topological inconveniences. The small eateries and alfresco cafés one would expect to find at street level in a big city are to be found here instead on the fourth and sixth floors, which are given over almost entirely to such enterprises. And again, this shift can be read as a mutation of an established line. Instead of the long straight line of restaurants one finds at street level in certain sections of the city, though not in the downtown any more, in the Bonaventure that line curls round on itself, becoming heliacal. The six-floor mezzanine is a vortex that concentrates the flow of lunchtime pedestrians, who, on the old system, would have been forced to pursue a line of dispersion. Accordingly, one might argue that rather than turn its back on the city, it actually taps into the inherent verticality of the new downtown, making it an active response to changes in the movement of people. One might also say, and indeed there would be no denying it, that this upward drive reflects a generalised fear and distaste for the street and the hapless souls condemned to it (something the sky cars envisioned by *Blade Runner* capture all too well).

Then again, one must wonder why in a city like Los Angeles where the dominant mode of movement is vehicular one would ever reckon the relation of a building to the street in terms of pedestrians. On this point, I think it is worth noting that the Bonaventure, according to its own proud boast, is built near the conjunction of six major freeways, and, it is implied, all the major conduits to other states, and of course other cities all over the world (at the endpoint of at least one conduit is LAX, where conveniently enough there is another Westin hotel), making it a nodal point in a nexus encompassing, if not the whole world, then at least the whole of Southern California. Whether it turns people away at ground level is thus immaterial beside the fact that it attracts people from much further afield – its pool of potential customers is not confined to happenstance pedestrians stumbling around the downtown in search of a place to eat or shop. Indeed, if it were, it doubtless could not support itself, so empty is the downtown on non-working days and after business hours. As such, it makes perfect sense for its sidewalk restaurant not to be anywhere near the curb – not even in sight of it, truth be told – because the flow of customers is downwards from the towers and outwards, not inwards from the street. There are thus two sort of flows here: the first is an influx, sucking in the hotel customers from all around the world, the second is an outflux into the hotel's own businesses and then the city itself. To put it in Deleuze's terms, the first flow creates a body without organs, while the second is its miraculate.

The body without organs is without doubt the least understood and the most easily misunderstood of all the key components of the Deleuzian hermeneutic apparatus. It is, though, readily translatable into more familiar terminology: it primarily functions as a principle of totalisation. It is produced by the 'synthesis of connection, as that which is going to neutralise – or on the contrary put into motion – the two activities, the two heads of desire'.[12] (These two heads, as I've already mentioned above, are flows and schizzes.) In this instance, the vortical action of the hotel is synthetic inasmuch as it brings enough people together to create a viable business centre, while its internal blockages encourage the dilatoriness needed for peaceful expenditure. What these people spend is thus a miraculate of this body of customers constricted into a commercial critical mass. (The true outflux is of course a flow of money.) The hotel itself thus looms before us as a whole, a full body as Deleuze and Guattari put it, but not in a way that can be used to subordinate the many and varied interests of the specific elements of that body. The fact that it is a hotel we are talking about is not sufficient in itself to explain the motivations and actions of all the people who visit, inhabit or otherwise make use of its space. Yet, clearly enough, the fact of it being a hotel is nonetheless crucial to our understanding of these selfsame activities. It is thus a totalisation *on which things occur and move*, but do so according to their own interests.

Interestingly, the hotel presents itself precisely as a body without organs – its own body (as imagined by its brochure) radiates outwards, in a glorious series of concentric rings encompassing landmarks such as Bunker Hill, Dodger Stadium, the MOCA, Chinatown, all the way out to the Venice Pier. Thus an image of itself as centripetal screens the reality of its vortical mechanism, whose pull, it needs to be emphasised, is weakest the nearer one is to the hotel itself, where in an important reversal of its effect it becomes actively repelling (I mean, it doesn't pull in the street-dwellers, who on some days would be the only people around the hotel itself).[13] On this score, I think Davis is right to reiterate Jameson's point (though, of course he does not recognise it as such!) that the Bonaventure Hotel, whatever its aesthetic qualities may be, is inserted into a cityscape and a city-life that it cannot but alter, at times savagely, whether symbolically, by once again figuratively asserting class difference (a luxury hotel amidst, but excluding the urban working-class people who live and work nearby), or directly, by displacing the homeless and the low-income earners who once occupied its infamous Bunker Hill site.[14] But to accuse Jameson of complacency, by suggesting he turns his back on the raw facts of the matter, is to miss the point of his paper altogether.

The disjunction of this hotel and its surrounds, which finds figuration in its reflective shell, is, Jameson argues, a function of its disaffection with the Utopian impulse at the heart of modernism.[15] Nothing could express his critical concern for the state of affairs we call postmodernism more succinctly or more patently. By the same token, Davis's equally evocative point that primitive modes of production surround the hotel like a sea of pity, is, however salutary, no less wrong-headed in terms of a critique of Jameson.[16] For one thing – as Jameson himself replies – sweatshops are not pre-capitalist; but even if they were, Davis would still be off-beam, because, as Mandel points out, such an uneven admixture of modes of production is precisely what one should expect of capitalism.[17] For another, it also glosses the admixture of modes of production internal to the hotel itself, by which I mean the new generation of (globalised) itinerant merchants and journeymen (i.e., sales representatives and technical experts) who make use of the hotel as way-station and home-away-from-home. It is one thing to speak of the permanently displaced persons who used to occupy the site, but however baleful that story is we shouldn't let it blind us to the new stories being told in their place. Today, we have to reckon into our account people who in contrast might be called perpetually displaced persons.

These modern-day nomads are like the associative flows of money (rather than the other way round) in that they move with the money, following its flux in the same way that once upon a time miners followed mineral seams.[18] Now, though, they

Section 5: Relations

follow a huge variety of sources of fantastic wealth in addition to that which is still available from mining; and, let's face it, few places offer as many sources of fantastic wealth as Los Angeles. One thing that Davis does illustrate exceedingly well in his 'biography' of the city of Los Angeles, is that its history of amazing growth is owed entirely to the way it has opened itself to profiteering at every level – from the initial land speculation boom that turned a parched beanfield into a city through to the very fact of supplying that parched land with water. From a diachronic perspective, the Bonaventure can thus be seen as still another way of mining the 'natural' resources of Southern California: its target is the transhumants (as Deleuze and Guattari call them) whose business it is to follow the money, and who might otherwise have slipped by without being profited from.[19] On this enlarged view, the Bonaventure is no longer a body without organs in itself, but an apparatus of capture operating on a far vaster stage, that of the being of capital itself (the most luminous of all the bodies without organs).[20] It is thus a breakflow in the middle of vortex, not a vortex in itself.

If it is true that the 'primary determination of nomads is to occupy and hold a smooth space' then the sad truth is that nomadism cannot save us anymore – if it ever could! – because it is now engendered by capitalism.[21] The smoothest of all smooth spaces today is that which the heady operations of finance capital (which miraculously conjures money from money without having to detour via production) creates. Aptly enough, Jameson has characterised it as a kind of cyberspace.[22] This brings us to Davis's most serious misapprehension of Jameson's account of the Bonaventure, which is a methodological one. His argument with Jameson rests on the absurd claim that totalisation 'homogenise[s] the details of the contemporary landscape' and thereby somehow extinguishes the phenomenal. In reality, Jameson's position is that the situation we call postmodernity has grown so complex and heterogeneous that an adequate totalisation of it is no longer possible.[23] Davis's lament feels all the more absurd when it is realised that what he seems to be calling for in chastising Jameson for not making adequate mention of the specific social and political context of the Bonaventure Hotel is in fact a *greater* totalisation. Not a little bemused with the fuss it continues to cause, but more than a little tired of defending it against all manner of wild accusations, Jameson has lately described 'totalization' as 'the hoariest of all negative buzzwords'.[24]

The itinerants who pass through the hotel are not the only elements missing from the fuller picture advocated, but not actually furnished, by Davis. There is also the staff of the hotel itself – that vast army of cleaners, waiters and waitresses, room-service attendants, bell-hops, concierges, middle managers and senior executives, who collectively and mostly invisibly comprise the majority of the working parts of the hotel machine.[25] A host of issues present themselves for consideration now because this labour force is composed of a politically fraught admixture of men and women, white and other, gay and straight, rich and poor, salaried and non-guaranteed, young and old, workers.[26] By promising work, the hotel draws employees to itself from near and far. In return for a wage, it demands they identify themselves with its corporate image, not merely by wearing a uniform, but even more profoundly by conforming to an ethos (the customer is always right; it takes more effort to frown than to smile; service with a smile; prompt service; efficient service; and so on).

The smiling face of the Filipino woman who brings you your $11 cocktail in the

Bona Vista bar is the face of the hotel – the hotel facialises itself by demanding from her a certain smile, a certain demureness and an unflappable tolerance for any idiosyncrasy whatever. And though you are only spending $11, and not even on her, she lets you act as though it were all the riches in the world you were doling out. Through inviting a vague but unmistakable libidinalisation her demure face encourages the fantasy that you somehow deserve what you're getting, that you've earned it, that you're worth it. Her face, her minutely calculated genuflections and conciliatory attentions are, as Dreiser scathingly put it, what 'Americans pay for'.[27] This drink is your reward for all your hard work. This is what Deleuze and Guattari are referring to when they say capitalism substitutes relative limits for the absolute limits of desire – there is something remarkable in the fact that a mid-level executive can happily work an eighty-hour week and still think an $11 drink is a privilege!

From an ideological perspective, it seems that the trouble with totalisation, which, as an analytic instrument, is simply a means of identifying and naming the connections between the various forces and interests that compose a society, and nothing more, is too easily confused with totalitarianism, and ends up, rather weirdly, being taken as one with fascism. But, if 'the meaning of a word is its use, we can best grasp "totalisation" [...] through its function – to envelope and find a least common denominator for the twin activities of perception and action'.[28] It is, then, in fact one of the means criticism has at its disposal of detecting and describing fascism, and is perhaps the only means with a scope broad and detached enough not to be ensnared or seduced by the very thing it names. Its principal aim is to develop a perspective from which the connectedness of all things can be seen; not, as is perhaps true of totalitarianism, the elimination of difference by the monstrous imposition of the same. Therefore, to describe postmodernism as a cultural dominant is not to suggest that an intrinsically alien cultural force – too simply identified as 'American' – is somehow depriving the world of its political, religious and ethnic variety, as James Clifford (among others) seems to fear, but rather to say, that it is the superstructural expression of a rapidly changing but undeniably pervasive base.[29] What is in fact dominant, of course, is not a particular aesthetic style, or even a way of thinking about the world, but a mode of production.

Philosophically, a totality is something which, whether because of its inconceivable size (too immense or too minute), or because it is yet to be actually invented, or simply because it is still to be imagined, is – *by definition* – unknowable to us. Methodologically, as structuralism instructed us, 'a totality is a combination or permutation scheme, endowed with a closure of its own no matter how ineffably fluid and dynamic its processes may be'. In the case of truly elastic processes like chaos or catastrophe theory, it is only the closure representation provides that in fact makes them thinkable.[30] Closure of this type is anything but the end of the story insofar as the analysis of certain hitherto undisclosed phenomena are concerned: obviously enough, insofar as it is what actually makes that phenomena visible it is the inauguration of a problem not a solution. Here an important contrast can be made between Jameson's philosophical position, which might cursorily be classified as Hegelian, though it should also be seen as a profound modification of Hegel, and the currently dominant Kantian tradition.[31] In the Kantian scheme, such unknowables as Nature, the Cosmos, Beauty and so on are converted into transcendental concepts,

Section 5: Relations

readymade Universals as it were, and made to serve as the fixed coordinates of thought. In contrast Jameson treats all concepts, including totalities, as problems, and in this respect adopts a position far closer to Deleuze than his repeated affirmations of Hegel would seem to allow. This is even true of postmodernism – for better or worse, the organising term of this discussion – which Jameson explicitly states 'is not something we can settle once and for all and then use with a clear conscience'.[32] On this definition, totalisation refers to the effort of thinking the structurally unthinkable, or more precisely the attempt to coordinate disparate data in such a way as to explain it without at the same time explaining it away.

Postmodernism, then, is a problem still to be fully worked out and while it is not without its problems, these are not to be found where they are commonly asserted to be. The problem is not that Jameson grounds his account of what he calls post-contemporary culture in a determining economic base, late capitalism. All theories must be grounded somehow (differance for Derrida, the plane of immanence for Deleuze, Being for Heidegger and so on), and that ground is always going to be (by definition) pre-philosophical, and therefore impossible to critique.[33] What can be critiqued, however, is the set of relations pertaining between a ground and its superstructure, and, observing that the term 'late capitalism' seems to collapse base and superstructure, necessitating a discussion of cultural phenomena alongside any and all discussions of economics, it is precisely as a set of relations that Jameson defines postmodernism.[34] So while the distinctions between such divergent philosophical grounds as differance, the plane of immanence and late capitalism are not lightly dismissed, or simply ignorable for the sake of producing an effective homology, they should not be fetishised either.[35] By the same token, however peculiar each of these grounds may be, we should not allow their individuality to blind us to the fact that each one represents a philosophical system consisting of a relation between a base and superstructure, which is to say, each one proposes an *a priori* totalisation – the plane of immanence, differance, just as surely as late capitalism, are all totalisations, even if they are not totalisations of the same type, with the same implications.[36]

On this view, the differences between these grounds become important only to the extent that they effect the specific nature of the receding of a given text or particular situation they produce.[37] Jameson calls this piece of dialectical manoeuvring transcoding (his updated word for what he elsewhere calls metacommentary).[38] The usefulness of this term lies not so much in what it names, though, as in the critical distance, or, better, estrangement, it creates. Although it may appear to be a homogenisation of all theories, or, even worse, an extreme form of relativism, it is in fact an attempt to historicise theory. By treating theories in this abstract way, their dependence upon a particular situation, and a certain formulation of a problem, can be emphasised. This, in turn, allows us to see that the real problem of postmodernism – and by extension, all theories – if indeed there is one, lies in the relational structure it proposes between itself and its base, late capitalism. Aesthetically, as is the case with what Jameson counts as its immediate predecessors modernism and realism, postmodernism is at once a reflection and registration of the conditions of the period it describes, which itself is determined, in the last instance, by the prevailing mode of production. If we take architecture as our example, which is – as is well known – the medium Jameson tends to favour in his own meditations on the subject, a very interesting second problem arises as soon as we try to describe the peculiarities of its aesthetic response.[39] For while it may be true that the Bonaventure Hotel is responding to the anomie of late capitalism by creating a kind of mini-city unto itself, in doing so, somewhat oddly, it actually seems to exacerbate that feeling, such that what began as the registration of a certain culturally felt ennui suddenly becomes one of its causes.

While it is tempting to see this as still another example of a perverse outcome, the fact that its underpinning logic – the aspiration to be a miniature substitute for a city – can also be found in the Eaton centre in Toronto and in the Beaubourg in Paris (to give only the examples Jameson uses), means that it is not an accident but a contradiction.[40] In short, it would confound the very logic of capitalism itself to deliberately create an environment that did not appeal in some way to consumers, so one has to assume, on the evidence of its repetition, that beyond its repelling first appearance there is something subtly compelling in the design of the mini-city. My speculation is that if it is true that the Bonaventure Hotel does in fact turn its back on the city in which it is situated, and I do not doubt this reading at all, then it is in view of becoming an enclave, a haven or refuge from the stresses of city life.[41] The implication I want to draw from this is that the so-called spatial turn of postmodern theory is in fact a reflection of an entrepreneurial counter-strategy to the unproductive chaos of modern life. As Deleuze and Guattari put it, what capitalism deterritorializes with the one hand, it reterritorializes with the other: it creates new forms of freedom by lifting old restrictions only to supplant them with profit-seeking axioms.[42] In what follows I want to suggest a different answer to the one Jameson proposes; rather than see this contradiction as a 'return of the repressed', I see it as a stratagem – not a 'distraction', which lacks the sense of manipulation I believe is at work in postmodern space – whose specific version of the age-old 'bread and circuses' logic is as yet undisclosed.[43] This will in turn necessitate an examination and re-evaluation of Jameson's important claim that postmodern space is schizophrenic.

Support for this hypothesis may be found in the widely documented shift in feeling that has occurred in relation to the city in the past century. Where once it was associated with freedom, contrasting favourably with the depressing restrictions of the arch-conservatism and economic stagnation of the countryside, now it feels crowded, dangerous and oppressive.[44] As Benjamin's analysis of Baudelaire illustrates, the city began to seem fearful and shocking as early as the middle of the nineteenth century. And the first and most decisive reactions to this change in perception were precisely architectural – the arcades and the boulevards. The first created charming cloisters for the bourgeoisie to shop in without fear of being mugged or pushed in front of moving carriages, while the second were meant to prevent barricading by the working class, though in reality they actually assisted in the task of gridlocking the city.[45] Today, for much the same reasons, these same architectural strategies persist in the shape of the mall and the freeway and while they no longer protect an *ancien régime* as such, they still serve the entrenched interests of capital. At bottom, both no doubt reflect a fear of urban concentration, which, as Jameson has speculated, is itself 'a twentieth-century variant, a coded or "sedimented" persistence, of that older, ideologically far more transparent, nineteenth-century terror of the mob itself, the revolutionary crowd'.[46] What the mall must do, as the arcade did before it, is create an environment conducive to consumption (it must halt the flow of pedestrians so as to extract the associative flow of money). Now if it is true that the mall in the Bonaventure actually turns customers away then not merely is it a failure in commercial terms, it is also utterly illogical in capitalist terms, and this latter point threatens in its illogicality to unravel the whole postmodern tapestry.[47]

The problem, as I see it, is this: the Bonaventure does not appear to express the logic of capitalism in its function, although it manifestly does so in its form. What we must ask now is if the Bonaventure's mall is in fact an attempt to create a enclave, which should be seen as a device, then why create an enclave that seems to call for the construction of yet another enclave, this time a personal one like an individual force-field? The feeling that still another enclave is required is precisely what Jameson is referring to when he says postmodern architecture has finally succeeded in transcending present human capacities to cognitively map their surrounds.[48] The feeling of dislocation induced by the seamlessness – and what I want to call the anti-modernity – of the Bonaventure mall that Jameson calls schizophrenia is, he says, analogous to the sense of incomprehension all of us feel today in face of globalisation.[49] This is without doubt Jameson's most important claim vis-à-vis the Bonaventure Hotel and postmodern space generally and, significantly, it relies on the very divergence of form and function I have highlighted above. The reason the individual cannot map the postmodern space he or she is thrust into upon entering the mall is that it no longer conforms to the accustomed spatial patterns of modernity, in which form and function are triumphantly unified. It is, I might add, precisely for the fact that postmodern space seems to suppress function in favour of form that I want to call it anti-modern. If this form/function disparity were to be resolved then Jameson's important analogon would be invalidated.[50] And although, as I will show in a moment, this disparity can be shown to be amenable to that strong form of comprehension called empathy, I do not want to thereby destroy the analogon because I agree with Jameson in thinking it has a vital Utopian function. In order to prevent that I want now to underscore something Jameson himself only fleetingly touches on and that is the fact that our incapacity to cope with postmodern space stems from our constitutional lack of preparedness for its characteristic features.[51]

As I have said, the trouble we have with postmodern space is twofold: on the one hand, it suppresses function, giving itself over entirely to form, thus making it virtually impossible to determine what it is for and accordingly how one should approach it and or utilise it; on the other hand, and ultimately, the problem is our expectation of transparency, our spatial complacency in other words. We are beset by the fact that our spatial habits were formed in modernity, not the postmodernity in which we actually live, so we are not constitutionally equipped for own environment.[52] The word that I want to underscore here is habit. It is, by his own admission, Jameson's lack of postmodern habits that leaves him unable to map the space of the Bonaventure mall, and which, I presume, compels him to view postmodern space in a modernist way, that is, to search out what is new in it, what is telling about it, and emphasise these aspects over its more mundane features – the fact that it still has shops, elevators and so on.[53] His reaction, in other words, is the reaction of somebody watching a strikingly original film for the first time, not the reaction of someone who has seen the film so often they have practically memorised it. My implication, of course, is that the requisite new habits have not been given sufficient time to form.[54] So while it is undoubtedly true that to be able to apprehend postmodern space in a single glance we would have to grow new perceptual organs, this emphasis on simultaneity can only be maintained if the perception of space is treated as analogous to the perception of film.[55] Such an idea can only hold if we assume that our current apparatus of perception was constructed by film.

Although Jameson does not explicitly state that he is treating as equivalent cinematic perception and what in contrast might be called ordinary perception, it is I believe implicit in the general claim that our perceptual apparatus was formed by modernity. One of the most distinctive features of modernity is assuredly the advent of cinema, not merely as a new aesthetic medium but also as a training ground for our collective perceptual habits. If, as Deleuze suggests, film improves on and, as it were, perfects perception, then one consequence of the pervasiveness of cinema must be a sense of perceptual inadequacy outside the darkened confines of theatre.[56] We cannot pull to a long shot or swoop in for a close-up with the apparent ease of film and are thus always trapped between a desire for detail and an urge for the big picture by our own weak bodies.[57] Even the elevator which rapidly lifts one up to the top of the building is not as fast as film and the lag between views spoils the montage; what in a film is a striking juxtaposition is in reality a tedious wait for a free elevator, a squeezed and stuffy ride and then a giddying stare at a shimmering city grid.[58] The more filmically literate we become the less able we are to perceive ordinarily, or at any rate, to feel satisfied that we are seeing all that we ought to see. So when we enter a space that enchants us, as Benjamin optimistically – and against the grain of his Frankfurt colleagues – argued the arcades are capable of doing, we are also struck by our inadequate means of apprehending it; we feel footsore and slow even as we feel delightfully bewildered.[59]

By the same token, cinema has also accustomed us to spectacle, so even as we are readily bewildered by fantastic new spaces we are equally easily bored and unimpressed by ordinary spaces. On the evidence of buildings already considered postmodern, the most boring aspect of what I am here loosely calling 'ordinary space' is its function, which is not to say that the non-functional or dysfunctional has in some strange way become desirable, but rather that it is no longer desirable for a building to look like what it is: office buildings should no longer look like office buildings, and art museums shouldn't look like art museums. (Better they look like binoculars, or crumpled aluminium foil if you're Frank Gehry.) What this aesthetic defies above all, including convention, and the need to be functional, is material constraints, the sheer material fact of pipes, glass, steel, supporting columns, stressed concrete, and so on.[60] Its confrontation with these ultimately determining facts is, then, a figuration of that daily confrontation we all face, the need to eat, to sleep, to shower and to work, and the extent to which it is capable of aestheticising its own material needs is an expression of the depth to which our bodily needs are similarly aestheticised, which is to say commodified by late capitalism. It is this aspect of it that evinces our empathy and secretly enables us to map what initially appeared unmappable. Against the background of the efficiency of modernity and the structural need in late capitalism to plan everything, including obsolescence, whimsical has come to mean free, and the most visible way of achieving this effect is to defy the evident good sense of modernist design.[61]

Section 5: Relations

In this respect, Deleuze is undoubtedly right to suggest that we have moved into a new age of invisible power – what he calls the society of control – because one rarely sees panopticons these days, they are too obvious. Mechanisms of control have deepened.[62] Postmodern space is delightfully bewildering because it responds to the boringly familiar with humour – the expected response to its designed inconveniences – but since this also entails disguising control mechanisms just who the joke is on is never clear. Boredom, as Jameson has argued, is the sign that personal habits have become fixed, invisible, and so deeply etched that it takes a profound shock to bring them into view.[63] Hence the desirability of an aesthetics of the boring, which would amount to a catalogue of the wilfully forgotten and the naturalised.[64] It is not difficult to see why the mini-city is in fact an excellent strategy. The mini-city is a satisfying containment of the vastness of the actual city, yet still large enough in itself not to disappoint jaded consumers. A delicate balance must be struck between overwhelming the visitor in a good sense and overwhelming them in a bad sense. And as Bachelard might have put it, since overwhelming is not an object as such, a phenomenology of it refers us directly to the imagining consciousness which, as Deleuze would surely remind us, we need to remember not to take for granted.

If a mini-city mall is not massive, then it would not have the conceptual appeal of an actual city, namely the allure of unlimited variety, the contemporary signifier of freedom. But, of course, if it is too monstrous, then unlimited variety suddenly becomes distressing and repelling. So the mini-city must be small enough to appeal to a longing for what Bachelard calls 'intimate immensity', for contained spaces, and it must be said, pedestrian spaces, where cars no longer rule and where the speed is human, and at the same time satisfy the desire for difference that consumer capitalism has trained us to believe a corner-store simply cannot satisfy any longer, and that anything less than a cornucopia is an impingement on personal liberty.[65] To satisfy this latter demand, the size restrictions on the mini-city have to be raised beyond what can humanly be mapped, at which point the mini-city ceases to be a city *in* a city and becomes *another* city, demanding to be cognitively mapped just as one would map any other city, a step at a time. The lack of convenience that Jameson cites is thus no accident or byproduct of postmodern space, but an integral feature of its appeal.[66] But the appeal of the mini-city is not only a matter of size, the design is important too, as Jameson stresses. However, what Jameson regards as confusing (and for that reason, either mistaken or misguided), the minimally signposted layout, I prefer to see as a cunning ploy.[67] In disguising the panoptic substratum with outrageously whimsical repositionings of long-established coordinates like lobbies and check-ins, by hiding their modernity in other words, post-modern buildings call on us to map their new space in a very old way – by power of local knowledge, not global or strategic knowledge. What this does is create the opportunity for one to acquire the feeling of empowerment (which is not the same thing as power) that comes with local knowledge, the ineffable sense of security one feels in knowing one's way around. This, finally, is the greatest dupe of them all.

This feeling of empowerment is achieved at the expense of ignorance of the interconnectedness of global capital and what it means to be imbricated in the world-system. The strategy here is to compel the consumer to accept the merely tactical as desirable. This is done rather easily, as it turns out, by playing on already sensitive ideological nerves and making everything planned appear undesirable, less richly textured than the more whimsical and contingent option. To this end, as Jameson has decisively shown, the communist world has been ruthlessly deployed as an analogon of the horror of conformity, distracting us from the structural homogeneity of our own far more conformist system that the infiltration of franchises (McDonald's, KFC, Burger King, but also Holiday Inn, Duty Free Shoppers and Ralph Lauren, not to mention the irrepressible Starbuck's, which, I note, has moved right into the heart of the Bona-venture too) into every corner of every city would seem astounding and incontrovertible evidence of, though it is frequently seen positively as the coming of modernity.[68] In this respect, indigenisation, despite the good press it has been getting lately, is in reality just another word for the penetration of the logic of late capitalism, for however positively you want to describe, say, the Indonesianisation of American franchises (notably Dunkin Donuts and McDonald's), the fact remains that it entails an Americanisation of the Indonesian too.[69] But, I hasten to add, Americanisation does not mean homogenisation, as such, it is rather the insidious implantation and intensification of a desire for the same. (This occurs, I would suggest, as something akin to what Russian formalism called a motivation of the device: the uniformity of McDonald's is a guarantee of taste, hygiene, convenience and availability, all of which are motivating values before being features.) And even if it were true that indigenisation did express a new logic of multiplicity, then it would still conform to the logic of late capitalism since its chief characteristic is precisely its diversity.[70]

Nowhere does Jameson say the experience of postmodern space is anything like delightfully bewildering, but, logically, as I hope I have shown, this must be the case. What is more, his utilisation of the notion of the Utopian impulse can be used here to transcode, literally to mediate, 'delightfully bewildering'. On the contrary, famously – and not a little controversially – Jameson describes it as schizophrenic, by which he means (borrowing his definition from Lacan and not, rather surprisingly, Deleuze and Guattari), 'a breakdown in the signifying chain, that is, the interlocking syntagmatic series of signifiers which constitutes an utterance or a meaning' and not, he is careful to point out, a clinical condition as such.[71] Basically this is another way of saying that postmodernism amounts to a loss of historicity, for what in effect schizophrenia is to Jameson is an absorption of the past into the present and, more damagingly, a disconnection of the present from the future as its hidden but uplifting potential.[72] The effect of this schizophrenising is twofold: first, it 'releases this present of time from all the activities and intentionalities that might focus it and make it a space of praxis'; and second, in consequence, the 'present suddenly engulfs the subject with undescribable vividness, a materiality of perception properly overwhelming'.[73] Politically, then, schizophrenia is paralysing: it makes impossible any effective connection of ideology with action, or to put it differently, it reduces the subject to being merely tactical. Worse still, the subject is so enthralled by the spectacle of postmodernity he or she no longer feels this desperate lack of political efficacy, except as bedazzlement.

However, despite this rather bleak picture, Jameson's purpose in describing this feeling as schizophrenic is to reinject politics into a domain that seems wholly given over to capitalism. Given that the scene I have just described is almost perfect from a capitalist point of view, full of happily duped consumers as it is, this must seem hardly possible, and although it is indeed only a potentiality for a radical politics that can be adduced in the end, not an actual revolution, the situation is not utterly hopeless. The stratagem at work in the mini-city would be perfect from a purely entrepreneurial point of view but for the fact that the awe these delightfully bewildered shoppers feel in the face of the mall's calculated grandeur is *estranging*. By defying established conventions of design, particularly those design elements that directly effect movement, such as the displacement of the lobby and check-in desk from the entry level of the hotel to a lower floor, the mall's idiosyncratic features bring into view the easily overlooked fact that a building constitutes a set of relations. And as Brecht says, breaking the environment into constitutive relationships 'corresponds to a new way of thinking, the historical way'.[74] In other words, if the design of a space is such that it casts what is usually taken for granted in an entirely fresh light, one that separates the various compositional elements from an unthought organic whole and presents them as objects with which we have relations, then its effect can be said to be estranging, which is to say historicising. It is historicising because it makes us aware that our spatial habits are tied to a conventional ordering of elements in space and that such an ordering is not naturally occurring, and, far from being immutable, is entirely contingent.[75]

So even as the apparent meaninglessness of postmodern space renders us schizophrenic, paralysing our ability to act, it nevertheless shocks us into seeing that space is available to ideological coding; it creates sufficient critical distance to allow us to place much needed inverted commas around words that roll too easily off the tongue (it is more 'efficient' to put the lobby on the entry level, more 'elegant' to have the check-in facing the door and so on). But, however hopeful this may be, even the most disconcerting design – as I have suggested above – is never entirely without the possibility of empathy; the trouble with that is empathy destroys estrangement by constraining it to sheer novelty. Attached to estrangement there is a permanent risk of recuperation, which brings me to a reconsideration of Jameson's use of schizophrenia. The problem that needs to be considered is what political potential can the concept and experience of schizophrenia (as process, not illness, to use Deleuze and Guattari's important distinction) have if the schizo it creates is politically awakened and paralysed in the same moment? A solution to this impasse obviously hinges on the nature of the relation between the two poles (what I will term, paralysis and conscience) attributed to schizophrenia by Deleuze and Guattari. My surprise above stems from the fact that Deleuze and Guattari's definition of schizophrenia as process does in fact accommodate this particular problem-position – indeed it is built around it – whereas Lacan's does not.[76]

You would think that this surprise would evaporate once it became clear just how resolutely anti-Hegelian and anti-dialectical Deleuze and Guattari's deployment of schizophrenia actually is. Yet, as I will show in a moment, even though Deleuze and Guattari define schizophrenia in such a way as to prevent any dialectical – or even dialectical-like – movement, resulting in some kind of raising up, or transformation, it is still not antithetical to the Jamesonian enterprise. For while their version of becoming as it is articulated in the idea of schizophrenia as universal process strictly precludes a terminal moment at which one thing becomes another thing, preferring the Marxian becoming-concrete, so too does Jameson's, as can be seen in his idiosyncratic conceptualisation of Utopian discourse as success by failure. The main difference, I want to say, is, finally, only terminological: Jameson permits himself to describe certain cultural processes as Utopian, although they do not result in or from any transcendent raising-up as such, while Deleuze and Guattari, in reference to more or less the same processes, do not. In other words, bringing these two models of thought together via schizophrenia basically means finding an impulse within schizophrenia as a process analogous to what in Jameson's work is deemed Utopian.[77]

Jameson's own reading of Deleuze and Guattari is not helpful in this matter.[78] For the most part, he uses their work to lend force to his correlation of period and style – famously, he equates decoding with nineteenth-century realism and receding with twentieth-century modernism – which although it has resulted in some powerful literary critical insights is achieved at the cost of a slight distortion that needs to be corrected if Deleuze and Guattari's model is to be of any use to us.[79] By grasping it as a primordial flux which as humans progress is left behind rather than a universal one that eternally haunts us, Jameson eliminates the crucial dialectical 'mechanism' on which Deleuze and Guattari's entire account of schizophrenia hinges. According to Deleuze and Guattari, the different stages of human organisation, the move through savage, barbarian and civilised societies in other words, occur not so much as a progression whereby one might say schizophrenia is pushed further and further behind us (like our reptilian selves on the evolutionary model), as a succession of modes, different ways of dealing with the same thing – schizophrenia as the uncoded flow of desire. The bottom line in all Deleuze and Guattari's thinking is the axiom that desire in its raw state is inimical to civil society and must be coded to be properly managed, but no code can be sustained forever.

Capitalist society, they say, 'can endure many manifestations of interest, but not one manifestation of desire, which would be enough to make its fundamental structures explode, even at the kindergarten level'.[80] Hence the fragility of the socius, whose prime function 'has always been to codify the flows of desire, to inscribe them, to record them, to see that no flow exists which is not properly dammed up, channelled, regulated'.[81] Sometimes, as is acutely the case in capitalism, the very process of regulation leads the socius into an invidious situation of having to unleash the very forces that will destroy it in order to stay afloat. Capitalism, as such, is not an administration of schizophrenia, but an investment in it. So, when Deleuze and Guattari say schizophrenia is the malady of our age, they do not mean it is modern life that drives people mad, but that the mode of production we call capitalism and the production of production called schizophrenia have been brought into a mad alignment that holds us constantly on the brink of dissolution and transformation – or what Deleuze and Guattari term 'breakdown' and 'breakthrough'.[82]

What we are really trying to say is that capitalism, through its process of production, produces an awesome schizophrenic accumulation of energy or charge, against which it brings all its vast powers of repression to bear, but which nonetheless continues to act as capitalism's limit. For capitalism constantly counteracts, constantly inhibits this inherent tendency while at the same time allowing it free rein; it continually seeks to avoid reaching its limit while simultaneously tending toward that limit. Capitalism institutes or restores all sorts of residual and artificial, imaginary, or symbolic territorialities, thereby attempting, as best it can, to recode, to rechannel persons who have been defined in terms of abstract qualities.[83]

A well-known economic conundrum will allow the truth of this insight to be seen. If it is true that commodity capitalism mobilises desire in order to promote consumption and consumption is by that equation an amortisation of desire, then, accordingly, an increase in consumption is bound to extinguish desire at an increasing rate. So to maintain itself capitalism must promote an ambiguous form of satisfaction: one that results in, to coin a term, insatiety. A purchase must result in customer satisfaction, otherwise they will not return to that store, or continue to use that product, but it cannot at the same time result in the extinction of the urge to repeat the act of purchasing or else capitalism itself would falter. In other words, the very thing that is posited as the goal of consumer culture, namely satisfaction, is radically decoded in consumer culture, which is to say, made to function in the interests of capital, not the consumer. Through a sequence of profound acts of abstraction, credit being perhaps the most insidious of all, in that it automatically decodes all people as consumers and does not hesitate to give them a precisely determining numerical rating, capitalism has succeeded in penetrating the process of self-realisation itself, enabling it to make it truly seem that you are what you buy, and correspondingly not what you lack.[84] This does not mean desire itself is intrinsically experienced as lack, however, only that desire must be transformed into lack if capitalism is to perpetuate itself.[85] What it shows above all is that the very notion of satisfaction is a capitalist-inspired concept, a fact perhaps reflected in Freud's frequent recourse to economic metaphors (especially in his discussions of the so-called perversions). It reduces all encounters to a simple transaction with afterglow; radical or subversive feelings are thus contained by a decoding of them as dissatisfaction, which implies a consumerist solution, that is, a satisfying conclusion, to whatever social problem is at issue by making all problems a matter of lack. Importantly, however, what this means is that the consumer is both permanently excluded from capitalist culture by their very means of participation, namely consumption, and protected from total absorption.

It is this 'included disjunction', to use Deleuze and Guattari's terminology, that – in the Jamesonian sense of succeeding by failure – I want to suggest can be read as Utopian. The included disjunction belongs to the second component (mode) of Deleuze and Guattari's tripartite description of the schizophrenic process (desire) as it is invested by capitalism, the disjunctive synthesis or production of recording; in addition there is the connective synthesis or production of production and the conjunctive synthesis or production of consumption-consummation. None of these modes are even relatively independent, so everything can be seen as production; indeed, it is an axiom of Deleuze and Guattari's thought that everything *is* seen as production, especially the conscious: 'production is immediately consumption and a recording process, without any sort of mediation, and the recording process and consumption directly determine production, though they do so within the production process'.[86] A pop song, for instance, is already consumption in the instant of its production, however original it may be, precisely because it is a consumable sound, by which I mean a sound that has already found expression, elsewhere and by other means, and is now clamouring to be heard, forcing its way into production. This can be seen in the transition between different genres of pop, from say disco to new wave, where a new rhythm emerges in the vacuoles of the older rhythm, first of all supplementing it, then complementing it, then finally supplanting it. Instead of a theory of succession, what this implies is a genealogy of experimentation. Disco set in motion a certain form of a musical production, or what we might perhaps better call channelled creative energy. From a free impulse to express, it fashioned a new form of expression, a different musical syntax to be explored. At disco's limits, new wave was formed as a detachment of energy, a freeing-up of a creativity beginning already to be stifled by the disco form. But new wave too soon produced its own syntax, and like disco before it, achieved its limit of becoming: consumption-consummation.

The schizo does not follow this path exactly. 'He is and remains in disjunction: he does not abolish disjunction by identifying the contradictory elements by means of elaboration; instead he affirms it through a continuous overflight spanning an indivisible distance. He is not simply bisexual, or between the two, or intersexual. He is transsexual.'[87] Schizophrenia, on this model, is pure, fully detached creative energy oscillating between a breakthrough to a new mode of existence and a breakdown into an already exhausted and spent mode. The model is anti-dialectical because any raising-up is also a tying-down: the breakthrough is the road to the breakdown. Yet, in that it proposes a dualism as a suppression of the dialectic it remains dialectical in spirit, as it were, albeit as a failed dialectic. Despite their suspicion of Utopia, and corresponding reticence to use it as a critical term, schizophrenia inasmuch as it oscillates between breakthrough and breakdown (where any form of breakthrough is a breakthrough to a new form of society, a new mode of living, and a breakdown a failed attempt to reach that new society) is precisely Utopian. And, however reluctantly, they do finally acknowledge as much in the 'group fantasy' section of their discussion of the included disjunction, where they admit to its Fourieresque qualities, and insist on its revolutionary character.[88] The schizo, they say, 'produces himself as a free man, irresponsible, solitary, and joyous, finally able to say and do something simple in his own name, without asking permission'.[89] To be sure, schizophrenia as process lacks a specific mechanism of raising-up, something that would enable the becoming to become, but then as Jameson has shown this is in fact in its favour.

For Jameson, insofar as Utopia is concerned, success is in fact to be found in failure; indeed, what is most striking about Jameson's writings on Utopia is his marked interest in its failings and failures rather than its strengths and successes. Yet he is not a pessimist. His paradoxical catchcry – Utopian thought succeeds by failure – is, I would argue, optimistic.[90] Instead of prophesying a bright future on the basis of a rosy present, Jameson uses the various futures art has so far been able to imagine to diagnose and indict (in precisely the clinical/critical sense that Deleuze gives these terms) what it is tempting to call the existential health of the present.[91] My implication is that for Jameson Utopia is not a place, a mythical island in an unknown sea, but a *process*. It is in this respect that it is analogous to schizophrenia, also a process. And, bearing in mind Jameson's salutary caution that dualisms are the strong form of ideology, and that it all too frequently appears that we are called on to side with the schizo, it is important that it be emphasised that it is not the schizo as such that is posited as revolutionary by Deleuze and Guattari, though they do allow that from time to time he or she makes certain escapes, but the process, the potential of its flux.[92] However welcome and fantastic (or even unappealing, as is sometimes the case too) specific Utopias may appear to Jameson, it is still the act of fantasising (the attempt to breakthrough, we might now say, together with the attendant risk of breakdown) itself that he prioritises not the actual fantasy.[93] As in the case of classic Hollywood films like *The Godfather* and *Jaws*, what impresses Jameson is the way they conceal a Utopian impulse ('that dimension of even the most degraded type of mass culture which remains implicitly, and no matter how faintly, negative and critical of the social order from which, as a product and a commodity, it springs').[94]

Jameson's method consists in discovering the best in the worst, Utopia in other words, and then asking why it is that it must be so deeply buried, and moreover, why it is that no-one else seems prepared to look for it? In this way, cultural analysis has been, through recourse to such ahistorical notions as pleasure, desire and gratification, thoroughly depoliticised.[95] Utopia is the critical means of reversing this trend. If it is accepted that Utopia (in the sense Jameson deploys it) is in fact analogous to Deleuze and Guattari's schizophrenia, then a very interesting reversal occurs, one which puts postmodernism through a change of paradigm. By exchanging Jameson's Lacanian definition of schizophrenia for a Deleuzian one, what was initially described as the experience one feels in the face of a loss of historicity is turned around 180 degrees and transformed into an intensification of historicity, or as (I have suggested above) what Brecht calls estrangement. Precedent for this move can be found in Jameson's own work, in his proposal for a schizophrenic historicism, but nowhere does he explicitly connect Utopia and schizophrenia as I have done here. The reason for that is fairly obvious: it is Jameson's practice to bracket schizophrenia as a critical and/or aesthetic term, whereas Deleuze and Guattari posit it as an unmediated ground, so to bring the two together involves a substantial epistemological shift. Utopia would have to be supposed an immanent concept for it to be properly equivalent to Deleuze and Guattari's schizophrenia, and this is exactly what I take it to be.

This move no doubt comes as something of a surprise because Jameson frequently defines Utopia in such a way as to make it appear transcendental: by placing it structurally beyond the capacity of writers and thinkers alike to imagine fully, Jameson makes Utopia seem transcendental in the classic Kantian sense, that is, something which must be posited because it is a necessary frame for thought but cannot be presented. Yet, crucially, it is not as a frame for thought that he actually uses it.[96] In his accounts of science fiction, Jameson follows Suvin in suggesting Utopia – or, more generally, the future – might serve the same function as Brecht's 'estrangement'.[97] In the case of Brian Aldiss's *Star-ship*, the futuristic substitution of culture (the starship itself) for nature (the real world, as it were), results in a twofold estrangement: 'on the one hand, it causes us obscurely to doubt whether our own institutions are quite as natural as we supposed, and whether our "real" open-air environment may not itself be as confining and constricting as the closed world of the ship; on the other hand, it casts uncertainty on the principle of the "natural" itself, which as a conceptual category no longer seems quite so self-justifying and common-sensical'.[98] Here it is the inability of the author, in spite of his evident imaginativeness, to create a truly alternative universe that for Jameson evokes a Utopian dimension, a dimension he ascribes to all science fiction. By force of its failure we are returned all the more intensively to the real.[99] This is what it means to succeed by failure; but what is important for our purposes, however, is the fact that it is an immanent dimension – immanent because it is a failure, because it never rises above the realm in which it is and can be thought.

Whereas for Lacan schizophrenia is the eradication of the relation, already arbitrary to begin with, between the signifier and the signified, and the consequent loss of semiotic cognition, for Deleuze and Guattari it is a heightened sense of semiotic relatedness that obtains, a feeling that there are no natural relations, that new ones can constantly form. It is semiotics without a bar. Instead of being lost in the funhouse, the postmodern schizo is for the first time in history aware that his or her environment is in fact a funhouse, a dead zone of images, false trails, bad deceptions. If they are happy there it is because they have finally learned to laugh at the madness that surrounds them on all sides, not because they have lost contact with reality.[100] 'Far from having lost who knows what contact with life, the schizophrenic is closest to the beating heart of reality, to an intense point identical with the production of the real.'[101] No doubt, then, Deleuze and Guattari are correct in believing that no one 'has ever been as deeply involved in history as the schizo, or dealt with it in this way. He consumes all of universal history in one fell swoop.'[102] Instead of being a malaise, schizophrenia turns out to be the sign we are in fact coping with postmodernism, adapting to its twists and turns, precisely as Jameson envisaged that we must. This is the moment then for me to return to the issue of the body, for what Jameson seems to be calling for in his account of postmodernism is precisely a hastened evolution of the human body.

Despite the obvious, though pernicious truism that the body is usually only positioned as a third term so it can be repressed (so that sticky questions of libinality and so on can be buried with it, something Jameson can hardly be accused of), it nevertheless remains tempting to see the omission of an extended meditation on the body anywhere in Jameson's output as a deliberate avoidance because the body does actually seem to stand between all the opposing terms in the various critical binaries Jameson utilises without ever being fully figured for itself. Nowhere is this more obviously true than in the account of postmodern space where the body plays no part beyond that of faulty apparatus. It is perception that is the primary term. This is even true of his use of the notion of bodily perception, which although it appears to foreground the body still positions it as, finally, in-between: it is in-between what is perceived and the perceiving apparatus itself, namely the eyes, and is figured only as the more diffuse registration of affect. Here then, as in Merleau-Ponty's work, the body really only serves as a means of deconstructing phenomenology, forcing it to reckon with the apparatus of perception as well as the phenomena of perception.[103] Bodily perception turns out only to mean that what we see, we feel, and that our response is visceral because it cannot be purely visual (our eyes cannot 'reply' as it were).[104] Yet all of this assumes that a body as such can at some stage be placed in evidence; that it has a known and knowable form, a precise reference point and an obvious sense; none of which his dialectical method could permit him to hold true. As Jameson has shown in relation to such apparently 'natural' sensations as pleasure, even affect, long held to be utterly spontaneous and instinctive, must be bracketed because far from being purely physiological it is thoroughly ideologically coded.[105]

I want to suggest therefore that Jameson's proposed moratorium on the 'body' is a considered response to a problem of description.[106] As I believe he must see it: the problem lies in the algorithm itself (perception + body + space) – or rather, in the insistence that an algorithm can apply in such a situation. It assumes that the body is a thing, that perception is an activity, and that affect is a second order response to perception that runs through the body like electricity. It also assumes that the body is distinct from the space it inhabits, both in a general sense of discrete solids, and in a genealogical sense. The next question then is whether or not the body is thinkable at all? Again, it would not be some ready-to-hand referent that was at issue, but a concept. And in this respect I think it is probably true to say for all its present attention that the body has become unthinkable, for Jameson at least, in postmodern theory. It is unthinkable because no new totalisation has been constructed to replace the now rejected idea of the natural body, except perhaps the cyborg but that is too additively conceived a concept (body + machine) to really serve as an adequate replacement. It is also unthinkable because capitalism separates the body from its attributes and abilities, turning it into a source of labour, a surface to be ornamented and displayed, and even more insidiously a problem to be solved (bad breath, obesity, fitness, health and so on). In trying to articulate this problematic cultural studies has simply turned the body itself into a way of totalising certain forms of consumer culture, from punk to crossdressing, thereby pushing it into even further abstraction. It has become an empty signifier, sadly capable of absorbing both the demands of consumer capitalism and the inquiries of critical theory.

The truly perverse outcome of the now legendary unmappability of the Bonaventure Hotel is not, I want to argue, finally, that it turns customers away; but that in attempting to lure them in, by disguising or else hiding its implicit connections to global capitalism in such a spectacular fashion, it actually brings to mind the enormity of capital, the very thing it hides so well. In this respect, schizophrenia is, though Jameson does not say as much, a Utopian concept; still another example of what Jameson refers to as succeeding by failure. My point in suggesting that postmodern space is delightfully bewildering is that its primary effect seems to be the suppression of inquiry, which is not to say false consciousness so much as the diminution of that political awareness we call conscience.[107] The distracted windowshopper is anything but politically conscious and certainly very far from being subversive, no matter how much unauthorised pleasure they gain from the marvellous displays, and the not incidental opportunity to display themselves malls afford. The mall, if it is to be seen in its proper light as a technology for the creation of surplus value, has to be seen as recuperating in advance any and all uses of its space, whether these result in direct sales or not, because it has by the fact of the presence of mall-users succeeded in its singular aim of attracting potential customers.

And although he makes the same observation himself, Jameson does not ask the one question that would seem to follow from this observation and that is, from the point of view of obtaining surplus profits, how does the mall in the Bonaventure Hotel actually work? Obviously enough, he does not ask this question because in a sense he has answered it already by saying the mall in fact does not work as it is supposed to. Yet, in the same breath, as it were, he also points out – contradictorily – that the general pattern it follows of being a city within a city is in fact a world-wide trend, so one must assume it is not generally speaking a bad strategy. In other words, far from depriving the subject of agency, in saying that customers are turned away by postmodern space, Jameson is probably endowing them with too much. By the same token, the very experience Jameson saw as resulting from a loss of historicity turns out to be the most intensely historicising experience available.

Notes

1. Derek Gregory, *Geographical Imaginations* (Oxford: Blackwell, 1994) p. 139. Cf. Stephen Pile, *The Body and the City: Psychoanalysis, Space and Subjectivity* (London: Routledge, 1996), p. 247 n.6.
2. Thus I extend Kellner's claim made in 1989. Cf. *Postmodernism/Jameson/Critique*, edited by D. Kellner (Washington D.C.: Maisonneuve Press, 1989), p. 2. Interestingly, the strongest competition for this title of most written about is probably Foucault's work on the prison, which obviously enough is also an inquiry into the coalescence of architecture and culture.
3. Sean Homer, *Fredric Jameson: Marxism, Hermeneutics, Postmodernism* (Cambridge: Polity, 1998).
4. For instance Pile, *The Body and the City*, op. cit., p. 247, n.6; Hans Bertens, *The Idea of the Postmodern: A History* (London: Routledge, 1995), p. 183, n.5.
5. Gilles Deleuze and Félix Guattari, *Mille plateaux* (Paris: Minuit, 1980), trans. by Brian Massumi, *A Thousand Plateaus* (London: Athlone, 1987), p. 15.
6. Jameson's errors of memory and map-reading, which were duly amended in subsequent versions of the essay, are recorded for posterity by Edward Soja, *Postmodern Geographies: The Reassertion of Space in Critical Theory* (London: Verso, 1989), p. 198.
7. Fredric Jameson, *Postmodernism, or, the Cultural Logic of Late Capitalism* (Durham: Duke University Press, 1991), p. 44.
8. See, for instance, two very interesting collections of papers, *Sexuality and Space*, edited by Beatriz Colomina (Princeton, NJ: Princeton Architectural Press, 1992); and *The Sex of Architecture*, edited by Diana Agrest *et al.* (New York: Abrams, 1996).
9. Gilles Deleuze and Félix Guattari, *L'Anti-Oedipe* (Paris: Minuit, 1972) trans. by Robert Hurley, Mark Seem and Helen R, Lane, *Anti-Oedipus* (New York: Viking, 1977), p. 316.
10. Ibid., p. 324.
11. In this respect, it obeys an important principle of schizoanalysis: 'the rule of the right to non-senseas well as the absence of a link' (Deleuze and Guattari, *Anti-Oedipus*, op. cit., p. 314).
12. Ibid., p. 326.
13. As we've seen, attraction and repulsion are in fact the twin actions of the body without organs (Deleuze and Guattari, *Anti-Oedipus*, op. cit., p. 9–11).
14. Mike Davis, 'Urban Renaissance and the Spirit of Postmodernism', in *New Left Review* (1985) 151, pp. 106–13. Homer, *Fredric Jameson*, op. cit., p. 176 reaffirms this point, as does Susan Ruddick, 'Heterotopias of the Homeless: Strategies and Tactics of Place-making in Los Angeles', in *Strategies* (1990)

3, pp. 184–201, p. 94. The history of Bunker Hill is explored by Edward Soja, *Thirdspace: Journeys to Los Angeles and Other Real-and-Imagined Places* (Oxford: Blackwell, 1997) pp. 211–15.

15. Jameson, *Postmodernism*, op. cit., pp. 41–2. For an interesting use of the Bonaventure's reflective exterior, which picks up on precisely its class-distinguishing function, see the 1998 film *Most Wanted*, which uses the mirrored surface of the hotel as a contrasting backdrop in a scene where the fugitive hero hides out in a homeless man's humpy.
16. 'At least 100,000 apparel homeworkers toil within a few miles radius of the Bonaventure and child labour is again a shocking problem', Mike Davis, 'Urban Renaissance', op. cit., p. 110. This is by means a problem peculiar to the Bonaventure, it is in many ways an implicit feature of the mall. As Anne Friedberg has put it, 'The mall is a contemporary phantasmagoria, enforcing a blindness to a range of urban blights–the homeless, beggars, crime, traffic, even weather'. Anne Friedberg, *Window Shopping: Cinema and the Postmodern* (Berkeley: University of California Press, 1993) p. 113.
17. Jameson, *Postmodernism*, op. cit., p. 421 n, 19; Ernest Mandel, trans. by J. de Bres, *Late Capitalism* (London: Verso, 1978) p. 23.
18. Deleuze and Guattari, *Thousand Plateaus*, op. cit., p. 412.
19. Ibid., p. 409.
20. Ibid., p. 10.
21. Ibid., p. 410.
22. Fredric Jameson, *The Cultural Turn: Selected Writings on the Postmodern 1983–1998* (London: Verso, 1998) pp. 154, 187.
23. Davis, 'Urban Renaissance', op. cit., p. 107; Even more puzzling is Gregory's endorsement, *Geographical Imaginations*, op. cit., p. 281.
24. Jameson, 'On "Cultural Studies"', in *Social Text* (1993) 34, pp. 17–52, p. 30.
25. For an interesting representation of this side of the Bonaventure, see the John Badham film, *Nick of Time* (1996).
26. Some of these issues are addressed in M. Morris, 'At Henry Parkes Motel', in *Cultural Studies* (1988) 2 (1): pp. 1–16, 29–47.
27. Theodore Dreiser, *Sister Carrie* (1900–reprinted Harmondsworth: Penguin, 1994).
28. Jameson, *Postmodernism*, op. cit., p. 332.
29. James Clifford, *Routes: Travel and Translation in the Late Twentieth Century* (Cambridge, MA: Harvard University Press, 1997) p. 32.
30. Fredric Jameson, *The Seeds of Time* (New York: Columbia University Press, 1994) p. xv.
31. As Jameson insists, there is a right and wrong way of reading Hegel; his own preference is not to condemn Hegel for his idealism, which is easily done, though not all that interesting or useful, but rather to look at those things he was capable of doing thanks to his idealism. Fredric Jameson, 'Notes on Globalisation as a Philosophical Issue', in *The Cultures of Globalisation*, edited by Jameson and Miyoshi (Durham, NC: Duke University Press, 1998) pp. 54–77, p. 75.
32. Jameson, *Postmodernism*, op. cit., p. xxii.

33. Gilles Deleuze and Félix Guattari, *Qu'est-ce que la philosophie?* (Paris: Minuit, 1991) trans. by Graham Burchell and Hugh Tomlinson, *What is Philosophy?* (London: Verso, 1994) pp. 40–42,
34. Jameson, *Postmodernism*, op. cit., p. xxi.
35. Dialectics teaches 'us that we cannot speak of an underlying "essence of things", of a fundamental class structure inherent in a system in which one group of people produces value for another group, unless we allow for the dialectical possibility that even this fundamental "reality", may be "realer" at some historical junctures than at others, and that the underlying object of our thoughts and representations–history and class structure–is itself as profoundly historical as our own capacity to grasp it'. Fredric Jameson, *Signatures of the Visible* (London: Routledge, 1992), p. 37.
36. It is Gasché who shows most clearly that 'differance' is an intellectual construct enabling a certain form of philosophy.
37. For instance, on the issue of the death of the subject, Jameson states that it is unproductive to take sides, 'except to observe that the kinds of criticism and interpretation generated on either side of this divide will be very different from each other'. Jameson, *Signatures of the Visible*, op. cit., p. 117.
38. Jameson, 'Notes on Globalisation', op. cit., p. viii.
39. Cf. ibid., pp. 103–13. This desire for an 'other' space is much more explicit in colonial and postcolonial situations. For example, the Hotel Indonesia in Christopher Koch's *The Year of Living Dangerously* (1978) is defined as a world complete unto itself, and sealed off from the world around it by prohibitive cost. Not surprisingly, it is the chosen haven of the white expatriate journalists. One can find a similar treatment of the hotel in Arundhati Roy's *The God of Small Things* (1996).
40. Jameson, *Postmodernism*, op. cit., p. 83.
41. Cf. Friedberg, *Window Shopping*, op. cit., pp. 111–15.
42. Deleuze and Guattari, *Anti-Oedipus*, op. cit., p. 303.
43. 'When you recall that Portman is a businessman as well as an architect and a millionaire developer, an artist who is at one and the same time a capitalist in his own right, one cannot but feel that here too something of a "return of the repressed" is involved' Jameson, *Postmodernism*, op. cit., pp. 44, 49. David Harvey, *The Condition of Postmodernity: An Enquiry into the Origins of Cultural Change* (Oxford: Blackwell, 1990) p. 88.
44. Jameson, *The Seeds of Time*, op. cit., p. 29; Jameson, 'Notes on Globalisation', op. cit., p. 89; Michel de Certeau, trans. by Brian Massumi, *Heterologies: Discourse on the Other* (Manchester: Manchester University Press, 1986) p. 121.
45. Walter Benjamin, trans. by H. Zohn, *Baudelaire: a Lyric Poet in the Era of High Capitalism* (London: Verso, 1997) p. 174.
46. Jameson, 'Notes on Globalisation', op, cit., p. 89.
47. Jameson, *Postmodernism*, op, cit., p. 44.
48. Jameson, *Postmodernism*, op, cit., p. 44.
49. 'It may now be suggested that this alarming disjunction point between the body and its built environment–which is to the initial bewilderment of the older modernism as the velocities of the spacecraft to those of the

automobile–can itself stand as the symbol and analogon of that even sharper dilemma which is the incapacity of our minds, at least at present, to map the great global multinational and decentered communicatuibal network in which we find ourselves caught as individual subjects' Jameson, *Postmodernism*, op, cit., p. 44.
50. The concept of the analogon is taken from Sartre's *Psychology of Imagination*. Jameson defines it as 'that structural nexus in our reading or viewing experience, in our operations of decoding or aesthetic reception, which can then do double duty and stand as the substitute and representative within the aesthetic object of a phenomenon on the outside which cannot in the very nature of things be "rendered" directly' Jameson, *Signatures of the Visible*, op. cit., p. 53.
51. In a later work, Jameson gives grounds for a different kind of speculation. In so far as America recognises itself as being somehow at the centre of globalised late capitalism, it also has to admit to a certain amount of blindness. As such, the figurative disorientation that Jameson's argument hinges on can now be reread as a kind of allegorical blindness that a theorisation of globalisation may help to correct. Cf. Jameson, 'Notes of Globalisation' op. cit., p. 59. Such blindness however should not be construed as weakness, or taken to mean that capitalism's effects are not felt at the ground level , as an early commentator, John Fiske, mistakenly reads Jameson. Cf. Fiske, 'Popular Forces and the Culture of Everyday Life', in Southern Review (1988) 21 (1), pp. 288–306, p. 297.
52. Jameson, *Postmodernism*, op, cit., p. 44.
53. While I have little sympathy with Goldstein's paper as a whole, on this point I do agree: 'If we were to see only the strangeness of the Bonaventure Hotel and not its ordinariness, we would be missing something important about the everyday cultural logic of late capitalism' J. Goldstein, 'The Female Aesthetic Community', in *Poetics Today* (1993) 14 (1), pp. 143–63, p. 159.
54. This is what I take to be the deeper implication of the otherwise facile observation Goldstein makes in saying Jameson responds to the Bonaventure mall as a theorist and not a consumer. Goldstein 'The Female Aesthetic Community' op. cit., p. 160. It also explains why Steve Pile found its space to be disappointingly uncomplicated: his mode of perception was different to Jameson's, postmodern where the latter was still modern. Pile, *The Body and the City*, op. cit., p. 247 n. 6.
55. So while I agree with Friedberg in thinking that the mall and the cinema are two different means of mobilising the gaze, I do not share her view that the gaze itself is a homogeneous function. For the same reason, I cannot agree with Baudrillard's claim that in order to properly examine the American landscape one should begin in the cinema and then work outwards; Jean Baudrillard, trans. by C. Turner, *America* (London: Verso, 1988) p. 56. My position is that each perceptual situation demands its own mode of perception. For a different comparison between Baudrillard and Jameson see Richard Lehan, *The City in Literature: an Intellectual and Cultural History* (Berkeley: University of California Press, 1998), pp. 276–80.

56. Gilles Deleuze, trans. by Paul Rabinow, 'Foucault and the Prison: an Interview with Gilles Deleuze', in *History of the Present* (1986) 2: pp.1–2, 20–21; p. 2; 'Foucault et les prisons', a retranscription from the original tapes published in French in Gilles Deleuze, *Deux régimes de fous: texts et entretiens 1975–1995*, edited by David Lapoujade (Paris: Minuit, 2003), pp. 254–62.
57. Conveniently, thanks to the film *In the Line of Fire* (1993) it is now possible to make a precise comparison between the actual experience of the lifts at the Bonaventure and the cinematic experience of them.
58. Jameson, *Postmodernism*, op. cit., pp. 42–3.
59. Susan Buck-Morss, *The Dialectics of Seeing: Walter Benjamin and the Arcades Project* (Cambridge, MA: MIT Press, 1989), pp. 253–60.
60. Jameson, *The Seeds of Time*, op. cit., p. 58.
61. Mandel, *Late Capitalism*, op. cit., p. 232.
62. Gilles Deleuze, 'Postscript on Control Societies', see above pp. xx-xx.
63. Jameson, 'Notes on Globalisation', op. cit., pp. 117–20.
64. Fredric Jameson, *Sartre: the Origins of a Style* (New York: Columbia University Press, 1961), p. 19; Jameson, *Cultural Turn*, op. cit., p. 68; Jameson, *Postmodernism*, op. cit., pp. 70, 303.
65. Gaston Bachelard, *La poétique de l'espace* (Paris: Presses Universitaires de France, 1958) trans. by Maria Jolas, *The Poetics of Space* (Boston: Beacon Press, 1969), p. 184.
66. Jameson, *Postmodernism*, op. cit., pp. 39–44. For an even more exacting description of this feature of the Bonaventure Mall see Soja, *Postmodern Geographies*, op cit., pp. 234–5. Baudrillard too has occasion to describe the Bonaventure Hotel, but his account is little more than a pastiche of Jameson's, makinf the same remarks about the exterior being like reflector sunglasses and the interior being confusing. The only difference is that Baudrillard is not able to decide whether this is a postmodern space or not. Baudrillard, *America*, op. cit., p. 59.
67. Jameson actually says there are no signposts, which may have been true when he visited, but is no longer the case. Interestingly enough, in one of the pictures of the interior of the Bonaventure that Jameson includes in his book directional signs can actually be seen.
68. Jameson, *The Seeds of Time*, op. cit., p. 30.
69. For an example of this particular form of privileging of the indigenous see Arjun Appardurai, *Modernity at Large: Cultural Dimensions of Globalization* (Minneapolis: University of Minnesota Press, 1996) p. 32.
70. 'The postmodern effect, on the contrary, ratifies the specializations and differentiations on which it is based: it presupposes them and thereby prolongs and perpetuates them.' Jameson, *Postmodernism*, op. cit., p. 371.
71. Jameson, *Postmodernism*, op. cit., pp. 26–7.
72. 'With the breakdown of the signifying chain, therefore, the schizophrenic is reduced to an experience of pure material signifiers, or, in other words, a series of pure and unrelated presents in time' Jameson, *Postmodernism*, op. cit., p. 27.

Section 5: Relations

73. Jameson, *Postmodernism*, op. cit., p. 27.
74. Berthold Brecht, trans. by John Willett, *Brecht on Theatre: the Development of an Aesthetic* (London: Eyre Methuen, 1964), p. 97.
75. Jameson, 'Notes on Globalisation', op. cit., p. 141.
76. It is worth pointing out here that in his account of the same conceptual frame, Harvey elides the crucial methodological and epistemological differences between Deleuze and Guattari's definition of schizophrenia and Lacan's because he interpolates a modernism/postmodernism period distinction not found in their work, nor in Lacan's either, effectively making the former paranoid and the latter schizoid, which is a profound misrepresentation. Harvey, *The Condition of Postmodernity*, op. cit., pp. 53–4.
77. For an alternative, much more rigorously dialectical (in the Hegelian sense) attempt at a *rapprochement* of Deleuze and Jameson, see Robert Miklitsch, *From Hegel to Madonna: Towards a General Economy of 'Commodity Fetishism'* (New York: SUNY, 1998), pp. 49–59.
78. Cf. Jameson, 'Notes on Globalization', op. cit., pp. 123–32.
79. Oddly, Jameson later dismisses this very apparatus altogether, condemning it as 'merely' existential, without any reference to his earlier instrumental use of it. In the same breath he then introduces yet another distortion into the picture by disenchaining codes from territoriality, when Deleuze and Guattari say that it is precisely the codes inbuilt in flows that makes territorialisation possible. Cf. Jameson, *The Cultural Turn*, op. cit., pp. 150–2; Deleuze and Guattari, *Anti-Oedipus*, op. cit., p. 285.
80. Ibid., p. 379.
81. Ibid., p. 33.
82. Ibid., pp. 34, 278.
83. Ibid., p. 34.
84. 'In a sense, it is the bank that controls the whole system and the investment of desire. […] That is why it is unfortunate that Marxist economists too often dwell on considerations concerning the mode of production, and on the theory of money as the general equivalent as found in the first section of *Capital*, without attaching enough importance to banking practice, to financial operations, and to the specific circulation of credit money–which would be the meaning of a return to Marx, to the Marxist theory of money', Deleuze and Guattari, *Anti-Oedipus*, op. cit., p. 230. For an example of just such analysis, one that emphasizes credit over mode of production, see Giovanni Arrighi, *The Long Twentieth Century: Money, Power and the Origin of our Times* (London: Verso, 1994) and also Jameson's commentary on it, Jameson, *The Cultural Turn*, op. cit., pp. 136–61.
85. 'We know very well where lack–and its subjective correlative–come from. Lack is created, planned, and organized in and through social production. […] The deliberate creation of lack as a function of market economy is the art of the dominant class. This involves deliberately organizing wants and needs amid an abundance of production; making all of desire teeter and fall victim to the great fear of not having one's needs satisfied; and making the object dependent upon a real production that is supposedly exterior to

desire (the demands of rationality), while at the same time the production of desire is categorized as fantasy and nothing but fantasy' Deleuze and Guattari, *Anti-Oedipus*, op. cit., p. 28.
86. Ibid., p. 4.
87. Ibid., pp. 76–7.
88. Ibid., pp. 63, 292.
89. Ibid., p. 131.
90. Fredric Jameson, 'Progress versus Utopia; or, Can We Imagine the Future?', in *Science Fiction Studies* (1982) 9, pp. 147–57, p. 153; Fredric Jameson, 'World-Reduction in Le Guin: the Emergence of Utopian Narrative', in *Science Fiction Studies* (1975) 2 (3) pp. 221-30, p. 229; Fredric Jameson, 'Generic Discontinuities in SF: Brian Aldiss' Starship' in *Science Fiction Studies* (1973) 1 (2), pp. 57–68, p. 59.
91. Postmodernism, for instance, can conjure fantastic digital paradises in which everything a person could want would be available instantly in virtual form (as well as a host of apocalyptic scenarios, to be sure, from total environmental collapse to thermonuclear Armageddon), but appears unable to conceive of a world-system other than capitalism. Cf. Jameson, *The Seeds of Time*, op. cit., p. xii.
92. Deleuze and Guattari, *Anti-Oedipus*, op. cit., p. 341.
93. Jameson, 'Notes on Globalisation', op. cit., p. 80.
94. Jameson, *Signatures of the Visible*, op. cit., p. 29.
95. In *The Seeds of Time* Utopia is given precisely a repoliticising, therapeutic task: 'There is,' Jameson says, 'a collective therapy to be performed on the victims of depoliticization themselves, a rigorous look at everything we fantasize as mutilating, as privative, as oppressive, as mournful and depressing, about all the available visions of a radical transformation in the social order', p. 61.
96. The suggestion that Utopia is an immanent rather than transcendental notion is Marin's. see Jameson, 'Notes on Globalisation', op. cit., p. 88.
97. Jameson, 'Generic Discontinuities', op. cit., p. 58.
98. Ibid., p. 58.
99. Ibid., p. 59.
100. [typesetter do not indent this]It should be noted that laughter and euphoria are not the same thing, and I agree with Jameson that the euphoria customarily associated with postmodernism is in fact merely a compensation formation. Jameson, *Postmodernism*, op. cit., p. 330.
101. Deleuze and Guattari, *Anti-Oedipus*, op. cit., p. 87.
102. Ibid., p. 21.
103. Jameson, *Postmodernism*, op. cit., p. 124.
104. Jameson, *Signatures of the Visible*, op. cit., p. 1.
105. Jameson, 'Notes on Globalisation', op. cit., pp. 62–3.
106. Jameson, 'On "Cultural Studies"', op. cit., p. 44.
107. This is how I interpet Jameson's claim that postmodernism may be characterised by a certain 'waning of affect'. Jameson, *Postmodernism*, op. cit., pp. 10–15.

Heinrich von Kleist

Kleist (1777–1811) was a contemporary of Goethe, born in Frankfurt into a military family. His father died when Heinrich was eleven, his mother when he was fifteen, and his life was restless. He wrote plays, poems and essays, but his output was not large. At the age of 34, he shot himself and his fiancée Henriette Vogel in a famous suicide pact beside the Wannsee in Berlin. The essay on the marionette theatre, printed here, was written in 1810, and shows no sign of restlessness or self-destruction. It is a series of parables about the idea of balance and grace, and it has a quality about it that lingers in the mind long after much else has faded away. In 1922 Hugo von Hofmannsthal – now best remembered as Richard Strauss's librettist, but a considerable cultural force in Vienna in his day – said that Kleist's essay was the most perceptive piece of philosophy since Plato, which seems hyperbolic, but might not be.[1] It suggests in images a way of approaching the problem of maintaining a balance in a world of irreconcilable complexities, remaining calm and indifferent to the incidental feints and gestures, but responding unaffectedly and spontaneously to the things that matter. It is perhaps better not to make claims for the importance of the essay, if it is an essay, but to invite you to allow yourself to be drawn into its narrative and see what happens – not immediately, but as years go by.[2]

Notes

1. Idris Parry, 'Kleist on Puppets', in *Hand to Mouth* (Manchester, Carcanet, 1981) p. 9.
2. For example, Deleuze draws on this essay for an apt image of the relation between a force and its effects. The movements of the puppeteer cause but do not represent the movements of the marionette. Gilles Deleuze, *Deux régimes de fous* (Paris: Minuit, 2003), p. 11.

The Puppet Theatre

In a public garden one evening in the winter of 1801, which I was spending in M., I met Herr C., recently appointed first dancer at the Opera there and enjoying an extraordinary success with the public.

I said to him that I had been surprised to see him – several times indeed – at a puppet theatre erected in the marketplace where little burlesques, into which were woven songs and dances, were being given for the entertainment of the common people.

He assured me that the puppets' silent acting gave him a great deal of pleasure, and hinted that a dancer wishing to improve his art could learn a lot from them.

Behind his words, so it seemed to me, by the way he said them, there was more than a passing thought, and I sat down beside him to question him more closely on the grounds he might have for such a strange assertion.

He asked me whether I had not in fact found the marionettes, especially the smaller ones, often very graceful in their movements as they danced.

I could not deny it. A quartet of peasants dancing a round in rapid time could not have been done more prettily by Teniers.

I asked how these figures were worked and how it was possible, without thousands of strings on one's fingers, to govern their separate limbs and particular points in just such a way as the rhythm of the movements or the dance required.

He answered that I should not suppose that every limb at all the different moments of the dance had to be separately positioned and pulled by the puppeteer.

Every movement, he said, had a centre of gravity; it sufficed if this, inside the figure, were controlled; the limbs, which were nothing but pendula, followed without further interference, mechanically, of their own accord.

He added that this movement was a very simple one; that whenever the centre of gravity was moved *in a straight line* the limbs described a *curve*; and that often, if shaken by accident, the whole thing was brought into a kind of rhythmical activity similar to dancing.

This observation itself seemed to throw some light on the pleasure he claimed to find in the puppet theatre. But I was far from suspecting how much further he would go.

I asked him whether he thought the man working the marionettes must be a dancer himself or at least have some notion of what constitutes beauty in dancing.

He replied that though an activity might in its mechanics be a simple one it did not follow that it could be conducted wholly without feeling.

The line the centre of gravity had to describe was indeed very simple and in most cases, he believed, straight. In cases where it curved the law of its curve did not seem to be more than of the first or at most of the second degree; and even in that latter case only elliptical, and a movement of that description was altogether natural to the

Section 5: Relations

extremities of the human body (because of the joints) and so would not require much skill on the part of the operator to achieve it.

However, in another sense that line was something very mysterious. For it was nothing other than *the way of the dancer's soul*; and he doubted whether it could be discovered otherwise than by the operator's putting himself into the centre of gravity of the marionette; in other words, by *dancing*.

I replied that the operation had always been presented to me as something rather mindless: rather like the turning of a handle to play a barrel organ.

'Not at all,' he replied. 'In fact the relationship of the movements of his fingers to the movements of the marionette is quite a subtle one, rather like that of numbers to their logarithms or the asymptotes to the hyperbola.'

He did however think that the last remnant of intelligence, of which he had been speaking, could itself be taken out of the marionettes; that their dancing could be shifted wholly into the realm of mechanical forces and produced by turning a handle, as I had supposed.

I said how astonished I was to see him honouring this popularized version of a noble art with so much attention. Not only did he think it capable of a higher development: he even seemed to have put his own mind to it.

He smiled and said he would go so far as to assert that if he could get somebody to make a marionette to his specifications he would perform such dances with it as neither he nor any other trained dancer of the day, not even excepting Vestris himself, would be capable of equalling.

'I wonder,' he said, as I looked down at the ground and was silent, 'whether you have heard of the mechanical limbs that craftsmen in England make for people who have lost their legs?'

I said no: such things had never come my way.

'A pity,' he replied; 'for if I tell you that those poor people can dance with them I am almost afraid you will not believe me. – Dance? What am I saying? The range of their movements is limited, I grant you; but those they are capable of they execute with an ease, grace and poise that every thinking person must be astonished by.'

I remarked, in jest, that there he had found the man he was looking for. For a craftsman capable of making such a remarkable leg would without doubt be able to construct him a whole marionette to his requirements.

'And what,' I asked, since he himself now, rather taken aback, was looking down at the ground, 'what exactly would you require of the skills of such a person?'

'Nothing,' he replied, 'that we don't see here already: balance, agility, lightness – only all to a higher degree; and particularly a more natural arrangement of the centres of gravity.'

'And the advantage that the puppet would have over living dancers?'

'The advantage? In the first place, my dear fellow, a negative one, namely this: that it would be incapable of *affectation*. – For affectation occurs, as you know, whenever the soul (*vis motrix*) is situated in a place other than a movement's centre of gravity. Since the puppeteer, handling the wire or the string, can have no point except that one under his control all the other limbs are what they should be: dead, mere pendula, and simply obey the law of gravity; an excellent attribute which you will look for in vain among the majority of our dancers.

'Watch P.,' he went on, 'when she is playing Daphne and, pursued by Apollo, turns to look at him: her soul is somewhere at the bottom of her spine, she bends as if she would snap, like a naiade à la Bernini. And watch young F. when, as Paris, he faces the three goddesses and hands Venus the apple: his soul – it is painful to see – is actually in his elbow.

'Such mistakes,' he added, breaking off, 'have been unavoidable ever since we ate from the Tree of Knowledge. But Paradise is locked and barred and the Cherub is behind us. We shall have to go all the way round the world and see whether it might be open somewhere at the back again.'

I laughed. – True enough, I thought. Your wits will not lead you astray if you have none. But I could see that he still had things to say, and begged him to go on.

'Also,' he said, 'these puppets have the advantage of being *resistant to gravity*. Of the heaviness of matter, the factor that most works against the dancer, they are entirely ignorant: because the force lifting them into the air is greater than the one attaching them to the earth. What wouldn't our friend G. give to be four or five stone lighter or to have such a weight working in her favour in her entrechats and pirouettes! Marionettes only *glance* the ground, like elves, the momentary halt lends the limbs a new impetus; but we use it to *rest* on, to recover from the exertion of the dance: a moment which clearly is not dance at all in itself and which we can do nothing with except get it over with as quickly as possible.'

I said that although he was defending his paradox very cleverly he would still never persuade me that there was more grace in a mechanical marionette than in the form and build of the human body.

He replied that it would be quite impossible for a human body even to equal the marionette. In dance, he said, only a god was a match for matter; and that was the point where the two ends of the round earth met.

I was more and more astonished, and did not know what to say to such strange assertions.

It seemed, he replied, taking a pinch of snuff, that I had not read the third chapter of Genesis attentively; and a man not familiar with that first period of all human education could not properly discuss those following it, let alone the last.

I said that I was perfectly well aware of the damage done by consciousness to the natural grace of a human being. A young man of my acquaintance had, I said, by a chance remark lost his innocence before my very eyes and had afterwards, despite making every conceivable effort, never regained that paradise. – 'But,' I added, 'what conclusions can you draw from that?'

He asked me what had happened.

'About three years ago,' I began, 'I was bathing with a young man whose development at that time had a wonderful grace about it. He would be in his sixteenth year, I should say, and only very remotely, brought on by the kind regards of women, were the first indications of vanity discernible. As it happened we had just seen, in Paris, the youth pulling a thorn out of his foot; the cast of the statue is well known, most German collections have it. Resting his foot on a stool, to dry it, and glancing at himself as he did so in a large mirror, he was reminded of the statue; he smiled and told me what he had seen. In fact, at precisely that moment, I had seen the same; but either because I wished to find out how securely grace dwelled in him or because I

Section 5: Relations

thought it would do him good if I combated his vanity a little, I laughed and answered: he must be seeing things. He blushed, and raised his foot a second time, to show me; but the attempt, very predictably, failed. In confusion he raised his foot a third time, a fourth, again and again, a dozen times: in vain. He was incapable of reproducing the movement – indeed, in the movements he made there was something so comical I could scarcely refrain from laughing at him:–

'From that day, or from that very moment forth, the young man underwent an unbelievable transformation. He began spending days in front of the mirror; and one after the other all his charms deserted him. An invisible and incomprehensible power seemed to settle like an iron net over the free play of his manners and a year later there was not a trace left in him of those qualities that had in the past so delighted the eyes of people around him. There is a person who witnessed that strange and unhappy episode and who word for word could corroborate my account of it.'–

'At this point,' said Herr C. with a smile, 'I must tell you another story. You will soon see its relevance here.

'On my journey to Russia I was staying at the country house of Herr von G., a gentleman of Livland, whose sons were just then busily engaged in practising their fencing. Especially the elder boy, just down from university, prided himself on his skills and one morning when I was in his room offered me a rapier. We fenced; but it happened that I was better than him; he became heated, confused; almost every thrust of mine hit home and at last his rapier flew across the room. With a laugh, but also a trifle piqued, he retrieved his rapier and said that he had met his match: but everybody would one day, and now he would take me where I should meet mine. The two brothers laughed out loud and cried: "To the wood store with him!" And they took me by the hand and led me down to a bear that Herr von G., their father, was rearing in the yard.

'The bear, when I approached him in astonishment, was reared up on his hind legs and leaning back against a post to which he was fastened, his right paw lifted in readiness and his eye fixing mine. That was his stance, for fencing. I thought I must be dreaming when confronted by such an opponent; but "Go on, go on," said Herr von G. "See if you can land a hit on him." Recovering a little from my astonishment I thrust at the bear with my rapier: he made a very slight movement with his paw and parried the thrust. I tried to mislead him with a feint; the bear made no move. I thrust at him again, swiftly and shrewdly, beyond any doubt had it been a human breast I would have hit: the bear made a very slight movement with his paw and parried the stroke. Now I was almost in the position of young Herr von G. And the bear's seriousness discomposed me. Now I tried a thrust, now a feint, the sweat was dripping off me: all in vain! Not only did the bear, like the foremost fencer in the world, parry all my thrusts; when I feinted – no fencer in the world can follow him in this – he did not even react: looking me in the eye, as though he could read my soul in it, he stood with his paw lifted in readiness and when my thrusts were not seriously intended he did not move.

'Do you believe this story?'

'Absolutely!' I cried, applauding him in delight. 'I should believe it from any stranger, it is so very likely. How much more so from you!'

'Well my good friend,' said Herr C., 'you now have everything you need if you are to understand me. We see that in the same measure as reflection in the organic world becomes darker and feebler, grace there emerges in ever greater radiance and supremacy. – But just as two lines intersecting at a point after they have passed through infinity will suddenly come together again on the other side, or the image in a concave mirror, after travelling away into infinity, suddenly comes close up to us again, so when consciousness has, as we might say, passed through an infinity, grace will return; so that grace will be most purely present in the human frame that has either no consciousness or an infinite amount of it, which is to say either in a marionette or in a god.'

'But,' I said rather distractedly, 'should we have to eat again of the Tree of Knowledge to fall back into the state of innocence?'

'Indeed,' he replied; 'that is the final chapter in the history of the world.'

Index

Abelove, Henry 150–1
Abercrombie, Patrick 264
Absolute, the, concept of 57–9
abstract painting 173
Aeschylus 28, 219
aesthetics 61–2
Alberti, Leon Battista 7
Aldiss, Brian 291
Allen, Woody 118
Amsterdam 275
anthropology 71, 74, 85
Aragon, Louis 88–9
Aristotle 46, 51, 67, 69–70, 177
Armstrong, Louis 222
art, nature of 174
Ashby, W. R. 83–4
Augustine, St 31
Avallon 10, 238–9

Bachelard, Gaston 33, 42–6, 88, 161, 234, 285
Bacon, Lord 27
Badovici, Jean 234
Bali 37, 72–85
Balzac, Honoré de 89
Basilica of the Madeleine, Vézelay 3–4
Bataille, Georges 4–6, 10–11, 15–16, 30, 36–7, 40, 71, 162, 237–8, 241
Bateson, Gregory 35–7, 71–2, 109–10
Baudelaire, Charles 282
Bazoches 3, 236
Benjamin, Walter 15, 33, 88–93, 282, 284
Berkeley, George 51
Bernard, Saint 240
Besançon 235
blackness 212–16, 221–5
Blake, William 12
Blanchot, Maurice 15
Bloom, Harold 9
Boetticher, Karl Heinrich von 89–90
Bonaventure Hotel, Los Angeles 272–82, 293
Borges, Jorge Luis 71
Bramante, Donato 39
Brecht, Bertolt 287, 291

Breton, André 15, 88
Buchanan, Ian 232, 259, 272
Butler, Samuel 42, 109–12, 124, 234–5

Caillois, Roger 15
Canetti, Elias 158, 203
capitalism 288–9
Cassirer, Ernst 169–71, 175–6, 203
Cather, Willa 213
Cézanne, Paul 115, 177–8
Chapin, S.J. 264
Chaplin, Charlie 221
Chicago school of sociologists 264
Clausewitz, Karl von 18
Clifford, James 280
Coleridge, Samuel Taylor 65
Colette 163–4, 166–7
Collins, James 152
common sense 110–11
Conrad, Joseph 275
Constantinople 235
control societies 248–51
Corman, Roger 203
Cronenberg, David 113
crowd behaviour 158–60, 182, 203
culture 37, 165
cyborgs 145–8

Dante 28
Darwin, Charles 9, 218
Davis, Mike 278–9
Debussy, Claude 72, 203
Delanda, Manuel 160
Deleuze, Gilles 10, 37–8, 43, 46, 71–2, 108–11, 114–18, 123, 159–62, 232–3, 245–6, 253, 256, 272–92 *passim*
denotation symbols 172
Descartes, René 70
development projects 262–6
Dewey, John 33, 53–5, 58, 61, 67, 114, 169
Diderot, Denis 120
Douglas, Ann 221
Doyle, Arthur Conan 123
Doyle, Laura 215, 218, 220

Eames, Charles and Ray 6–7, 11, 238
ecology and eco-systems 36
Eluard, Paul 43
Emerson, Ralph Waldo 30, 67, 150–1
Empire State Building 216, 219, 221
empiricism 51, 57, 59
ethos 34, 38–9
Euclid 52
Euclidian space 253–6, 264
eugenics 215, 218
Euro currency 246
'event-cities' 38

Favro, Diane 35, 93
Feyerabend, Paul 110
Fitzgerald, F. Scott 108
Foucault, Michel 37–8, 107, 146, 248–50
Fraser, T. J. 7
Freud, Sigmund 34, 71, 118, 120, 289
Frye, Northrop 42
futurology 144–5

Galton, Francis 217
Gangs of New York 159–60
Gehry, Frank 284
Giedion, Sigfried 90
Glass, Philip 72
Gobineau, Comte de 217
Godwin, William 112
Goodman, Nelson 165, 169–80, 259
Gray, Eileen 234–5, 238
Gray, Thomas 1
Greek art 62–3
Greenfield, Susan 144
Gregory, Derek 274
group identity 157–60
Guattari, Félix 10, 36–7, 71–2,
  108–11, 115–18, 123,
  159–62, 240, 245, 251,
  256, 272, 278–82, 286–92

habitat 36
Hampshire County Council 265
Haraway, Donna 145
Harlem 221–3, 227
Harrison, Lou 72
Haussmann, Baron 235
Haydn, Franz Joseph 72
Healey, Patsy 259
Heelan, Patrick 42
Hegel, G. W. F. 9, 22, 70, 120, 280
Heidegger, Martin 9, 15, 179, 281
Hemingway, Ernest 213
Heraclitus 21, 23
Hesse, Hermann 162

Hobbes, Thomas 70, 157–8
Hodgson, Shadworth 51
Hoffmansthal, Hugo von 301
Hölderlin, Johann 180
Homer, Sean 274
house, the, conceptions of 44–6,
  64, 151–2, 161–2, 233–5
humanism 55
Hume, David 51, 107

identity, concept of 107–9;
  see also group identity
Les Invalides 3, 5
Irigaray, Luce 118

James, Henry 203
James, William 33, 42, 48, 67, 169
Jameson, Frederic 272–94
Jeanneret, Charles Édouard 163,
  165
Jefferson, David 107
Jencks, Charles 9, 272
Job, Book of 28
Joughin, Martin 245
Julius Caesar 98–9
Jung, Carl Gustav 161

Kafka, Franz 249
Kahn, Louis 240
Kant, Immanuel 46, 67–8, 70,
  120, 171, 175–9, 280
Keaton, Buster 221
Kepler, Johannes 52
King, Rodney 237
Klein, Hilary 147
Kleist, Heinrich von 111, 301
Knight, Richard Payne 1–2
Koolhaas, Rem 38
Kristeva, Julia 111, 120–1
Kubrick, Stanley 112

La Mettrie, Julien Offray de 112
Lacan, Jacques 118, 286–7, 291–2
Laing, Samuel 151
Last, Hugh 120
Le Corbusier 11, 113, 162–6,
  210–27, 234–5
Leibniz, Gottfried 46, 201, 253
Leiris, Michel 15
Leviathan 157
Livy 159, 182–5, 191, 197
Locke, John 51
Loos, Adolf 240
Los Angeles 236–8, 277, 279
Louis XVI 198

Index

Luxemburg, Rosa 245–6
Luxor 23

machines, Butler's view of 126–43
McDonald's 286
Mahler, Gustav 72
Manhattan 214–16, 219–24, 236
Marcus Antonius 95
Marx, Karl 34, 91, 110, 245–6
Marxism 39, 147
Massumi, Brian 253
mathematics 67–9, 160, 253
Mead, Margaret 71, 74
Merleau-Ponty, C. 177–8, 292
metaphors 172–3
metaphysics 42–3, 51–2, 231
Michelangelo 39
Mies van der Rohe, Ludwig 11
Minsky, Marvin 109, 158
Montaigne, Michel Eyquen de 90, 120
monuments 35–40, 100, 158
Morrison, Toni 212–13
music 72

Nabokov, Vladimir 9
Nagel, Thomas 123
Napoleon 3, 90, 198, 248
Negri, Antonio 245
New York 214–27, 236–7; see also Gangs of New York
Newton, Isaac 9
Nietzsche, Friedrich 17, 21–3, 26, 30, 34, 107, 210
nihilism 30
nominalism 52

obelisks 18–24

Paine, Thomas 107
Palladio, Andrea 166
paranoid state of mind 159
Parc de la Villette 38
Paris arcades 89–91
Parthenon, the 65
Pearson, Karl 217
Peirce, Benjamin 68–9
Peirce, Charles Sanders 33, 42, 50, 67, 110
Pevsner, Nikolaus 115
phenomenism 179
Philibert, Nicolas 162
philosophy of science 42–3
Place de la Concorde 4, 18, 20, 23–4
planning systems 259–68
Plato 38, 203, 301
Plotinus 120

Plutarch 94
Poe, Edgar Allen 161, 203, 213
poetry 8–9, 26–8
Polanyi, M. 177
Portman, John 272
positivism 52
postmodernism 272, 275, 281–5, 293–4
poststructuralism 38, 266
Powers of Ten 6
pragmatism 33, 48–60, 67–9
Proust, Marcel 9, 121
psychoanalysis 147
pyramids 19–20, 38, 150, 155

Rameses II 19
rationalism 42–3, 52, 55–9
Ravel, Maurice 72
realism 42–3
Reich, Steve 72
Renaissance thought 38
Richards, Simon 210
Richardson, L. F. 75–6
Ricoeur, Paul 165, 169
Robespierre, Maximilien de 198
Rome 7–8, 35, 38, 93–100, 118–20, 159, 182–202, 235
Rorty, Richard 9, 33, 61, 169, 240
Rousseau, Jean-Jacques 26, 189
Roy, Jules 4
Royal Opera House, Covent Garden 37
Ruskin, John 34

St Peter's, Rome 38
Schiller, Friedrich 53–5, 58
schizoid state of mind 159
scientific method 39
Scorsese, Martin 159
Semper, Gottfried 239–40
Serres, Michel 159–60, 182
Shelley, Mary 26, 112–13
Shelley, Percy 8–11, 26, 30, 33, 67, 110, 112, 160, 259
Shusterman, Richard 33, 61
Social Darwinism 215, 218
Socrates 21–2, 51
Sofoulis, Zoe 147
Sophocles 203
South Hampshire Structure Plan 264–5
Speer, Albert 11, 158
Stertinius, L. 99
Stevenson, Robert Louis 108
Stokes, Adrian 121
Swedenborg, Emanuel 48
Swift, Jonathan 71
Syndicalism 226

tendency, concept of 64
Tennyson, Alfred 7
Thoreau, Henry David 150–1, 169
topology 253–7
Tournier, Michel 46–7
transcendental deduction 177
Trump, Donald 36
truth, concept and theorisation of 54–60, 175
Tschumi, Bernard 38
Twain, Mark 213

utilitarianism 52

values 39–40
Van Gogh, Vincent 178–9
Vauban, Maréchal 3, 8–10, 235
Veblen, Thorstein 67

Versailles 38, 115, 236
Vesta, temple of (Rome) 7–8
Vézelay 3–4, 10, 15
Villa Savoie 165–7, 213
Virilio, Paul 248
Vitruvius, Pollio Marcus 26
Vogel, Henriette 301
Von Neumann games 82–3

Washington DC 38
Wigley, Mark 224
Wilson, Mabel 210, 232
Winckelmann, Johann Joachim 10, 237
Wittgenstein, Ludwig 123
Wollstonecraft, Mary 112
Wordsworth, William 115

Žižek, Slavoj 123